Operations Strategy

OPERATIONS STRATEGY

DESIGN, IMPLEMENTATION AND DELIVERY

ALEX HILL

TERRY HILL

BLOOMSBURY

NEW DELHI • LONDON • OXFORD • NEW YORK • SYDNEY

BLOOMSBURY INDIA
Bloomsbury Publishing India Pvt. Ltd
Second Floor, LSC Building No. 4, DDA Complex, Pocket C–6&7,
Vasant Kunj, New Delhi 110070

BLOOMSBURY, BLOOMSBURY ACADEMIC INDIA and the Diana logo are
trademarks of Bloomsbury Publishing Plc

First published in India 2023
Published 2018 by PALGRAVE
Reprinted by Bloomsbury Academic

This edition published with permission from Bloomsbury Publishing Plc,
50 Bedford Square, London, WC1B3DP, UK

ISBN: 978-93-56403-28-4
10 9 8 7 6 5 4 3 2 1
For sale in the Indian subcontinent only

Typeset by Deanta Global Publishing Services, Chennai, India
Printed and bound in India by Thomson Press India Ltd

To find out more about our authors and books
visit www.bloomsbury.com and sign up for our newsletters

BRIEF CONTENTS

CONTENTS

LIST OF FIGURES

CASE FIGURES

LIST OF CASE STUDIES

Chapter	Case	Title	Industry	Focus
1	1.1	Giordano	Apparel and accessories	Overview of setting objectives and strategy development
2	2.1	Price leadership strategies at Aldi	Supermarket	
2	2.2	Giordano – Providing value for money merchandise	Apparel and accessories	Sound strategy development – three illustrations
2	2.3	Restructuring within the health care industry	Health care	
2	2.4	Customer segmentation in the electricity industry	Electricity	Essential task of identifying differences in market segments
2	2.5	Market position of bottled water labels	Bottled water	Illustrating market segmentation and customer insights
2	End of Chapter	ING Direct	Banking	Operations supporting a business's market
3	3.1	ING Direct – matching customers to service delivery systems	Banking	Matching customers to service delivery system design
3	3.2	Reducing vehicle maintenance costs at Alpha Engineering Construction	Engineering	Using benchmarking to improve performance
3	End of Chapter	Babcock and Wilcox	Energy and environmental technologies	Operations strategy development
4	4.1	Improving service delivery through use of front and back offices	Banking	Service delivery system design
4	4.2	Providing personal service online at Garden Escape	E-commerce (Nursery)	Online shopping
4	4.3	Self-scanning in supermarkets	Supermarket	Using customers in service delivery
4	End of Chapter	Amazon	E-commerce	Delivery services
5	End of Chapter	Cirque du Soleil	Entertainment	Delivering products

Chapter	Case	Title	Industry	Focus
6	End of Chapter	Rumack Pharmaceuticals	Pharmaceutical	The use of profiling in operations strategy
7	7.1	Triplex Electronics	Electronics	Focus – an illustration
7	7.2	Maintaining focus in maturing markets	Motor	Examining the basis of focus
7	7.3	Refocusing as products mature and diversify	Pharmaceutical	Focus – an illustration
7	7.4	Strategic review resulting from increased demand for a product group	Electronics	Focus – an illustration
7	7.5	Benefits of allocating infrastructure	Food	Allocating infrastructure as part of focusing operations
7	7.6	Creating an operation-within-an-operation arrangement	Packaging	Focus – an illustration
7	End of Chapter	M2	Communications	Focus
8	8.1	How to create your own competition	Multiple	Outcomes of some make-or-buy decisions
8	8.2	The dominance of the cost argument	Castings	Trade-offs in buy decisions
8	8.3	Suppliers that grow to be competitors	Mobile phones	Disadvantages of outsourcing
8	8.4	Direct alpine approach	Mountaineering	Reducing lead times
8	End of Chapter	Lego	Children's toys	
9	9.1	Analyse markets using cross-functional perspectives supported with data	Construction	Inventory management
9	9.2	Do not issue across-the-board inventory reduction directives	Motor	Inventory management
9	9.3	Computer system makes operations more expensive and less effective	Furniture	Simple controls replace by computer system
9	9.4	Systems not modified to meet changing business and market needs	Telecommunications	Make-or-buy decisions require appropriate systems
9	9.5	One system used to support different market needs	Aerospace	Different systems for different sets of needs
9	9.6	Konsuke Matsushita on why the West will lose	Multiple	Observations from Japan

Chapter	Case	Title	Industry	Focus
9	End of Chapter	Riviona Bank	Banking	Restructuring service delivery systems
10	10.1	Uber	Transportation	Impact of new service provision
10	10.2	Atos: zero email	Technology	Using ambitious targets
10	10.3	*South Park*'s number one rule of story telling	Entertainment	Rules for presentations
10	10.4	Pixar's rules of storytelling	Film	Some rules of storytelling
10	10.5	Some great TED talks	Entertainment	Presentation tips
10	10.6	The power of a good story	E-commerce	Building a story to enhance a proposal
10	End of Chapter	Fowlers of Earlswood	Food	Evaluating investment proposals

TOUR OF THE BOOK

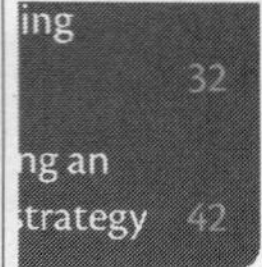

INTRODUCTION

Faced with the pressures of increasing competition, businesses need, more than ever, to coordinate the activities of their principal **functions** effectively in order to perform at their best in their chosen market(s). This involves developing a unified business strategy that embraces all parts of the organization. As a large function in most companies and one that delivers the services and products

Introduction
Sets the scene for the chapter and explains the key topics that will be covered.

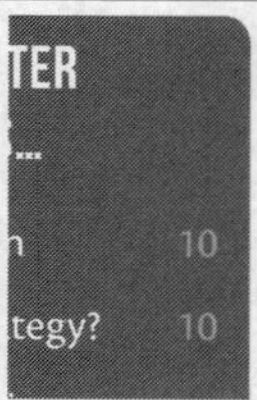

SUMMARY

This chapter outlines and explains the principles and concepts that underpin the role and content of operations strategy. In so doing it

- Clarifies the purpose and contribution of strategy within organizations
- Identifies the role of different functions in business strategy development

Summary
Provides a concise overview of the key points of the chapter.

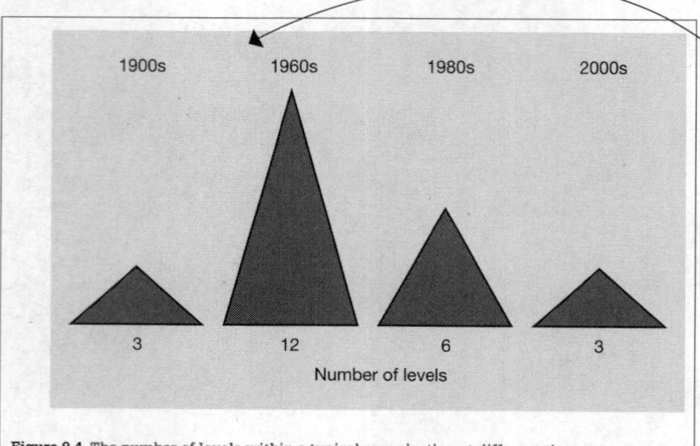

Figure 9.4 The number of levels within a typical organization at different times

Figures
Data or concepts in a tabular or graphic format to provide a deeper illustration of the issues being discussed.

Case 9.1 – Analyse markets using cross-fun supported with data

The marketing function within a US company believed its cons steel customers wanted products to be supplied in two days. I hold finished goods and work-in-progress inventory for all its p operations lead time. However, sales failed to increase as fore was left with high levels of slow-moving inventory. An operati highlighted the inventory and questioned whether a two-day l

Cases
Illustrate current business practices and show how the ideas and concepts discussed in the chapter can be applied in practice. Questions at the end of each case encourage critical reflection.

Discussion Questions
Each chapter offers a set of questions that can be used as class exercises or for self-testing and evaluating your knowledge about the chapter topic.

 DISCUSSION QUESTIONS

1 Whereas changes to existing or the introduc
manufacturing processes are readily recogniz
often appear questionable and overstated, b
timescales involved. Discuss.
2 Businesses can make infrastructure developn
in nature. Explain the advantages and disadva

Reflections
Discuss the issues addressed in each chapter and encourage critical evaluation and reflection on the key topics that have been discussed.

REFLECTIONS

This short introduction sets the context for
is useful and appropriate to summarize the

1 Whereas the skills and expertise require
built up over time, the skills to complete
content and orientation. These need to l
by executives as they move up the orga
responsibilities.
2 To effectively develop strategies to mee
to be clarity by having shared definition
within the executive group. Although st
is one where often the level of clarity is
characterized by generalized discussion
need to ensure that the debate uses clea
meanings and understandings. In this w

Exploring Further
Provides journal articles, books, films and websites that allow you to explore further the ideas and concepts discussed within the chapter content.

 EXPLORING FURTHER

Barber, F. and Strack, R. (2005) 'The surprising
Business Review, 83(6): 80–90.
Berry, W.L. and Hill, T.J. (1992) 'Linking systems to
Production Management, 12(10): 3–15.
Bryan, L.L. (2007) 'The new metrics of corporate
Quarterly, 1: 57–65.

End of Chapter Cases
As well as the smaller cases within the chapter, there is also a longer case at the end of each chapter. This can be used for a tutorial, study group or class discussion based on the aspects covered within the chapter. Questions at the end of each case encourage critical reflection.

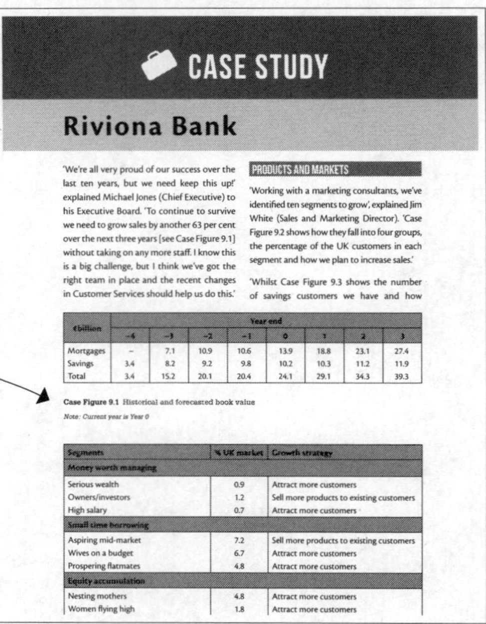
CASE STUDY

Riviona Bank

'We're all very proud of our success over the last ten years, but we need keep this up!' explained Michael Jones (Chief Executive) to his Executive Board. 'To continue to survive we need to grow sales by another 63 per cent over the next three years [see Case Figure 9.1] without taking on any more staff. I know this is a big challenge, but I think we've got the right team in place and the recent changes in Customer Services should help us do this.'

PRODUCTS AND MARKETS

'Working with a marketing consultants, we've identified ten segments to grow', explained Jim White (Sales and Marketing Director). 'Case Figure 9.2 shows how they fall into four groups, the percentage of the UK customers in each segment and how we plan to increase sales.'

'Whilst Case Figure 9.3 shows the number of savings customers we have and how

€billion	Year end							
	−4	−3	−2	−1	0	1	2	3
Mortgages	–	7.1	10.9	10.6	13.9	18.8	23.1	27.4
Savings	3.4	8.2	9.2	9.8	10.2	10.3	11.2	11.9
Total	3.4	15.2	20.1	20.4	24.1	29.1	34.3	39.3

Case Figure 9.1 Historical and forecasted book value

Note: Current year is Year 0

Segments	% UK market	Growth strategy
Money worth managing		
Serious wealth	0.9	Attract more customers
Owners/investors	1.2	Sell more products to existing customers
High salary	0.7	Attract more customers
Small time borrowing		
Aspiring mid-market	7.2	Sell more products to existing customers
Wives on a budget	6.7	Attract more customers
Prospering flatmates	4.8	Attract more customers
Equity accumulation		
Nesting mothers	4.8	Attract more customers
Women flying high	1.8	Attract more customers

Companion Website
The book's companion website at www.palgravehighered.com/Hill-OS offers a wealth of resources for both lecturers and students.

1 OPERATIONS STRATEGY: INTRODUCTION

THIS CHAPTER DISCUSSES...

SUMMARY

To provide the context in which an operations strategy is developed and implemented, this opening chapter

- Highlights the key role of developing an appropriate strategy in an organization
- Outlines the relationships between corporate/business objectives and strategy
- Explains the levels of strategy (corporate, business unit and functional) within an organization, the respective responsibilities for their development and how they relate one to another
- Explains how the day-to-day and strategic purposes of using the key resources of time and money differ

Managing business organizations is difficult due to the complexity and dynamics that characterize the task. The dynamics are driven by the changing nature of demand, the actions of competitors, the decisions and requirements of customers and the potential uncertainties of supply chains. The complexity comes not from the technical dimensions of the business but the number of dimensions involved, their changing nature and the interfaces between and across them. This level of difficulty is further enhanced by the need to set business objectives going forward and to agree and implement strategies to achieve these as well as managing the organization in terms of the ongoing and demanding day-to-day tasks. This book concerns one key aspect of these tasks. It discusses and explains how to develop and implement a strategy for one of the functions within a business, that of operations. This introductory chapter is designed to help set the context in which an operations strategy sits and to highlight some of the key features that need to be recognized and taken into account in its development.

Given the difficulty of undertaking this strategy task and the sizeable contribution it will typically make to the success of the business, then the outcomes need to be based on an analysis of relevant data and ongoing, in-depth discussions within the business about the issues and alternatives involved and progress being made. This requires each executive involved to think as a business person first and a functional expert second. Furthermore, clarity of discussion and relevance of insights are essential, and one of the key skills that executives need to develop. This clarity has its base in using words and data with shared meanings and common understandings. As with the other aspects of managing a business, if the words and concepts used to discuss and agree options have more than one meaning then the discussion and outcomes do not, in fact, have meaning. They lead to apparent agreement, future misinterpretations and a lack of shared outcomes. Given the complex nature of managing a business and the inherent uncertainties and dynamics highlighted earlier, then executives need to develop the skill of being clear and consistent in the difficult process of forging a strategy. They also need to clearly explain their own function's perspectives, opportunities, limitations, potential investments and timescales while ensuring that they understand these same key dimensions for the rest of the business.

Throughout the following chapters this clarity will be explained and illustrated, and will become a key takeaway in your greater understanding of and ability to contribute to strategy development and implementation in your own organization. To start this process, the rest of the chapter introduces some key background perspectives and positions the content of the book within a business and within the role of the operations management task.

ORGANIZATIONAL LEVELS AND THEIR STRATEGIC ROLES

As businesses grow the roles involved in designing, selling and delivering the services and products provided and accounting for the outcomes are separated out into functions as a more effective way of managing the larger business. Similarly, with further growth it will make sense at some point to run the total enterprise as more than one business. At this point the organization would now comprise three levels – corporate, business units and functions.

However, the various functions make up the business unit and the different business units make up the corporate whole. Although they have been separated out as explained above, they comprise the same whole and, therefore, the strategic direction and tasks to be undertaken need to be linked within one level and between one level and the next. Before we discuss how this works let's explain objectives and strategy and how they interface. Objectives are the targets that are set going forward while strategy is the way(s) of achieving them. And, note here that strategy is not an expression of importance alone but is a statement of how the business objectives are to be achieved. As a term, therefore, it should only be used when discussing or stating the actions and developments that concern how a function would deliver its part in meeting agreed business objectives.

As with the organizational tie-up of one level to the next, corporate objectives reflect and are a composite of the objectives of the different business units. Similarly, a business unit's objectives reflect the opportunities that are available, what the different functions can deliver and the investments and timescales involved. Now let's look at the role within these three organizational levels in setting objectives and agreeing relevant strategies to achieve them.

1 **Corporate level** – reflects the combined forward look of all the business units, discusses and determines the priorities between them and sets the objectives for the total organization. Discussions will take into account the proposals by each unit and the outcomes may, in fact, change the objectives initially put forward by one or more of the businesses. Each business will then be tasked with meeting its part of the total corporate objectives. The executives responsible for developing a corporate strategy will be the chief executive officer (CEO) of the whole organization, the CEOs of each business unit and possibly some specialists.
2 **Business unit level** – reflects the forward look of a business unit. The executives responsible will be the CEO of the unit, the heads of the different functions and possibly some specialists. The discussion will take into account a range of options and the forecast outcomes of these, the associated investments and timescales involved and the views and perspectives of all the functions. As at the corporate level, the discussion on objectives and strategy will be iterative in nature, with what is achievable and the investments and timescales involved tempering agreed outcomes. As explained above, the agreed objectives may then be modified by subsequent discussions at the corporate level.
3 **Functional level** – embodies the actions (strategies) proposed by functions to meet the business unit objectives and includes investments and timescales.

The content of this book concerns the operations function within a business unit. It reviews the role of the operations executive in, and the approach to, developing an operations strategy, and the contribution in agreeing the objectives and strategy for the business unit as a whole. The corporate level discussions and outcomes are the subject matter of other books.[1] Where corporate strategy issues are included here it is to help set context for the business unit and functional levels of strategy.

A business unit sets objectives going forward that can range from financial targets to improving its performance on chosen dimensions of its corporate social responsibility programme. While these objectives are set by the executive group at the top of a business, they are delivered by the various functions that make up the business as a whole. Operations is one of these and, as with other functions within a business, it is tasked with providing those aspects of performance for which it is responsible and with developing a strategy to accomplish these and deliver the results.

This short introduction to 'operations strategy' is designed to set the scene and establish the context for what follows. It is intended to help separate your understanding of the task facing functional executives into its components parts and, in that way, to help clarify the content of each and highlight the boundaries between them.

BUSINESS OBJECTIVES AND STRATEGY

Before addressing the executive roles within an organization let us first look at the components of the strategy task.

Business objectives – are set by the business unit as a whole and typically take the form of financial targets (such as the level of sales revenue, profits and return on investment) and non-financial targets (such as aspects of its corporate social responsibility programme).

Within the process of setting objectives, functions such as marketing and operations would be involved in agreeing the targets for the business unit.

Functional strategies – within the business-unit strategy process, each function will work through the detail of the targets set, what can be achieved and how it would be achieved, while identifying any additional resources the function would need to meet the targets. As you would imagine, the process of setting targets and agreeing strategies to achieve them is an iterative process as executives work through the detail and assess the outcomes. You will see in the following chapters that this task moves from business unit-wide outcomes to functional detail and back with all relevant executives involved in assessing and choosing from alternatives, testing proposals, challenging forecasts and examining outcomes.

EXECUTIVE ROLES – DAY-TO-DAY AND STRATEGIC TASKS

As businesses grow, activities are separated out into clusters of similar tasks. These are then managed as functions, which provides a workable structure to handle the growing complexity that comes with larger organizations, including the opportunity for relevant staff to specialize in one part of the business.

Within each of these functions senior executives have two sets of tasks:

- **Day-to-day** – to manage and control the range of activities that fall within their area of responsibility as well as the crossovers between functions. Also known as the 'operational' task.
- **Strategic** – to be a part of the executive group that determines the business objectives going forward and then develop an appropriate, functional strategy in line with these decisions.

The tasks that make up the day-to-day role within operations are covered by the content of books with the appropriate title 'operations management'.[2] In simple terms this concerns managing and controlling those tasks within the operations function that are necessary to provide the services or make the products and deliver them to customers and will range across the whole supply chain. However, there is an equally essential role that concerns developing an operations strategy to support the needs of agreed markets and, although part of the same executive task, this role is different in orientation. For operations management:

- The day-to-day or operational role is to manage and control the various, wide-ranging tasks involved in providing services and making products and to do this by the efficient management of these tasks and by bringing about developments and improvements.
- The strategic role is to contribute to the debate about and agreement on the non-financial and financial objectives to be addressed by the business. Regarding non-financial targets, operations would develop a strategy (the actions to take and the investments and timescales involved) to accomplish those for which it was responsible. Regarding financial objectives, operations would be party to agreeing the markets in which to compete in terms of retaining customers, growing market share and entering new markets. Operations then needs to develop and invest in the delivery systems and infrastructure to provide those competitive dimensions for which it is solely or jointly responsible, for example

price and delivery speed. In this way, operations' capabilities (such as people skills, delivery systems and processes) are guided by strategic requirements (to deliver the needs of agreed current and future markets) and so help provide competitive advantage and contribute to meeting the objectives set by the business as a whole.

Thus, while day-to-day or operational tasks are built on internal efficiency, strategic tasks need to be oriented to external effectiveness. Put another way, the day-to-day role is doing things right and the strategic role is doing the right things.

USE OF RESOURCES

Undertaking either strategic or day-to-day tasks involves using key resources in terms of time (staff, systems and processes) and money (costs and investments). It is the reasoning behind the decisions and the end goals served that determine whether the use of resources is day-to-day or strategic:

- The use of resources is day-to-day if they are used to deliver services or make products, schedule customer requirements, record activities, monitor costs, supervise staff and manage the daily tasks of a business. Similarly, improving activities, procedures or systems to reduce costs by making these areas more efficient is also a day-to-day task.
- The use of resources is strategic if they are used to maintain or improve a function's performance so that a service or product more adequately meets customer expectations or gives it an advantage over its competitors (and thereby influences a customer's decision to buy).

Let's look at an example of where the agenda concerns using resources to reduce cost. The intent will be:

- **Day-to-day** if the benefits of the cost reduction are retained in the business and used to improve internal efficiency or swell profits
- **Strategic** if the benefits of the cost reduction are passed on to customers in the form of a reduction in price and in that way make relevant services/products more competitive on that dimension.

DEVELOPING THE MANAGEMENT COMPETENCES TO UNDERTAKE THE STRATEGIC ROLE

When executives first begin to work in organizations they typically establish themselves within a particular function that matches their training and orientation. Over time they progress in their careers, in part through gaining the necessary expertise in managing the day-to-day tasks assigned to their role. In this way, executives accumulate this necessary expertise over time and, in a somewhat essentially incremental way, build up their competences to handle this part of their job.[3]

As they progress to higher levels in an organization, executives need also to recognize the demands of the strategic role that their position increasingly entails and purposefully develop the appropriate set of skills to successfully discharge this key part of their job. This book is intended to help executives in this essential part of their development.

This short introduction sets the context for the book and highlights some key issues. It is useful and appropriate to summarize these here

1 Whereas the skills and expertise required to undertake the day-to-day tasks are built up over time, the skills to complete the strategy tasks are different in both content and orientation. These need to be recognized and purposefully developed by executives as they move up the organization and take on these additional responsibilities.
2 To effectively develop strategies to meet agreed business objectives there needs to be clarity by having shared definitions of the data and language used by and within the executive group. Although strategy development is a critical task, it is one where often the level of clarity is low and the debate is in danger of being characterized by generalized discussion and conclusions. Consequently, executives need to ensure that the debate uses clear language that is based on shared meanings and understandings. In this way, clarity and rigour will characterize both the discussions and the outcomes.

Now take a look at Case 1.1.

Case 1.1 – Giordano

Giordano International Limited is a Hong Kong (HK)-based retailer of men's, women's and children's apparel and accessories. Founded in 1981, it now employs over 8,000 staff; with 2,400 outlets in more than 30 countries and current sales of HK$5,381 million (see Case Figure 1.1).

Year	Sales (HK$ million)	Net profit margin (%)
2005	4,413	4.7
2008	5,048	6.6
2012	5,673	14.6
2014	5,548	7.4
2015	5,381	7.9

Case Figure 1.1 Giordano – sales revenues 2005–2015

Originally founded as a wholesaler for HK-based manufactured clothing going to the US, it scaled back this part of its operation in the mid-1980s to set up its own retail shops in Hong Kong. Initially selling men's apparel, it soon expanded to selling discounted casual unisex apparel.

Giordano's success is based on its well-trained, frontline customer service staff that have always focused on exceeding customers' expectations in terms of merchandise and service. As part of this, it has initiated many additional services such as complimentary alterations to clothing, a global exchange policy and a customer service toll-free hotline. In 2007 it launched its global, cardless loyalty programme where the mobile phone number becomes a person's membership number, and the programme now has over 8 million members worldwide. The company adopts a mix of product and thematic marketing as a way to build and maintain its brand name. These campaigns change frequently and include celebrity endorsements, cross-over programmes with partner organizations (for example, a range of Monsters University-designed apparel when it teamed up with Disney-Pixar in 2013 to celebrate the launch of the Monsters University movie), in-store activities and selected ranges of merchandise.

In 2005 the company formally published its corporate social responsibility (CSR) policy statement. It is committed to maintaining and developing this programme throughout all its retail outlets as well as the other parts of its organization, The company highlights a number of key areas including ethical sourcing, employee relations, environmental protection and community involvement.

Questions

1. What are the company's objectives as outlined in the case, and which functions would be responsible for delivering them?
2. Given the data in Case Figure 1, what are some of the possible strategies open to the company going forward?

NOTES AND REFERENCES

1 Books dealing with corporate strategy include Horovitz, B. (2014) *The Hard Thing About Hard Things: Building a Business When There are no Easy Answers*, Harper Business; Lynch, R. (2006) *Corporate Strategy*, 4th edn, Pearson Education; Porter, M.E., Kim, W.C. and Renee, R. (2011) *HBR's 10 Must Reads on Strategy*, Harvard Business School Publishing, Boston; Rumelt, R.P. (2011) *Good Strategy Bad Strategy: The Difference and Why It Matters*, Crown Business; Stern, C.W. and Diemier, M.S. (eds) (2012) *The Boston Consulting Group on Strategy: Classic Concepts and New Perspectives Audio Studios*, 2nd edn, Wiley; Johnson, G., Scholes, K. and Whittington, R. (2014) *Exploring Corporate Strategy*, 10th edn, Prentice Hall.

2 See, for example Melnyk, S.A. and Denzler, D.R. (1996) *Operations Management – Value-driven Approach*, Irwin; Hill, A. and Hill, T. (2018) *Essential Operations Management*, 2nd edn, Palgrave Macmillan; Brown, S., Blackman, K., Cousins, P. and Maylor, H. (2012) *Operations Management – Policy, Practice and Performance Improvement*, Routledge; Hill, A. and Hill, T. (2012) *Operations Management*, 3rd edn, Palgrave Macmillan; Jones, P. and Robinson, P. (2012) *Operations Management*, Oxford University Press.

3 Smith, A.D., Plowman, D.A., Duchon, D. and Quinn, A.M.I. (2009) 'A qualitative study of high reputation plant managers: political skills and successful outcomes', *Journal of Operations Management*, 17: 237–46.

EXPLORING FURTHER

Beckman, S.L. and Rosenfeld, D.B. (2007) *Operations Strategy: Competing in the 21st Century*, McGraw Hill.

Brown, S. and Blackmon, K. (2005) 'Linking manufacturing strategy to the strategy mainstream: the case for strategic resonance, *Journal of Management Studies*, 42(4): 793–815.

Brown, S., Squire, B. and Lewis, M. (2010) 'The impact of inclusive and fragmented operations strategy on operational performance', *International Journal of Production Research*, 48(14): 4179–98.

Collis, D.J. and Rukstad, M.G. (2008) 'Can you say what your strategy is?', *Harvard Business Review*, 86(4): 82–90.

Fitzsimmons, J.A. and Fitzsimmons, M.J. (2010) *Service Management: Operations, Strategy, Information Technology*, McGraw Hill Higher Education.

Goddard, J. and Eccles, T. (2012) *Uncommon Sense, Common Sense – Why some organisations consistently outperform others*, Profile Books Limited, London.

Jessen, M. et al. (2007) *Strategy Execution: Passion & Profit*, Copenhagen Business School Press.

Johnson, G., Scholes, K. and Whittington, R. (2010) *Exploring Corporate Strategy*, 8th edn, Prentice-Hall.

Kaplan, R.S. and Norton, D.P. (2008) *Execution Premium: Linking Strategy to Operations for Competitive Advantage*, Harvard Business School Press.

Lencioni, P. (2006) *Silos, Politics and Turf Wars: A Leadership Fable About Destroying the Barriers that Turn Colleagues into Competitors*, Jossey-Bass.

MacLennan, A. (2010) *Strategy Execution: Translating Strategy into Action in Complex Organisations*, Routledge.

Mintzberg, H., Ahlstrand, B. and Lampel, J.B. (2008) *Strategy Safari: The Complete Guide Through the Wilds of Strategy Management*, Financial Times Prentice Hall.

Parry, K.W. and Bryman, A. (2006) 'Leadership in organisations', in Hardy C., Lawrence, T.B. and Nord, W.R. (eds), *Handbook of Organisational Studies*, 2nd edn, London: Sage, pp. 447–68.

Porter, M.E. and Kramer, M.R. (2007) 'Strategy and society: the link between competitive advantage and corporate social responsibility', *Harvard Business Review*, 84(12): 78–92.

Rosenweig, E.D., Laseter, T.M. and Roth, A.V. (2011) 'Through the service operations strategy looking glass: influence of industrial sector, ownership and service offerings on B2B e-marketplace failures', *Journal of Operations Management*, 29(1/2): 33–48.

Slack, N. and Lewis, M. (2015) *Operations Strategy*, 4th edn, Pearson Higher Education.

Van Mieghem, J.A. and Allon, G. (2015) *Operations Strategy: Principles and Practice*, 2nd edn, Dynamic Ideas.

Yukl, G.A. (2013) *Leadership in Organisations*, 8th edn, Prentice Hall.

2 OPERATIONS STRATEGY: PRINCIPLES AND CONCEPTS

THIS CHAPTER DISCUSSES...

SUMMARY

This chapter outlines and explains the principles and concepts that underpin the role and content of operations strategy. In so doing it

- Clarifies the purpose and contribution of strategy within organizations
- Identifies the role of different functions in business strategy development
- Highlights everyday misnomers in both business strategy and operations strategy and examines the reasons for current approaches to developing strategy
- Explains how to link business objectives and functional strategies through markets
- Outlines the approach and procedures for understanding markets
- Illustrates how to implement an operations strategy

INTRODUCTION

Faced with the pressures of increasing competition, businesses need, more than ever, to coordinate the activities of their principal **functions** effectively in order to perform at their best in their chosen market(s). This involves developing a unified business strategy that embraces all parts of the organization. As a large function in most companies and one that delivers the services and products sold to customers, operations has a key role in the development and implementation of strategy. This chapter will define strategy in relation to the organization and explore the levels within a business at which strategy must be developed and implemented, the relationship between strategy and **day-to-day tasks**, and the key step of understanding markets in the strategy development process. It will then go on to look at how operations can contribute to developing a successful strategy and the steps involved.

WHAT IS STRATEGY?

Strategy embodies the aspects of both direction (what to do) and implementation (how to do it). The element of direction concerns the approaches a company can use to help it choose the markets (today and in the future) in which to compete, understand the competitive drivers in these markets while also assessing how it can influence its market position vis-à-vis its competitors. Implementation concerns how it can match or better meet the competitive drivers involved by prioritizing where and how to spend its key resources of time and money. Integral within this strategy process is the development of a number of functional strategies (such as marketing strategy and operations strategy) that have the responsibility for implementing those aspects of the business strategy for which that function is solely or jointly responsible.

To help appreciate what this means it is useful to reflect on the meaning of the word itself. Derived from the Greek word *strategos*, a general, from *stratos*, army, and *aegin*, to lead, the origin of strategy concerned the art of planning and directing large military movements and operations of a campaign of war. The transfer of the word to business activities is understandable and appropriate, where the market becomes the theatre of competition.

The parallels don't stop there. The Greek general would also have divided his army into different units, for example archers, chariots and foot soldiers. As with functions in a business this leads to specialist skills and capabilities being enhanced. However, the general also quickly found out that to win a battle it was much better if the different parts of his army faced the same direction and their roles and activities in battle were agreed and coordinated. The same parallels also transfer to business and the same need to interface the different aspects of strategy and ensure cooperation and coordination between the parts is one key to success.

EVOLUTION OF STRATEGY WITHIN A BUSINESS

As companies grow, they cope with the greater level of complexity that results by splitting the total business activity into parts that are called **functions**. As organizations grow further, they invariably broaden the range of markets in which they compete. To cope with this growing complexity, organizations will typically arrange these different activities into separate **business units**, each made up of relevant functions such as operations, sales and marketing, and finance. For example, within a bank, business units might include corporate banking, retail banking, financial markets, mortgages, pensions and insurance – each will serve a different market or a similar set of markets or market segments. One outcome of these changes is that strategy development now takes place at three levels – corporate, business unit and functional. The substance of this chapter concerns the development and implementation phases of one of the key functional strategies, that of operations. But first, let's look at the three levels of strategy.

LEVELS OF STRATEGY

For most businesses, strategy needs to be developed at three levels (see Figure 2.1).

1 **Corporate** – concerns decisions by the business as a whole in terms of the sectors in which it wishes to compete. At this level, companies decide where to invest or **divest** in terms of the overall business mix they wish to develop today and in the future. Such decisions relate to aspects including where to allocate investment funds, the buying of relevant companies and the selling of all or parts of existing businesses.

Level of strategy	Distinctive tasks
Corporate	Strategic activity at the corporate level concerns the direction of the total business and addresses issues such as where to invest and/or divest, and priorities in terms of sales revenue growth. Implementation concerns the allocation of investment funds in line with these priorities.
Business unit	Business units comprise different parts of a total business. For example, corporate banking, retail banking, financial markets, mortgages, pensions and insurance would be separated into different business units within a bank. For each business unit, strategic direction concerns identifying the markets in which it competes, agreeing where it intends to grow (including new markets), the nature of competition and the relevant competitive criteria in its current and future markets, in terms of maintaining and growing share. Implementation concerns discussing and agreeing how and where to invest, in terms of functional tasks and alternative approaches.
Functional	Each business unit will comprise a number of functions such as sales and marketing, operations and IT that together make up the total activities within a business unit. The strategic role of each function is to provide, improve where necessary and maintain those competitive dimensions within a market for which it is wholly or partly responsible. In this way, the market comprises the agenda for functional strategies and becomes the mechanism for determining development and investment priorities. Implementation concerns consistently meeting the competitive norms involved and improving where necessary while selecting from alternative approaches to attain the improvement goals laid down.

Figure 2.1 Levels of strategy and their distinctive tasks

2 **Business unit** – within each chosen sector, an organization will usually have, depending on the terminology used, one or more firms, companies or business units. Each will serve different segments within a sector, although there may be some overlap. Such overlap could be for reasons of history, convenience, preference or failure to reach agreement within the overall business. Each business unit will need to develop a strategy in terms of its markets. Agreement on the current and future markets in which to compete is an essential strategic task and one in which all relevant functions must be involved. On the basis of the markets it has identified, the business as a whole discusses and agrees which customers to gain and retain, with which to grow (as well as the competitive factors involved in gaining, retaining and growing these customers) and the increased market share that would result. It is in these debates that functional differences need to be recognized and reconciled, and where resolution of strategic direction is taken. In that way, appropriate decisions on the markets in which to compete are taken at the business rather than the functional level.

3 **Functional** – functional strategies prioritize developments and investments in line with the needs of agreed current and future markets, and the strategic task for a function is consistently to meet or improve its level of support for relevant competitive criteria. These can either be the sole responsibility of a function (for example, meeting the delivery speed requirements of customers is solely an operations management responsibility) or the joint responsibility of two or more functions (for example, shortening service/product development lead times could be the joint responsibility of several functions such as design, marketing, engineering, IT and operations).

After the markets and customers have been agreed and the competitive factors involved in retaining and growing market share have been identified, functional strategies aim to:

- Assess how well each function currently provides those competitive factors for which it is solely or jointly responsible.
- Agree their relative importance in chosen markets.
- Assess the gap between the provision of these factors and the level required to retain and/or grow the company's share of the market.
- Establish how to close the gap (the investments and timescales needed).
- Implement the resulting plan.

The role of functions in supporting the needs of customers and markets differs from market to market in terms of their scope (the aspects involved) and level of importance. Thus, working within the context of the business as a whole, functions will agree priorities, the levels of investment involved and the timescales needed to complete the process. Figure 2.2 provides some examples of functional strategic responsibilities.

KEY STRATEGIC INTERFACES

While separating strategy development into three levels is appropriate in terms of orientation, helpful in terms of providing clarity and useful in terms of distinguishing the varying levels of contribution, there understandably exist key interfaces between them. Figure 2.3 illustrates these.

Function	Examples of criteria for which it is solely responsible
Research and development	Product and service design*
IT	System developments
Marketing	Brand name, customer relationships and pricing
Operations	Delivery reliability, quality conformance, price (in terms of cost reduction) and delivery speed

Figure 2.2 Examples of functional strategic responsibilities

**In a service company, the design function is typically part of marketing's strategic responsibility.*

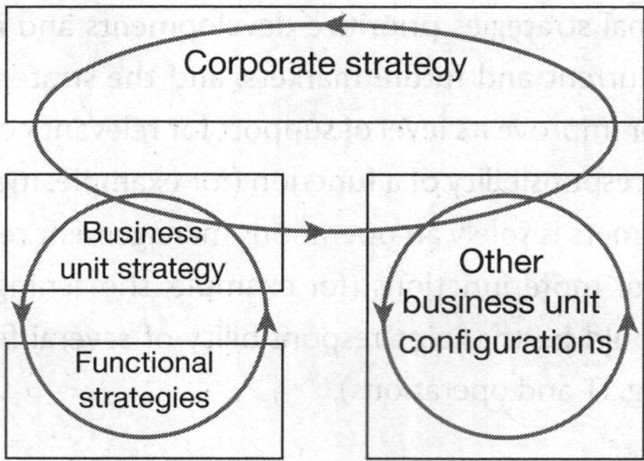

Figure 2.3 Essential interfaces between different levels of strategy

The corporate strategy and business unit strategy interface involves the chief executive officer (CEO) of the whole company, other executives with corporate responsibilities and the CEOs of each of the business units. Based on this group's understanding of all the business units in terms of their markets, their position vis-à-vis competitors and their investment needs, the strategic decisions addressed by these executives include where best to allocate investment funds within and between all the business units and whether to purchase other companies or sell off parts or all of existing businesses.

The second key interfaces are those within each business unit. The strategy group within a business unit comprises the CEO of the business unit, other executives with business unit-wide responsibilities and the heads of each function within the business unit. Based on their shared understanding of the unit's markets and customers, its position vis-à-vis its competitors, where it wishes to grow, where its current market share is under threat, any opportunities to gain new customers, increase its current market share or enter new markets, investment decisions will be made.

This book concerns the latter interface, that between business unit strategy and functional strategies using operations strategy as an in-depth example of the latter. This does not in any way imply that the strategic outcomes and contributions for functions will be similar one to another. In one company a particular function may be required to make little contribution whereas the same function in another company may be required to make a significant contribution to implementing strategy. Similarly, a function in the same business may be a key provider of strategic advantage in one market or for one customer and yet be of little strategic consequence in another market or for another customer. However, the one key strategic contribution that all functional executives need to provide is their part in discussing and analysing markets, helping to provide and review market and customer data and setting the strategic agendas for relevant functions.

ESTABLISHING STRATEGIC DIRECTION

Sound strategic direction (and subsequent implementation) is built on two key factors – robust content and the rigour applied to those discussions by the executives responsible for formulating and implementing strategy. An overview of these is now provided, while a more in-depth explanation of the process is given later in the chapter.

1 **Content** – competing successfully in chosen markets is the essence of the strategic task. This comprises the two independent but related tasks of:

- determining the factors (described as order-winners and qualifiers) that enable a business to compete effectively;
- functions developing and implementing appropriate strategies to bring this about.

Identifying and clarifying customer/market needs, therefore, is at the root of this task and involves establishing the order-winners and qualifiers (and their respective weightings) for customers/markets while recognizing that these will typically vary for different customers/markets and whether it concerns:

- today or the future;
- retaining or growing market share;
- entering new markets or gaining new customers;
- being market-driven or market-driving;
- being the primary or secondary supplier to a customer.

2 **Executives** – as mentioned earlier, those responsible for formulating a business unit strategy comprise the CEO of the business unit, other executives with business unit-wide responsibilities and the heads of functions (see Figure 2.4).

Executives begin their careers in the function that reflects their training, orientation and professional education. As they are promoted and assume higher positions in that function their role and contribution need to change.

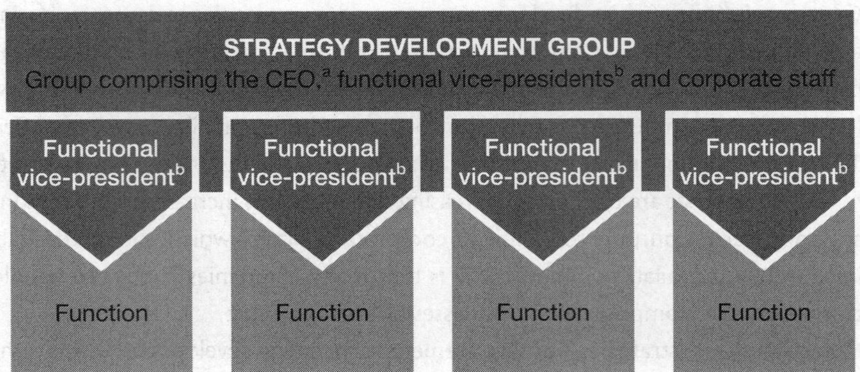

Note: [a]*CEO means corporate executive officer, also known as 'managing director'.* [b]*Vice-president is the term for the head of a function and is also known as 'director'.*

Figure 2.4 Strategic group composition

While in junior positions their role concerns exercising their technical expertise, which is both essential and appropriate. However, as they take on higher positions their contribution needs to broaden. This is particularly so when they are involved in business-wide discussions and particularly those regarding the strategic direction of the company. In these roles they need to think and behave like business executives first and technical experts second. In that way, while they bring appropriate expertise to the discussion and ensure that options and decisions are technically robust, they also need to contribute to the strategic debate from a business perspective. The rigour now required needs to comprise both a business and technical perspective to ensure that sound strategic direction is the outcome.

MISNOMERS IN STRATEGY DEVELOPMENT

With the essential role of strategy development in the prosperity of businesses there has been a corresponding and appropriate increase in attention to its development and formulation. That has resulted in new insights and approaches being proposed. While many of these are useful and usable, some of the contributions are misleading and unhelpful, resulting in a number of misnomers in the areas of both business and operations strategy.

This section is included here to draw your attention to these as a prelude to detailing how operations strategy should be developed and its role within a business. As the misnomers include key aspects of business as well as operations strategy development, then what follows has been provided as two separate sections.

1 Business strategy development

- Lack of integration – in many organizations, business strategy is developed as a series of independent statements. Lacking essential integration, the result is a compilation of distinct functional strategies which sit side by side, layer on layer in the same corporate binder. Integration is not provided if, in fact, it was ever intended.[1]
- Generic solutions – when developing strategy, many companies review their businesses as a whole, which allows them to undertake the business strategy development task by overlaying the diversity inherent in their businesses with generic, strategic solutions. Niche, low-cost, core competence-type arguments are seductive in their apparent offerings. The promise of uniformity is appealing to those with the task of developing strategies for businesses that are typified by increasing difference not increasing similarity. In fact, such approaches purport to identify a corporate similarity which, though desirable, is inherently not available. The outcome is that many companies choose to handle the complexity that comprises their businesses by setting it aside.
- Objectives versus strategies – often statements on strategy development include phrases such as 'improving customer service', 'meeting customer expectations' and 'delighting customers'. These types of statement illustrate a fundamental misunderstanding of strategy because such phrases are, in fact, corporate objectives. They describe the intended outputs of strategy but do not identify what a business has to do (its strategy) for meeting such objectives.

2 Operations strategy development

- Solution versus problem (or the cart before the horse) – as highlighted earlier, businesses compete with one another for customers and market share. The problem at the heart of strategy development then is for companies to determine the order-winners and qualifiers that reflect customers' needs in the various markets in which they compete while recognizing that these may change over time, vary from customer to customer and differ with regard to retaining as opposed to growing market share, or entering new markets (see the earlier section, 'Establishing Strategic Direction').

  The approach put forward by many writers and contributors in the field of operations strategy is to ignore this vital first step of problem resolution (that is, identifying the relevant order-winners and qualifiers). Instead they move on to the next step, that of solutions or the action(s) to take to provide the range of order-winners and qualifiers for which operations is responsible. As such they put the cart before the horse. Although the words used by various contributors and writers to describe each element of operations strategy may vary, in essence the dimensions listed are the same. This list comprises the aspects of operations' performance that satisfy market requirements, and are subsequently proposed as the performance objectives that constitute operations strategy. Typically there are five performance objectives listed by many contributors in the field of operations strategy – cost, dependability, flexibility, quality and speed. There are several serious flaws in this approach. Some are dealt with in the next section but one fundamental issue is addressed here: if operations strategy is proposed as the provision of the factors that satisfy all the market requirements for which operations is responsible, then this will create a perception within a business that operations' strategic role is to cover all its bases and that all the competitive factors that fall within operations' remit need to be provided at the same level irrespective of time (today or in the future), whether to retain or grow market share, whether to enter new markets and so on.

  Such levels of similar emphasis are clearly untenable given the differences that characterize markets, the size of investment (time and money) involved, the constraints of reality and the changing nature of competition. Companies need to be aware of the relevant order-winners and qualifiers and their respective importance and how well these criteria are being provided, the size of the gap and the investment and timescales necessary to close the gap. In this way strategic tasks can be understood and assessed, options can be considered and consequences evaluated. Furthermore, the formulation of all functional strategies is a business and not a functional responsibility. While functions put forward data and recommendations, the business (as did the Greek general) chooses between options and determines the level of importance. While functions are at the heart of the analysis and discussion, choosing between options and determining priorities are business-based decisions. Implementation of a functional strategy, on the other hand, is the task of that function. Operations strategy (as with other functional strategies) is the business's operations strategy, while implementation is an operations task.
- Components of operations strategy are described and explained by the same dimensions. Building on the last point, putting forward operations strategy as comprising the

same list contributes to undervaluing the role of the operations executive in strategy development while misleading businesses by implying that all market requirements will be met by those five performance objectives. This has the following outcomes:

- Operations' contribution to the difficult but most essential task of determining the order-winners and qualifiers of markets and customers is set aside.
- The trade-offs that accompany strategic choices within operations are neither recognized nor addressed. As the list of five performance objectives above covers the major contributions from operations, then the rest of the business, being presented with such a list, is led to believe that there are no apparent issues to address, no choices to make, no concerns to consider and no limits to what operations can contribute.
- Where constraints are not identified then choosing which customers to shed, retain or grow and which new markets to enter are inadequately reviewed and which order-winners and qualifiers are critical to supporting these options are not determined.
- Decisions regarding the size of investment (time and money) and the priority (which tasks to complete first) are left with operations and not, as they should be, determined by the business. Making these key decisions at the level of the function and not at the level of the business will invariably lead to
    - inappropriate priorities and allocation of resources;
    - operations being exposed to criticism, not with regard to what it has done but with regard to those aspects that are yet to be improved because it will invariably fall short of the 'total provision' mandate that this approach implies.
- Where operations investment priorities are left to operations to decide then insights and opportunities of where best to invest and where best to start so as to maximize sales revenue and profits are bypassed. Without a business mandate, operations understandably will invest in line with its own, and not necessarily the business's, perspective of what is best.

- Use of words with more than one meaning – the lack of clarity highlighted in an earlier section is also repeated in the way that contributors to operations strategy also blur discussion by using words with more than one meaning.

  Examples include

  - Quality: does this refer to the service/product specification or providing the service or product to specification? While the former falls within the remit of sales/marketing (for services) or research and development (for products), the latter is part of operations' strategic contribution (see Figure 2.2).
  - Delivery: is this on time (delivery reliability) or a need for short lead times (delivery speed)?
  - Flexibility: does this, for instance, relate to accommodating new service/product introductions, providing a wide range of services/products, handling a range of volumes or readjusting schedules to cope with changes in delivery lead times? The operations capabilities to handle these differ but expressing its contribution as providing 'flexibility' leaves both operations and the business exposed to misinterpretation, unfounded expectations and the subsequent failure to meet customer promises or requirements and market needs.

To handle the complexity and dynamics that characterize today's markets requires clarity in terms of the order-winners and qualifiers that reflect customer needs and the corresponding functional tasks to provide them. Being clear is a core requirement of a successful strategy process.

A RECAP ON FUNCTIONAL STRATEGY DEVELOPMENT

At this point, let's pause and reflect. This chapter principally concerns the development of an operations strategy. As a key function within a business, one role of operations (as with other functions) is to contribute to meeting the corporate objectives set by a business and, in so doing, it needs to be party to their agreement in order to exploit available opportunities while recognizing the timescales and constraints involved. As Figure 2.5 shows, strategy development is an interactive process linking all parts of a business with one another and with the objectives set within a given period. And core to this are the markets (recognizing the driven and driving dimensions discussed in the next section) in which a company competes. Note that the separation of operational strategy in Figure 2.5 from the other functional strategy elements is merely to reflect the orientation of this book. It is important to remember that what needs to dominate strategy development is the business itself and not one functional view. Similarly, the Wal-Mart and Kmart illustrations in the next section are not intended to imply that emphasizing one functional strategy is better than emphasizing another but are provided to show the key roles of market understanding in giving direction and the implementation of functional strategies in bringing this about.

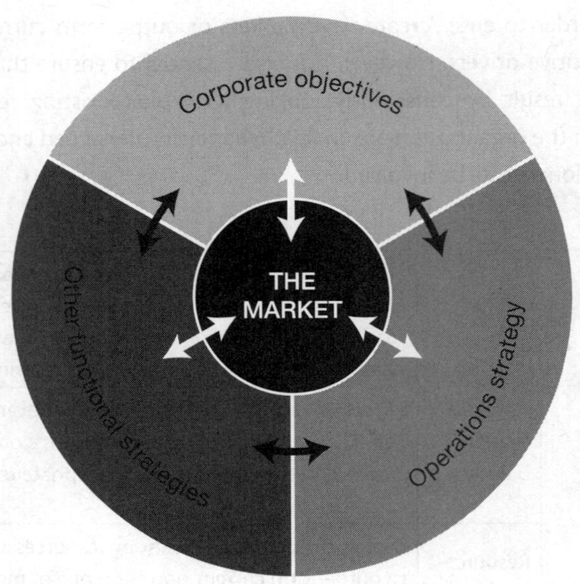

Note: The phrase 'corporate objectives' here refers to the objectives set at the level of the business unit

Figure 2.5 The market at the centre of strategy development

MARKET-DRIVEN AND MARKET-DRIVING STRATEGIES

At this early stage in our discussion on operations strategy, it is useful also to distinguish between **market-driven** and **market-driving strategies**.

Market-driven

Being market-driven concerns providing the competitive criteria in a market to the required levels, for example meeting the delivery lead times that customers require or expect, such as keeping queue lengths in a bank to (say) three minutes or less.

Market-driving

Market-driving concerns proactively seeking ways to change the competitive norms and hence create a situation where a company can influence its market position vis-à-vis its competitors. In this way, an organization can improve on current, required levels of a given driver to gain a competitive edge. The ways to do this can be either a market-based or a resource-based approach[2] as explained below and summarized in Figure 2.6.

- Market-based – here companies proactively identify where market advantage could be gained by outperforming the current norms on one or more relevant market drivers and then allocating resources to this end.
- Resource-based – continuing the theme of being more proactive in arriving at appropriate strategies has seen the emergence of resource-based competition. Again the emphasis is to be knowingly proactive in seeking ways to change the competitive norms for market advantage. The orientation here is to exploit the potential of existing resources and capabilities in order to enter/create new markets or outperform current norms on one or more competitive drivers. However, it is also essential to ensure that the competitive advantages that result by consciously looking to exploit existing resources or create **synergies** within the organization are, in fact, what customers need and are willing to pay for should additional costs be involved.

The strategic mix	Market-driven		Strategy based on understanding current and future markets and recognizing how the competitive drivers are time- and market-specific. Will differ depending on whether it concerns maintaining share, growing share or entering new markets
	Market-driving	Market-based	Proactive approach to identify where advantage can be gained by outperforming current norms on one or more drivers and then investing in appropriate resources and capabilities
		Resource-based	Exploit the potential of existing resources and capabilities to outperform current norms on one or more competitive drivers

Figure 2.6 **Market-driven and market-driving strategies**

The market-driven and market-driving strategic mix

Most companies' approach to current and future markets will comprise a mix of both market-driven and market-driving strategies. Much of what a company sells, the customers it sells to, the markets in which it competes and how it competes within these today will be similar to yesterday and the same for tomorrow. But, being aware of the need to proactively seek ways to drive markets and exploit resource-based opportunities is an essential element of the strategic task in times when markets are increasingly different and competitive. For this reason, most companies will need to have a strategy that is a mix of the market-driven and market-driving approaches, as illustrated in Figure 2.6.

BUSINESS UNIT STRATEGY

Functional strategies are an integral part of a business unit and, in that way, the two levels of strategy need to interface (see Figure 2.3). While this chapter concerns developing an operations strategy, let us first look at how a business unit strategy should be developed compared to how it often is in practice.

As discussed earlier, organizations use functions in order to facilitate the management task involved. However, businesses are not a number of different parts or functions, but are wholes. An essential task, therefore, is to rebuild the parts back into a whole and nowhere is this more critical than at the strategic level. Also, as Figure 2.4 illustrated, the heads of functions will appropriately form part of the strategy development group as these parts form the whole business.

Discussion and agreement about current and future markets have already been highlighted as an integral part of strategy development. This step requires functions to discuss their views on markets, address and resolve differences and agree on what is best for the business overall. Similarly, the outcomes of this debate would be major inputs into developing a strategy at the business-unit level, with the desired process being in line with that outlined in Figure 2.7.

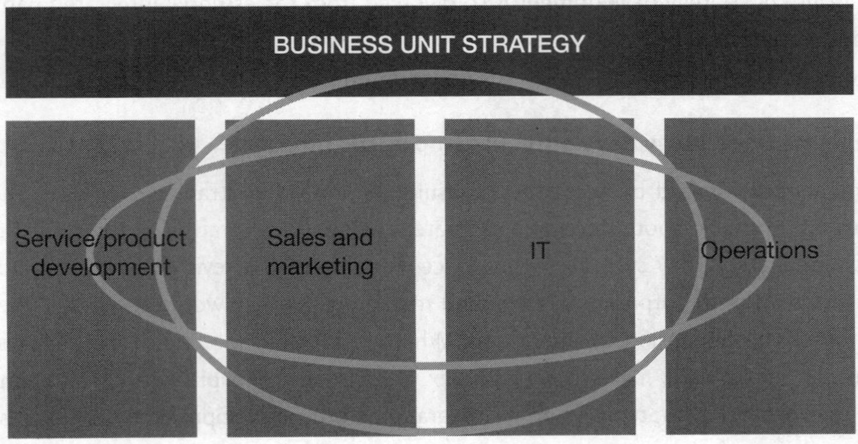

Figure 2.7 Ideal business unit strategy-making process

Figure 2.8 Real-life business unit strategy-making process

Functions would debate current and future markets, and highlight constraints and opportunities as part of their input into developing a strategy for the firm while again providing both market-driven and market-driving orientations. Similarly, opportunities and strategic initiatives would be signalled at the business-unit level and form part of the essential debate and strategic outcome.

Reality is often far from this. As mentioned earlier, the lack of integration that too often characterizes business strategy development results in outcomes more similar to that represented by Figure 2.8 than that shown in Figure 2.7.

Some of the reasons why this occurs were highlighted in the section 'Misnomers in strategy development'. Other reasons for the approach to developing strategy with outcomes similar to that in Figure 2.8 are now provided.

Reasons for current approaches to developing strategy

If the reality of strategy development is so divorced from the essential integrated nature of the task, the question which at once comes to mind is Why? There are several reasons – some were discussed earlier while the other key ones are summarized below.

Statements on strategy developments stop at the interface

Statements put forward by academics, consultants and other strategy specialists on how companies should go about developing a strategy allude to integration, but in reality ignore this essential step. They stop at the interface. For example, a review of major textbooks and articles on both corporate strategy and marketing strategy would show that they fail to embrace the dimension of operations. Whether it would inhibit the approaches and arguments put forward, make it too complex to describe and explain or signal an implicit belief that delivering strategy is not an integral part of its development, the reality is that the essential interfacing central to Figure 2.7 is never aspired to, let alone delivered, in most approaches to corporate and marketing strategy development.

History of functional dominance

Approaches to developing corporate strategy have a history of being dominated by single functions. In many manufacturing companies, for example, the operations function dominated the corporate strategy process until about the mid-1960s. In a world where, up to that time, there was in the manufacturing sector undercapacity relative to demand, selling what you could make was typically the dominant thrust of strategy. As the capacity/demand imbalance redressed itself, selling into markets became more difficult and heralded the birth of marketing's key role in the success of companies. This strategic role has, in many firms, been strengthened with the continued growth in competition, especially where markets are increasingly characterized by overcapacity as emerging nations develop or companies enter existing markets in which they previously did not compete. As with operations before, marketing has acquired the mantle of providing strategic direction, not only in its own eyes but typically in the eyes of others and the firm as a whole. The outcome is that much of the time marketing's view goes undiscussed and unchallenged.

Markets versus marketing

Coupled with the last point is the fact that many firms fail to make the critical distinction between markets and marketing. Whereas markets comprise the business itself, marketing is a function. Thus, while marketing will play a necessary role in the debate and agreement about markets, it is critical that its views of market needs are challenged and enlarged, or changed where necessary. While its insights are essential to the understanding of markets, they are limited in the perspective they offer on two counts:

1 The reality of delivering the needs of markets is only fully understood by those functions charged with undertaking those tasks. While marketing has responsibility for meeting several of these criteria, there are many that are in the domain of others. In fact in some, if not several, instances, marketing's strategic role is limited, in that other functions are responsible for supporting most, if not all, of the needs of a company's chosen markets.
2 The constraints, timescales and investment implications involved in maintaining or improving support for those performance criteria that relate to market success can only be gauged and assessed by the function involved in that provision.

Not recognizing these essential differences and not incorporating all relevant perspectives within the strategy debate will only lead to inadequate and superficial outcomes.

THE PROACTIVE ROLE OF MARKETING IN STRATEGY DEVELOPMENT

One consequence of the last two points is that marketing expects to, is expected to and consequently does take a proactive role in strategy development. While this is the desired stance to be adopted by all relevant functions, many organizations, in acknowledging and supporting marketing's proactive role, fail to recognize the need to incorporate other perspectives essential to the discussion and agreement on markets and strategic direction. The proactive stance adopted by marketing is seen as an implicit (if not explicit) statement that markets and marketing are one and the same, and that marketing has a singular role in these essential strategy decisions that are central to the business as a whole.

THE REACTIVE ROLE OF OPERATIONS IN STRATEGY DEVELOPMENT

The fact that the operations function has an exacting and critical corporate role to play is never in dispute. Couple this with the high cost and fixed nature (changes take a long time to bring about) of its investments, then it is paramount for a company to understand the business trade-offs involved in operations decisions. As operations is the principal player in providing those criteria that maintain and improve market share and successfully allow the company to enter new markets, then not knowing how operations will ensure the provision of that support is risk-taking of a higher order, especially given the highly competitive and fast-changing nature of today's markets and the fixed and high-cost dimensions involved in development and investment.

Reasons for the reactive role of operations in strategy development

Given this scenario, why is it that today's operations executives typically adopt a reactive role in strategy development, and why does the situation appear not to improve? There are several reasons, including those listed below.

Operations managers' view of themselves

A major contributing factor to the current position is that operations managers also see themselves as holding a reactive business brief. Too often they believe that their role concerns a requirement to react as well as possible to all that is asked of the operations delivery system. They see their role as the exercise of skill and experience in coping effectively with the exacting and varying demands placed on the system and reconciling the trade-offs as best they can. But rarely do they explain or provide data to illustrate the relative size and impact of these trade-offs that would form an essential insight and part of the business strategy debate. As a result, these decisions are inappropriately made at the level of the operations function rather than the level of the business.

The company's view of the operations manager's role

The view held by operations of its own role is reinforced by the company's view of its strategic contribution. Although chief executive officers (CEOs), managing directors or their equivalents are actively (and appropriately) engaged in discussions with marketing about decisions on markets and customers, the same level of time investment is typically not given to understanding key operations decisions and their impact on market support. A lack of recognition is, therefore, reflected in the typically low level of involvement that results.

Too late in the corporate debate

Very often, operations executives are not involved in business unit strategy discussions until the decisions have started to take shape. The result is that they have less opportunity to contribute to decisions on strategy alternatives. Consequently, operations finds itself in a reactive role, unable to affect strategic alternatives or direction, and to be on the back foot in terms of providing appropriate levels of market support while defensively complaining about the unrealistic demands made of them and the problems that will invariably ensue.

Lack of language

Underpinning these organizational barriers is the added difficulty that, on the whole, operations managers do not have a history of explaining the strategic contribution of their function clearly and effectively to others within the company. Reasons for this failure, however, cannot wholly be placed at the operations executive's door. The knowledge base, concepts and language so essential to providing, explaining and positioning operations' perspectives and insights have not been developed in the same way. Surrogates for operations strategy in the form of panaceas (see the earlier section 'Misnomers in strategy development') have more often than not taken the place of strategic inputs, and the support given to these approaches by academics and consultants has reinforced this stance. For example, the regular heralding of just-in-time (JIT), lean operations and total quality management (TQM)-type initiatives has been seen, in part at least, as comprising the strategic contribution of operations. In a similar way, calls to become 'flexible', for instance, point to an apparent state in operations that offers a capability to do most (if not all) things. Purposefully general, such overtures as these are without essential definition and direction and, more importantly, purport to offer the rest of the business an operations' capability to support any strategic alternative equally well and without involving any trade-offs. Furthermore, when the superficiality of this state is exposed, the pundits for such strategic alternatives merely switch the phrase (to become 'versatile' and 'agile' are two such), arguing that the subtle differences provided remedy the serious misgivings inherent in the discarded phrase. The cycle then restarts.

LINKING MARKETING AND OPERATIONS

For many businesses, strategy comprises the independent inputs of different functions. However, this invariably leads to functional conflicts that, without a way of being resolved, will result in inappropriate business decisions being taken. Where this concerns process and/or infrastructure investments, it involves two important characteristics. These investments are large in size and fixed in nature. Consequently, they typically take a long time to determine and install, and a long time to change. Thus, it is essential that companies understand the relevance of proposed investments in terms of their current and future markets.

This chapter addresses the need to close the gap by providing approaches to strategy building that bring together marketing and operations, facilitate open discussion about the business and enable the sensible resolution of functional differences at the business level.

The importance of linking marketing and operations is as paramount as it is logical. They are, after all, two sides of the same coin. Together, they constitute the basic task in any business – the sale and delivery of services and products. On the surface it would seem simple to unite their efforts to meet the needs and expectations of customers. The reality is often far removed from what should be the desired goal of those involved.

Many current strategy approaches reinforce business misunderstandings and promote interfunctional differences and rivalry. Functional dominance in business strategy development is a typical source of such problems. The result is that key functions tend 'to treat one another as competitors for resources rather than coming together to serve external customers'.[3] This is well illustrated by Figure 2.9 that lists the different, often opposing, views held by operations and marketing on a range of issues. In markets that are increasingly competitive, there is an urgent need to close the gap, increase business awareness of the differences and difficulties involved in the status quo and facilitate discussion based on an improved understanding of functional perspectives, business options and overall consequences. The way forward is to resolve interfunctional differences not at the level of the function, as is often the case now, but at the level of the business. These genuine conflicts need to be addressed and resolved in terms of what is best for the business as a whole. In that way, the tensions, concerns and rivalries that typically characterize the marketing/operations relationship can be set to one side. The focus can then shift from competing functional views about what is best overall, to each function doing its part to implement the chosen strategy.

The question is how? Before addressing this issue, however, Cases 2.1–2.3 illustrate how the link has been established and the successful outcomes that result.

Case 2.1 – Price leadership strategy at Aldi

The advent of the warehouse model for distributing food and dry goods provides a good example of companies competing on a price leadership strategy.

Aldi, the German-based grocery chain, provides an example of how an integrative approach to marketing and operations has been successful as the company has supported its chosen price leadership strategy with a clear integration of marketing and operations so that they cooperate rather than compete. The basis of Aldi's retail offering is a no-fuss concept. The design is simple, making it easy to shop. Wide gangways, bare floors, inexpensive lighting (basic, bright and abundant), basic displays (often displayed in the manufacturer's original packaging), comprising warehouse-style racking and sturdy wire mesh cages, and limited support staff keep costs down. Of the product range on offer, Aldi keeps a limited (typically about 25 per cent of the range offered by traditional supermarket competitors), mainly own-label range of goods.

Issues		Perspectives and goals	
		Operations	**Sales and marketing**
Services/ products	Range	Restricting range enhances volumes, helps reduce costs and simplifies control	Customers typically seek variety. Restricting range reduces segment coverage and sales revenues
	Standardization versus customization	Lack of change reduces uncertainty and room for error. Limiting server discretion maintains cost and throughput targets	Customization is often important, particularly in mature markets. Server discretion personalizes service, often at little cost, and enhances customer retention
Costs and profit		Measured on meeting cost budgets. Resists orders that increase costs. Has no control over pricing	Sales revenue is the key performance measure. Profit implications are not part of the decision or evaluation. Higher costs are not part of its budget considerations
Productivity improvements		Reduce unit costs	May cause a decline in the provision of quality conformance
Location of facilities		Considerations relate to costs and the convenience for suppliers and staff	Customers may find it unattractive, undesirable and, for a service business, inaccessible
Managing capacity		High utilization of capacity has an effect on costs and assets. Pressure to manage capacity and thereby keep investment as low as possible	Service/product may be unavailable when needed. Quality compromised in high demand periods
Job design		Oriented to minimizing errors and waste. Simplify tasks and use technology where possible	Employees are oriented to operations task and not customer need. Restricts the ability to meet changing requirements as they occur
Queues		Optimize the use of available capacity by planning for average throughput	Increases customer lead times. Customers facing long lead times or queues may go elsewhere

Figure 2.9 Operations and marketing perspectives on key issues

Case 2.2 – Giordano – providing value-for-money merchandise

Giordano, the Hong-Kong-based clothes retailer, provides value-for-money merchandise through the careful selection of suppliers, strict cost control and holding down its in-store prices, For example, its average retail outlet in the Middle East is between 1,000 and 2,000 square feet. In these locations, where retail space is expensive, the company works without a storeroom by replenishing stock from a central distribution centre. When an item is sold, the bar code information on the garment lists size, colour, style and price and is transferred to the company's computerized system through its point-of-sale cash registers and used to compile the store's order for the next day. With orders filled during the night, the new inventory is in the store the following day. The IT system similarly provides real-time information to production facilities, an essential input into manufacturing schedules.

Furthermore, the company has maintained its policy of keeping the range in store to no more than 100 items of which some 20 are classed as core items. The narrow range helps keep inventory levels low, reduces discounts and enables the company to be more responsive to market changes. As Giordano expands into different markets, the need to understand these customer tastes and preferences for different fabrics and colours has been recognized and built into its systems.

Case 2.3 – Restructuring within the health-care industry

Restructuring within the health-care industry grew apace in the 1990s, with worldwide annual mergers and acquisitions. However, delivering the potential is proving harder to bring about. Those that have are looking to change the delivery of care and the operations support involved.

Quantum Health Resources, an Indianapolis-based firm specializing in the treatment of haemophiliacs, reduced by over 20 per cent the typical annual patient bill of $100,000 by assigning 'personal care managers'. In this way, drugs are now managed, hospitalization due to lack of personal care is cut and drug regimes are under constant review, improving fit and eliminating waste.

Paradigm Health is a California-based company specializing in caring for people with catastrophic injuries such as brain damage and serious burns. Annual patient care costs can run as high as $2 million but this has been cut by half through specializing support for patients, treating more people at home and assigning support teams to sets of patients, thereby improving operational support and lowering costs.

The growing need to control and reduce the operational costs of delivering health care has led, in the US, to a spurt of vertical integration by insurance companies moving into the management of hospitals and health clinics. In that way, they recognize that the essential need to link sales and operations can be made, enabling businesses to grow, deliver a better service and become more profitable.

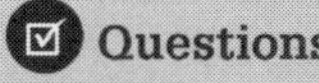

Review Cases 2.1, 2.2 and 2.3 and consider the following questions.

1 Identify the key way in which operations supports each company's markets.
2 Now compare your three reviews and tabulate the similarities and differences involved.

LINKING BUSINESS OBJECTIVES AND FUNCTIONAL STRATEGIES THROUGH MARKETS

Functional strategies concern investing and developing in ways that support the needs of markets in terms of being both market-driven and market-driving. The role of functional strategies is to contribute to meeting agreed business objectives. The form and size of contribution will vary from market to market but the strategic development process for all functions is similar:

- **Phase 1 – understand markets** and ensure both a market-driven and a market-driving approach while maintaining an ongoing, rigorous review throughout this first critical step.
- **Phase 2 – translate** the reviews into strategic tasks. For example, if price is an order-winner, then the task is to reduce costs; similarly if on-time delivery is a competitive factor, then improving the reliability of meeting customer due dates is the task.
- **Phase 3 – check** that what is currently provided matches what is required in a market-driven scenario or the new level in a market-driving scenario.
- **Phase 4 – develop a strategy** (the prioritizing of investments and developments) to close the gap where the level of provision falls short of the requirement or achieve the new level of performance in a market-driving scenario.
- **Phase 5 – implement** the necessary investment and development priorities.

Typically, companies are in more than one market or market segment with different sets of order-winners and qualifiers. As a consequence, there will invariably need to be more than one set of functional strategies and so the strategic development process for functional strategies outlined above will need to be repeated for each market or market segment. Where the order-winners and qualifiers of two or more markets/market segments are similar then one operations strategy will meet these needs, assuming that there are no delivery system technology constraints. Separating operations into clusters of capabilities to serve similar performance objectives is one way to handle this diversity within businesses. The concept is entitled 'focused facilities' and is addressed later in the book.

In this way, companies are better able to coordinate functional contributions, with markets appropriately providing the common agenda for all. Invariably, two functions that are central to this task are operations and marketing, as emphasized in the last section.

BUSINESS OBJECTIVES	MARKETING STRATEGY	HOW DO YOU QUALIFY AND WIN ORDERS IN CHOSEN MARKETS?	OPERATIONS STRATEGY	
			Delivery systems choice	Infrastructure choice
Sales revenue growth Survival Profit Return on investment Other financial measures Corporate social responsibility targets Environmental targets	Product/service markets and segments Range Mix Volumes Standardization versus customization Leader versus follower alternatives	Price Quality conformance Delivery: speed reliability Product/service range Design leadership Technical support Brand name New services and products – time to market	Choice of delivery systems Trade-offs embodied in these choices Make-or-buy decisions Capacity: size timing location Role of inventory in the delivery system	Operations scheduling systems IT systems Procedures Work structuring Organizational structure

Notes

1 *The entries in each column are to provide examples and are not intended to be a definitive list.*

2 *Although the steps to be followed are given as finite points in a stated procedure, in reality the process will involve statement and restatement, because several of these aspects will impinge on each other.*

3 *Column 3 concerns identifying both the relevant order-winners and qualifiers for customers or markets/market segments.*

Figure 2.10 Framework for reflecting operations issues in business strategy decisions

The framework given in Figure 2.10 is intended to help explain what needs to take place, so that the link between business objectives and marketing and operations strategies can be made. The framework has five columns, each representing a step, while Figure 2.11 shows the interactive, ongoing nature of the strategy debate.

The middle column in both figures concerns analysing and understanding the market, and is at the core of the framework. In Figure 2.10 the arrow going from left to right represents the need to link objectives and marketing strategy to the market, while the one going from right to left represents the need to link operations strategy to the market. In this way, how a company competes in its markets and how it may wish to drive the market is at the centre of the debate. This allows functions to discuss current and future markets, how competitors behave and their potential responses in the future, alternative ways of competing in these, the

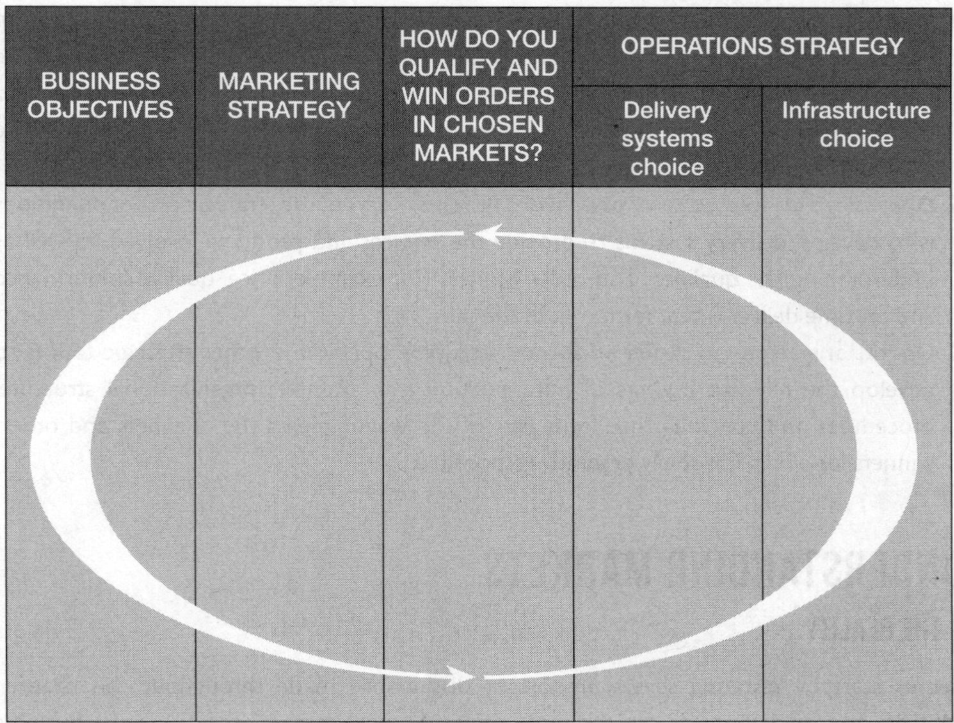

Figure 2.11 The interactive ongoing nature of the strategy debate

constraints, developments, investments and timescales involved and how they can coordinate their strategic efforts to meet the agreed objectives for the business as a whole. As Figure 2.11 illustrates, this is an interactive approach and needs to be an ongoing process forming an integral part of senior executives' roles.

How the framework operates

The objective of using the framework in Figure 2.10 is to develop an operations strategy for a business. The steps involved are outlined below. Although presented here in a sequential form they will, in fact, constitute an ongoing set of discussions, with statements and restatements of corporate or business objectives and functional strategies comprising the outcome of the process.

1 **Business objectives** – these are set by the business as a whole and typically take the form of targets for sales revenue growth, profit, return on investment, social responsibility and other financial measures. They may well include non-financial objectives such as corporate social responsibility and environmental targets.
2 **Marketing strategy** – developed by the marketing function to meet relevant corporate, business objectives. It would typically be concerned with approaches to growing sales in existing markets and strategies to enter new markets.

3 **How do you qualify and win orders in chosen markets?** Addressing this question constitutes the core step in the development of functional strategies, where the executive group (see Figure 2.4) debates and agrees markets (to include both the market-driven and market-driving dimensions) and the qualifiers and order-winners involved. This step will be expanded in the following sections.
4 **Operations strategy: choice of delivery systems** – part of the strategic task of operations is to develop delivery systems to provide the services and products involved, as well as underpinning the qualifiers and order-winners (for example, price, quality conformance and on-time delivery) that form part of the sale.
5 **Operations strategy: choice of infrastructure** – operations' other strategic task is to develop the relevant aspects of infrastructure (for example, organizational structure, procedures and controls) that form part of the way it meets the qualifiers and order-winners for which it is solely or jointly responsible.

UNDERSTANDING MARKETS

1 THE REALITY

Let us start by restating several important distinctions made throughout this chapter. Markets and marketing are not the same thing. Whereas markets constitute the business itself, marketing is a function. As there will typically be several markets served by a business, the relevant competitive criteria to retain and grow existing market share, change the rules (become market-driving) and enter new markets will differ from market to market. As emphasized throughout, the strategic role of functions (including marketing and operations) is to debate and agree the markets in which to compete, the qualifiers and order-winners and respective weightings involved, and to support those criteria for which they are solely or jointly responsible. In this way, the company becomes market- (as opposed to marketing-) driven.

And, once again, the cornerstone in all of this is understanding markets. Markets are the essence of a business, the very reason for its existence and, consequently, you can never know too much about them. Identifying differences, supporting these insights with clear explanations and descriptions, and verifying them with supporting data would, therefore, be reasonable to expect. The reality is, however, that the necessary clarity is too often not provided. The case examples given earlier are the exception rather than the rule. Instead, current approaches to business strategy development typically fail to provide sufficiently adequate insights on which to build functional strategies. One outcome of this is that, without the necessary clarity, each function's investment and development priorities are in line with what it thinks are the best aspects to improve. The essential link between market needs and functional strategies is consequently not provided.

Current approaches to market reviews, as explained earlier, are usually only looked at and described from a marketing point of view. Markets or market segments are typically based

Case 2.4 – Customer segmentation in the electricity industry

A major UK electricity distributor segmented its customers into large businesses, small and medium-sized enterprises (SMEs) and domestic consumers. The basis for the segmentation was the relative size of sales revenue per customer account. The initial marketing strategy was to grow sales revenue and, as a consequence, its efforts were directed towards increasing its large business customer portfolio as the best way of meeting this objective. However, a noticeable decline in profits as a percentage of sales followed and led to a review. Operations data revealed that profit margins in the large business segment were, on average, more than 40 per cent lower than for SME customers. Marketing's successful drive to increase sales revenue had also led to a lack of effort to retain, let alone grow, SME customers. The outcome was an increase in overall sales revenue but a decrease in profit percentages. The marketing-led strategy had pursued sales growth in a below-average profit margin segment.

Questions

1. List side by side the market dimensions used by marketing and operations.
2. How would you use both perspectives to arrive at an operations strategy?

on factors such as geographical regions and the sectors in which a business's own customers operate. A pause for reflection will lead you to a recognition that this is both an inappropriate and an inaccurate inference to draw. Although from the viewpoint of marketing, customers clustered by a region or country or customers' own standard industrial codes represent coherent segments. From an operations point of view, there will invariably be different sets of demands from groups of customers within these segments and hence these will constitute different customers in terms of the order-winners and qualifiers to be provided, as illustrated by Case 2.4.

In summary, what typically happens now is that:

- Market descriptions are limited to the views of marketing. While these views give essential insights from a marketing perspective, they fail to yield the key differences and provide essential insights into markets from the view of other functions, particularly that of operations.
- The words and phrases used to describe markets are not sufficiently precise to provide the clarity needed to yield essential insights.
- The procedures used are not sufficiently exacting to expose and challenge these critical deficiencies, and inadequate outcomes result.

Given the pivotal role of market understanding to strategy development, how does a company improve its approach in this key phase of the process? This question is answered in the following section.

2 UNDERSTANDING CUSTOMER REQUIREMENTS

Before we explain the approach to follow in the process of understanding markets (the subject of the next section), let's first reflect on what customers buy when making a purchase.

When customers purchase a service or product, they buy a combination of:

1 The service/product itself which has a specification (what it comprises), and
2 A number of related criteria such as:
- **Price** – it matches or betters an acceptable price, or the purchase price set by competitors;
- **Delivery speed** – it meets its customers' lead-time requirements;
- **Quality conformance** – the service/product is provided to the stated specification (see point 1);
- **Customer relationships** – the company/staff have established relationships with customers;
- **Delivery reliability** – the service/product is delivered on time.

In some instances, the specification of the service/product may be the only or the dominant factor influencing a customer's decision to buy, for example a custom-made wedding dress, an expensive automobile or choice of restaurant. But, in most instances, the purchase is made on the basis of the specification together with a mix of related criteria such as those listed above, and is illustrated in Figure 2.12. The criteria and their relative importance in securing the sale will differ from one service/product to another and from customer to customer.

3 THE APPROACH TO FOLLOW

Clarity about markets is essential. Companies are in multiple markets and the outcome of the debate on markets should identify, and provide a clear understanding of, the differences that exist.

The purchase	The service/ product specification	Examples of related criteria				
		Price	Delivery speed	Quality conformance	Customer relationship	Delivery reliability
The business task	Meet/better the design of competitors	Reduce costs	Shorten lead times	Meet the specification	Develop customer relations	Deliver on time
Function responsible	Marketing for services, research and development for products	Operations	Operations	Operations	Sales and marketing	Operations

Figure 2.12 The purchase: the make-up of customer choice

The steps to secure these insights are as follows:

1 **Avoid general words and phrases** – again we emphasize the fact that using general words and phrases needs to be consciously and rigorously avoided. Each dimension should be expressed on its own and a single definition needs to be associated with each word or phrase used. In this way, each competitive dimension put forward as being relevant can be discussed separately and its relevance assessed. One classic example of this that was highlighted earlier is the phrase 'customer service'. While a desirable objective, the answer to the question 'what does it mean?' is not self-evident because it embodies a number of potential meanings. Using 'customer service' to describe the competitive nature of a market thus confuses rather than clarifies.
2 **Long lists denote poor strategy process** – the outcome of the discussion on how a company competes in its markets is typically a long list. The intention seems to be to leave nothing off the list, thereby covering all aspects. Nothing could be further from the truth. This phase of the strategy development process concerns distilling the very essence of how a company has to compete. In this way, essential clarity is provided.
3 **Separate out order-winners and qualifiers** – a further step to improve a company's understanding of its markets is to separate relevant competitive criteria into:
   - **Qualifiers** – these criteria get a service or product into a marketplace or onto a customer's shortlist and keep it there. They do not in themselves win orders but provide the opportunity to compete. Conversely, the failure to provide qualifiers at appropriate levels will lead to a loss of orders. In this way, qualifiers are order losing in nature because failure to provide a qualifier results in not being on the list – the opportunity to compete is not in place. In such situations, competitors do not win orders from a rival, rather the rival loses orders to its competitors.
   - **Order-winners** – these criteria enable the company to sell their service or product. Gaining entry to a market or onto a shortlist is only the first step. The task then is to know how to win orders against competitors who have also qualified to be in the same market. With qualifiers, you need to match customers' requirements (as do competitors), whereas with order-winners you need to provide them at a level better than your competitors.

Finally, when applying this concept there are some key points to remember:

- Qualifiers are not less important than order-winners, they are different. Both are essential. With qualifiers, a company needs to qualify and requalify at all times to stay on a customer's shortlist. If you are not on the list, you cannot compete.
- Order-winners and qualifiers are time- and market-specific – they will be different from market to market and will change over time within a market.
- The relevance and importance of order-winners and qualifiers will typically be different for retaining market share, growing share in existing markets and entering new markets.
- The relative importance of qualifiers and order-winners will change when moving from being market-driven to being market-driving.
- As highlighted earlier, not all criteria will be either a qualifier or an order-winner. Some criteria do not relate to some markets.

4 **Weight qualifiers and order-winners** – to improve clarity still further, it is necessary to weight qualifiers and order-winners in the following way:
  - **Qualifiers** – it is adequate and appropriate to limit the classification of qualifiers to two categories – qualifiers and order-losing sensitive qualifiers. The latter is intended to alert a company to the fact that failure to provide criteria which are considered to be 'order-losing sensitive' will lead to a rapid loss of business.
  - **Order-winners** – the appropriate step here is to allocate 100 points across all the order-winners within a market. This forces the different levels of relevance to be exposed and provides an essential step in distilling out importance. It is essential, therefore, to avoid procedures where stars (for example) are allocated as a way of indicating importance. Such approaches bypass the need to discriminate between the relative importance of one criterion vis-à-vis another – as any level of importance can be attributed to any criterion.

4 WHAT IS GAINED FROM UNDERSTANDING THE MARKET?

After gaining an understanding of the market and customer needs, and identifying the relevant qualifiers and order-winners, the strategic task of functions can be developed. Clarity in terms of recognizing the market helps to identify the most appropriate direction (which qualifiers and/or order-winners need to be provided), their relative level of importance, emphasis (the size of the gap between what is required and what is currently provided), resource allocation and timescales. For example, the greater the order-winner weighting, the more emphasis and importance it is given. Similarly, because qualifiers indicate a need to match competitors' norms, any gaps between a company's performance and the market norm need to be closed quickly, especially where a qualifier is order-losing sensitive in nature.

To illustrate this point, let's take the role of price in a particular market:

- When price is an order-winner, a company competes on price. The higher the weighting, the more emphasis is placed on reducing costs, which, in turn, allows a company to be more competitive on price while sustaining its profit margins.
- When price is a qualifier, a company needs to be price competitive (that is, at an acceptable level within market norms). For example, highly skilled specialists who win business primarily on the uniqueness of their skill sets will be able to pitch their fee rates at the top end of the acceptable range for their sector. In such instances, there will be limits on how high they can set their fees (because of the order-losing nature of failing to qualify by setting fees at an unacceptably high level) and this will, in turn, relate to the level of their skills compared with those of their competitors. Here, the key task regarding costs would be to control them within the agreed budget rather than seeking to lower them as a strategic objective. Here, acceptable profit margins would be created by the high level of price and not by cost reduction.
- Having agreed the markets and relevant qualifier/order-winner mix and weightings, then, as mentioned earlier, the steps in developing functional strategies are to:

- Assess how well the relevant qualifiers and order-winners are being provided.
- Identify the gap between the provision of a criterion, its relative importance and the level required to retain or grow a company's market share or to enter new markets.
- Work out how to close the gap – in terms of the level of investment alternatives, costs and timescales.
- Implement the plan.

In order to illustrate this, Figure 2.13 outlines some typical areas for review and the type of improvements to make against a list of possible operations-related qualifiers and order-winners.

Relevant qualifiers and order-winners	Typical areas for review and improvement
Price	Reduce costs in all areas, particularly regarding materials and overheads, which can make up to 70–90 per cent of total costs
Quality conformance	Provide services or make products to specification. Build quality into the process and delivery system rather than checking conformance after the event. Improvements here also reduce costs
Delivery reliability	Assess on-time delivery performance by service/product and customer. Review current approaches to meeting orders – involves discussions on the extent to which services and products can be or are made-to-order or made-to-stock and the role of activities and investments such as scheduling and inventory in meeting these requirements
Delivery speed	Review the elements of the operations process with the purpose of reducing the lead time of the various steps making up the service delivery system or manufacturing process
Service/product range	Review the process capability and staff skill base in relation to current and future service/product range requirements. Identify and supplement capabilities in line with current and/or future needs
Demand spikes	Assess current capacity provision in terms of the ability to rapidly increase output in line with known or anticipated changes in demand. Approaches include short-term capacity and inventory-holding alternatives
New services/ products – time to market	Identify the elements of lead time within the new service/product development process for which operations is responsible. Assess the tasks involved and the opportunities to reduce the work content, bring forward the start times in relation to the overall procedures, and identify the possibility of completing part or all of the task in parallel (rather than in sequence) with other elements of the process
Meeting specific customer needs	Assess current approaches to identify how standard services and products can be modified in line with specific customer requirements and the impact on costs, lead times, quality conformance and the overall schedule

Figure 2.13 Translating qualifiers and order-winners into actions

5 THE PROCEDURES FOR ANALYSING MARKETS

Understanding markets is a difficult task and one that is made more so by the conflicting views often held by the principal functions such as marketing and operations. As highlighted earlier, the inherent lack of market clarity is further confused by the failure of many companies to distinguish clearly between markets and marketing. This lack of insight shows itself in several ways. Often the strategy debate ends when Steps 1 and 2 of the framework in Figure 2.10 – setting business objectives and determining marketing strategy – have been completed. The assumption is that marketing's view of the market is how the market is. The key nature of Step 3 in Figure 2.10 – deciding how to qualify and win orders in chosen markets – lies in its role of facilitating the important distinction between marketing (the functional perspective) and market (the business perspective) by undertaking a 360° review that incorporates testing initial opinions by other views in the business and, most importantly, by checking opinions with relevant service/product and customer data.

Before outlining the procedure to follow, let's first challenge existing perspectives and so arrive at the insights that support the use of the approach that is detailed afterwards.

Markets

As highlighted earlier, to help understand their total business, companies group customers together using criteria such as the standard industrial code (SIC) of their customers' own services/products or the country/region in which their customers are located.

For example, a carton maker will supply packaging to a range of customers. These will be bespoke products in that the carton design and what is printed on a carton will be customer specific.

To help understand its total business, a carton maker will often group customers into clusters (known as segments) based on what the customers themselves sell. For example, the cartons made by a carton maker may go to customers who use them to package food, beverages, pharmaceuticals or industrial products. When analysing its market, the carton maker would then group all its customers who produce food products into its food segment and so on. Then, all food product-related customers would be treated as one segment of the carton maker's market and the same for the beverage, pharmaceutical and industrial customers in their corresponding segments. Case 2.5 provides an illustration. Alternatively, companies may split their customers into geographical areas (by country such as Italy or Spain or regions such as Scandinavia and South America) and all customers in a country or region (depending on the chosen split) would be treated as being in one segment.

The purpose of this splitting is, in part, to help a company simplify the complex task of understanding its total market. However, such approaches are arbitrary in that each one has merits and can be deemed most suitable. While there are clear benefits to be gained by reducing the total market into parts or segments (for example, the SIC approach to segmentation enables aspects such as advertising, technical data gathering and market analysis to be directed and focused in specific ways), such approaches have one major flaw.

Case 2.5 – Market position of bottled water labels

Imagine that you are the CEO of a manufacturing company. One of your customers is a company that produces and sells bottles of mineral water, and your organization has been employed to provide the labels to go on the bottles. Into which segment would your sales and marketing department place the customer for whom you are producing the labels?

The likelihood is that this customer would be placed in the 'beverage' or 'soft drinks' segment (that is, the sector in which your customer operates). From a marketing perspective, this makes sense, but from an operations point of view, the kind of product to which your customer attaches the label is actually of little consequence. Instead, the key issues for operations relate to factors such as the level of price sensitivity, the length of delivery lead times and the size of demand peaks throughout the year. By segmenting markets based on the sector in which a company's customers operate, the implication is that all customers in this beverage segment are equally price sensitive, require similar delivery lead times and have similar demand profiles throughout the year. As you can see, taking the view of only one function gives insufficient insight and leads to unfounded assumptions – and these will result in inappropriate strategic decisions.

Questions

1 Why would marketing place this customer in a 'beverage' or 'soft drinks' market segment?
2 Why is operations' view of customers focused on qualifiers and order-winners such as price sensitivity, length of delivery lead-times and size of demand peaks?
3 How would you use both perspectives to arrive at an overall strategy?

Once the approach to segmentation has been agreed, companies then treat a segment as being homogeneous in terms of customers' needs, and this is often (indeed, more than likely) not the case. When reviewing markets then, such analysis needs to be completed at the level of customer activity.

Customers

Understandably, customers are at the centre of an analysis of markets. However, although clearly an appropriate perspective to take, it rests on the premise that customers behave in set ways and their requirements are the same. Such assumptions need checking as orders from one customer may be from more than one location and may, in fact, be different from the same site. While the total purchases from a group of companies may be used when negotiating supplier discounts, say, day-to-day transactions will be handled by each independent site.

In such instances, this may well (and invariably does) result in different sets of order-winners and qualifiers from site to site. The outcome is that, although there is a single customer name, there are several sets of order-winners and qualifiers to support.

Customer orders

It is then at the customer-order level of activity that customer needs can be assessed. The orders, in fact, embody the reality of customer needs and are the source of the key data essential to identifying the competitive requirements of markets.

Orders are statements of customers' needs and expectations such as volumes, lead times and profit margins (reflected in the price of the services and products). It is these details that together make up the competitive factors to be provided and are the basis for differentiating one customer from another and assessing the extent to which customers' requirements differ or are similar. With this information now available, companies can discuss what has to be provided so as to retain or grow share, which customers to drop or renegotiate fresh terms, what it would anticipate having to do to enter new markets or gain new customers and so on.

With the context now provided, let's review the procedure for establishing the order-winners and qualifiers and look at some examples.

The procedure used to gain these insights is now outlined.

- Marketing is requested to separate the company's business into different segments as it perceives them. The procedure, as with other aspects of strategy debate, is iterative in nature. Thus marketing's separation of the business is requested to give relevant insights and market distinctions as a way of providing the initial inputs into the debate that follows. These are then considered and invariably revised as strategy formulation progresses.
- To focus discussion, marketing is asked to select services/products and/or customers that represent these market segments, together with two future time periods for each segment. Note that the selected periods may differ as they are chosen to reflect the characteristics of each segment. This step allows specific data to be collected in preparation for analyses to be completed on the representative sample of services/products or customers chosen for each segment.
- Actual and forecast sales volumes/revenues for chosen representative services/products or customers are provided to help identify the relative importance of each segment and the expected future growth or decline.
- Based on the representative sample of services/products or customers, the executives in the strategy-making group (see Figure 2.4) determine the relevant order-winners, qualifiers and weightings. A good starting point is to ask these executives to independently record their own views, including the use of the weighting system for order-winners and qualifiers. Listing the views of individual executives highlights the level of difference initially involved. This will often be sizeable and, where this is so, the iterative nature of strategy discussion kicks in.
- When agreement on the order-winners, order-winners' weightings and qualifiers has been reached, a final, essential check is made. This concerns analysing the previously collected data from actual representative customer orders to verify the order-winners and qualifiers and their respective weightings. The way to approach this step is to request marketing to select a period (3, 6 or 12 months, say) that represents the market and then agree a representative sample from the selected period.

- Analysing customer order data yields many insights that allow the order-winners and qualifiers and their respective weightings to be checked and executive opinions challenged or verified.

  For example:
  - If price is considered to be a heavily weighted order-winner, this should result in low margins (for these analyses, it is recommended that contributions – invoice price less variable costs – are used); alternatively, if price is considered a qualifier, margins should be high.
  - Similarly, a check on delivery speed can be made by comparing customer lead times (the date an order was placed compared to the requested delivery date) against the current or preferred operations lead time. Customer lead times that are shorter than operations lead times indicate a delivery speed factor – the customer wants delivery of the service or product in a time shorter than the scheduled operations lead time.
  - Checks on on-time delivery, providing services or making products to specification (quality conformance) and other relevant competitive criteria would follow a similar pattern by checking actual performance and comparing it with the order-winner/qualifier category and the respective weightings used by executives.

Such analyses provide several benefits, including:

1 Allowing the strategy-making group to check their initial views one with another.

2 Providing a check on whether the outcome of the analysis of representative orders (the way customers behave) differs from the reconciled views of the strategy-making group. This serves to emphasize the need to always check opinion with data analysis. As Figure 2.14 illustrates, whereas customer contracts are agreed towards the top of the supplier and customer organizations, actual customer requirements are embodied in the orders that customers subsequently place. It is only by analysing orders that actual requirements (customer behaviour) can be identified and compared to contractual requirements (customer voice).

3 The addition of data helps clarify the views on markets or customers and enables differences to be evaluated and reconciled. In this way, it further ensures that an in-depth discussion takes place on identifying market or customer needs and the strategic response that is required.

4 Highlighting that the essential task of the strategy-making group is to understand the markets in which the company competes and what it will take for the company to retain or grow market share today and in the future and to enter new markets.

5 Underscoring the fact that market reviews form the agenda for all functional strategies. Without this, functions will lack insight and have no alternative but to pursue strategies they believe to be appropriate. While the business debate sets the agenda, the functional role is to implement and fulfil the strategy agreed by the strategy-making group.

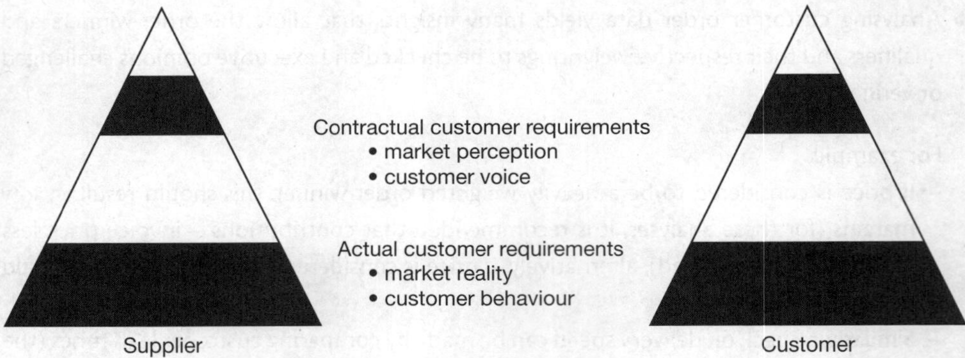

Figure 2.14 Contractual versus actual customer requirements

IMPLEMENTING AN OPERATIONS STRATEGY

The reality of implementing a functional strategy is to translate the order-winners and qualifiers for which that function is solely or jointly responsible into relevant actions. Translating from order-winners and qualifiers into actions is a straightforward step. Implementation, on the other hand, is typically far from easy, as highlighted in Figure 2.15.

Knowing which approach to follow for the best results and then making developments happen is a capability that management needs to have and develop. The place to start in terms of operations strategy is linking the strategic tasks to courses of action. Figure 2.13 gave typical areas to be revised and improved.

OPERATIONS STRATEGY – ILLUSTRATIONS

Let us now look at two short illustrations (one from the services sector and the other from the manufacturing sector) of what is involved in the approach to and outcomes of operations strategy developments.

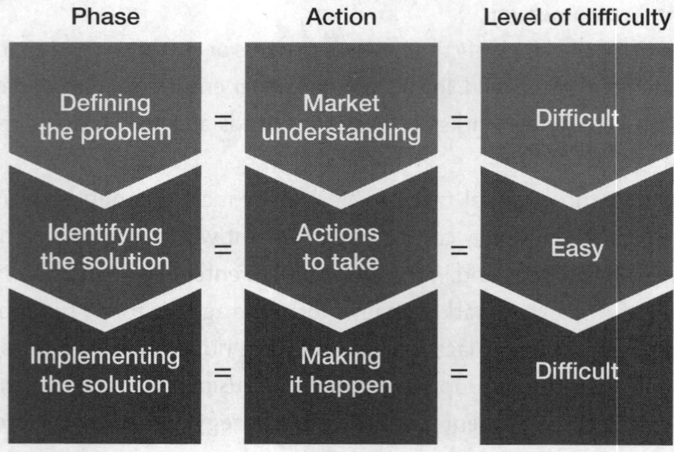

Figure 2.15 Phases and characteristics of strategy development and implementation

Illustration 1

Figure 2.16 shows part of a major European bank's review of its Corporate Banking Services (CBS) Division, a key contributor to the bank's overall sales revenue and profit performance. The bank identified three segments within this sector (termed Small, Medium and Large Corporates) which reflected the size of a customer's own annual sales revenues.

- The bank's overall strategy for its CBS Division is to grow the Small and Medium Corporates segments while retaining the current size of Large Corporates. This in-depth review enabled CBS to assess current levels of support, to influence clients' expectations and to highlight the key criteria within each corporate banking segment. To keep the example to a manageable size, the details in Figure 2.16 are only for the 'Small Corporates' and 'Large Corporates' segments. In Figure 2.16, qualifiers are denoted by 'Q' and order-losing sensitive qualifiers by 'QQ'.

Some of the key distinctions include

1 **Tailored products** With Large Corporates the essential characteristics for relationship management is to have in place the capability to develop bespoke product solutions in line with a customer's precise needs together with a proactive, high level of after-sales support. For Small Corporates the task of the relationship manager is to select from the bank's range of standard products to best meet a client's business needs and involves a simple documentation process supported by after-sales as required.

2 **Staff availability** For Large Corporates, relationship managers are the primary contact. These managers are supported by direct access to specialist staff within the bank, thus allowing the team to build up a detailed knowledge of clients' business strategies and their non-financial as well as financial needs.

Competitive factors	Small Corporates	Large Corporates
Brand name	Q	Q
Price-interest rates, margins and fees charged	40	Q
Lending facilities – terms and conditions	30	Q
Relationship management – expertise	Q	50
Provision of tailored products	Q	50
Easy to complete documentation	10	–
Availability of skilled staff	20	QQ
Percentage of total number of CBS clients	81	3

Notes

1 Q denotes a qualifier, QQ denotes an order-losing sensitive qualifier and a number denotes the weighting attributed to that order-winner.

2 The CBS business strategy group also identified the order-winners and qualifiers (and respective weightings) for two years out, but these have not been included here.

Figure 2.16 CBS: order-winners and qualifiers for the 'Small and Large Corporates' segments

For Small Corporates, the relationship manager provides most, if not all, of a client's financial needs with very occasional specialist involvement. What is offered is financial advice in a broad business context while responding to clients' lead times as and when required.

3 **Price and lending facilities** For Large Corporates, the outcome of the financial advice given by the bank and the overall performance of the tailored products are the prime ways in which the bank is judged. On the other hand, the price and terms negotiated with the bank are the more overt way by which Small Corporates judge the bank as a provider of financial services.

The bank's in-depth analysis of its CBS Division has enabled this key sector to review its current levels of client support in line with the key performance factors in each of the three segments. In addition, CBS is now alert to the need to:

1 ensure that banking staff understand the relative roles of the order-winners and qualifiers for their respective clients;
2 track clients so as to identify ahead of time if and when any should be recategorized;
3 test whether in the future the CBS Division should be split into four segments to embrace the top end of Small Corporates/bottom end of Medium Corporates;
4 measure the performance of staff in line with the order-winners and qualifiers (and their respective weightings) within each segment;
5 discuss and agree on the order-winners, qualifiers and their respective weightings that the executive group put forward as reflecting the CBS position two years out (not shown in Figure 2.16).

Illustration 2

Figure 2.17 shows the outcome of a US graphic supplies company's review of its markets and provides details of two customers as representing the range involved.

Criteria		Customer A			Customer B		
		CY	CY + 1	CY + 2	CY	CY + 1	CY + 2
Design (product specification)		40	40	40	30	40	50
Price		Q	Q	Q	40	20	Q
Delivery	Reliability	QQ	QQ	QQ	QQ	QQ	QQ
	Speed	30	20	Q	30	20	QQ
Quality conformance		QQ	QQ	QQ	QQ	QQ	QQ
R&D support services		30	40	60	–	20	50

Figure 2.17 US graphic supplies company: order-winners and qualifiers for two customers considered by the company as representative of its customer range

Customer A represents the relationship this graphic supplies company seeks to develop with all its customers. The distinguishing competitive approach by the company is to support its customers with high-level design and R&D capability, which would not only provide development help in meeting their ink product needs but also, as part of the sale, provide fast, technical support in the field. To provide this level of technical expertise and support, high margin sales are necessary. To its customers, while ink is a relatively small percentage of their total costs, having printing presses not making saleable products due to ink problems impacts both costs and their ability to deliver on time.

Customer B on the other hand, typifies customers who are price sensitive. The strategy for this company is to convert customers like Customer B into a Customer Type A relationship. Where this fails, the company would proactively decide not to continue supplying such customers in the future.

THE ITERATIVE NATURE OF STRATEGY DEVELOPMENT

The key to developing business unit and functional strategies is to recognize the iterative nature of their development. And key to this is the need for regular and frequent discussions based on the analysis of customer data. Customer reviews based on order-winners and qualifiers and checked by the analysis of representative orders are an essential element of this process.

Too commonly, strategy development is undertaken infrequently and is characterized by discussions based on the opinions of executives that are typically functional in orientation and insight. While contributing views is a key element of the strategy debate, the role of opinion is to serve as a pointer to the relevant data that need to be analysed to check whether or not a view is correct.

Markets are difficult to understand, so regular and frequent discussions underpinned by relevant data are critical to gaining essential insights. Meeting regularly (monthly should be the maximum time gap) and reviewing part of the total market (taking manageable slices is key here) makes this difficult, but fundamental, task manageable. Furthermore, regular customer-based discussions and functional reviews help to overcome the inherent sensitivity that typically characterizes the challenging question and fact-based approach so essential to strategy formulation.

THE OUTPUTS OF DEVELOPING AN OPERATIONS STRATEGY

Three basic outputs accrue from using this approach, and are now discussed.

1 Setting the strategic task for operations

As emphasized throughout, the market/customer needs set the agenda for all functions. Figure 2.13 (p. 37) lists some of the order-winners and qualifiers that fall within the remit of operations and some typical areas for review and improvement that will form part of operations' strategic task. As highlighted earlier, prioritizing where operations spends its time and money will be provided by the order-winners, qualifiers and their relative weightings that make up a market or market segment. When it comes to strategy, it is not about doing things right but doing the right things.

2 Assessing operations' alignment with service/product or customer needs

Assessing operations' degree of alignment with the service/product or customer needs today and in the future concerns reviewing how well these needs are provided by operations' delivery system(s) and infrastructure investments while meeting expected margins, as depicted in Figure 2.18.

This check should also be done for all future service/product proposals or new customer agreements. This essential, regular review should be used to pick up any volume or order-winner/qualifier changes which may be significant as measured against the relevant base year. By checking on and assessing competitors' moves and actions and reviewing customer behaviour changes and trends, then the relative levels of match and mismatch are monitored, thus detecting incremental market changes that have occurred over time and would often otherwise go unnoticed. Only by reviewing current and future requirements against the original decisions can the full change be assessed.

3 Operations' input into the business strategy debate

Once determined, the operations strategy and the necessary investments and time period for change form part of the business strategy debate, as illustrated in Figure 2.19.

As a consequence, a company as a whole is now required to review the business in both marketing and operations terms. It changes the style and substance of business decisions from functionally based arguments and perspectives to ones that address functional differences at the business level and where the trade-offs involved are resolved. This business-level resolution, therefore, leads to an agreed understanding of the business objectives, marketing

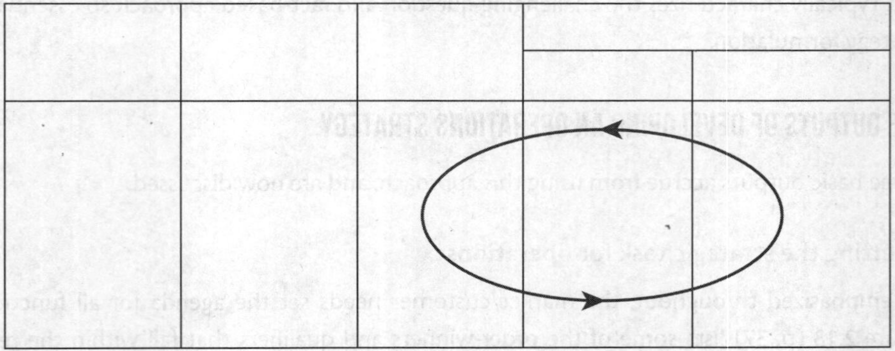

Figure 2.18 Assessing the implications for operations delivery systems and infrastructure of the order-winners and qualifiers for which operations is solely or partly responsible

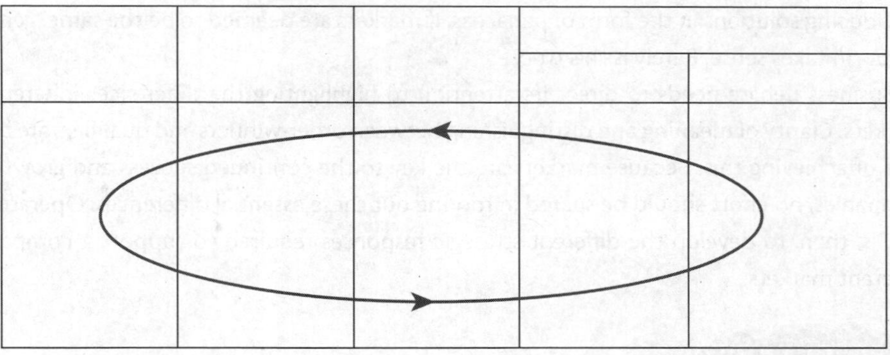

Figure 2.19 Operations' input into the business strategy debate

strategy and operations strategy. In reality, it will lead to one of five positions based on the degree of fit between the market and operations strategic interface:

1 Where the interface is sufficiently close and requires little, if any, adjustment.
2 Where the interface is not sufficiently close, but the business decision is not to invest the required time and money to bring it closer to position 1.
3 Where the interface is not sufficiently close, and the decision is to change the marketing strategy to reduce the mismatch and move towards position 1.
4 Where the interface is not sufficiently close and the decision is to allocate the time and investment to enable operations to bring its processes and infrastructure to that required to support the marketing strategy and so move towards position 1.
5 A combination of alternatives 3 and 4 to move towards position 1.

In situations 3 and 4, the company decides to reposition marketing and operations, respectively, to bring about the position described in 1. In the case of 2, it is essential that the reality of the mismatch is translated into operations targets and budgets and so present a manageable, achievable and hence controllable task. In this way, the inadequacies of operations' performance against budget are separated from the consequences of the business strategy decision to accept the mismatch involved. The business is, therefore, able to learn the extent of the consequences resulting from the operations/marketing interface mismatch and use this vital information in its future strategic decisions.

OPERATIONS TYPICALLY DEVELOPS MORE THAN ONE STRATEGY

Because markets are different, the order-winners and qualifiers relating to these markets will also be different. Consequently, operations (as well as other functions) will need to develop different strategies to support these different sets of market needs.

Typically in the past, this diversity has neither been recognized nor provided. The failure of business strategy approaches to identify difference has led to general strategic approaches being adopted. This, in turn, has fuelled the trend for operations to fulfil its strategic role by introducing solutions in the form of panaceas. If markets are deemed to be the same, generic support makes sense. Rarely is this true.

Business debate needs to direct its attention to highlighting the differences inherent in markets. Clarity of meaning and distinguishing between order-winners and qualifiers are both part of achieving this. Because markets are the key to the continued success and growth of companies, no effort should be spared in rooting out these essential differences. Operations' task is, then, to develop the different strategic responses required to support a company's different markets.

Developing an operations strategy involves a number of phases, the first of which is the most critical; it is one in which operations must be involved, ensuring that its perspectives on and insights into customers and markets are taken into account and form part of the discussion and agreement. Being proactively part of and contributing to the ongoing debate about markets, agreeing the order-winners and qualifiers involved in current and future markets, and being party to market-driving opportunities comprise the first critical step.

Operations helps gain the first sale while also securing the second

An important strategic task for operations concerns its role in retaining customers. As Figure 2.20 shows, although sales and marketing may have a key role in gaining the first sale, fulfilling the order or contract and thereby securing repeat business principally falls within the remit of operations.

Let's explain with an example. Wishing to eat out one evening on some special occasion and not knowing where to go, you ask a friend for suggestions. The restaurant recommended is duly booked, but the reality of the evening doesn't match your expectations – your table is not quite ready, the service is slow, and the food is nothing special. So next time you wish to celebrate, where will you go? While your first visit to the restaurant arose from it being recommended (the reputation it had established), any subsequent visits will be based on your own experience of the delivery of the service. In this way, how well a service is delivered results in:

1 Creating the reputation (the equivalent of a brand name) that leads to customers' recommendations to others (the first sale).
2 Customers returning to repeat-buy (the second sale).

Because operations is central to creating the customer experience (the reputation) and repeat purchases, its critical role in the selling process cannot be overemphasized.

Market- or marketing-led?

Markets are the common denominator of functional strategies. With markets analysed in depth and agreement reached on the current and future directions to follow, the strategic task in operations is to develop the capabilities to support relevant order-winners and

Task	Gaining the first sale		Fulfilling the order or contract		Securing the second sale	
Function(s) responsible	Sales and marketing	Through customer contacts and relationships, advertising, promotions and selling Creating a good business reputation based on past performance in meeting customer orders and customer needs leads to existing customers recommending a business to others	Operations	Operations fulfils a mix of requirements such as meeting the service/ product specification, delivering on time and supporting the relevant degree of price sensitivity	Operations	Operations – as a consequence of fulfilling an order and meeting customers' needs, customers typically return and repeat their purchase. If operations fails to meet customer orders and needs, it is likely that customers will go elsewhere – and may tell others!

Figure 2.20 Operations' role in gaining the first sale and securing the second

qualifiers. However, as highlighted earlier, companies do not always keep in sharp focus the critical differences between being market-led and being marketing-led. Substituting the business (market) perspective with a functional (marketing) perspective will invariably lead to distorted strategies and eventually to the company losing out. Unfortunately, in many businesses, marketing is increasingly characterized as having the perceived role of creating ideas, with the rigour of testing whether the business will fit the market being left to others. This trend not only trivializes the important functional perspective of marketing, but also detracts from its fundamental strategic contribution.

MOVING TO A BUSINESS-LEVEL STRATEGIC DEBATE

Choosing the markets in which to compete is a business and not a functional decision. Whatever the strategic mix between being market-driven and marketing-driving, markets lie at the very centre of strategy development, interconnecting corporate objectives with their delivery and connecting functional strategies, as illustrated in Figure 2.5 (p. 19). In this way, markets form the agenda for the development of all functional strategies and help ensure that differences and alternatives are appropriately resolved at the level of the business. Companies need to continuously seek to line up their functional strategies with market needs, and one of the major players in delivering strategy is operations (see Figure 2.20). As shown in the case examples given throughout the chapter, getting it right in operations results in a sizeable and sustainable advantage. Although it is not the only strategic player, in most organizations the role of operations will be important, and in many it will be central to the continued success of the overall business.

CHARACTERISTICS OF STRATEGY DEVELOPMENT

To be effective, strategies must display the following characteristics that are central to the procedure and the outcomes:

- **Congruence of purpose and function** As illustrated in Figure 2.5, the markets in which a company competes should link business objectives and functional strategies. Otherwise, functions will base strategies on their own perspectives and understanding, which disrupts the essential gains of coherent direction of the parts and the whole. Congruence of purpose and function, therefore, is an essential ingredient of strategy formulation and implementation.
- **A focus on key priorities** The coherent direction in which functional strategies need to be formed will lead to an agreement on which developments and investments are the most important for supporting given markets. Priorities for timescales and costs are agreed on and functions base subsequent actions and activities on these outcomes. This prioritizing mechanism is a key characteristic of effective strategies. It gives essential context, orients actions, keeps the list of tasks small and manageable, focuses attention on what is critical and promotes coordination and cooperation between the different functions in the core task of being competitive within agreed markets.
- **Commitment through understanding** Knowing where the company is going and why is essential if strategies are to be effective. In addition, knowing where and why builds commitment among participants. An understanding of the rationale underpinning the strategies to be taken and the priorities to be pursued gives essential and appropriate direction in the short term, while providing the basis for strategic rethinking that the future will undoubtedly demand.
- **Regular review and revisions** Strategy development is an essential executive task. It is unique to this level within a business and cannot be delegated in terms of insight, review and direction. An integral part of successfully undertaking these developments is the frequency and nature of the discussion. Regular and frequent reviews of one part of the market at a time make the task manageable and keep it in the forefront of everyone's mind. Underpinning these difficult debates with data on services/products and customers provides the insights necessary to create sufficient understanding to give appropriate direction and the informed commitment of the scarce resources of time and money.
- **Routine performance measurement** Strategy leads to appropriate direction, the pursuit of priorities and the essential commitment to see them through. As part of the

continuous reappraisal of strategy decisions, performance needs to be monitored on a regular basis. Routine checks are vital in themselves. Adherence to and progress towards agreed strategies is essential for all development and close and continuous monitoring of performance is integral to a successful strategy. Furthermore, strategy is not a once-and-for-all development that remains unaddressed between one review time and the next. Continuous reassessment needs to be undertaken and the routine measurement of performance is an integral part of this procedure.

OPERATIONS STRATEGY

In the past, companies have often seen operations' role as being the provider of corporate requests. Business strategy debate has stopped short of discussing the implications of decisions for operations. This behaviour has been based on two incorrect assumptions:

1 Within a given technology, operations is able to do everything.
2 Operations' contribution solely concerns the achievement of efficiency rather than also including the effective support of market needs.

The result for many companies is that not only have the profit margins they once enjoyed been eroded, but also the base on which to build a sound and prosperous business in the future is no longer available. A company is exposed and vulnerable without the frequent operations strategy checks necessary to evaluate the fit between the business and operations' ability to provide the necessary order-winners and qualifiers of its various services, products and customers. In times of increased world competition, being left behind can be sudden and fatal. In many instances, averting the end is the only option left. Turning the business around, however, will only be achieved by switching from an operational to a strategic mode, which will require a corporate review of the marketing and operations perspectives and the financial implications of the proposals.

Operations strategy comprises a series of decisions concerning delivery system and infrastructure investment, which, over time, provide the necessary support for the relevant order-winners and qualifiers of the different market segments of a company. It is built on keeping the strategic development relevant to the business, that is, it must reflect the aspects of operations' performance critical to those segments of the firm under review. Identifying the pertinent aspects, and setting aside those that are not, provides for a strategy that is oriented to the market and the simplicity and clarity of direction this affords.

On the other hand, operations strategy is not:

- A list of aspects typically comprising an operations function and an attempt to develop a strategic statement about each. Differentiating the important from the less important aspects in terms of market needs is a key feature of sound strategy development.
- A list of potential operations improvements such as flexible, lean and agile. Although sound investments to make, they are not, by rights, strategic in orientation. Such arguments are not strategic (that is, related to market needs) in origin, and imply that this is, in essence,

operations' strategic task. Essential difference is now excluded and operations' contribution to strategic discussion is limited.

- An exhortation that the strategic perspectives of the operations function should be paramount

Operations' strategic task is to transform, over time, support for a company's markets into an appropriate collection of facilities, structures, controls, procedures and people skills. This chapter has provided essential insights into the principles and concepts that underpin this task, while Chapter 3 looks in depth at the methodology to develop an operations strategy.

CASE STUDY

ING Direct

It was a beautiful summer day and bankers working in the ING Direct cafe in Madrid served coffee, orange juice and Danish pastries to potential customers while advising them on savings and mortgages. Throughout the cafe, various ING Direct merchandise, such as mountain bikes, coffee mugs and volleyballs, is for sale, all in their trademark bright orange colour. It doesn't take long to realize that this is not a typical bank. 'Many organizations have tried to enter the banking industry with innovative business models, but the traditional players have always managed to defend their markets', comments the analyst Will Foster. 'But', all that changed when ING Direct was launched in 1997.'

THE STORY

ING Direct is one of the three business lines of ING Bank, a division of ING Group that offers a wide range of insurance, banking, and asset management services to individuals, families, small businesses, large corporations, institutions and governments (see Case Figure 2.1).

In May 1997, ING Direct launched its first operation in Canada because it had no presence there and the market was dominated by a small number of players. It appointed a new management team, led by Arkadi Kuhlmann, a Harley-riding painter and poet who was previously a professor at the American Graduate School of International Management in Phoenix (Arizona), a President of North American Trust, CEO of Deak International Incorporated, and who had held various executive positions at the Royal Bank of Canada.

The experiment in Canada was a great success and ING Direct now has operations in nine countries (Australia, Austria, Canada,

Measure	Annual performance						
	2004	2006	2008	2010	2011	2012	2013
Income (€m)							
Banking	12,663	14,190	12,177	17,901	17,908	16,102	15,296
Insurance	55,614	59,642	39,142	15,900	16,589	12,946	11,136
Total	68,277	73,832	51,319	33,801	34,497	29,048	26,432
Profit (€m)							
Banking	3,402	5,024	533	5,983	6,016	4,347	4,191
Insurance	4,322	4,935	(1,282)	596	443	(272)	(83)
Total	7,724	9,959	(749)	6,579	6,459	4,075	4,108

Case Figure 2.1 ING Group performance (2004–13)

Measure	Annual performance						
	2004	2006	2008	2010	2011	2012	2013
Income (€m)							
Commercial	5,871	4,738	4,107	6,033	4,494	4,963	4,994
Retail	5,062	7,166	7,399	7,650	7,480	7,441	9,536
ING Direct	1,709	2,289	878	3,782	3,423	1,648	626
Other	21	(3)	(207)	436	718	458	181
Total	12,663	14,190	12,177	17,901	16,115	14,510	15,337
Profit (€m)							
Commercial	1,945	2,052	533	2,390	1,986	1,635	1,817
Retail	1,175	2,364	1,420	2,176	1,945	1,502	2,415
ING Direct	435	691	(1,155)	1,450	999	461	188
Other	(153)	(83)	(265)	(33)	56	153	(55)
Total	3,402	5,024	533	5,983	4,986	3,751	4,365

Case Figure 2.2 ING Direct's performance by business area (2004–13)

France, Germany, Italy, Spain, UK and the US), with more than 17 million customers and over €200 billion deposits (see Case Figure 2.2).

SIMPLE PRODUCTS

The last thing ING Direct wanted was to be a replacement provider for traditional current accounts (also known as debit or checking accounts) as these are expensive to service with a large number of transactions and tasks such as verifying customer identification and handling payment slips, cash and cheques. Nor did it want to offer products where there was a risk of bills not being paid, such as credit cards or unsecured loans. Instead, ING Direct wanted to be 'your other bank' where customers can get simple, high-return savings accounts and simple, low-interest loans.

When it initially launched, the interest rates on its savings accounts were typically 50 per cent higher and its mortgage rates significantly lower than those offered by other banks. Instead of posting a mortgage rate and then allowing potential customers to 'haggle' through financial advisors, it advertised its best 'no-haggle' rates for all to see. It also wanted to move away from the 'small print' and fees used by traditional banks as ways to generate their income. As Molly Stewart (a financial analyst based in New York) comments, 'Often, customers with traditional banks suddenly find that their fees have increased or their interest rate has been reduced because they have less than €1,000 in their account. ING Direct wanted to move away from this philosophy by creating products that are easy to understand, simple to use and have no "no fees" or "small print" that you need to check on page 12!'

PENETRATING NEW MARKETS

ING Direct carefully selects and then targets the wealthiest regions in countries that have large numbers of middle-income customers who want to earn more interest on their savings. For example, it has targeted Sydney in Australia, Toronto in Canada, Paris in France and Barcelona and Madrid in Spain. It selects countries with at least €100 billion in savings and then tries to get 5 per cent market share (€5 billion) because experience has shown that this is necessary for a business unit to be profitable and to able to operate as a self-contained organization.

'Unlike traditional banks, ING Direct avoids wealthy customers', explains the analyst, Molly Stewart, 'as they want special treatment and a level of service that ING Direct is not prepared to deliver. Rather than selling solutions, ING Direct sells commodities and it expects its customers to appreciate this and the level of service this involves. In fact, it typically "fires" 5,000 to 8,000 customers a year for calling too often or asking for too many exceptions from its standard operating procedures. Managing its market in this way gives it a real clarity and focus. People know what to expect and they get what they expect!'

When entering a new country, ING Direct hires a local management team and supports them with experienced personnel from other countries until they are up and running. Initially, only simple, high-interest savings accounts are on offer because these are clearly understood by potential customers and tend to give higher returns than the existing products available in the market. This strategy enables ING Direct to rapidly penetrate the market and gain sizeable assets before starting to cross-sell other products to these customers (see Case Figure 2.3).

However, before starting to cross-sell products it seeks a customer's consent (typically only 30 per cent of customers say 'yes') and only sells products to customers who are likely to want them. For example, ING only approaches customers with those products it thinks they will want to buy. As a result, 85 to 90 per cent of customers still only have an ING Direct savings account.

ATTRACTING NEW CUSTOMERS

Not only is ING Direct's bright orange colour (a link to its Dutch heritage) distinctly different from the conservative blues or greens used by most of its competitors, so is the rest of its marketing. It believes that most people

Order of selling products to customers	Target market (% retail market)	Ease of		
		Direct selling	Servicing by phone or web	Typical profit (% sales)
1. Savings	100	***	*	***
2. Mutual funds	<10	**	**	***
3. Mortgages	50	**	**	**
4. Consumer loans	60	**	*	***
5. Online brokerage	<10	**	***	*
6. Insurance (Life or Pension)	20–50	**	**	**

Case Figure 2.3 Market penetration strategy

are sleeping, so you have to wake them up, get them to switch their money and then get them to go back to sleep again.

To do this, it uses unconventional campaigns such as providing 'free' services and then asking people to put the money they have saved into an ING Direct savings account. These experiences attract lots of free press coverage and help create a sense of 'theatre' that sets the bank apart from its competitors. For example, there was a 3 km queue of cars by the end of its 'free gasoline' promotion to 1,000 drivers at three selected Shell stations in Baltimore. It also attracted over 8,000 people with its 'save your money at the movies' campaign in Washington DC and has organized a number of events such as the 'movie on the beach day' in California, the 'freedom ride' in San Francisco (with Harley Davidson to raise money for a children's fund), and a 'hot air balloon ride' in Phoenix, Arizona.

Despite these high profile events, ING Direct typically spends only €75 to attract a new customer compared with the €250 typically spent by most banks. In fact, its products almost sell themselves with 40 per cent of new customers coming through word-of-mouth recommendations from existing customers. To reduce marketing costs it reuses literature and advertising campaigns across different countries while also giving each regional operation freedom to tailor campaigns to the needs of local markets, provided that they stay consistent with the overall brand. It has also developed the 'Planet Orange' website where children, parents and teachers can learn about the best ways to save and invest their money. Furthermore, it is one of the first banks to start using social media properly and has the largest 'fan base' of any bank in the US, which helps strengthen its brand name and gives it instant customer feedback on anything it does.

'Educating customers about your products is time consuming and expensive', comments the London-based analyst Will Foster. 'ING Direct doesn't have to do this as customers don't have a wide range of products to choose from. Instead of trying to solve all a customer's financial needs, they have decided to solve just one or two of them very well!'

DELIVERING THE CUSTOMER EXPERIENCE

The idea for the cafes came in the late 1990s when a Canadian couple wanted to meet Kuhlmann to ensure they were dealing with a legitimate company before putting $2 million into a savings account. He met them in his office and afterwards took them to Starbucks for a coffee. It took Kuhlmann a while to convince the senior executives at ING in Amsterdam to set up 'coffee shops', but it now has cafes in all its largest cities such as Toronto, Vancouver, Sydney, Barcelona, Madrid, New York, Philadelphia and Los Angeles. For many customers, the cafes give the bank a physical presence, whereas for others they are just a place to buy cheap coffee, surf the internet for free, check information on their existing ING Direct products or discuss new ones with trained bankers.

As well as going into its cafes, customers can set up accounts and transfer money over the phone. Within its call centres, ING Direct tries to create a positive, spontaneous and 'principle-driven' (rather than 'rules-based') customer experience. It does this by not employing more than 200 people in any one location, giving staff instant access to customers' recent histories as soon as they call and empowering them to solve customers' problems rather than getting 'someone to call them back'. As a result, 70 per cent of calls are answered in 20 seconds, calls last for an average of 4 minutes and each customer is only 'called back' on average 1.6 times each year.

However, ING Direct would rather customers interacted with them through the internet and it tells customers that they shouldn't call as this will lead to higher fees and lower interest rates. As a result, 50 per cent of customer accounts are opened online with no client contact and 85 per cent of customer contact is through the internet or Interactive Voice Response (IVR) system. Once customers have set up a savings account, they can electronically transfer money into this account from other bank accounts or post a cheque to a central ING depot.

CREATING THE RIGHT CULTURE

ING Direct makes every effort to hire people that are willing to do things differently. Instead of recruiting bankers, they would rather employ artists, jazz musicians or dancers. They believe that people without a classical business training are more open to new approaches and will look for creative ways to meet customer needs. 'I think about it as casting rather than staffing', comments Kuhlmann. 'We like to employ artists whenever we can because they are always thinking about what's next. What is the next painting, the next song, the next score I want to do? They are always searching for something beautiful and different. When you apply this thinking to business, you end up with something elegant, fit for purpose and right for the customer.'

Once ING Direct has found the right people, then it starts to inspire them with the same set of values it uses to connect with its customers. Every new employee, no matter what level, spends their first five days taking customer calls and learning about the ING Direct culture described by the 12 statements in the 'Orange Code' shown in Case Figure 2.4.

We are here

Every day is a new beginning. A new set of challenges. A chance to reinvent ourselves.

Our mission is to help people take care of their wealth

Money is the fruit of work and saving it is fundamental to freedom. Few missions could be more important to the lives of our customers than this one.

We will be fair

Everyone has value. Everyone deserves a chance at independence. So, everyone will be treated equally here.

We will constantly learn

Every experience we have will make us wiser and better at what we do. That will always be true.

We will change and adapt and dwell only in the present and the future

The world does not stand still. Neither will we. We will not resist change. We will be exhilarated by it. The value of the past lies in what it has taught us. Our greatest treasure is our potential. We are nourished by thinking about what can be.

Case Figure 2.4 The 'Orange Code'

We will listen. We will invent. We will simplify

Our customers can make us better if we let them. But we must first understand them. We can find a solution or create one, but if our invention does not make our customers' lives better, it will not make our business better.

We will never stop asking why. Or why not

Nothing can be sacred here except for our mission. To be challenged is not to be criticized. It is to be invited into the process of invention.

We will create wealth for ourselves too, but we will do this by creating value

Our customers want us to succeed. Profit is the proof that we are fulfilling our mission, and it is only rewarded when it is earned.

We will tell the truth

We cannot succeed without the trust of our customers and of society.

We will be for everyone

To be our customer, people need only a dollar and the will to be independent. Though we welcome everyone, we will have the courage to accept that not everyone will hear the call, and remain true to ourselves.

We aren't conquerors. We are pioneers. We are not here to destroy. We are here to create

We have competitors, not enemies. We will respect them. We came here to offer people a choice. It is for them, not us, to decide who will prevail.

We will never be finished

Every generation will have its own hunger for independence, and its own challenges in achieving it. We will be there for them, as new then as we are today.

Case Figure 2.4 (Continued)

For example, in keeping with the statement 'We will be for everyone', no one in the company has a job title or an office, even though they have clear responsibilities. Therefore, everyone has to accept a degree of flexibility in the amount and type of work they do each week. The company believes that this helps break down the silos that typically exist in businesses and encourages people to work better together. After their first week, some people realize that this is not the place for them, but the ones who want to stay then embark on a 90-day 'Maiden Voyage' where they have to volunteer in the local community, work in one of the ING Direct cafes and read *The Alchemist* by Paulo Coelho. These are all pretty unusual business practices, but in a recent staff survey 99 per cent of the employees said they were proud to be part of ING Direct because of its 'non-banking' culture, flat organization and feeling empowered to make a difference.

Even though ING Direct is a cost leader, its staff salaries are higher than the industry average with substantial bonuses (up to half the fixed salary) offered to everyone based on them meeting financial, customer and operational targets. Despite this, the expense to asset ratio for its branches is 40 compared with 250 for its competitors, and its income per employee is $48 million compared with $5–6 million for traditional banks.

All aspects of ING Direct's organization are measured to ensure it meets its five key objectives: growing profit, savings assets and mortgage funds; reducing non-marketing expenses; and increasing call-centre service levels. Performance against these key measures are posted on an intranet site every day for everyone in the organization to see and its operations centres compete against each other for recognition and monthly bonuses based on their ability to meet sales and service targets.

THE FUTURE

ING Direct's unique approach has made it a huge success. However, like its competitors, the ING Group was hit hard by the 2008 financial crisis and, as part of a restructuring agreement to get state aid from the Dutch Government, the ING Group had to sell ING Direct's US operation to Capital One, its Canadian operation to Scotiabank and its UK operation to Barclays in 2012.

'Being part of the ING Group gives ING Direct financial strength and stability', comments the analyst Will Foster. 'However, as it continues to grow and become more important to the ING Group as a whole, more stringent reports and controls will be put in place that may well threaten its lean and entrepreneurial spirit. It also must resist the temptation to diversify and increase its product range as this will reduce its simplicity, increase its risk and defocus its people. A person working with seven products cannot know and understand them as well as a person focused on just one product. In the end, its success has been built on simplicity and efficiency. If it loses this, then it loses its competitive edge in the market.'

QUESTIONS

1 What are the factors that have made ING Direct so successful?

2 How can it continue to be successful in the future?

DISCUSSION QUESTIONS

1 Choose a well-known organization or one for which access to relevant information is easy to obtain and then summarize:

   a Its corporate objectives.

   b The key elements of its marketing and operations strategies.

   Next, review the three aspects of corporate objectives, marketing strategy and operations strategy, and assess how well (with examples) they form a coherent whole.

2 What are the key decision areas that organizations need to address when determining their operations strategies? Give examples.

3 Why is an organization's operations function crucial to its strategic success? Give three examples to illustrate the points you make.

4 Using an organization you know well, list three examples that illustrate how operations decisions have helped it to succeed and three examples that have hindered its success.

5 What is the difference between being market-driven and market-driving within the context of strategy development?

6 Do all functions necessarily have a strategic role? Explain and provide two examples to illustrate your views.

7 Give three key reasons for operations' reactive role in strategy development. Explain your choice.

8 What are the steps in developing a functional strategy using operations as the example in your answer?

9 What is the essential difference between order-winners and qualifiers? Could a competitive criterion be an order-winner in one market or market segment and a qualifier in another market or market segment? Explain.

NOTES AND REFERENCES

1 Hill, T. (1998) *The Strategy Quest*, AMD Publishing, p. vii. Email: amdpublishinguk@gmail.com.

2 See, for example, Gagnon, S. (1999) 'Resource-based competition and the new operations strategy', *International Journal of Operations and Production Management*, 19(2): 135–8; Grant, R. (1991) 'The resource-based theory of competitive advantage: implications for strategy formulation', *California Management Review*, 33: 114.

3 Hill, A. and Hill, T. (2003) 'Customer service: aligning business to markets' Executive Briefing, Green Templeton College, University of Oxford.

EXPLORING FURTHER

Bettley, A., Mayle, D. and Tantoush, T. (eds) (2005) *Operations Management: A Strategic Approach*, Sage Publications.

Fitzsimmons, J.A. and Fitzsimmons, M.J. (2010) *Service Management: Operations Strategy and Information Technology*, McGraw Hill Higher Education.

Prajogo, D.M. and McDermott, D. (2008) 'The relationship between operations strategies and operations activities in a service context', *International Journal of Service Industry Management*, 19(4), 506–20.

Rudberg, M. and West, B. (2008) 'Global operations strategy: coordinating manufacturing network', *Omega*, 36(1), 91–106.

Savitz, A.W. and Weber, K. (2006) *The Triple Bottom Line: How Today's Best-run Companies Are Achieving Economic, Social and Environmental Success*, Jossey Bass.

Schwientek, R. and Schmidt, A. (eds) (2005) *Operations Excellence: Smart Solutions for Business Success*, Palgrave Macmillan.

Tan, K.H. and Matthews, R.L. (2009) *Operations Strategy in Action: A Guide to The Theory and Practice of Implementation*, Edward Elgar Publishing.

Van Meighem, J.A. and Allon, G. (2014) *Operations Strategy: Principles and Practice*, Dynamic Ideas.

3 DEVELOPING AN OPERATIONS STRATEGY: METHODOLOGY

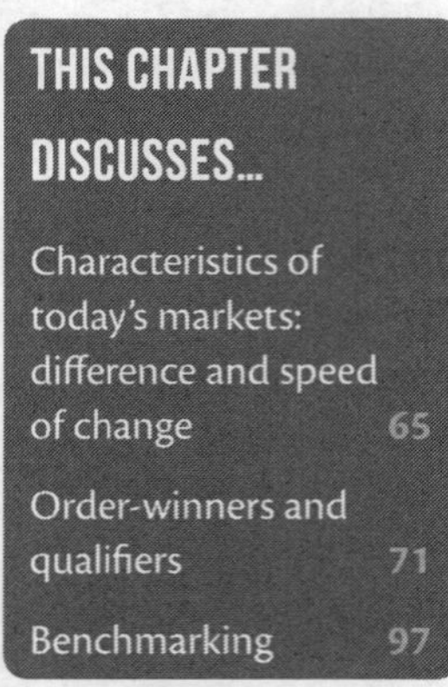

THIS CHAPTER DISCUSSES...

SUMMARY

This chapter explains the methodology for developing an operations strategy and details the following key aspects

- Explains the specific characteristics and dimensions of order-winners and qualifiers and the insights they provide
- Details the steps in developing an operations strategy
- Reviews the content and ways to improve the provision of the specific order-winners and qualifiers for which operations is solely or jointly responsible
- Discusses the characteristics of the non-operations-related criteria in markets
- Outlines the role of benchmarking in strategy formulation

INTRODUCTION

The previous chapter introduced the principles and concepts underpinning the development of an operations strategy. This chapter explains how to develop an operations strategy, together with a range of analyses and actions to be undertaken to illustrate what an operations strategy comprises.

Functions manage, control and develop the resources for which they are operationally and strategically responsible. The operational tasks concern managing and controlling the day-to-day, short-term aspects of a business. The strategic tasks concern investing in and developing those capabilities to provide the qualifiers and order-winners necessary to compete in agreed current and future markets. Let's start by restating the steps involved in operations strategy development while remembering that it is iterative in nature and business-based in substance and outcomes. Figure 3.1 provides an outline of the steps described here.

Step 1 Agree markets – agree the current and future markets in which a business wishes to compete. This, in turn, will often take the form of identifying current and new customers or current and new services/products as the means of retaining and growing market share and entering new markets.

ANALYSE MARKETS		DEVELOP AN OPERATIONS STRATEGY		
Agree markets	Determine market order-winners and qualifiers	Identify key strategic task	Review current performance and identify improvements	Prioritize investments and developments
Agree current and future markets in which to compete	Determine the order-winners and qualifiers for these markets	Identify key order-winners and qualifiers supported by operations and translate them into strategic tasks	Assess how well operations currently supports these strategic tasks and identify areas for improvement	Prioritize the investments and developments to improve support of strategic tasks

Figure 3.1 Analysing markets and developing an operations strategy

Step 2 Determine the order-winners and qualifiers – discuss and agree (with executive opinion being checked by actual data, as explained in Chapter 2) the set of order-winners and qualifiers for the range of markets or customers served while recognizing that these will differ throughout. For example, the order-winners and qualifiers and their respective weightings will differ depending on the task in hand, such as:

- time dimensions – current or future market(s)/customers;
- market share – shed, retain or grow market share;
- customer/market – existing or new customers/markets;
- position – #1 or #2 supplier.

Step 3 Identify operations' strategic tasks – identify the order-winners and qualifiers for which operations is solely or jointly responsible and translate them into strategic tasks.

Step 4 Review current level of performance and identify improvements – assess how well operations currently supports these strategic tasks and identify areas where improvements need to be made. Here it is important to broaden the discussion to identifying whether the source of improvement is solely within operations' remit or potentially best met by working with other functions (see the later section entitled 'Trade-offs').

Step 5 Prioritize investments and developments – prioritize the investments and developments necessary to improve the level of support for relevant strategic tasks, agree the timescales involved and determine the plan to implement the agreed changes.

Steps 1 and 2 were the subject of Chapter 2. It is these key first steps that set the strategic agenda for functions. Steps 3, 4 and 5 then follow, and they are the subject of this chapter. As highlighted earlier, functional strategies are agreed and set by the business as a whole with each function, understandably, taking the lead in its own area of responsibility by providing insights, data and alternatives. Each function is then tasked with implementing the agreed agenda in terms of investments and timescales.

CHARACTERISTICS OF CURRENT APPROACHES TO DEVELOPING AN OPERATIONS STRATEGY

It is useful to highlight the issues that were addressed in the previous chapter and to introduce other drawbacks that characterize current approaches to developing an operations strategy. These are often proposed in the literature and were also cited in Chapter 2.

Generic strategies – searching for the alchemist's stone

Academics, consultants and other third-party advisors too often appear to search for generic strategies in much the same way as those who sought to change base metal into gold. Firms themselves perpetuate this by seeking simplistic solutions to their complex problems. Perhaps this quest will only be set aside when firms realize that the diverse and dynamic needs of their markets cannot be met with the selection and application of one or more generic options.

Niche, low cost, differentiation and core competence are seductive offerings, but the uniformity they promise does not reflect the nature of business. Instead, organizations must recognize differences across their market and develop multiple strategies to address these separate needs. Strategy is not a process leading to generalizations. It is a distillation process that identifies the very essence and purpose of a business before building the capability to achieve this.[1]

Markets set the strategic agenda

Though functions may have different strategic roles they share the same strategic agenda – contributing to the company's capability so as to compete effectively in its chosen markets. Without a market agenda functions may pursue good practices but not necessarily sound strategies – they will be working to their own, rather than the business's agenda.

Failure to understand markets

Some of the characteristics that point to an organization's failure to understand its markets include market reviews that are:

- infrequent and irregular in nature;
- not an integral part of the corporate agenda;
- characterized by discussions about customers that are reactive in nature and triggered by day-to-day events such as problems, complaints, upcoming customer meetings or impending customer contract renewals;
- fuelled by opinion, resulting in unclear insights that go unchallenged and outputs that fail to identify the essential differences that characterize most companies' markets.

Motherhood and apple pie strategies

Much of the literature includes 'motherhood and apple pie' statements on strategy such as 'customer service', 'the customer is king', and 'delighting the customer'. While these contain the spirit of meeting the needs of a market, such approaches:

- close down the debate about how a company wins orders;
- set aside the discussion essential to identifying differences in markets by overlaying the total with single, overarching descriptions and thereby circumvent the complex nature of businesses;
- fail to distinguish the outputs of strategy (for example, serving/delighting customers) from the content (how you serve or delight customers);
- allow sales and marketing to disengage from the debate;
- imply that all customer orders are as good (in terms of revenue and profits) as one another when invariably they are not;
- induce a sales revenue-driven mentality that sits well on the sales and marketing agenda because maximizing revenue is typically its prime measure but invariably ignores the key dimensions of profit and cash flow;
- go against the iterative nature of the strategy development process because such outcomes brook further discussion.

MARKETS AND MARKET SEGMENTS

In Chapter 2, the terms 'market', 'market segments', 'products', 'services' and 'customers' were used as ways of describing markets. For operations, a market is a cluster of one or more customers for whom the order-winners, qualifiers and weightings are similar. Such a group represents a similar strategic task in terms of what operations needs to provide in order to retain and grow share. Consequently, the term 'market' and 'market segments' are deemed interchangeable.

CHARACTERISTICS OF TODAY'S MARKETS: DIFFERENCE AND SPEED OF CHANGE

In the past, markets were characterized by similarity and stability, but current markets are characterized by difference and rapid change.

The market characteristics of today place a greater need on gaining clear insights into how companies have to compete than was required for markets in the past, and one theme throughout is the need to attain the necessary level of understanding. Chapter 2 outlined a framework for gaining more detailed market insights. A wide range of methodologies has been put forward by academics, consultants and other advisors specifying approaches that would lead to strategic insights and appropriate answers. Driven by a need for generic solutions, these approaches too often set aside the overriding differences that exist in companies in order to offer a universal way of developing strategy that typically overarches a range of very different businesses. Failing to recognize and cope with difference, and avoiding the essential interface between corporate, business unit and functional strategies and between functions themselves, has resulted in approaches that appear complete but which, when applied, are unable to cope with the complex nature of today's businesses and their markets. Strategy development is not that easy.

Companies will not arrive at successful and workable strategic decisions unless they adequately understand their markets. Only then will they be able to identify the strategic alternatives to meet the needs of their different markets and thus move away from prescriptive approaches. The solutions developed by academics and consultants are very attractive in what they offer. However, the all-embracing and solution-oriented characteristics of these approaches invariably do not provide executives with the insights necessary to cope with their complex businesses. Neither do they warn them that these approaches have limitations, and that strategy development will be ongoing, difficult, time-consuming and necessitate continuous months of exacting work. Because advocates of these approaches invariably fail to start with sufficient emphasis on understanding markets then executives are impeded in their strategy development task by their failure to complete this fundamental step. Also, as with most aspects of management, an essential ingredient in doing a task well is hard work. Understanding today's varied and fast-changing markets is no exception. As Figure 3.2 highlights, defining the problem – understanding market requirements – is difficult. Finding the solution – identifying the action to take, such as reducing cost where price is a significant order-winner – is easy. Finally, implementation – in this example, undertaking the necessary investments, decisions and actions to reduce cost – is difficult. Too much of the time, the focus is on the solution phase.

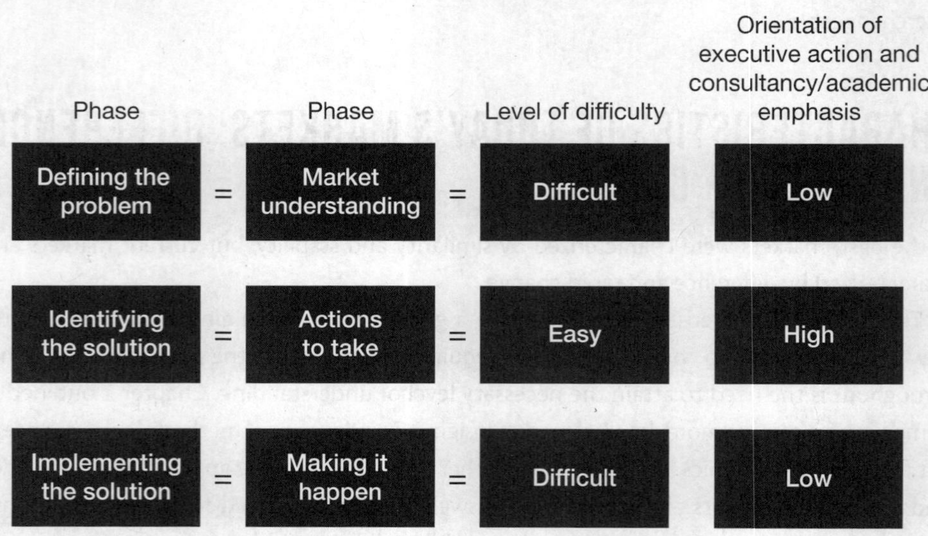

Figure 3.2 **Phases and characteristics of strategy development and implementation**

TRADE-OFFS

The trend towards increasingly competitive markets brings with it the question of whether it is possible to improve on all competitive fronts at the same time or whether companies need to recognize and select between the trade-offs inherent when choosing alternative investments.

The concept of trade-offs has received much interest since the late 1960s when Skinner put the issue at the centre of the operations strategy paradigm.[2] Researchers still take significantly different positions on the existence[3] as well as the implications of trade-offs for a business and the relevance of these issues for operations strategy and the company as a whole.

The concern with the proposition that trade-offs can be set aside, reduced to a level that no longer restricts options or strategic direction, or even that they are somehow manageable now and in the future, ignores the fact that trade-offs are an integral feature of business decisions.

The investment of time and money to change, develop or improve elements of delivery systems or infrastructure within operations always involves choices, and with choices there are trade-offs – relevant performance dimensions that are better served by one approach compared to another, allocating investment resources to improve one qualifier or order-winner as opposed to another and so on. Compromise is inherent in choice and so to put forward a view of operations' business contribution that is in denial of this introduces a premise that is unsustainable and misleading in several ways.

- Operations' inputs into strategic discussion need not include the issue of choice nor an explanation of the constraints that follow.
- Similarly, the rest of the company may assume that operations' contribution to meeting the competitive needs of a company's markets is neither constrained nor limited such that these must be taken into account.
- Consequently, the compromises that are inherent in choice and that need to be fully understood by a business when making strategic decisions are taken out of the corporate arena and are, in fact, subsequently made within the organization at the level of the function rather than the level of the business.

But that situation cannot be supported. Where a company allocates resources and how these investments are spent will impact on what offerings a business can provide and how well it can provide them. When addressing these issues companies, whether consciously or not, make choices at several levels. Some concern direction, others concern means but, as the next section explains, all embody trade-offs. Although, for ease of explanation, these choices have been separated into discrete statements at different levels, they are part of a whole that would require iterative discussion as part of the selection process.

Level 1: Which business unit?

Where companies are of a size that makes splitting the whole into two, or more, business units, the investment decision at the corporate level concerns to which business unit(s) the resources should be allocated. These decisions around investment (and similarly divestment) concern critical issues about future sales revenue and profit growth.

Level 2: Which market?

Because businesses are typically in two or more markets, prioritizing the investments made by functions such as operations needs to reflect the corporate importance of the market choices involved.

Level 3: Which order-winner or qualifier?

The competitive drivers in markets typically differ. Thus having made choices at level 2, the next set of choices concerns which order-winner(s)/qualifier(s) in the chosen market(s) to prioritize in terms of where investments will be made.

Level 4: Which function?

To improve the company's ability to better provide a chosen order-winner or qualifier, the next choice is how to achieve this most effectively. The first step is to determine how this will be provided in terms of the two or more functions that can contribute to improving support for a competitive driver in a company's market(s).

To illustrate these options, let's overview the contribution that different functions could make to two possible competitive dimensions, that of price and delivery speed.

Price

Where price is an order-winner, the strategic task of relevant functions is to reduce cost in terms of the service/product specification itself, or the operations processes used in its provision. The trade-off decision facing a business at this level includes deciding which function or functions are best able to contribute to this requirement in terms of investment (time and money) and return. For example:

- **Service sector**
  1. **Marketing**, as the function typically responsible for determining the service specification, could be tasked to simplify or lower the service specification itself so as to reduce the total time (and associated costs) spent to provide the service.
  2. **Operations** could be required to improve/simplify the existing system for delivering the service in order to:
     - reduce the time required to deliver the service;
     - simplify the system to lower the skill sets (and consequently staff costs) necessary to deliver the service.
  3. **IT** could be set the task of simplifying the process so as to:
     - shorten the service delivery lead time;
     - reduce the staff time (and consequently costs) spent to deliver the service.
- **Manufacturing sector**
  1. **Design** could be tasked to simplify the current design in order to:
     - take out material cost, for example by reducing the material content or substituting a lower cost material, while still meeting the required product specification;
     - reduce the labour cost involved by, for example, reducing the number of parts in the product and thus the time needed to make and assemble it.

2 **Operations** could be required to improve the existing process so as to:
   - reduce waste, for example reducing the number of rejects or the level of process waste;
   - reduce the time to make the product by increasing process speed while maintaining quality conformance levels.

3 **Engineering** could invest in modifying, or retrofitting, the existing process in order to:
   - increase throughput speed;
   - reduce the number of people to run the process;
   - reduce the level of rejects or process waste.

Delivery speed

Where delivery speed is an order-winner, the strategic task concerns reducing the operations lead time involved. Again the trade-off decisions concern which function or functions would best be able to contribute to this requirement in terms of investment (time and money) and return. For example:

- **Service sector**

  1 **Operations** could arrange its staff schedules to better match the times when customers can more easily attend. For example, veterinary and medical practices could arrange the time when patients (their customers) can book appointments more in line with their customers' typical working hours. In that way, the time from request to appointment would be shortened.

  2 **Operations** could seek ways to reduce delivery system lead times with the aim of matching or improving on customer lead-time expectations. For example, part-preparing food in a restaurant prior to opening so as to reduce customer waiting times and introducing a checkout system in a store to equate staff numbers at the tills to customer queues in a highly sensitive and responsive manner.

- **Manufacturing sector**

  1 **Operations** could invest to reduce lead time through a better production planning and control system, or through improved integration with suppliers.

  2 **Operations** could trade lead time for inventory and move from, say, a make-to-order to an assemble-to-order position.

  3 **Design** could modify the product structure and increase modularization, thus allowing a change from a make-to-order to an assemble-to-order position with little or no increase in inventory.

At this point, it is worth recalling that trade-offs at different levels are not independent of one another. The above examples do not affect the selection of which market, or which order-winners/qualifiers; these are still open options. For example, when addressing the need to improve delivery speed, there is the option of redefining the business so as to, say, reduce the available range of offerings and move to a make-to-stock policy with zero delivery lead times.

Level 5: Which investment?

The evaluation of alternative investments has to take into account not only the trade-offs inherent in the investment itself but also a comparison between each investment and its alternative. Investing in an advanced manufacturing system (AMS) is a way to meet a wider range of products and the high- and low-volume demands that would be involved. However, this proposal ignores the trade-off discussion to assess the outcome of spending the money in other ways. For example, by spending $3m on an AMS a company would be able to meet its current product range. An alternative for this company would be to spend part of this investment on a process to meet the high-volume products within its current range while continuing to make other products on existing processes using the increased available capacity that would result. One benefit of the latter approach would be to lower the unit costs of its high-volume products, thus enabling the company to compete more effectively in this part of its market. It is clear that investing in delivery systems and manufacturing processes that can meet the demands and volumes of a range of products will bring one set of trade-offs. Investing part or all of the same funds in the high- or low-volume segment of the total market involved will bring another set of trade-offs. Here again, choice brings alternatives and issues of compromises that highlight the trade-offs on hand and the alternative decisions to be taken.

Investment for strategic versus operational reasons

Investments and developments can be made to meet either strategic or operational goals and some illustrations are given in Figure 3.3. Both approaches involve sound decisions but are

Activity	Strategic considerations	Operational considerations
Cost reduction	Lowers costs to lower price	Lowers costs to increase margins and profits
Inventory reduction	Could increase operations lead time	Improves cash flow
Change from a make-to-stock to a make-to-order position	Increases operations lead time	Improves cash flow
Improve quality conformance levels	Right first time	Lowers costs to increase profits
Improve delivery reliability levels	Improve on-time delivery performance	Simplifies scheduling and reduces waste

Figure 3.3 Examples of the different strategic and operational outcomes that may result from activities

undertaken for different purposes and to deliver different outcomes. Part of the operations executive task is to ensure that these differences are understood and form the basis of the executive decision process. As already emphasized, the executive task is to ensure that time and money is spent on the 'right things'.

ORDER-WINNERS AND QUALIFIERS

BASIC CHARACTERISTICS

Identifying relevant order-winners and qualifiers, and the relevant weightings to be attached to them, helps companies to achieve the critical insights needed to ensure that money is spent effectively. The following sections describe what these criteria are and how they work. The first section provides important background for the discussion of specific criteria that follows. When discussing markets, a company should keep in mind the following:

- General statements about markets embody imprecise meanings. As a result, executives take away from strategy discussions their own understandings that are typically based on their own functional perspectives. Thus, a prerequisite for sound strategy development (that is, agreement by all on what markets the company is and should be in, and the competitive characteristics of those markets) is missing.
- Order-winners and qualifiers are market-specific. The criteria relating to one market will carry different order-winners, qualifiers and weightings from another market. It follows, therefore, that there are few general rules.
- When developing order-winners and qualifiers, companies must distinguish the level of importance for individual criteria for each market. To do this, they weight order-winners by allocating points; for qualifiers, a distinction is made between a qualifier and an order-losing sensitive qualifier (that is, one that will cause a business to lose customers' orders quickly). Examples of these dimensions were given in Figures 2.16 and 2.17, together with supporting text (see pp. 43–5).
- Order-winners and qualifiers and their relative weightings will change over time. To assess these potential changes, a company must weight each criterion for the current period and two future periods. The latter will need to reflect the nature of the market; for example, for a printing company, the future time periods may be next year and the year after, but for an aerospace company, they would need to be several years ahead, so reflecting the product life cycles involved. Again, Figures 2.16 and 2.17 illustrate these points.
- Differences typically exist between the criteria and the weightings necessary to retain existing market share, those necessary to increase market share and those to gain new customers. These differences need to be reflected in the relevant order-winners and qualifiers and their respective weightings.
- Similarly, the criteria that relate to winning orders for a primary supplier will differ from those for secondary or other supplier categories. Although customers tend to infer that the criteria are the same, common sense challenges that logic. The large percentage share of demand that typically goes to a primary supplier creates very different contractual

demands and opportunities from those for other suppliers. The way in which secondary or other suppliers win their part of the contract needs to reflect this.

- Not all order-winners and qualifiers relate to operations. However, over time, operations-related criteria will often come to the fore, for example price, on-time delivery and quality conformance.

SPECIFIC DIMENSIONS

There is a range of order-winners and qualifiers, and, as highlighted above, not all of them form part of operations' strategic task. Consequently, this section separates the different categories and reviews typical criteria within each category. As stressed earlier, strategy is market- and time-specific and, therefore, not all order-winners and qualifiers will relate to, or be of the same importance to, all companies.

Operations-related and operations-specific criteria

This category concerns those order-winners and qualifiers that are specific to operations and will, where relevant, form part of operations' strategic role.

Price

In many markets, and particularly in the growth, maturity and saturation phases of a service or product life cycle (see Figure 3.4), price typically becomes an increasingly important order-winner. When this is so, operations' task is to provide the low costs necessary to support the price sensitivity of the market, thus providing the level of profit margin necessary to support the business investment involved while creating opportunities for the future. As in many of the pertinent analyses in operations, highlighting the pockets of significant cost will give direction toward the areas where resource allocation should be made and management attention given, and these details will be covered in the next section.

Since price is an omnipresent factor in most markets, companies are reluctant to consider that price may not be a relevant order-winner. This misunderstanding often stems from the fact that price comparisons with alternatives will typically form part of a customer's evaluation. However, where price is an order-winner, margins will be low. Only then will cost

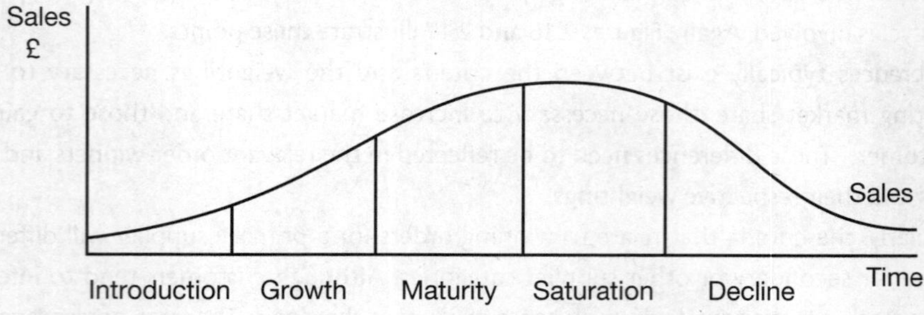

Figure 3.4 Generalized service or product life cycle

reduction be a priority. Where service/product margins are high, price is not an order-winner but a qualifier. In such markets, customers will compare one price to another, not to seek the lowest price but to check that the quoted price is within an acceptable range. Therefore, companies need to recognize the key difference between being price competitive (a qualifier) and competing on price (an order-winner).

Such an evaluation is not unique to the aspect of price. Customers will typically cross-check all relevant criteria. In the case of qualifiers, this is to ensure a ballpark fit, whereas for order-winners, customers will typically be looking for a 'better than' performance.

As explained earlier, qualifiers get a company into and maintain it within a market. As such, they do not win orders but are essential prerequisites for a company to be considered as a potential supplier. Where price is a qualifier, a company cannot simply charge whatever it wishes. The company must price the service or product according to what the market will bear, keeping exploitation within sensible bounds. Failure to do so will result in lost orders to competitors that are more price competitive. In such situations, a company will have turned a qualifier (that is, a service or product highly priced within acceptable limits) into an order-losing criterion (the price has become too high).

Where price is an order-winner, low (or anticipated low) margins give operations the clear task of reducing costs in order to maintain or improve available margins. Where companies decide to reduce price significantly, altering its role (from a qualifier to an order-winner) or its importance as an order-winner, they must similarly change related elements of operations strategy. Companies electing to alter the role of price would need to assess the lead times involved for operations to respond to the increased emphasis on cost reduction, any associated investments and the cost reduction potential. Deciding to reduce price without assessing these factors will invariably lead to inappropriate strategies. On one hand the decision to reduce price, although difficult to evaluate, is easy to make; cost reduction, on the other hand, is easy to evaluate but difficult to achieve.

Cost reduction

When price is an order-winner, a strategic role for operations is to reduce costs. To this end, companies need to concentrate their efforts in those areas where costs are greatest.

- *Service sector*

In service organizations, staff costs are often a significant portion of the total. Where this is so, it follows that, in price-sensitive markets, investing to reduce staff costs would become a key strategic task for operations. Approaches to meeting this requirement include simplifying the provision of a service, developing systems to complete all or parts of a service and identifying aspects of a service that can be completed by less skilled staff or customers.

Where offerings are towards the non-repeat end of the service continuum, developing the skill sets of those involved, while ensuring that these staff skills are only used, as much as possible, on the right level of work, ensures that these 'scarce resources' are fully and appropriately utilized. This approach is termed 'maximizing the use of a scarce resource', and ensures that profits are maximized.

- *Manufacturing sector*

As highlighted earlier, in many developed economies labour costs in manufacturing companies are relatively small as a percentage of total costs. Here, since materials and overheads typically account for some 80–90 per cent of the total, these will be the areas that will typically yield the best results and should receive the pro rata attention they deserve. Companies need to ensure that the emphasis on controlling and reducing direct labour costs has not been carried forward from the past. Too often, this traditional orientation unduly influences the direction of cost reduction initiatives.

- *Lean operations*

The drive towards reducing waste within operations is encapsulated by the term 'lean operations'.[4] As the term implies, the aim is to seek out and eliminate waste in all its forms, including the elimination of non-value-added activities and inventory reduction.

Many organizations have undertaken continuous improvement efforts to increase productivity. The key areas for re-evaluation, however, are broadly based as they reflect the more significant areas of expense and cost reduction opportunities within each company. Typical lists include eliminating waste (for example, doing necessary tasks wrong the first time; doing unnecessary tasks; data errors; missing information and unnecessary approval cycles – and the typical costs associated with these non-value activities typically range from 20 to 30 per cent of total cost), service/product redesign, quality conformance at source, process redesign, just-in-time (JIT) production control systems, quicker set-ups, overhead reduction and the involvement of people in continuous improvement activities. The outcomes create significant improvements and underpin high performance organizations. Examples of this are increasingly common. One study investigated the relative performance of 18 automotive component plants, 9 in Japan and 9 in the UK. Figure 3.5 shows the difference between those plants categorized by the report as being 'world class' (note that all world-class plants were Japanese but not all Japanese plants were world class) and the remainder of the sample.

While initially the drive for lean systems and procedures was used and developed in the manufacturing sector, the application of these principles is equally appropriate in service organizations. For example, Jefferson Pilot Finance, a leading US full-service life insurance and annuities company and, since 2006, part of Lincoln National Corporation, initiated an improvement programme using lean principles. Some of the results reflecting the improvements gained are listed in Figure 3.6.[5]

Dimension		Relative plant performance (100 = best)	
		World class	Other
Units per	hour	95	54
	m² floor space	89	64
Level of rework (% direct labour force)		1.5	4.1
Hours of inventory		11	75

Figure 3.5 Relative average performance of world class and other manufacturing plants against selected dimensions

Dimension		% reduction
Turnaround time[1]	APS[2]	70
	Non-APS[2]	84
Total staff costs – all applications		26
Re-issues due to errors		40

Notes
1 Turnaround time is the time taken from receipt of an application to the insurance policy being issued.
2 APS – a policy requiring an attending physician's statement.

Figure 3.6 Performance improvements in a life insurance and annuities company

A key factor in the approach to driving out costs is to avoid concentrating on one aspect of cost rather than total cost because this can lead to missed opportunities. For example, Heinz, the US-based food company, introduced a labour cost reduction plan at its Starkist tuna factories in Puerto Rico and American Samoa. With increasing competition from low labour-cost areas, this policy seemed to make sense. But a study revealed that the staff were so overworked that each day they were leaving tonnes of meat on the bone. Adding workers, slowing down production lines, increasing supervision and retraining increased costs by $5m but cut waste by $15m to give a $10m saving each year. A similar example is provided by a Dutch-based food preparation company. The growing importance of high-volume demand from large supermarket chains in Europe had brought an increased emphasis on price as an order-winner. The company's response was to seek direct labour productivity improvements. But this diverted attention from controlling costs elsewhere. Further reviews revealed high levels of waste in preparation. For example, lettuce loss was four times higher than the standards set. Additional training and close monitoring of actual performance compared to standards soon got waste down to acceptable levels and, with it, associated costs.

- *Continuous improvement*

Going hand in hand with the drive to cut costs and reduce waste is the recognition that improvement should not only be the result of business-level activity led by specialists (and resulting in stepped changes and significant breakthroughs) but should also be continuously sought by all involved. Continuous improvement[6] describes the ongoing drive to seek improvements (no matter what their size) in all aspects of a business and for this to be set within the domain of the staff undertaking the work involved. In this way, improvement becomes an integral part of a person's job and is ongoing in nature. The success of this approach has been clearly demonstrated in Japanese automobile companies over several decades. Known as 'kaizen', a Japanese term meaning 'continuous improvement', the benefits have been clearly demonstrated and maintained over time. Increasingly, Western companies have adopted this approach with significant benefits. While typically the changes that result are small and lead to incremental improvements, the wealth of ideas leads to sizeable results overall with immediate and identifiable benefits. Toyota, for example, typically implements an average of 30 ideas per employee per year, generating significant savings; Boardroom Inc., a US publishing company, receives on average 100 ideas per employee. Similar levels of ideas were also recorded by Milliken Inc., a US-based textile and chemicals company, while Wainwright Industries, an aerospace and automotive group, typically implements an annual average of 65 ideas per employee.

Continuous improvement also signals a change in management style, where responsibility and authority to seek out and implement changes is pushed down the organization. Undertaking these improvement activities is built into the job, with appropriate training and development being provided and time set aside to carry out these tasks.

- *Experience curves*

Evidence clearly shows that as experience accumulates, performance improves, and the experience curve is the quantification of this improvement. The basic phenomenon of the experience curve is that the cost of delivering a service, processing a document or manufacturing a given item falls in a regular and predictable way as the total quantity produced or delivered increases. The purpose of this section is to draw attention to this relationship and its role in the formulation of an operations strategy. It is helpful to note that while the cost/volume relationship is the pertinent corporate issue, one example, in fact, relates price to volume because the information, not being company derived, uses average industry price as a convenient substitute.

The price of a new service or product almost always declines after its initial introduction and as it becomes more widely accepted and available. However, it is not so commonly recognized that over a wide range of services or products, costs also follow a remarkably consistent decline. The characteristic pattern is that the cost declines (in constant $s, €s, or £s) by a consistent percentage each time the cumulative unit throughput or production is doubled. The effects of learning curves on staff and labour costs have been recognized and reported over more than 70 years, beginning with studies on airframe production in the United States in the 1930s. However, experience curves are distinctly different from this. The real source of the experience effect is derived from organizational improvement. Although learning by individuals is important, it is only one of many improvements that accrue from experience. Investment in operations delivery systems and processes, changes in methods, service/product development, and improvements in all functions in a business account for most of the significant experience-related gains.

The experience curve is normally drawn by taking each doubling of cumulative unit provision or production and expressing the unit costs or price as a percentage of the cost or price before doubling. So an 80 per cent experience curve would mean that the cost or price of the one-hundredth unit of a service/product is 80 per cent of that of the one-fiftieth; of the two-hundredth, 80 per cent of that of the one-hundredth and so on. Figure 3.7 illustrates the basic features of experience curves.[7]

Figures 3.7a and 3.7b show the same information but plotted on different scales. Both show the cost or price per unit on the vertical axis and the cumulative quantity produced on the horizontal axis. The graph in Figure 3.7a is plotted on a linear scale, and reveals a smooth curve

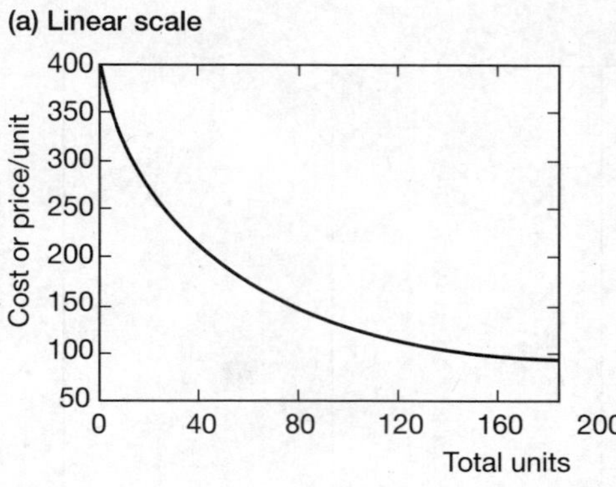

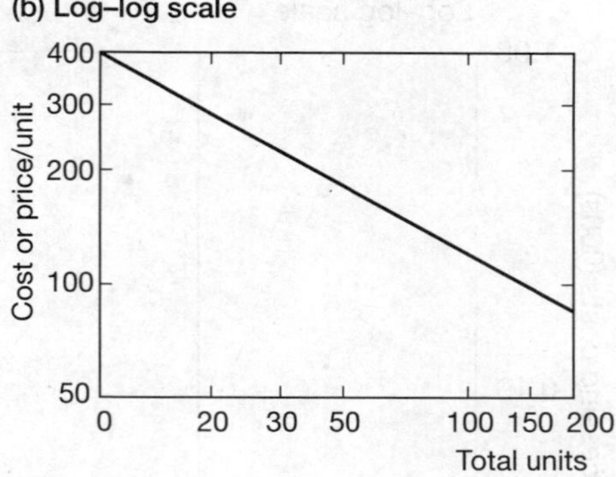

Figure 3.7 Cost/volume or price/volume relationship

Source: Based on Hill, A. and Hill, T. (2009) Manufacturing Operations Strategy, *3rd edn, Palgrave Macmillan.*

which demonstrates the implied regularity of the relationship between unit cost and total volume. However, Figure 3.7b shows the same information plotted on double logarithmic (log–log) scales. This presentation shows percentage changes as a constant distance, along both axes. The straight line on the log–log scale in Figure 3.7b means that a given percentage change in one factor has resulted in a corresponding percentage change in the other. The nature of that relationship determines the slope of the line that can be read off a log–log grid.

Figures 3.8 and 3.9 show the experience curves for voucher processing and for colour film produced by Japanese companies, respectively, and give the following insights:[8]

- Plotting the graphs on the logarithmic scale shows that many doublings of voucher processing or production can be achieved early on but, later, vastly larger quantities are needed to double the cumulative unit volumes then involved. This implies, as one would expect, that movement down the experience curve slows with time. Initially, additional growth in annual volumes can offset this, but the levelling in demand associated with the mature stage in a service/product life cycle will slow the rate of progress down the curve.
- The vertical axis of an experience curve is usually cost or price per unit and is also expressed logarithmically. However, the cost or price per unit must be adjusted for inflation to allow comparisons to be drawn over time. Figures 3.8 and 3.9 show that improvements further down the curve become, in absolute terms, quite small. Thus, as progress is made down the curve, each incremental improvement will take longer and yield less.

The characteristic decline in cost or price per unit was established by the Boston Consulting Group's (BCG) work in the 1960s and early 1970s as being between 20 and 30 per cent for each doubling of cumulative production. Although the BCG claims that this can go on (in constant $s, €s or £s) without limit and despite the rate of experience growth, in reality, this tends not to happen for the reasons given earlier.

Furthermore, it is important to stress that the experience curve characteristics are phenomenological in nature. They portray a relationship between cost or price and volume that can, but does not necessarily, exist. Consequently, the BCG concludes that:

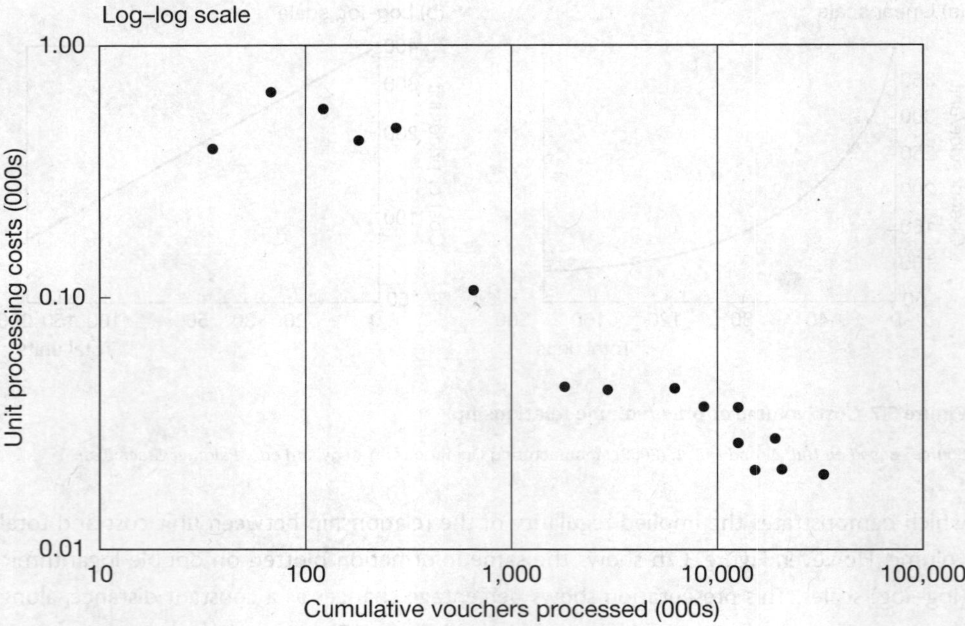

Figure 3.8 Experience curve over a six-year period – voucher processing centre

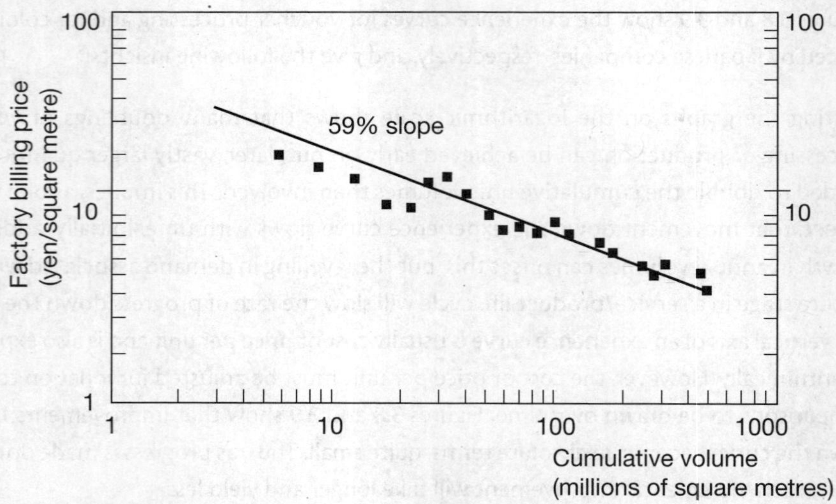

Figure 3.9 Experience curve for colour film produced by Japanese companies over a 23-year period

Source: Photo Electric News and *Japanese Economic Journal*.

these observed or inferred reductions in costs as volume increases are not necessarily automatic. They depend crucially on a competent management that seeks ways to force down costs as volume expands. Production costs are most likely to decline under this internal pressure. Yet in the long run the average combined cost of all elements should decline under the pressure for the company to remain as profitable as possible. To this extent the relationship is one of potential rather than one of certainty.[9]

Delivery reliability or on-time delivery

Delivery reliability or on-time delivery (OTD) means supplying the services or products ordered in full and on the agreed due date. It is, therefore, a major task of the operations function. In many businesses, this criterion now constitutes a qualifier. Very often, in fact, it is order-losing sensitive in nature, in that if companies miss due dates, customers will quickly respond by reducing the amount of business they allocate to them or even take them off the potential supplier list altogether. As companies seek to reduce inventory levels, certainty of suppliers meeting agreed delivery dates is paramount. The role of OTD as a qualifier or often an order-losing sensitive qualifier is a consequence of the improvements made by suppliers in this regard in response to increasing pressure from customers. OTD performance is now an important prerequisite, with its measurement by customer, sector and, overall, a key factor in most businesses. The need to identify different OTD expectations is a critical step here as with other order-winners and qualifiers.

For the operations function, this involves consideration of capacity, scheduling and inventory, particularly regarding work-in-progress and finished goods. Such checks need to be supplemented by regular reviews of those dimensions affecting a company's record on delivery reliability, such as completed line-item reviews and checks on lead-time performance throughout the total delivery system.

The exactness of the due date can vary from an appointed hour on a given day to delivery in an agreed week or even month. The level of data collection and the timing and proactive nature of the feedback to customers will need to form part of this decision. As a rule, the more exact the delivery, the more proactive a supplier should be in the data collection and the more regular the performance summaries and feedback to customers should be.

These data are the source of information about reporting stage completions where parts of a service are delivered over an agreed period of time, the size of 'call-offs' (what a customer actually wants rather than the total quantities expressed in any contract or agreement) and the lead times associated with deliveries. The former concerns the issues of costs and price agreements and part payments while the latter leads into the criterion of delivery speed.

Delivery speed

A company may win orders through its ability to deliver more quickly than competitors or to meet the delivery date required when only some or even none of the competitors can do so. Services and products that compete in this way need an operations delivery system that can respond to this delivery speed requirement. The key measurement here is to compare a customer's lead time (the time between the order or call-off being placed and required delivery date) with the operations lead time (OLT). As shown in Figure 3.10, the OLT is a combination of the material lead time (MLT – the time taken for a supplier to deliver) or order backlog (OBL – the number of orders already accepted and waiting to be processed or made), whichever is the greater, plus the delivery system lead time (DSLT) or the process lead time (PLT – the length of time it takes operations to complete the order), whichever is the greater. Note that a further possible element of lead time is delivering the order to a customer's premises, and it would need to form part of the calculations. It is addressed in a

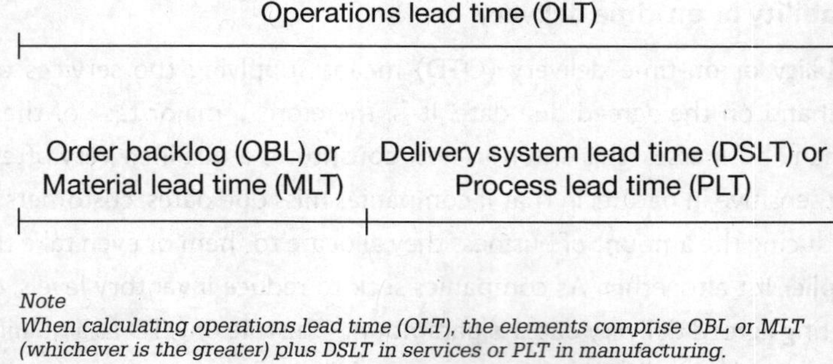

Figure 3.10 The components of operations lead time

later section but has been omitted here to simplify the discussion. As shown in Figure 3.11, such comparisons can result in the customer lead time (CLT) being shorter than the OLT (Situation 1) or the reverse (Situation 2).

Situation 1 – CLT shorter than OLT

In Situation 1, once an order is accepted, operations will need to select from a number of options so as to shorten its lead time norms in line with the promised delivery date. These include actions to:

- Increase short-term capacity, for example by overtime working.
- Change customer priorities in the existing order backlog/queue or jobs going through the operations delivery system.

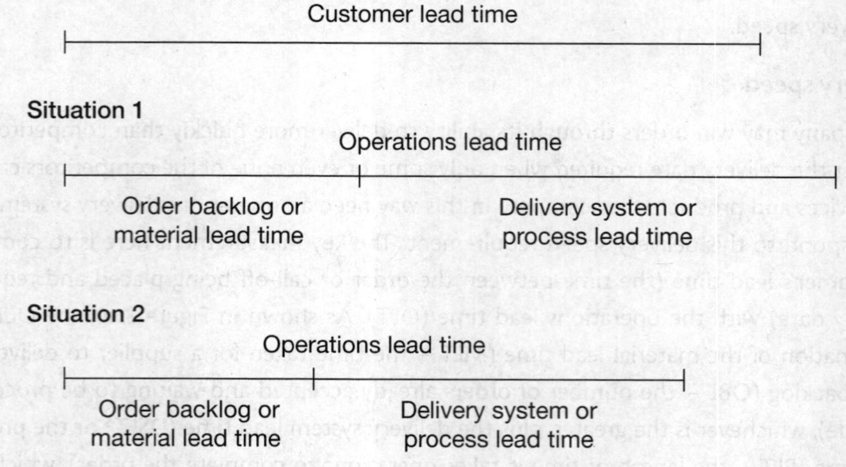

Figure 3.11 Customer lead time and operations lead time comparisons

Where such situations are infrequent, short-term responses such as these will often suffice, with the former increasing costs and the latter increasing the scheduling pressures within operations. However, where Situation 1 represents an increasing trend, such short-term options become unsustainable and will need to be replaced by a strategic solution that will move the business back to the position where Situation 2 is the norm.

Such a trend would, in turn, be reflected in the order-winner weighting allocated to delivery speed in the regular review of markets and allow the strategy-making group (see Figure 2.4) to select from a range of options based on the investment required, the timescales involved and the benefits provided. (Note that the options below do not include reducing the company's existing DSLT or PLT because it is assumed that this would already form part of operations' ongoing activities.) These include actions to:

- Increase capacity either on a permanent (additional staff or the purchase of additional equipment) or a semi-permanent (for example, a move to increased daily working hours for a given period) basis and hence reduce the DSLT or PLT.
- Hold selected materials in stock and hence reduce the material lead time (MLT) element of the OLT.
- Move from a make-to-order position to either an assemble-to-order (and associated work-in-progress inventory) or make-to-stock (and associated finished goods inventory) position and hence reduce the DSLT or PLT.
- Contract with suppliers to guarantee a given level of orders so as to enable them to prioritize their own requirements within this portion of each supplier's OBL and thereby reduce the OBL element in that supplier's own OLT.
- Similarly, arrange for a supplier to hold selected material inventory (with guarantees of usage or compensation) and hence reduce the material lead time (MLT) element of a supplier's own OLT.

Figure 3.12 helps explain the last two options: it shows how the elements that make up a supplier's OLT (which, in turn, forms the MLT of the company) are the same as those in the

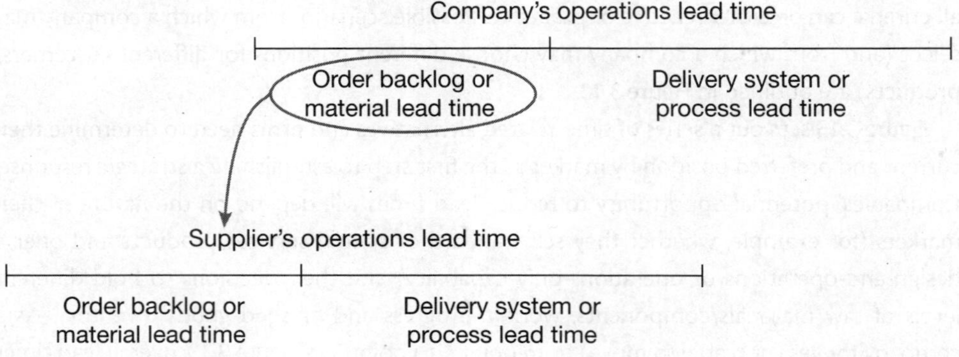

Figure 3.12 The elements making up a supplier's operations lead time that constitute the company's own material lead time

company's own OLT. What the latter two options offer is a way of helping a supplier reduce the OBL or MLT (respectively) of its own OLT, and hence reduce the MLT element of the company's own OLT.

Situation 2 – CLT longer than OLT

In Situation 2, there is no delivery speed element. The task in operations is to schedule customer orders to meet the promised due dates.

A market-driving option

Falling within a company's market debate should be a discussion around reducing its own existing OLT by a range of alternatives where it is considered that customers would value shorter lead times, or to change the accepted current market norms on suppliers' lead times to disadvantage competitors and in that way increase market share. The market-driving nature of such an alternative should form part of a company's strategic options.

An organization's response to reducing lead times needs to be corporate wide, and often the lead times associated with operations, before and after the actual service delivery or processing activity can be a substantial part of the time it takes from order entry to customer delivery. (Note: lead-time reduction in service/product development is addressed under the section on design later in the chapter.) From the moment an order is received, all elements of lead time need to be reviewed, with the aim of reducing each component involved in the total process. To succeed, companies must transform themselves and simply break the paradigms that hold current procedures and norms in place.[10]

Companies can knowingly offer short lead times to customers by holding, for example, excess capacity, maintaining low or zero order backlogs (queues) or holding inventory at any or all stages in the process. As highlighted earlier, such decisions would fall within the domain of the business strategy-making group, with operations' role to implement and maintain the chosen alternatives.

With customers typically reducing their own lead times, many companies are finding that the element of delivery speed is becoming an increasingly important factor in their markets (Situation 1; Figure 3.11). As discussed earlier, a company's response to delivery speed, as with all criteria, can be either reactive or proactive. Possible scenarios from which a company may select (and from which a company may choose different positions for different customers/products) are outlined in Figure 3.13.

Figure 3.13 sets out a series of time-related alternatives and firms need to determine their current and preferred position by market as the first step to establishing a strategic response. Companies' potential opportunity to reduce lead times will depend on the nature of their markets (for example, whether they sell standard or special services/products and offer a design-and-operations or operations-only capability) and their decisions to hold different levels of raw materials/components, work-in-progress and finished goods inventory. As a company moves (or is able to move) from point 1 to point 5 in Figure 3.13, overall lead times will reduce. However, as explained above, any repositioning is a corporate decision directly affecting the element of delivery speed. Adjusting its position on this continuum so as to

Initial positions	Length of lead time
1. Design to order – new service/product response where companies design and provide a service or product to meet the specific needs of a customer	Long
2. Engineer to order – changes to standard services or products are offered to customers and only provided to order. Such changes would be substantial in nature and customer specific. Lead times include the relevant elements of design, technical functions (e.g. IT) and all operations	↓
3. Make to order – concerns providing a standard service or product (any customization is nominal and does not increase total lead times) only on receipt of a customer order or against agreed schedules or call-offs	↓
4. Assemble to order – parts of a service or components and subassemblies for products have been prepared ahead of time. On receipt of an order (or against an agreed schedule or call-off), the required parts are drawn from work-in-progress/component inventory and assembled to order	↓
5. Make to stock – finished goods are made ahead of demand in line with sales forecasts. Customers' orders are met from inventory	Short

Figure 3.13 Alternative responses to markets and their lead-time implications

eliminate or reduce the impact of delivery speed would need to be supported by shortening each element of lead time within the overall process. Some everyday examples to illustrate how lead times are being universally shortened are provided in Figure 3.14.

The opportunity to reduce lead times is often provided by technology developments, as with the introduction in the 1980s of mini labs to develop photographs on site. Other improvements come from simply changing the delivery system itself. Take, for example changing a tyre on your car. The quick change systems have reduced the actual lead time to no more than 15 minutes but add in the time taken before and after the fitting and the total time for a customer increases significantly. However, companies such as Tyres On The Drive now (as the name suggests) bring the facility to you at home or at work. Customers save on time while also getting their tyres at a competitive price.

Service/product	Lead time (days)		
	1990	2000	2017
Personal computers	Up to 21	3	2
Photographic development	5	3	1
Spectacles	Up to 14	3–4	1–2

Figure 3.14 Examples of service and product lead time reduction

Quality conformance

Quality conformance (providing services and products to specification) as a competitive criterion has been thrust centre stage over the last three or four decades. Although its importance has been recognized throughout this period, many companies were slow to respond to the new quality conformance levels provided by competitors. In part, this was not helped by the lack of definition of the word 'quality' that has been broadened to encompass many dimensions. This lack of clarity contributed to some companies subsequently failing to recognize the size of the competitive threat. The new, sustained level of quality conformance represented a stepped change in performance that, in some sectors, redefined the role of quality conformance from a qualifier into an order-winner.

The spearhead for this change came predominantly from Japanese manufacturing companies. In the immediate postwar period, the need to address the poor image of the quality of most of Japan's manufacturing sector became a national as well as a corporate priority. The outcome of the investment and development initiatives changed that image and raised the threshold in both the national and international arenas. The results were instrumental in changing customers' expectations, and access to the large and growing markets of Western economies followed. Now, Japanese companies have a significant share of the major markets in many sectors, including automobiles, motorcycles and electrical and electronic products.

At the business level, the strategy-making group needs first to recognize the different dimensions that fall under the quality umbrella[11] and then the function(s) with prime responsibility for providing each of these (see Figures 3.15 and 3.16). Once the role and importance

<table>
<tr><th colspan="2">Dimensions of product quality</th><th>Function(s) with prime responsibility for their provision</th></tr>
<tr><td>Performance</td><td>A product's primary operating characteristics</td><td rowspan="5">Design</td></tr>
<tr><td>Features</td><td>Secondary characteristics, the 'bells and whistles'</td></tr>
<tr><td>Reliability</td><td>The probability of a product malfunctioning within a given period</td></tr>
<tr><td>Aesthetics</td><td>How the final product looks</td></tr>
<tr><td>Durability</td><td>A measure of a product's life in terms of both its technical and economic dimensions</td></tr>
<tr><td>Conformance</td><td>The degree to which a product is manufactured to the agreed specification</td><td>Operations</td></tr>
<tr><td>Serviceability</td><td>The ease of servicing (planned or breakdown) to include the speed and provision of after-sales service</td><td>Design and after-sales</td></tr>
<tr><td>Perceived quality</td><td>How a customer views the product</td><td>Marketing and design</td></tr>
</table>

Figure 3.15 The dimensions of product quality and the functions typically responsible for their provision

Dimensions of service quality		Function(s) with prime responsibility for their provision
Core elements	A service's basic provision	Sales/marketing
Customizing elements	Changeable core elements plus 'add ons' to better meet a customer's needs or preferences	
Structural preferences	Ambience, décor, and layout to reflect an organization's desired image	
Staff	Style, presentation, dress code, know-how and level of discretion of front-office staff	
Customer/system interface	Service delivery system design and ease of customer use	Operations
Fulfilment	Delivery meets customers' actual requirements	
Duration	Meet service targets related to queuing/waiting time and lead time for completion	
External compliance	Meet relevant professional bodies' and trade associations' standards for work and after-sales care	
Service experience	Match customer's perceptions with operations' performance (what a service delivery is designed to provide)	
Conformance	The percentage of occasions when a service is provided to specification	
After-sales care	The built-in provision (or response as required) of an organization's after-sales care	
Perceived quality	How a customer views the service	

Figure 3.16 The dimensions of service quality and the functions responsible for their provision

for a customer of a dimension within a market has been established, the current level of provision and the gap between requirement and current performance creates the task. With strategic direction provided, appropriate resources can be allocated, so ensuring that a company can match competitors (market-driven) or create new norms (market-driving), whichever approach the business decides is appropriate.

In the context of this section, the aspect of quality that principally concerns operations is conformance – delivering a service or making a product to specification.[12] Linked closely to sales and marketing for services and the design function for products (which determine the specification itself: see Figures 3.15 and 3.16), quality within this definition is a key operations task. Its role in most markets is now or has reverted to that of a qualifier (customers expect a service or product to meet the specification) and the order-losing characteristics of such dimensions often provide opportunities for newcomers to enter markets and take share from established players.

One example of losing market share to newcomers is provided by the automobile sector. The growth in Japanese companies' share within the volume and luxury sectors of this market has been outstanding. This is partly due to the continued high levels of quality conformance achieved compared to their principal competitors. Link this to their superior productivity performance, and the reasons for their success begin to emerge. Toyota being the world's number one car maker from 2008 to 2016 endorses these points.

The recent attention attracted by quality-based approaches in management has further emphasized the advantages of completing tasks correctly the first time. This, in part, has been an extension of the improvements in quality conformance and the significant benefits that have been secured. Much has been written on the approaches that have underpinned success.

Demand fluctuations

In some markets, a company's ability to respond to increases in demand is an important factor in winning orders. These sales may reflect the high seasonality of customers' requirements, be a demand profile of a spasmodic or one-off nature or a by-product of some service companies using queues to help manage the demand/capacity interface. The factors here include the level of predictability surrounding demand itself, the level of variability of service times, a product's shelf life and the frequency of service/product modifications in line with market requirements. All will affect operations' response.

Knowing the pattern of seasonal demand makes it possible to reach agreement between supplier, manufacturer, distributor and customer about inventory holdings throughout the delivery system, delivery system capacity and planned increases in staff (for example, overtime working or additional shifts). With one-off or spot business (for example, during an influenza epidemic when demand is for the same product that may have a short shelf life, thus limiting viable inventory levels, or where a product is customer specified at some point in the process and, therefore, cannot be made ahead of demand, or a significant order for a product over and above agreed call-off quantities or simply an unexpected, sizeable order for a given product), holding materials or forms of capacity, arranging short-term increases in staff (for example, through overtime), moving staff from back-office to front-office tasks, rearranging priorities or some combination of these will typically be a supplier's response.

The phenomena described here provide another example of the way that a lack of essential clarity can lead to serious levels of corporate misunderstanding. The generalized discussion surrounding these key aspects of a business typically involves words such as 'flexibility'.[13] However, the extent to which a company intends to respond to such significant increases in demand is a strategic decision of some magnitude. To allow each function to respond according to its own interpretation invariably reduces the benefits of corporate cooperation on the one hand and leads to mismatches on the other.

Service/product range

As highlighted earlier, markets are increasingly characterized by difference, not similarity. However, the balance between levels of customization and the volume base for repetitive operations has to be addressed by the business as a whole. That markets are increasingly segmenting is a given. Operations' role is to continue to develop delivery systems and processes that can cope with service/product range differences and provide low costs. It needs to be able to bridge these essential differences in order to retain the volume base so essential to efficient operations.

Where service/product ranges are widening, delivery system developments need to reflect the broadening nature of the service/product base and the lower-volume implications that tend to go hand in hand with these trends. While the former needs to be recognized at the time that delivery system investments are made, the latter is reflected in reduced set-up times, whether manual or automated (for example, a numerically controlled facility), so enabling companies to cope with the lower-volume nature of these changes while retaining the necessary levels of cost.

Examples of these trends are seen in the automobile industry. The pressure on car makers at the lower end of the volume scale is to continue to differentiate their products as a way of competing not only with their traditional competitors but with makers at the higher end of the volume scale as well. BMW's 7 Series offers a marked uplift in customization, more akin to the very low-volume luxury car makers such as Rolls-Royce and Aston Martin. Handcrafted leather interiors and its 'any colour' option are examples of this. Competition based on increasing the product and option range is also coming from traditional, high-volume car companies. Several Japanese car makers (for example, Toyota) have been and are continuing to develop a production system capable of responding to individual customer requirements. As a result, to support increases in product-range options successfully, operations needs to develop its processes to provide these in a cost- and time-efficient way.

At the non-repeat end of the service continuum (this concept is addressed in more detail in Chapter 4) companies sell expertise and consequently are organized to meet whatever needs a customer may have, with the range on offer only limited by in-house capability. At the other end of the service continuum, companies need to ensure that low-cost delivery systems are in place and developed in order to maintain the volumes and costs base that underpin the price sensitivity of these markets. Invariably such systems involve customers as part of the delivery mechanism so as to help lower costs. In such designs part of the maintenance task is to ensure that additional costs are not incurred as a consequence of customers frequently requiring fringe services that add cost, as illustrated in Case 3.1.

Figure 3.17 now provides an overview of some of the reviews and typical improvements to meet some order-winners and qualifiers.

Operations-related but not operations-specific criteria

Although businesses separate clusters of activities into different functions, in reality they are, and need to form, part of the same whole. Thus, many functions within a company will directly support operations or will undertake tasks that link or directly affect operations' strategic and operational (day-to-day) roles.

Case 3.1 – ING Direct – matching customers to service delivery systems

ING Direct is one of ING Bank's three business lines with more than 17 million customers and over $200 billion in deposits worldwide. Its business model is to target the wealthiest regions in countries that have large numbers of middle-income customers and to offer high interest rates on savings accounts. To support this, its approach is to sell commodity products, and it expects its customers to appreciate this and the basic level of support this entails. In order to align its customer base it adopts two principal positions. On the one hand it steers away from wealthy customers who want a tailored approach to meet their needs and a level of support that ING Direct is not designed to provide. On the other hand, each year it typically cancels accounts with 5,000 to 8,000 customers for making too many enquiries or requesting too many exceptions to its standard operating procedure. In that way it maintains the required level of fit between its customers' expectations and requirements and the low-cost service delivery system that underpins its high interest offerings.

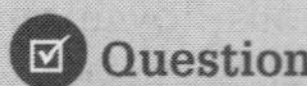

Question

1 What strategies does ING Direct use to help maintain alignment between its operations and marketing strategies?

Order-winner or qualifier	Review current performance	Typical improvements
Price	• Review actual material, direct and overhead costs • Map current system and identify areas of waste • Review mix of volumes in an operation • Review annual volumes within a service product range • Review production run lengths • Review contribution per staff or machine hour • Review service/product pricing	• Reduce large areas of costs – note the typical increase in overheads as a percentage of total costs • Reduce material and staff waste • Reduce system changeover and set-up times • Reallocate services/products across operations • Focus operations on markets
Quality conformance	• Review quality conformance levels for services, products, orders, customers and market segments	• Reduce quality conformance errors • Build quality into the delivery system rather than checking conformance after the event

Delivery reliability	• Review delivery performance for services, products, orders, customers and market segments • Analyse and compare customer requested and operations actual delivery lead times • Compare actual processing with overall operations lead time	• Improve scheduling of activities • Improve delivery system reliability • Hold inventory at various stages in the delivery system
Delivery speed	• Analyse and compare customer requested and operations actual delivery lead times • Compare actual processing with overall operations lead time • Map actual operations process and identify areas of material and staff waste	• Eliminate waiting time between steps in the system • Reduce lead time of system steps • Eliminate wasteful activities
Service/product range	• Review the delivery system capability to meet required current and future service/product range	• Develop delivery system capability to cope with service product range
Demand fluctuations	• Assess ability of operations capacity to respond to known or anticipated demand changes	• Invest in capacity or inventory
Time to market	• Map new service/product development process and identify areas of waste • Determine length of activities and their dependence on other activities or key resources • Identify activities for which operations has responsibility	• Eliminate wasteful activities • Increase capacity of constraining resources • Reschedule activities so they are completed in parallel (rather than in sequence) with other parts of the delivery system

Figure 3.17 Examples of how to review performance and typical improvements to meet some order-winners and qualifiers

Design

The links between designing the service or product, operations (delivering the service or product) and markets are the very essence of a business. The way that these interrelate, therefore, is fundamental to sound strategy development and implementation. The aim of marketing (for services), design (for products) and operations is to provide services and products according to their technical and business specifications. In addition, these functions combine to provide the service/product development phase that comes before the ongoing selling and operations activities that form the commercial substance of companies. Three of the more important dimensions involved are addressed in this section and have been chosen because they are fundamental to this basic corporate activity.[14]

Low cost

The design activity is increasingly important in providing essential support for several criteria relevant to today's markets. Services and products have to be designed with both process characteristics and cost reduction in mind. Design not only concerns functionality but has a critical impact on costs. For example, for products where direct materials typically account for some 40–60 per cent of the total costs, the opportunities to reduce costs at source are substantial. In addition, this essential link reinforces the need to meet the design for operations' requirements in terms of labour cost reduction through increased use of IT and other labour-saving opportunities. For many years, corporate appeals by Western firms to design for manufacture have been more exhortation than accomplishment, a view confirmed by a committee of the National Research Council in the early 1990s.[15] It found the overall quality of engineering design – the process of turning a concept into a finished product or determining how to make a new toaster, dress or computer as efficiently as possible – to be poor. Long before a product reaches the store, 70 per cent or more of its cost is determined by its design. However, responses to these issues and overtures have been spasmodic.

Any third-rate engineer can design complexity. The emphasis on making designs simple needs to be part of the designer's task and the corporate demands placed on this function. In the twenty-first century, pressure on price has continued and will continue to be an important competitive factor in many segments. Thus, design's role in the total corporate response is fundamental in more ways than one.

Service/product range

The increasing level of service and product diversification has already been highlighted as an important factor in today's competitive markets and central to this provision is the design function. The pressure on design will vary from market to market but the interpretation and execution of these will always be central to a company's ability to remain competitive. The tendency for Western designers to be more interested in functionality than the commercial facets of design is in marked contrast to competitors, particularly the Japanese. As Hiroyuki Yoshida, head of Toyota's design centre, reflected:

> Whatever the merits of a design, it has to be robust enough to go through our engineering and manufacturing system. The commercial point of design has not been lost. We are in the business to make low-cost high-quality cars for a mass market. We are making cars, not art.[16]

Within this context, markets are increasingly segmenting. Design needs to be able to meet these changes and to recognize, certainly in terms of attitude and speed of response, that change is a fundamental characteristic of today's markets.

It is now the age of diversification and those companies unable to keep pace with this growth of diversity will decline. Many companies are directing much more attention to incorporating the perspectives and preferences of customers into future designs. A classic example of this is provided by Toyota and Mazda. Both have built complexes in Tokyo that incorporate vehicle design studios in which the visitors are invited to 'design' their own cars. Thus, ideas on what constitutes a potential customer's ideal vehicle are included as inputs into future designs.

However, the demand for styling and product features has to be reconciled with other pressures. Environmentally friendly products are not only a growing concern of customers but also high on the agenda of legislative bodies. For example, clean air legislation in the US and the European Union (EU) is at the forefront of changing pressures on vehicle design. Their requirements for minimum percentage sales of low-emission vehicles and ultra-low-emission vehicles have been an added stimulus for improvements on all car emission standards. The targets for 2020 will mean that unless there is a major breakthrough in existing engine technology, companies will have to develop a viable electric car by 2023. The advent of hybrid cars now introduced by many of the major auto companies is the first step to meeting these demands.

Time to market

The reduction of lead times within the operations process has already been highlighted as an increasingly important order-winner. Similarly, speed to market with new designs and developments has become a significant competitive factor. The increasing priority of speed is based on a recognition that it can simply negate the competition. The results of such improvements, as shown in Figure 3.18, speak for themselves. In addition, companies receive a number of distinct advantages from reducing design and development lead times, including the following:

1 **Benefits of double gain**: Being first in the market brings advantages of both higher volumes and higher margins – the opportunity for double gain – as explained below.

- **Life cycles are extended** – If a service/product is introduced sooner, rarely will it become obsolete sooner. This advantage accrues even more so where customers incur high switching costs. The usual outcome of early introduction is to gain more customers who, in turn, stay longer (see Figure 3.19).

Company	Product	Development time (months)	
		Old	New
AT&T	Telephones	24	12
Hewlett-Packard	Computer printers	54	21
Honeywell	Thermostats	48	12
Ingersoll Rand	Air-powered grinders	42	14
Warner Electric	Clutches and brakes	36	9

Figure 3.18 Examples of reduction in product development lead time

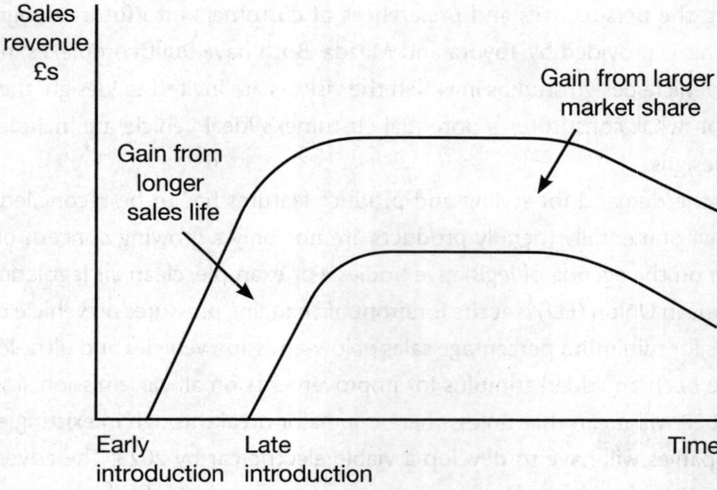

Figure 3.19 Increased sales revenue element of the benefits of double gain

- **Increased market share** – The first producer will, in the beginning, command 100 per cent market share. Thus, the earlier a service or product appears, the more likely the prospect of obtaining a large market share. Link this to the previous factor and the impact on total life cycle volumes is marked.
- **Higher profit margins** – A company will naturally enjoy a higher level of pricing freedom in the early stages of a service/product's life cycle. This will provide higher margins in the early stages, with the opportunity for operations to provide lower costs in light of the volume advantages highlighted above (see Figure 3.20 and also the earlier section on experience curves).
- **Double gain** – The first three factors combine to give a situation of double gain – companies gain higher sales and also achieve a higher margin on each sale.

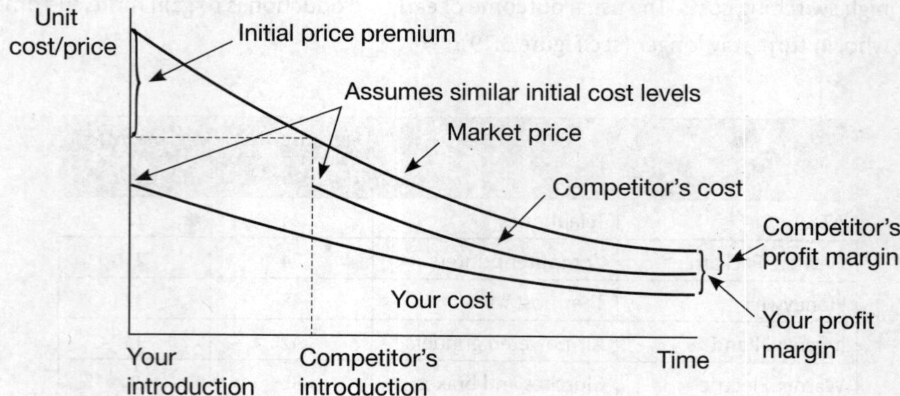

Figure 3.20 The higher profit margin element of the benefits of double gain

2 **Technology, consumer preference and corporate image**: Reductions in service/product development lead times also provide opportunities for companies to sustain technology leadership and corporate image:

- **Exploiting technology opportunities** – Where organizations develop services or products quickly, they are more able to synchronize such developments with the latest technologies and thus exploit these opportunities fully.
- **Matching consumer change** – Short service/product development lead times help a business to match market changes, thereby tracking more closely changes in consumer preferences and demands.
- **Corporate image** – Developing services and products more quickly will help a firm to maintain its corporate image of being a progressive frontrunner in developments and technology excellence.

3 **Reduction in design costs**: Compressing development lead times also results in a reduction in design costs. This is achieved in part by increased levels of cooperation, which reduces misunderstandings and ensures the incorporation of functional perspectives throughout. In addition, the changed role and contribution of design within the process also lead to less time being spent within the design stages, with associated reductions in cost.

Figure 3.18 provided examples of what can be achieved, while Figure 3.21 shows how this is accomplished. A glance at the latter shows a two-pronged approach to reducing lead times:

- shorten the time to complete each step in the process;
- start the steps earlier while running some in parallel.

Although some steps in the revised approach are much shorter, the gain is more cumulative in nature and a combination of the two elements above, as clearly shown in Figure 3.22. This compares approaches to product development by Japanese, US and European car makers. A close look at the details illustrates the two-pronged approach, and reflects the different approaches and values of those involved, as explained below:

- Western designers typically expect to develop products that require little or no modification. As perfection is rarely, if ever, achieved, any necessary changes must be identified in

Stage	Original start and competition times to market (months)	New start and completion times to market (months)
Develop	0–13	0–6
Approve	13–17	2–7
Self-test	15–20	4–7
Manufacture	21–26	3–7
Total elapsed time (months)	26	7

Figure 3.21 **Digital Equipment Corporation's reduced competition time for a new product**

Development phase	Japanese		US		European	
	Lead time (days)	Percentage reduction	Lead time (days)	Percentage reduction	Lead time (days)	Percentage reduction
Concept study	42	86	62	71	62	76
Product planning	38	76	57	68	57	76
Engineering	100	39	128	38	129	49
Pilot run	7	43	9	33	9	33
Total	187	56	256	52	257	60

Note: Sample sizes are Japan 12; US 6; and Europe 10.

Figure 3.22 Initial average project lead times and percentage reductions for Japanese, US and European car makers

Source: Clark, B. and Fujimoto, T. (1989) 'Overlapping problem-solving in product development', in K. Ferdows (ed.) *Managing International Manufacturing*, Elsevier Science.

later phases. However, part of the typical design function's attitude is a resistance to change since, given the 'achieve perfection' approach, a need for change implies failure. The result is long first-phase lead times, which are subsequently further increased because of the later resistance to change.

- The Japanese alternative is based on a different set of expectations. Knowing that perfection is impossible, designers conclude their proposals much more quickly than their Western counterparts and, ready to accept change, respond to the demands of the modification stages with appropriate expectations and corresponding speed. The result is a significant overall reduction in development lead times.

A look back at the examples of product development lead time reduction clearly illustrates the shared responsibility for two or more functions to provide this criterion, as highlighted in Figure 3.23.

Competing on time is a key aspect in many markets and has several dimensions. Delivery speed and product development lead times have been highlighted so far. Another aspect is also emerging: plant start-ups. Automotive research[17] highlighted the gap between Japanese and US car makers in terms of the length of time needed to change over a factory to produce a new model. Figure 3.24 shows the significant differences, part of which comes from the insistence by Japanese car makers that their engineers adapt designs to a plant's existing capabilities.

Distribution

Distribution's role in quick and reliable delivery has been mentioned earlier. As part of the total process, distribution plays an essential role in delivery. In addition, the costs of this facet of overall provision (including those of storage, warehouse administration and movement) typically have been rising both in themselves and as a percentage of the total. Highlighting the

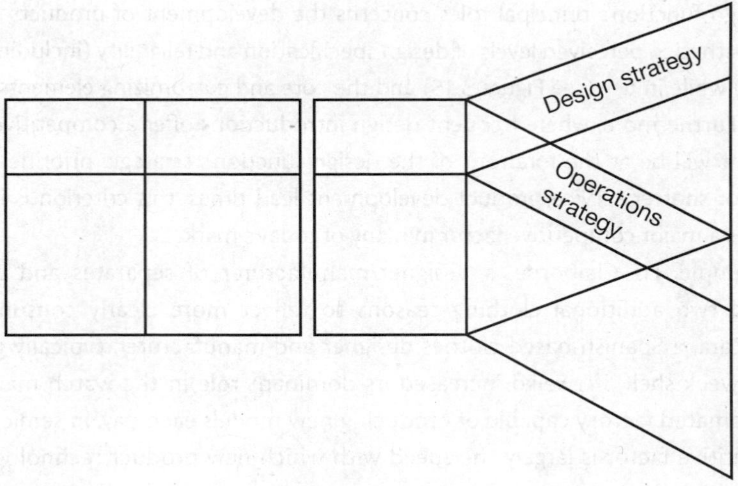

Figure 3.23 Shared functional provision of relevant order-winners and qualifiers

Plant	Car model	Elapsed times (days)
US		
Oshawa, Ontario	Chevy Lumina	87
Kansas City	Ford Contour/Mercury Mystique	60
Japanese		
Georgetown, Kentucky	Toyota Camry	18
Marysville, Ohio	Honda Accord	3

Figure 3.24 Comparative changeover times to produce a new model, US and Japanese car makers

potential source of cost reduction inherent in distribution-related activities has not, however, received the attention that other supply chain activities have.

Non-operations-related criteria

It is not unusual for companies to be in markets whose relevant order-winners are not directly related to operations. In these types of markets, operations will be required to support one or more qualifiers. Some of the more important non-operations-related criteria that frequently characterize markets are now briefly discussed. In all instances, each function responsible for the criterion reviewed would have the task of providing and maintaining the required level of support.

Design leadership

The task of design and its relationship to competitive issues such as service/product development lead times and service/product costs have already been discussed. However one of the design function's principal roles concerns the development of products in terms of features, aesthetics, perceived levels of design specification and reliability (including maintenance costs) while in use (see Figure 3.15) and the core and customizing elements of services (see 3.16). Furthermore, where frequent design introductions offer a competitive edge, this requirement will be at the forefront of the design function's strategic priorities. Linked to the need for shorter service/product development lead times, this criterion is increasingly emerging as a major competitive factor in many of today's markets.

For example, Liz Claiborne, a designer/manufacturer of separates and sportswear, introduced two additional clothing seasons to reflect more clearly consumer buying patterns; Zara, a Spanish-based clothes designer and manufacturer, typically gives products a six-week shelf life. Seiko increased its dominant role in the watch market with a highly automated factory capable of producing new models each day. In semiconductors, the competitive factor is largely the speed with which new product technologies can be applied to chips.

The importance of product design has always been recognized. Markets can be dominated by this dimension and unique design, particularly in the past, has been considered the principal order-winning provision of this function. However, companies are increasingly recognizing the other contributions that the design function can make in winning orders, the key elements of which have been discussed in earlier sections.

Being an existing supplier

Where a company is an existing supplier, it may continue to win orders in part or solely because of this factor. The criterion tends to be relevant to both low-volume and spares markets. In the former, operations needs to continue to support the relevant order-winners and qualifiers, while in the latter, it needs to recognize the impact that its performance on relevant criteria will have on orders for any new or existing products in the future.

Marketing and sales

The marketing and sales functions' principal orientation is towards the marketplace. Its important links to customers and its insights into the characteristics of relevant market segments – including issues of pricing, competitive threats, growth and/or decline of existing segments and identification of new opportunities – is an essential part of a company's strategic provision.

The role of marketing and sales in the design of services was discussed in the earlier sections on Design, Service/product range and Time to market.

Brand name

Through a variety of activities, including design, advertising and increasing or maintaining market share, companies seek to establish brand names for their services and products. Where this has been achieved and maintained, companies will win orders partly due to the image its services and products have in the markets in which they compete.

Technical liaison and support

In certain markets, customers will seek technical liaison from suppliers during the precontract phase and technical support thereafter. The quality and extent of a supplier's in-house technical capability to support service or product development, particularly towards its introduction in the early stages of its provision or manufacture, will be an important criterion in these markets.

After-sales support

Companies may look for ways of differentiating their total service/product by offering, for instance, a high level of customer support (see Figures 3.15 and 3.16). One example is BMW. The company has a fleet of 30 cars funded jointly with its dealers and strategically placed throughout the UK. The purpose is to go to the support of any BMW that has broken down by the roadside. The company will continue to increase this standby fleet until it can deal with the 80 per cent of breakdowns occurring in all the BMWs in the UK that can actually be solved at the roadside.

A further example of after-sales support is the motor repairs sector. IT systems enable a mechanic to call up information on any component or car by typing in the relevant part number or the vehicle's chassis number. In repair procedure terms, the mechanic can find out which faults cause which problems and what procedures should be followed. Service sales staff are similarly able to investigate customer details and vehicle records to help in their service support provision. Companies using these customer support systems include Volkswagen, BMW, Opel, PSA (Peugeot and Citroën), General Motors and Toyota.

BENCHMARKING

The failure of a company to assess and monitor its competitors is at best a mark of corporate complacency and at worst a sign of strategic naivety. For a company, such a monitoring process comprises:

- a continuous updating of the level and dimensions of competition within its markets;
- seeking proactively to improve its own business performance by learning from other companies about what can be done and how to do things better.

Benchmarking[18] is an approach that was identified and highlighted in the 1980s and since that time many organizations have used this as one of the ways to enhance their competitive position. Its contribution is to redirect the corporate spotlight from assessing internal performance (typically using internal measures) to checking externally how its performance compares with best practice. In this way, it reinforces the clear need to identify market requirements, to differentiate importance and to establish the level of performance that needs to be achieved within each competitive dimension.

As shown in the earlier section on experience curves, all companies tend to learn and improve through time, but the key question is whether the rate of improvement is adequate to become and remain competitive. Benchmarking forces organizations to look outwards and recognize this external perspective as a way to identify the levels of performance that need to become their new targets. Furthermore, checking against performance in other businesses (and particularly in unrelated sectors) leads to further distinct advantages:

- It describes the 'what' rather than the 'how', presenting companies with targets and not solutions. This increases the aspect of ownership and reinforces the inappropriateness of solution-oriented approaches.
- Having targets helps to create a uniform response from all parts of a business; when goals are common, improvement becomes a shared task.
- It reinforces the executive role, rather than that of support staff, as the key element to bring about sustained performance improvements.
- External, and particularly ex-sector, comparisons are often perceived as being more objectively derived and therefore more readily accepted.
- It opens up new improvement horizons that frequently represent a stepped change in performance. In so doing, it gives the opportunity to leapfrog competitors in selected and relevant dimensions of performance.

Benchmarking is concerned with the search for best practices, whatever their source, in order to achieve superior performance. It involves continuously measuring a company's services, products and practices both against competitors and the leaders in any business sector. It is not an end in itself, but a means to help to achieve higher levels of competitiveness. In this way, it offers an important dimension within the domain of order-winners by ensuring that corporate performance against relevant criteria is measured against externally derived, best practice norms. Benchmarking moves a company from having an inward bias to incorporating external perspectives, and this invariably introduces a stepped change in terms of performance horizons and targets. These external antennae help a company to assess what is going on and also to manage itself within its own competitive environment.

The first step in implementing benchmarking is to determine the key functions within a business that need to be reviewed. When the relevant performance variables to measure these functions have been agreed, identifying best-in-class performances sets the target. What follows is the task of assessing the action programmes to bring corporate performance into line with and then to surpass best-in-class companies. Cases 3.2 provides an example

For benchmarking to be successfully implemented, key elements need to be in place. These include:

- **Rigour:** Companies need to ensure that the targets to be achieved are set high enough, with targets derived from data not intuition.
- **Overcoming disbelief:** In the initial phases of this process, companies need to convince themselves that they can not only do better but can meet the daunting tasks that benchmarking reviews typically identify.
- **Accountability:** Benchmarking represents an ongoing procedure for measuring performance and ensuring improvement. A prerequisite is to instil in everyone the

Case 3.2 – Reducing vehicle maintenance costs at Alpha Engineering Construction

The annual maintenance cost for Alpha Engineering Constructions' (AEC) fleet of 425 pieces of rolling stock (on-road and off-road) was $6.2 million. With its fleet valued at $73 million then the annual maintenance cost as a percentage of the fleet replacement value was 8.5 per cent compared to the industry average of 15 per cent. Although below the industry average, AEC's performance was twice that of the best-in-class of 4 per cent and so offering a potential saving in maintenance costs of up to $3.1 million if it could match the best. A look at why its costs were twice that of the best in the sector revealed that AEC used 62 per cent of its total maintenance hours on emergency work, twice that of the industry average and fifteen times that of the 4 per cent used by the best-in-class.

However, further analysis revealed that AEC only used 9 per cent of its total maintenance hours on planned maintenance compared to 42 per cent for the industry average while the best-in-class spent 55 per cent of its total on this aspect of maintenance.

These data clearly pointed to a need for AEC to implement a robust planned maintenance programme involving not only technicians and mechanics but also operators and vendors.

 **Question**

1 Review the AEC case and identify how it used benchmarking to help it understand where and the extent to which it could reduce its maintenance costs.

responsibility and authority for identifying, checking and implementing the changes necessary to achieve this improvement.

- **Culture change:** Managers typically spend most of their time on internal issues. Reorienting companies to be externally rather than internally focused is essential to the successful introduction and ongoing development of this approach and associated improvements.

BEST-IN-CLASS EXEMPLARS

Companies need to assess themselves against externally derived standards and these can be identified from a number of different company classifications, including:

- other parts of the same company – internal benchmarking;[19]
- direct competitors;
- companies in the same business sector but not direct competitors;
- latent competitors;
- companies outside the business sector.

Recognizing the different categories enables a business to identify a broader range of potential best-in-class sources, thereby improving the quality and representative nature within this critical phase.

WAYS TO CLOSE THE GAP THEN SURPASS EXEMPLARS

Improving performance results from a number of coordinated actions across key functions. But there are different levels of achievement and these need to be part of the targets set:

- **Try harder** – A classic approach that, if adopted, implies a failure to recognize the principles underpinning benchmarking.
- **Emulate** – Involves setting achievement targets on a par with competitors and/or best-in-class exemplars.
- **Leapfrog** – Means setting targets higher than existing exemplar norms.
- **Change the rules of the game** – Entails setting the pace in driving the order-winners and qualifiers in relevant markets.

These constitute target levels of change but at the beginning the difficulty many companies face is identifying the different levels of achievement. Many find that looking outside helps to identify more clearly the levels of higher achievement, as shown in Figure 3.25.

COMPETITORS ARE MOVING TARGETS

That order-winners and qualifiers change over time was highlighted earlier. This is because markets are dynamic and competitors are moving targets. Companies that set their sights without taking these dimensions into account may fall further behind. Failing to identify the rate of improvement of competitors may lead to companies setting targets, only to find that the goalposts have moved. At best they will have closed the gap but more often they will find themselves even further behind and less able to catch up.

In today's markets, it is less likely that companies will have a sustainable competitive advantage. To compete effectively and continue to be successful, businesses need to fully understand their markets. But strategy debate has been and continues to be general in nature. Typical outcomes are broad descriptions that foster independent responses from each function. Unless individual functions are able, and are required, to develop strategies

Exemplar	Level of achievement	
	Emulate	Change the rules of the game
Internal benchmarking	80	20
Direct competitors		
Industry sector but not competitor		
Latent competitor		
Outside the industry	20	80

Figure 3.25 Source and levels of targeted achievement

that directly support the company's markets, these businesses will lose substantial and essential advantage. Organizations that fail to provide coherent strategies will continue to lose out.

Identifying and weighing order-winners and qualifiers forms a key element of this strategic provision. Without such insights, agreement on what constitutes markets is replaced by individual views grounded in the biases and preferences of different functions. This leads to unsophisticated responses and allows, even encourages, unrelated functional initiatives to be developed.

For operations, investments in both delivery systems and infrastructure are expensive and fixed. Once commitments have been made, it is difficult and sometimes impossible to make changes, certainly within the allowable timeframes of current commercial environments. The overall effect on corporate performance will be significant. In the short term, it can lead to substantial disparity in performance while, in the long term, it can be at the root of corporate success or failure.

Determining order-winners and qualifiers

It takes time for companies to gain an understanding of their markets. In fact, allowing sufficient calendar time is a prerequisite for gaining sound insights. The characteristics of markets and the perspectives of functions must be allowed adequate time, both in their explanation and reception. Going away for a corporate strategy weekend or arranging one-off discussions will lead to generalized statements but little insight.

Similarly, identifying and weighting relevant order-winners and qualifiers require these same characteristics to be in place. Seeking to clarify and understand these key insights will take time and requires soundings from the following different sources:

- **Functional perspectives** – The internal perspectives of those functions that are engaged in the provision of services and products or that interface with the marketplace hold important insights into customer requirements. This needs to be a 360° review. Too often companies limit this internal review to the marketing function. In part, this is based on the historical perception that marketing's view of the market represents the market, and other functions have added to this by failing to assess customers and markets from their own perspectives. As a result, these other functions (and particularly operations that invariably contributes much that helps to retain and grow market share) contribute little to the market debate and fail to improve the insights on markets. One consequence has been that companies have given undue weight to marketing's view, which typically emphasizes the need to respond to customers' actual or perceived wishes and demands. Checking the impact of fulfilling these responses on a business has not usually been part of its overall assessment of a market, segment or customer.

  When developing strategy, the roles and expectations of a company and customer differ before and after the point at which an order/contract is placed, as shown in Figure 3.26. Up to that point, a company is in control of whether it takes on an order/contract and,

Player	Before		After
Customer	Selects which supplier	Order/contract placed	Is right
Supplying company	Decides, as a business, whether to take on the order	Order/contract accepted	Must meet the promise

Figure 3.26 The roles of a company and customer before and after an order/contract is placed

equally, a customer is in control of with whom an order/contract is placed. After that point, a customer is right to expect the promise to be fulfilled. Such discussions are often not easy and need to take account of current and future opportunities, relationships, market share and similar issues.

- **Customers' views** – Checking with customers on what they believe they require can invariably lead to a distorted view of reality. Setting aside the aspect of self-interest, customers place orders on suppliers in one system and make demands on supplier's plants in another. Furthermore, customers are unlikely to acknowledge that the business they offer to a supplier is anything other than favourable. Equally, they typically fail to make distinctions concerning different criteria – it is safer to ask for everything at the highest level or provision.

  Most times, those involved in agreeing contracts do not know the critical dimensions of the contracts being discussed. Few have attempted to find out. All present their business in its best light. To seek the views of customers can only be one part of an assessment of a company's market.
- **Actual orders** – The real demands on a supplier are embodied in the characteristics of the individual orders, call-offs, and/or scheduled deliveries placed by customers. Tracing the volumes, lead times, margins and other relevant aspects of these will bring essential insights because analysing these key data will show the characteristics of the basic commercial transactions that comprise a company's markets.
- **Customer reviews** – Working with customers is essential to maintain and grow sales. Discussion with customers is a key component of this process. However, seeking customers' views is typically restricted to the sales and marketing function and is characterized by the criticisms listed above. This traditional approach needs to be replaced. Reviews of customers should be undertaken by executives from sales/marketing, operations and other relevant functions, be based on data that analyse the real demands of customers and be ongoing in nature and frequent in occurrence.

  The purpose of such reviews is to highlight the nature of the actual demands made by customers, to discuss ways to improve customer support (including possible changes in a customer's own activities and procedures), to proactively develop customer relationships that are business rather than functionally based, and to agree the improvement priorities for functions that would now form part of a coordinated corporate approach.

The most important orders are the ones to which you say 'no'

The orders a company declines mark its commercial boundaries by declaring the market in which a company decides to compete. Without this level of clarity, all orders are deemed to be equally attractive. This cannot be the case, but without a mechanism for knowing how to judge the orders received, appropriate decisions cannot be made.

The capsizing effect

The need for companies to be proactively alert stems from the nature of today's markets. Whereas companies in the past could recover from being outperformed and strategically outmanoeuvred, this is increasingly less likely. An ever-increasing phenomenon of the current competitive environment is the capsizing effect. Companies find that one day they are confident, secure and well directed and the next capsized, bottom up and sinking. The capsizing effect is often due to a lack of corporate awareness of competitive performance. Not being alert to the dimensions and extent of competitive performance leaves a company vulnerable to significant reversals of fortune and, hence, irretrievably disadvantaged.

To avoid being competitively outmanoeuvred (or sinking altogether), a company must understand its markets with sufficient insight and undertake this task on an ongoing basis. This not only provides understanding of sufficient adequacy on which to base corporate strategic directions but gives the essential inputs from which coordinated functional strategic outputs are formed.

Hitting singles versus home runs

One essential feature of management that is singularly omitted from its many descriptions is hard work. Clearly identifying markets, establishing functional strategies to support these and implementing the outcomes is a demanding role. One characteristic essential for completing these necessary parts is persistence. Winning teams build on hitting singles and do not rely on home runs.

Little is new, even less is complex

Earlier it was pointed out that any third-rate engineer can design complexity. The same holds true for strategy. Moving from what is complex and uncertain to what is understood and clear is the result of hard work – the same requirement as for a designer to get from the initial complex design to the simple.

Sound foundations for strategy are built on understanding; to respond to changing markets, a company must know where it is. In the past, companies have tolerated an inadequate understanding of their markets, with the result that they have been unable to respond and have lost market share or even lost out altogether. Complexity is an inherent feature of most aspects of business and none more so than markets. But it need not be so.

Similarly, nothing is new. The issues and criteria (even the aspect of time) discussed in this chapter are not revolutionary. For example, in the 1920s, Henry Ford highlighted the 'meaning of time' as an essential and integral competitive factor in all stages of his business from raw materials to distribution.[20] With lead times at every stage from ore extraction to sold product of a little over four days and average shipping times between factory and branches of just over six days, the meaning of time was well understood and exercised as long ago as the 1920s. What is new is the need to identify markets in terms of what wins orders and then to develop functional strategies to support these. Every long journey begins with a first step – in strategy this first step is understanding your markets.

CASE STUDY

Babcock and Wilcox

On 30 June 2015, Babcock and Wilcox (B&W) was spun off from BWX Technologies. It was the end of a 15-year journey to turn the business around after it filed for bankruptcy in 2000 due to thousands of asbestos personal injury claims from its 12,700 employees. 'This is a key day for the business', commented James Fynch (analyst). 'It's performing well and looks like it has a good future with sales back up to over $3 billion and an operating profit of $536 million. However, it needs to ensure it doesn't repeat any of the mistakes it made 40 years ago when it first moved into the nuclear market. I know that was a long time ago, but its core business isn't really that different and the problems it encountered resulted from the management decisions it made rather than the technology it used.'

ENTERING THE NUCLEAR MARKET

B&W was set up by Stephen Wilcox and George Herman Babcock in 1867 to design and make their patented non-explosive boiler, which was significantly safer and more efficient than its competitors' boilers. B&W didn't move into the nuclear market until 1956 when it set up a research and development facility at Lynchburg, Virginia that helped it win some early contracts to design and build nuclear reactors for Consolidated Edison and the US Navy. It lost money on these, but gained experience which was vital to entering this market.

George Neilson took over as Chief Executive Officer (CEO) in 1957. He was a large, flamboyant leader with a reputation for using salty language. He had joined B&W in 1924, making boilers for central power stations, and described his co-workers as, 'Goddamn rough people, hard drinkers and fighters who lived by their wits.' He felt right at home.

Over the next thirty years, Neilson progressed up the organization supervising the installation of over 4,000 boilers in US navy and merchant-marine ships during the Second World War before leading the Boiler Division and then becoming CEO. In the following six years, Neilson significantly improved B&W's profitability by centralizing activities and systematizing how it operated with clearly defined policies, procedures, objectives and responsibilities. Although sales remained constant between 1958 and 1963 at about $360m, its profits doubled from $13m to $22m.

BUILDING MOUNT VERNON

With annual demand for energy in the US increasing by 10 per cent, Neilson decided in 1960 that it was time for B&W to start building a $25 million factory in Mount Vernon, Ohio to produce one nuclear pressure vessel a month. At the time, people said he was crazy and would never be able to fill the plant's capacity. However, a few months later the US utility companies decided to increase their use of nuclear power to generate electricity because it promised to be cleaner and more efficient than the energy sources they were currently using. By the end of the year B&W had firm orders for 28 pressure vessels, filling its capacity for the next three years.

Although nuclear pressure vessels (used to contain atomic reactions) were similar to the fossil fuel boilers B&W was used to making, their higher technical specification meant they had to be assembled and welded before they could be transported to customers (see Case Figure 3.1). Mount Vernon seemed the perfect location to do this as it was on the Ohio River with reliable accessible to deep-water barges that could be used to deliver the 70-feet-long, 700-tonne pressure vessels to customers after they had been made. B&W knew the area well because it had owned the land for a number of years and already had a small plant there making components for its fossil fuel boilers. However, it lacked the skilled labour pool required to make the nuclear pressure vessels. As an executive observed, 'Workers required a higher level of knowledge, intelligence and judgement to operate the machinery, perform operations and maintain the very high quality standards.'

B&W decided to overcome this skill gap through automation (using a sophisticated machining centre) and embarked on an extensive training programme ($1 million per year) to entice farmers from their cornfields and turn them into skilled machinists and welders. However, many of the people they recruited soon left (546 of 1,060 taken on in the first three years) because they were ill suited to the job, untrainable, didn't enjoy working in heavy industry or felt they were underpaid. The plant was closed several times by labour strikes over wages and working practices with a 40-day closure to negotiate a new employment contract in 1967. However, under the new contract, wages were still too low to stop workers leaving or to attract qualified workers into the business. As one executive commented, 'Even for experienced workers, welding two pieces of 8-inch steel together is difficult, especially when each weld is examined by an x-ray machine. Most factories have to rework less than 10 per cent of welds, but at Mount Vernon 70 per cent had to be "mined out" and redone!'

B&W also had problems sourcing and installing the equipment it needed, with the linear accelerator (used to detect welding flaws) and the automated machine centre both delivered 12 months late and then taking almost a year to get fully up and running. This meant the plant was run on a makeshift basis for the first two years and produced

Fossil fuel boilers

Made using a 'line' process where materials enter at one end and flow through a defined sequence of work stations until completed. Production is relatively easy to schedule as all products follow the same path and require a similar amount of work at each station. Once the components have been made, they are shipped to customers and then assembled at their facilities.

Nuclear pressure vessels

Made using a 'low volume batch' process where components are manufactured and assembled into large modules before being shipped to the customer's site for final installation. This makes production more difficult to organize and plan.

Case Figure 3.1 Making fossil fuel boilers and nuclear pressure vessels

only three vessels in its first three years. By May 1968 all of its 28 nuclear pressure vessels were behind schedule, some by 17 months. Customers urged B&W to increase the number of supervisors (who often worked one-and-a-half to two shifts a day) to keep a closer watch on the welds as they were built up, but B&W refused.

RISING SALES AND PROFITS

Despite Mount Vernon's problems, B&W's sales continued to rise and by 1967 it was the 157th largest company in the US Fortune 500 with sales of $648m (compared to $366m in 1963) and profits of $33m (compared to $22m in 1963) and its shares at $2.69 (compared to $1.05 in 1957). However, managers felt they were stretched too thin and didn't have the authority to match their responsibility. As one executive explained, 'Neilson created an atmosphere where engineers and technical people were not treated with respect. Top management weren't interested in the technical problems they faced, didn't understand them and didn't trust those who did!'

NEILSON STEPS DOWN

In September 1968, before the seriousness of the crisis was announced, Neilson stepped aside as CEO and sold 15,000 of his 20,000 B&W shares at $33 a share. His replacement, George Zipf, came from B&W's steel manufacturing tubular products division in Pennsylvania and was a stranger to the power generation division, how it operated, the challenges it faced and the large corporate customers it served.

The man directly responsible for Mount Vernon was John Paul Craven (Vice-President of the Power Generation Division) who many thought might one day become president of B&W. Craven felt head office didn't understand the difficulties he faced at Mount Vernon and he was not given the necessary authority, budget or personnel to get the job done. Less than a month after taking over from Neilson, Zipf called a meeting with Craven and Austin Fragomen (Vice-President for Manufacturing at Mount Vernon). The weekend before the meeting, Craven told his friends the job was getting beyond him and on the evening before his planned meeting with Zipf, he committed suicide. Soon afterwards, Fragomen and Norman Wagner (Mount Vernon's Plant Manager) both resigned, so Zipf had to put a whole new management team in place.

CUSTOMERS GET NERVOUS

Customers were now starting to get nervous, but B&W brushed their fears aside by saying that things at Mount Vernon were not as bad as they seemed. Customers who met with Zipf felt he didn't appreciate the seriousness of the delays and seemed to regard them as 'bothersome intruders'. 'He just sat there like a Buddha not saying a word!', exclaimed one customer.

As a precaution, GE and Westinghouse (B&W's two largest customers) started looking for other manufacturers to take over from B&W, but there weren't many alternatives. Combustion Engineering had some unused capacity and Chicago Bridge & Iron was setting up a plant in Memphis, but there was no one else in the US who could make nuclear pressure vessels. So they started looking abroad.

PROBLEMS ANNOUNCED

In November 1968, B&W announced its profits were expected to be 30 per cent less than predicted due to losses in its nuclear business and its share price fell into the $20s.

One month later, it contacted its customers saying the situation at Mount Vernon was worse than suspected and their orders would be delayed by a further 2 to 12 months. This was the final straw and its customers started ordering them to offload production to other organizations. One customer, Philadelphia Electric, estimated it was losing $50,000 a day because it had to provide the power due to be generated by the delayed nuclear units from other high-cost sources such as gas turbine generation.

Westinghouse managed to get B&W to agree to transfer two of its vessels to Rotterdam Dockyard (a large shipbuilder in the Netherlands). However, they were horrified when they were ordered back to Mount Vernon by B&W after negotiations broke down. To stop this happening, Westinghouse decided to pay B&W for the work completed so far and take over production of the vessels themselves, but it was not able to discuss this with senior management because Neilson was 'not available' and Zipf was 'out of the country'. It therefore had to take B&W to court to win a temporary restraining order preventing them from taking the vessels back to Mount Vernon. Part of the exchange in court between Judge Gourley and John Black (B&W's Commercial Nuclear Components Manager) is shown in Case Figure 3.2.

Judge Gourley:	What would you expect to make on this contract for $2,542,000?
John Black:	This specific contract?
JG:	Yes.
JB:	We don't expect to make a profit.
JG:	You don't expect to make a profit?
JB:	No, sir.
JG:	Why would you want to do the work if you are not going to make a profit? You are not in the business of losing money for your stockholders.
JB:	We don't expect to make a profit.
JG:	In other words, on this contract for $2,542,000, you don't expect to make a cent for your corporation if you went ahead and finished it?
JB:	No, sir.
JG:	How about this other contact for $2,304,789. What profit would you expect to make on this contract if you finished it?
JB:	I would think that one is probably in the same condition.
JG:	If you went ahead and finished this, you wouldn't make a cent?
JB:	I think we would cover our direct labour and shop expenses.
JG:	I meant after everything, would you or would you not make any money on this?
JB:	No.
JG:	I don't think your stockholders would want you to finish it. I certainly wouldn't.

Case Figure 3.2 Judge Gourley and John Black's exchange in court

TURNING THE BUSINESS AROUND

After Westinghouse won possession of the two pressure vessels reallocated to Rotterdam, B&W started working with other customers to transfer their vessels out of Mount Vernon. Over the next two months, customers moved 12 partially completed vessels (worth $35 million) and cancelled orders for four vessels, leaving only 12 in production. Westinghouse moved five to Combustion Engineering (Chattanooga, US) and two to Société des Forges et Ateliers du Creusot (France), while GE moved three to Chicago Bridge & Iron (Chicago, US) and two to Harima Heavy Industries (Japan).

In an attempt to steady the ship, Zipf appointed an experienced person from Westinghouse as Vice-President of the Power Generation Division (John Craven's old job). This was the first time B&W had made an external appointment at such a high level. Customers seemed happy with these changes, but the shareholders weren't and the share price dropped from $2.04 to $0.22.

THE FUTURE

'Although the rest of its non-nuclear business wasn't directly affected by the Mount Vernon disaster, its reputation never really recovered', commented James Fynch (analyst). 'In some ways, going bankrupt was possibly the best thing that could have happened as they can now put the past behind them, clear the decks and try to re-emerge like a phoenix from the ashes. I hope the recent spin off is the right decision to take the business forward from here, but only time will tell. Every organization has a history of successes and failures that they need to learn from so they keep developing and moving forward.'

QUESTIONS

1 What were the key events building up to B&W's shareholder announcement in November 1968?

2 What went wrong and why did this happen?

3 What can B&W learn from its mistakes going forward?

DISCUSSION QUESTIONS

1 What are the key elements when developing a functional strategy?
2 What constitutes a market from an operations perspective?
3 What is the result when an operations strategy development process is not in place?
4 What is a trade-off? Select two levels within an organization where trade-off choices will need to be made and discuss the issues involved.
5 What are the basic characteristics of order-winners and qualifiers?
6 Select two operations-related and operations-specific criteria and explain, using illustrations, some of the issued involved.
7 What is the difference between operations-related and operations-specific and operations-specific but not operations-related criteria? Illustrate your answer.

NOTES AND REFERENCES

1 This section is based on remarks in the foreword (pp. vii and viii) of Hill, T. (1998) *The Strategy Quest*, AMD Publishing. Email: amdpublishinguk@gmail.com.

2 Skinner, W. (1969) 'Manufacturing: missing link in corporate strategy', *Harvard Business Review*, May–June: 136–44.

3 Some question the existence of trade-offs: for example, Schonberger, R.J. (1982) *Japanese Manufacturing Techniques: Nine Hidden Lessons of Simplicity*, Free Press and Womack, J.P., Jones, D.T. and Roos, D. (1990) *The Machine that Changed the World*, Rawson Associates. Others take the view that it is possible to overcome trade-offs: Ferdows, K. and De Meyer, A. (1990) 'Lasting improvements on manufacturing performance', *Journal of Operations Management*, 9(2): 168–84; New, C.C. (1992) 'World class manufacturing versus trade-offs', *International Journal of Operations & Production Management*, 12(6): 19–31; Corbett, C. and Van Wassenhove, L. (1993) 'Trade-offs? What trade-offs? Competence and competitiveness in manufacturing strategy', *California Management Review*, Summer: 107–21: Hayes, R.H. and Pisano, G.P. (1996) 'Manufacturing strategy: at the intersection of two paradigm shifts', *Production and Operations Management Journal*, 5(1): 25–41; and Clark, K.B. (1996) 'Competing through manufacturing and the new manufacturing paradigm; is manufacturing strategy passé?', *Production and Operations Management Journal*, 5(1): 42–58.

4 There are many books and articles addressing the area of lean operations, including: Womack, J.P. and Jones, D.T. (1996) *Lean Thinking: Banish Waste and Create Wealth in your Corporation*, Simon & Schuster; Womack, J.P., Jones, D.T. and Roos, D. (1990) *The Machine that Changed the World*, Rawson Associates; Hines, P., Bicheno, J. and Rich, N. (2000) *End to End Lean*, Productivity Press; Hines, P., Lamming, R.C., Jones, D.T. et al. (eds) (2000) *Value Stream Management: The Development of Lean Supply Chains*, FT/Prentice Hall; Taylor, D. and Brunt, D. (eds) (2001) *Manufacturing Operations and Supply Chain Management: The Lean Approach*, Thomson Learning; Gladwell, M. (2002) *The Tipping Point: How Little Things Can Make a Big Difference*, Back Pay Books; Womack, J.P. and

Jones D.T. (2005) 'Lean consumption', *Harvard Business Review*, March: 59–68; Staats, B.R. and Upton, D.M. (2011) 'The "Toyota" Principles can also be effective in operations involving judgement and expertise', *Harvard Business Review*, October: 101–10; Staats, B.R., Brunner, D.J. and Upton, D.M. (2011) 'Lean principles, learning and knowledge work: evidence from a software service provider', *Journal of Operations Management*, 29: 376–90; Miller, J., Wrobleski, M. and Villafuerte, J. (2013) *Creating a Kaizen Culture*, McGraw Hill.

5 For a fuller review of this application of lean principles in Jefferson Pilot Financial, refer to the article by Swank, C.K. (2003) 'The lean service machine', *Harvard Business Review*, October: 123–9.

6 There are many articles and books on continuous improvement and references to some are provided in Note 4.

7 The computation of an experience curve is clearly detailed in 'Experience and cost: some implications for manufacturing policy', Harvard Business School paper, 9–675–228 (revised July 1975).

8 Other examples of experience curves in the public domain include those for the crushed-bone and limestone industry, 1925 to 1971, in Henderson, B. (1974) 'The experience curve reviewed v. price stability', in Boston Consulting Group, *Perspectives*, 149; 'The Model T Ford, 1909 to 1923', in Abernathy, W.J. and Wayne, K. (1974) 'Limits of the learning curve', *Harvard Business Review*, 52(5): 109–19; and random access memory (RAM) components, 1976 to 1984, in Ghemawat, P. (1985) 'Building strategy on the experience curve', *Harvard Business Review*, 42: 143–9. Examples from other sectors include: LeMorvan, P. and Stock, B. (2005) 'Medical learning curves and the Kantian ideal', *Journal of Medical Ethics*, 31: 513–18; Junginger, M., van Stark, W. and Faaij, A. (2010) *Technological Learning in the Energy Sector: Lessons for Policy, Industry and Science*, Edward Elgar; Maruthappin Metal (2015) 'Surgical learning curves and operative efficiency: cross-speciality observational study', *British Medical Journal Open*, 15(38).

9 Boston Consulting Group (1972) *Perspectives in Experience*, Boston, MA, p. 12.

10 Further details and approaches are to be found in Stalk, G.S. Jnr and Hout, T.M. (1990) *Competing Against Time: How Time-based Competition is Reshaping Global Markets*, Free Press; Schmenner, R.W. (1988) 'The merit of making things fast', *Sloan Management Review*, Fall: 1–17; and Blackburn, J.D. (1991) *Time-based Competition; The Next Battle-ground in American Manufacturing*, Business One Irwin; Vickery, S.K. et al. (1995) *Time-based Competition in the Furniture Industry, Production and Inventory Management Journal*, 4: 14–21; and Ozer, O. and Uncu, O. (2013) *Competing on Time Production and Operations Management*, 22(3): 473–88.

11 The dimensions of quality listed in Figure 3.15 were originally identified by Garvin, D.A. in his 1987 article 'Competing on the eight dimensions of quality', *Harvard Business Review*, November–December: 101–10.

12 Books or articles that specifically address approaches to quality conformance include: Juran, J.M. (1974) *Quality Control Handbook*, McGraw-Hill; Crosby, P.B. (1979) *Quality is Free*, McGraw-Hill; Juran, J.M. and Gryna, F.M. (1980) *Quality Planning and Analysis*,

McGraw-Hill; Deming, W.E. (1982) *Quality, Productivity and Competitive Position*, MIT Press; Feigenbaum, A.V. (1983) *Total Quality Control: Engineering and Management*, 3rd edn, McGraw-Hill; Taguchi, G. (1986) *Designing Quality into Products and Processes*, Asian Productivity Organization.

13 The basic misunderstandings surrounding the word 'flexibility' are highlighted in Hill, T.J. and Chambers, S.H. (1991) 'Flexibility: a manufacturing conundrum', *International Journal of Operations & Production Management*, 11(2): 5–13.

14 The dimensions of quality listed in Figure 3.15 that relate to the design function are addressed in a later section.

15 Hoover, C.W. Jnr co-chaired the committee that studied engineering design in the United States. The critical findings were embodied in his 1991 article, 'US products designed to fail', *Chicago Tribune*, 6 July, p. 15.

16 Quoted in Leadbetter, C. (1991) 'Toyota's conundrum: creating a global car for a niche market', *Financial Times*, 17 July, p. 16.

17 Treece, J.B. (1994) 'Motown's struggle to shift on the fly', *Business Week*, 11 July, p. 103.

18 Readings on benchmarking include Osterhoff, R. et al. (1991) 'Competitive benchmarking at Xerox', in Stahland, M.J. and Bounds, G.M. (eds) *Competing Globally Through Customer Value*, Quorum Books, pp. 788–98; Francis, G. and Holloway, J. (2007) 'What have we learned? Themes from the literature on best practice benchmarking', *International Journal of Management Review*, 9(3): 171–86; Camp, R.C. (2006) *Benchmarking: The Search for Industry Best Practices that Lead to Superior Performance*, Productivity Press; Stapenhurst, T. (2009) *The Benchmarking Book*, Butterworth Heinemann; Zairi, M. and Leonard, P. (2011) *Practical Benchmarking: The Complete Guide*, Springer Science and Business Media.

19 Internal benchmarking is an idea based on identifying the best-in-class within one's own total company in terms of concepts, usefulness and speed of introduction.

20 Ford, H. ([1926]1998) *Today and Tomorrow*, Productivity Press, particularly Chapter 10, 'The meaning of time'.

EXPLORING FURTHER

Adler, P.S., Goldoftas, B. and Levine, D.I. (1999) 'Flexibility versus efficiency? A case study of model changeovers in the Toyota production system' *Organisation Science*, 10(1); January–February.

Ahistrom, P. and Westbrook, R. (1999) 'Implications of mass customerization for operations management – an exploratory survey', *International Journal of Operations & Production Management*, 19(3): 262–74.

Anderson, M.M. and Poulfelt, F. (2014) *Beyond Strategy: The Impact of Next Generation Companies*, Routledge.

Beach, R., Muhlemann, A.P., Price, D.H.R., Paterson A. and Sharp, J.A. (2000) 'A review of manufacturing flexibility', *European Journal of Operations Research*, 122: 41–57.

Brown, S., Bessant, J. and Lamming, R. (2013) *Strategic Operations Management*, 3rd edn, Routledge.

Furnham, A. (2008) *Management Intelligence: Sense and Nonsense for the Successful Manager*, Palgrave Macmillan.

Goddard, J. and Eccles, T. (2012) *Uncommon Sense, Common Nonsense*, Profile Books.

Lowendahl, B.R. (2000) *Strategic Management of Professional Service Firms*, 2nd edn, Copenhagen Business School Press.

Miller, D. and Harthwick, J. (2002) 'Spotting management fads', *Harvard Business Review*, October.

Ozer, O. (2002) 'The role of flexibility in online business', *Harvard Business Review*, Jan/Feb: 61–9.

Simichi-Levi, D. (2013) *Operations Rules: Delivering Customer Value Through Flexible Operations*, MIT Press.

Sminia H (2014) 'The Strategic Manager', Abingdon.

Stevenson, M. and Spring, M. (2007) 'Flexibility from a supply chain perspective: definition and review', *International Journal of Production and Operations Management*, 27(7): 685–713.

4 SERVICE DELIVERY SYSTEM CHOICE

INTRODUCTION

The two principal areas of investment in operations are those concerning which delivery system(s) to use and those that together make up the operations infrastructure (see Figure 2.10 for examples). This chapter deals with the decisions concerning which type(s) of delivery system best meets the needs of a business while making the business aware of the trade-offs inherent in such decisions. As with most operations investment decisions, changing delivery systems after the event is both costly and time-consuming and so ensuring fit, monitoring changes and making adjustments are key aspects of this task.

Whichever systems are selected they have to meet both the 'technical dimensions' as well as the 'business dimensions' of a service or product. Although services and products have to be provided according to their technical specification(s) (the technical dimension), they also have to be supplied in ways that fulfil the qualifiers and order-winners within their respective markets (the business dimension). Because operations is a business-related rather than a technically related function, it is the business dimension (that includes providing but not determining the technical specification) that is the concern of operations.

This chapter describes the operations and business implications of delivery system choices and highlights the importance of these issues when making such decisions. In this way, it helps to broaden the view of operations currently held by senior executives and provides a way of reviewing the operations implications of marketing decisions and proposals, hence facilitating the operations input into business strategy. This ensures that the necessary marketing/operations interface is made and that the strategies adopted are business rather than functionally led.

As the choices within and between service delivery systems and manufacturing processes are different and wide ranging then they will be discussed separately. However, within each section similar issues inherent in these choices will be highlighted and parallels drawn.

Delivering services

Transforming inputs into outputs is central to the operations management task, and the system used for delivering services or products is a vital part of this transformation process. In this chapter, we will look at how the characteristics of services affect the design of service delivery systems, the different methods available to an organization for delivering services to customers and the task of choosing and designing a service delivery system. In the next chapter, we'll go on, in a similar way, to look at the process of making and delivering products.

Factors affecting service delivery system design

The service delivery system will (as you might imagine) often involve different designs, depending on the type of service that is being delivered. We'll explain how particular aspects of services affect service delivery system design shortly but, as an introduction, let's look at how two more general aspects of services impact the design – the complexity of the offering itself and the characteristics of the market in which the service is sold.

- **Service complexity** – this will directly affect the number of steps needed to complete the delivery of the service. In many organizations, the provision of a service is completed as a single step (for example, borrowing books from a library, buying a newspaper or getting cash at your local bank), whereas the processes involved to meet the needs of different patients in a hospital will invariably be made up of several steps and combinations of steps. The design of the service delivery system will, therefore, reflect this complexity.
- **The market** – a delivery system must provide the following dimensions to meet market needs:
  - The technical requirement – what the service comprises. For example, in a bakery, bread needs to be baked and cash transactions need to be processed. Completing these tasks requires appropriate technology (in the form of skills and equipment) within the delivery system – in these instances, a baker and ovens, and skilled staff and cash-processing equipment, respectively.
  - The business requirement – how operations decides to provide a service will reflect the volumes involved and the order-winners and qualifiers to be supported.

In order to gain an idea of how market requirements might affect a business in practice, consider how the approach to service delivery might differ between a village bakery and a large bakery company that bakes and delivers bread throughout a city and its suburbs, with several sites around the country. Both businesses must consider:

- The technical requirements that comprise the specifications (recipes) of the bread to be made. These will include the types and quantities of ingredients, and the processing and baking cycles for the range of breads in order to provide the desired taste and texture of the products.
- The business requirements that comprise the order-winners and qualifiers that, along with the technical dimension, make up the sale. These will include quality conformance (making bread to the specification), the price and the availability of the products on the shelf.

All these requirements are dealt with by operations. In order to deliver the service, operations needs the support of technical experts such as systems and IT specialists. For example, the large bakery would have engineering specialists to maintain the equipment and be on hand to respond to technical problems. Similarly, operations managers in call centres would not themselves meet the technical requirements of IT systems used by their staff but would look to specialists to fix any technical problems and undertake technical developments.

Operations managers use the necessary system technologies together with other inputs, particularly staff capabilities, to meet a market's needs and the cost profiles and profit targets of the business. Working hand in hand with technical specialists, a key role of operations managers is to choose and develop the service delivery systems that best meet customers' needs. Each delivery system has trade-offs (things it can do well and less well), and these need to be understood by a business and form part of making these key investment decisions.

CHARACTERISTICS OF SERVICE OPERATIONS

Before discussing alternatives, let's look at the characteristics of services that have to be taken into account when designing delivery systems. These include the service/product mix, the nature of what is processed (that is, customers, customer surrogates or information), the time-dependent nature of service capacity (that is, the fact that service capacity cannot be held over for use at a later time), the role of customers and managing customers within the delivery system. The extent to which these characteristics will affect the design will, as you would expect, differ from one service offering to another.

SERVICE/PRODUCT MIX

There are two important dimensions of services that need to be borne in mind when discussing delivery system design:

- Customer purchases are a mix of both services and products. As Figure 4.1 illustrates, the ratio between these two elements within the mix will vary. In some instances, there will be a heavy accent on services, in others, the reverse.
- The service component of the mix is a package of explicit and implicit benefits performed within a supporting structural facility. The need to identify these three elements and the meaning and concepts involved are now explained.

When developing a specification, it is useful to separate the elements of the specification into explicit and implicit dimensions.[1] When customers purchase services, they perceive that they are receiving one or more explicit services. For example, a bank provides the explicit service of money transactions; a hotel provides food and accommodation; and a hairdresser the styling of hair. Customers may choose from a range of levels related to the provision of a service, and this will typically influence their selection of which organization will provide it for them.

In addition, the offering may also include a range of implicit dimensions: for example, security and privacy within a banking system; the level of attention, promptness and

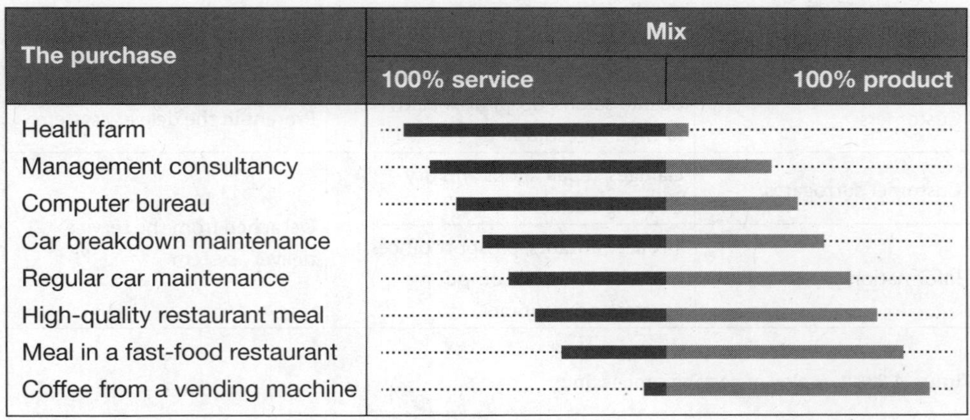

Note: The purchase mix represented here is meant as a broad indication only; others may consider the balance to differ from that shown.

Figure 4.1 Service/product mixes in a range of purchases

recognition of a regular customer on the part of restaurant or hotel staff; and the magazine and drinks provision and levels of cleanliness within a hairdressing salon. In fact, in some markets the implicit services may be more important in influencing a customer's selection than the explicit service that lies at the core of the purchase. But no matter what the relative importance of the explicit and implicit dimensions is, recognizing those differences helps in developing a specification and in signalling in detail what the organization's offering should involve.

Developing a specification also involves determining the supporting structural facilities that are required. These reflect the nature of the service provided and customers' perceptions of what it entails. Typical examples include the quality of buildings, reception areas, meeting rooms, furniture, fittings and equipment, appropriate décor, level of maintenance and general upkeep, delivery vehicles, and the appearance and technical know-how of sales support staff.

Customers receive impressions about an organization through their experience of the way a service is delivered. These impressions will affect repeat business and will be created by how well the specification (the technical dimension) and its delivery fit with a customer's expectations, together with the experience a customer has within the service delivery itself.

THE NATURE OF WHAT IS PROCESSED

As highlighted in Figure 4.1, organizations provide a mix of services and products. Although the examples given here relate to service companies, the same product/service mixes may also be (and often are) present in manufacturing businesses. For example, a company making and installing bespoke, high-specification kitchens would have a different product/service mix profile from a company making standard items of furniture that are delivered in the form of flat packs. In addition to this factor, in a service organization operations may process customers, customer surrogates or information. Which of these makes up the business will have a significant effect on the design and management of the operations delivery system.

What is processed	Examples	Customer involvement in the service delivery system
Customers	Beauty salons, hospitals, health farms and restaurants	Present in the delivery system
Customer surrogates	Garages, repair shops and dry cleaning outlets	Detached from the service delivery system
Information	Tax accountants, passport offices, financial advisors, computing centres and insurance	

Figure 4.2 Examples of service processing

As Figure 4.2 illustrates, the presence of the customer in the system will impact its design and the operations management task involved. The examples given in Figure 4.2 have been chosen to illustrate these differences, whereas in reality the operations function must often need to process a combination of customers, customer surrogates, information and products. For example, car servicing will involve contact with the customer as well as processing the automobile (the customer surrogate), updating a vehicle's records, and invoice preparation and payment (information). Similarly, purchasing furniture will involve advising the customer, completing the relevant paperwork for the invoice and guarantee as well as the product itself.

But what does all this mean for the operations function? Well, broadly speaking, its aim remains the same (its objective is always to provide the services that are sold), but the nature and characteristics of the operations function vary significantly depending on whether it is required to process a customer, process a customer surrogate, process information on behalf of a customer, or some combination of these. Embodied in these alternatives are different characteristics that either facilitate or restrict what operators can or cannot do in the processing task. For example, in services the opportunity to store capacity is limited. If a retail outlet (say) is not busy, the assistants' time cannot in some way be transferred to a future time period when customers are waiting. Similarly, the presence of a customer necessitates the system to respond as quickly as possible, whereas in a manufacturing company the product eliminates the need for an immediate response (as the customer is not physically present), which allows the process to be managed to best meet the output and efficiency targets set by the business.

TIME-DEPENDENT CAPACITY

Linked to the last point is the fact that capacity in a service firm is time-dependent. If a hotel room, passenger airline seat, or space on either a container ship, goods train or truck is not used at the time it is available, that capacity is lost for ever. Similarly, if a restaurant cannot seat you for dinner, that sale is lost for ever. Therefore, a service firm has to find ways to handle the fact that unused capacity is perishable (and thereby expensive), while insufficient capacity will lose sales.

Capacity also involves a complex set of issues, as decisions on how much is needed have to be made during the different phases of a delivery system. These design issues include not only how much capacity there needs to be in terms of structural facilities (for example, teller windows in a bank) and staff, but also the shape of the capacity, for example the hours worked and mix of part- and full-time staff in a bank, and which aircraft sizes are needed to best meet the demand profiles of a passenger airline's routes.

CUSTOMERS AS PARTICIPANTS IN THE SERVICE DELIVERY SYSTEM

In most service firms, the customer forms part of the delivery system and is often actively engaged in the system itself. The popularity of supermarkets, self-service stores, internet purchasing and online banking illustrates this phenomenon. From the firm's point of view, the customer provides capacity within the system that helps lower costs and also helps some aspects of the operations management task. For example, where customers undertake part of the role of a server, staff costs and the need to plan staff capacity at this phase of the delivery system are both reduced.

CUSTOMER MANAGEMENT

Relating to the last point, the design of the delivery system is such that customers and staff are linked. Customers are not just onlookers; their presence creates a dynamic that needs to be managed. For example:

- The supporting structural facilities (such as décor, furnishings and cleanliness) need to meet customer expectations.
- Staff need to be conscious of their roles, how they affect a customer's experience and sense of participation, and the lasting impression that they make.
- The level of server discretion (the extent to which staff are permitted to customize the offering) within the service specification needs to be identified, agreed and managed.
- The social dynamics of the customer experience, from entering to leaving the delivery system, need to be accommodated by and accounted for within the system itself. The approach adopted to meet these dimensions needs to form part of the service delivery system design, part of the people skills development and part of the operations management task.

UNDERSTANDING HOW SERVICES DIFFER

Understanding how services differ is an important prerequisite when designing delivery systems, especially in organizations that offer a range of services that typically require different delivery systems. Here, we will highlight key differences between services.

The role of technology in service provision

A company needs to select the delivery systems that it will use to provide the services it sells. As highlighted earlier, this concerns the technical dimensions of the items involved, for example:

- A restaurant will need to prepare food in line with the menus on offer and customers' requirements. It will, therefore, need the equipment and skilled staff to undertake the food preparation involved.
- A computer services bureau will need the hardware and skilled staff to enable it to process customers' information requirements.

While the need for appropriate equipment and levels of skilled staff is obvious, a suitable mix and suitable levels further depend on the volumes of sales involved. As we saw in the earlier example of a village baker and a large company bakery, the lower the sales levels, the less justification there is for investing in equipment to complete the task. Figure 4.3 illustrates this point while also giving examples of the mix of equipment and staff in a range of service businesses.

Predominant base	Level of automation and people skills	Examples
Technology	Automated	Cash dispensing
		Ticket machines
		Vending machines
		Mechanized car washing
	Monitored by unskilled/semi-skilled people	Photocopying
		Dry cleaning
		Gardening
		Tree surgery
		Taxi firm
	Operated by skilled people	Air traffic control
		Computer time-sharing
		Data-processing
People	Unskilled	Cleaning services
		Security guards
	Skilled	Catering
		Vehicle maintenance
		Appliance repairs
	Professional	Lawyers
		Management consultants
		Accountants

Figure 4.3 Range of operations requirements within the service delivery system

The nature of the services to be delivered

The services to be processed by the operations system are different not only in themselves (for example, fast-food and high-quality restaurants provide a different service and product mix), but also in terms of the nature of what is involved. The key dimensions that make up these differences are listed below, and illustrated in Figure 4.4.

- The complexity of the service to be provided (that is, the number of steps to complete it)
- What is processed in the delivery system – customers, customer surrogates, products, information or some combination of these.

Categorizing services

The key dimensions that help to classify services are provided in Figure 4.5. This shows why the system design to deliver a professional service needs to be different from that used in a retail bank or supermarket. Such differences, therefore, need to be taken into account when

Nature of the service	Examples
Customers	Hairdressing, passenger airlines and health care
Customer surrogates	Car maintenance and repair, dry cleaning and furniture restoration
Products	Retail outlets and vehicle purchases
Information	Mortgage applications, insurance claims and tax advice

Figure 4.4 The nature of service processing

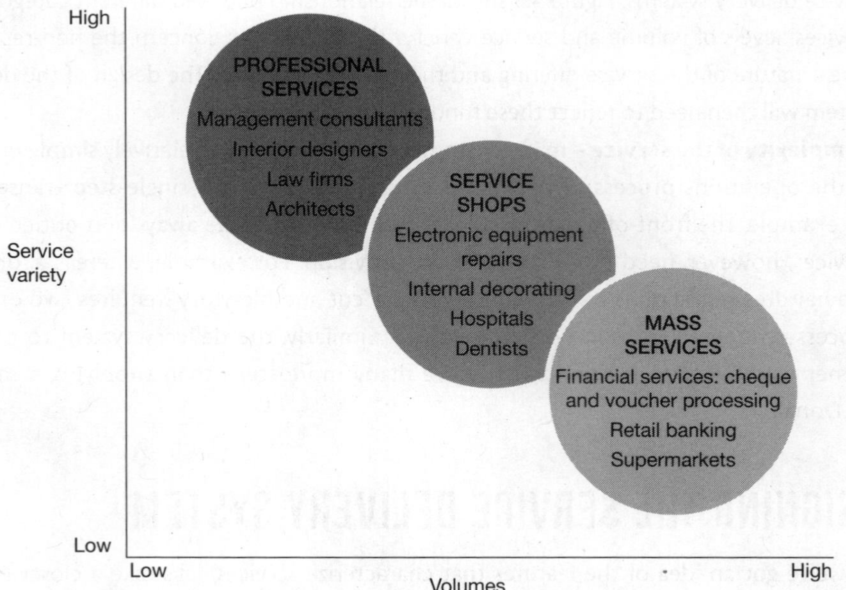

Figure 4.5 Service categories

designing service delivery systems. For example, volumes, levels of service variety and the degree of customization will differ significantly and will need to be catered for within the delivery system design.

From service categories to service delivery system design

While separating services into the three categories given in Figure 4.5 is useful, it is important to recognize that these service categories do not translate into types of service delivery systems. The reason is that, while some firms (for example, fast-food restaurants and supermarkets) provide services that are within a single service category, these are the exception rather than the rule as many firms provide services that fall into more than one category. For example, while banks offer mass services (such as cash dispensed from cash machines), they will also provide financial advice to individual customers (service shops) and professional and financial advice to their large corporate clients (professional services). Similarly, law firms may brief a barrister on behalf of a client (professional service) while also handling the legal aspects of house purchases and sales (mass services). Such firms will, therefore, need to develop service delivery systems that reflect these differences.

Designing the appropriate service delivery systems within a firm needs to take into account:

- **Relevant order-winners and qualifiers** – service delivery system design needs to reflect the order-winners and qualifiers for which operations is responsible. These comprise the business dimensions of the offering, and the system design needs to be built around this as well as the technical aspect of the service specification.
- **Volumes** – we have already introduced the idea of the impact of volumes when designing service delivery systems. Figure 4.5 shows the relationship between different categories of services, levels of volume and service variety. The key factors concern the non-repeat or repeat nature of the service offering and the volumes involved. The design of the delivery system will then need to reflect these fundamental dimensions.
- **Complexity of the service** – many customer-based services are relatively simple in terms of the operations process involved and can be delivered as a single-step transaction, for example, the front-office process in a retail bank or a take away food outlet. Other services, however, need multi-step process provision. For example, whereas a 'dry cut' in a hairdressing salon is a single transaction, a 'cut and blow dry' requires two or more processes depending upon what is involved. Similarly, the delivery system to provide dinner at the Ritz in London will involve many more steps than supplying a meal at McDonald's.

DESIGNING THE SERVICE DELIVERY SYSTEM

Now we've got an idea of the features that characterize services, let's take a closer look at service delivery design. We'll first deal with aspects of the overall design and then go on to look at the more detailed design of service delivery systems.

OVERALL DESIGN

Figure 4.6 shows a way of analysing and developing the overall design of a service delivery system.[2] The principal phases are:

- **The market** – provides the external context in which the service delivery systems need to be set, and is where the process of design and development starts. Identifying volumes and the relevant order-winners and qualifiers to retain and grow the company's share in chosen markets, together with the service mix and design specifications, are the requirements to be met when designing the system.
- **The service encounter and service experience** – the service encounter (where and what is delivered) and the service experience (the reality of the service delivered) are the essence of the delivery system. Each dimension needs to take into account both customers' expectations and what the service delivery system has been designed to provide. For example, the service encounter needs to consider customers' expectations of what will be provided which, in turn, needs to be set against what the delivery system has been designed to provide (the operations standards that the organization has set). Similarly, the reality of the service delivered (the service experience) needs to match customers' perceptions with operations' performance. In this way, customers' needs and the reality of provision will be in line with one another.

  Where customers' expectations exceed what the delivery system has been designed to provide, organizations need to work to adjust customers' expectations. Unless this happens, even though the delivery system meets the specification set, it will fall short of what is expected and customers will be dissatisfied.
- **Retention** – one aim of the service delivery system is to help retain and grow market share. The delivery system design, therefore, needs to monitor its level of success while determining what to do to recover failure situations. As Figure 4.7 shows, although failure impacts retention rates, a recovery of the service by satisfying customers' complaints can help to counteract the loss of repeat business when customers are dissatisfied and complain.[3]

DETAILED DESIGN

Some firms provide services that are similar in scope while others offer a range that differs markedly in terms of what is required. As services differ, so will their delivery system designs. This section describes the different systems and the types of service they are used to support. The key characteristics underpinning these differences are:

- the non-repeat or repeat nature of a service and the range of volumes involved in the latter;
- whether the delivery system is designed as a single- or multi-step process;
- which part(s) of the service is (are) delivered in the front office and which in the back office.

Non-repeat services

As the name implies, services in this category are unique (known as 'specials') and will not be provided in the same format a second time. Examples include interior design, legal advice for

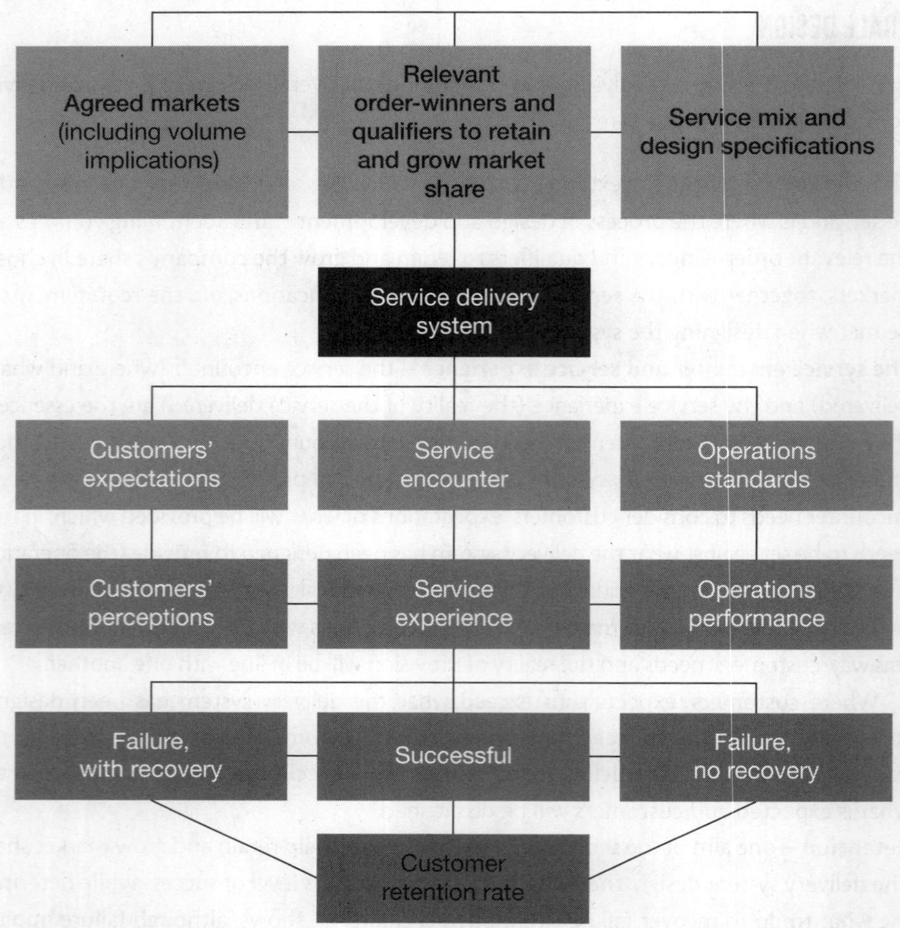

Figure 4.6 Elements within service delivery design

Level of service recovery	Percentage of customers who will buy again by level of complaint	
	Major	Minor
Complaint not resolved	19	46
Complaint resolved	54	70
Complaint resolved quickly	82	95

Figure 4.7 Repurchase intentions of dissatisfied customers

a business merger or takeover, financial advice for a stock exchange placement and the design and installation of tailor-made IT systems.

Providers of non-repeat services sell their skills and capabilities to meet a customer's specific needs. In this way, the service specification is determined by the customer, with changes to what is required often being made throughout its delivery. Order-winners such as having a unique set of skills (being the best), referrals and repeat business are characteristics of the way this type of market works. Although customer orders will not be price sensitive, the price for a service will need to be competitive (that is, in an acceptable price band) but one that yields high margins. In that way, price is a qualifier (prices have to be competitive) and not an order-winner.

The delivery system used for non-repeat services involves one person or a small group of skilled people providing all the service. The provider's role will include helping to identify what is required, determining the best process to follow and undertaking all the other steps involved through to and including implementation of the service. As the service will not be repeated, the opportunity to invest in the delivery system is not available and could not be justified, given the volumes involved. What is transferred from one service provision to the next is the provider's capability and skill base, and the experience gained from providing other one-off services in the past.

Repeat services

Most organizations provide services that are deemed standard (that is, they have been provided before) rather than special. The repeat and higher-volume nature of standard services signals a need to consider a different delivery system designed to take advantage of these characteristics. The volumes involved, however, can range from low to very high, and this factor will be reflected in the design of the delivery service system used.

To illustrate this, let's take a transcontinental air flight. At the extremes, there will be first-class and economy cabins. Although all passengers are travelling to the same destination and both classes of seat are repeat service offerings, the delivery system will show marked differences. Check-in arrangements, pre-boarding lounge facilities, carry-on luggage allowances, cabin staff to passenger ratios, the range of food, drinks and beverages, the level of customization provided, choices of in-flight entertainment, and disembarkation and luggage collection priorities will all differ, and the design of the service delivery systems will reflect these differences.

Figure 4.5 provided other examples of repeat services and illustrated the different volume levels associated with these offerings. Where volume is higher, factors such as service variety, level of price sensitivity and degree of customization will change as shown in Figure 4.8. Higher volumes justify the higher levels of process investment necessary to support the associated order-winning nature of price. Where possible, work is deskilled, with the process investment completing more of the task; this, in turn, will result in lower staff costs in terms of both skill levels and work content. Figure 4.8 summarizes some of the principal factors in delivery system design that reflect the non-repeat/repeat nature of the service offering and the levels of volume involved.

Single-step or multi-step process

A key decision in the design of a system concerns the number of steps to be taken in delivering the service. A **single-step design** implies that the complete service is delivered as a single transaction – for example, getting cash from an ATM or purchasing a newspaper from a shop. In a **multi-step delivery system**, the first part of the design process is to break down the service into a number of steps. How many steps there are will depend on the complexity of the service involved. The activities in each step that make up the total service will then be determined. These will be done separately, by different staff and normally in different parts of the system. Splitting the task into a number of smaller steps is a form of investment in itself, and is one way to help undertake the task more efficiently by accumulating similar activities from a range of services and completing these in the same part of the delivery system (for example, the pharmacy and X-ray departments in a hospital). This also provides the potential for staff specialization and process investments.

Now let's address the question of why organizations choose a multi-step rather than a single-step delivery system design. The factors to be taken into account include the following:

- **Delivering the service involves a range of staff skill levels** Where delivering a service comprises a range of skill levels, organizations seek to keep costs low by allocating the activities

Factors reflected in service delivery system design		Non-repeat services	Repeat services: Low volume	Repeat services: High volume
Service variety		Wide	→	Narrow
Level of customization		High	→	Low
What does a company sell?		Expertise	→	Standard offering
How are orders won?	Typical order-winners	Unique skills Repeat business Recommendations	→	Price
	Typical qualifiers	Price On-time delivery and quality conformance*		
Prior knowledge of task		Not well defined	→	Well defined
Volumes		Low	→	High
Delivery system	Design	Unspecified system	→	Specified system
	Level of flexibility	High	→	Low
Level of system investment		Low	→	High
Ability of system to cope with change	New service	High	→	Low
	Service change	High	→	Low
Staff skill levels		High	→	Low
Operations key strategic task		Enhance skills/ respond to change	→	Reduce costs

*The qualifiers 'on-time delivery and quality conformance' are typical of all markets, as shown.

Figure 4.8 Business implications in service delivery system design

and tasks involved to staff with the relevant skill sets. For example, in a hospital, healthcare specialists restrict their involvement to their area of specialism, with other tasks being completed in a more cost-effective way in terms of staff skills, and with each step of the process being provided by specialized and more effective procedures and approaches to completing the tasks involved. By processing customers step by step, the capacity at each step in the process is used and reused to meet the different requirements of different customers, with volumes justifying process investment and leading to a more cost-effective provision overall.

- **The service specification is complex** Where services are relatively simple, they lend themselves to being delivered by a single-step system. Where services are more complex, companies typically provide them in a multi-step format.
- **Volumes can be enhanced** Using a multi-step design to provide a number of services brings together similar steps from two or more services to be completed in the same function or area. The higher volumes that result will provide scope for cost reduction by creating the opportunity to invest in the process, develop specialist skill sets and match each step in the service to the required skill levels and salary grades that go with these.

The point of customer interface: back office or front office?

A service organization may process one or more customers, customer surrogates, information or products. Where customers are processed, in order for a service to occur the customer will at some point interface with the delivery system. But at what point and for how long a customer is involved are important factors in its design. The phase of a delivery system where customers are present is referred to as the 'front office' (or sometimes 'front of house'), and the phase where they are not present is known as the 'back office' (or sometimes 'back of house').

In some instances (for example, a hairdresser and a restaurant), customer involvement is not the subject of a decision. Here the service can only be provided with the customer present. In other instances, how long a customer is involved in the delivery system's front office is, to some extent, a matter of choice. In some circumstances, a company may decide to limit the front-office service provision to what is essential and complete as much of the service as possible in the back office.

What then are the characteristics of the back office and front office that influence the design of a service delivery system?

Back office

As we have just mentioned, the key distinction between back office and front office is that in the former, the activities take place without the customer being present or involved. For this reason, the separation of the front and back office is sometimes referred to as the **line of visibility** highlighting what parts of the delivery system a customer can and cannot see. Some of the advantages of completing work in the back office include:

- **Easier scheduling** – undertaking tasks in the back office means that the system is not required to respond immediately to customer demands and so allows the completion of work to be planned to best suit the system itself.

- **Higher processing volumes** – similarly, delaying completion allows the back-office system to cumulate volumes and provides the opportunity to undertake tasks more efficiently as all the work can be done at the same time. Furthermore, some back-office tasks can be cumulated still further; for example, in a bank, by bringing together the demands of many high street bank branches for bank statement preparation. These higher volumes justify more process investment leading to lower overall processing costs.

Front office

On the other side of the 'line of visibility' is the front-office portion of the system in which customer contact occurs. The characteristics inherent in this part of the system include:

- **Structural facilities** – because the customer is present in this part of the system, the structural facilities need to reflect the standards of the organization and meet customers' expectations. Ambience, décor, staff presentation and the speed of response to customers need to reflect the company's desired image and its customers' expectations.
- **Lead times** – because customer contact occurs here, the system needs to be able to meet the service specification while having sufficient capacity to meet the service targets relating to queuing (the time a customer waits), the length of time it takes to deliver the service and the costs of having too much capacity.
- **Ease of customer use** – the design must make it easy for customers to interface with the system because customers will then be encouraged to use an organization's preferred method of delivering the service. If not, customers will choose delivery systems which, from a provider's viewpoint, are less preferred in terms of effectiveness and cost, for example getting cash from an ATM vis-à-vis getting cash from inside the bank branch.

To help illustrate how organizations split delivery systems into front and back offices, Case 4.1 provides two examples of how companies have changed the front office/back office mix so as to influence customer perceptions on the one hand and improve the service provision on the other.

Figure 4.9 summarizes our discussion of service delivery systems and also relates the different delivery systems to the service categories introduced in Figure 4.5. You will see that the transition from professional through to mass services given in Figure 4.5 relates, in general, to the types of delivery system used. When reviewing Figure 4.9 you will need to bear in mind that the examples used will often be firms providing services that fall within two or even all three of the service categories. However, in order to make these distinctions clear, the service examples have been chosen to reflect the category under discussion.

We now reflect on the link between service type, delivery system type and volume.

Non-repeat delivery systems for professional services

This segment of the market comprises customers with specific requirements that initially may not be well defined, with changes to what is required being made throughout its delivery.

Case 4.1 – Improving service delivery through the use of front and back offices

Example 1 Positioning tasks in either the front or back office

Royal Bank of Canada believes that customers' perceptions are a critical factor in service provision. The bank considers that, when queues form, customers' attitudes to waiting are affected by both the server's attitude when they are eventually attended to and by the level of staff attendance shown in the front office. Thus, if bank staff in the front office are doing jobs other than attending to customers and the queues are long, customers' attitudes to the bank's overall regard for service quality are affected. Thus, the bank's aim is to transfer as much paperwork as possible to head office or the back office of a branch.

Example 2 Changing the point where customers interface with the delivery system

An electrical repair shop recently changed the customer interface point in the delivery system. Whereas previously the customer explained the repair needs to staff in the front office, the customer now takes the repair to the back office and discusses the problem with the person who will complete the repair. Everyone gains. The repair person can now ensure that all pertinent questions are covered and the customer is able to discuss the repair both before and after the service is completed. This, of course, has long been the arrangement in many good quality dressmakers and tailors.

QUESTIONS

1 How do these two examples differ?
2 What are the benefits and disadvantages of the alternative approaches in the two examples?

Typically, one or a small group of staff provide these services involving high levels of skills that include contributing to defining a customer's requirements as well as providing the service itself. As sellers of expertise, professional service firms need to continuously enhance the skills of their staff and respond quickly and positively to the ongoing changes that invariably characterize the process of meeting their customers' needs.

Low volume repeat delivery systems for service shops

Most organizations provide services that are deemed standard (that is, they have been provided before) rather than special. The repeat and higher-volume nature associated with this segment signals a need to select a different delivery system that is designed to take advantage of these characteristics. Typically, multi-step systems allow the range of tasks involved to be matched by different staff skills that helps ensure that staff costs are proportionate to the varying levels of skills required and the utilization of highly skilled staff is

Service delivery system type	Service		Delivery system description
	Category	Examples	
Non-repeat	Professional services	• Management consultants • Law firms • Architects • Interior designers • Receivership administrators	One or a small group of skilled staff deliver all elements of these services, including interpreting the service specification, clarifying issues with the client and ensuring that what is delivered meets the specification and is on time. The non-repeat nature of the service makes investment unviable with the experience gained by delivering these services being transferred to future services by the skilled staff
Repeat low volume ↓	Service shops	• Hospitals • Dentists • Veterinary practices • Vehicle maintenance	Higher volumes of increasingly standard services are typically delivered using established procedures that facilitate the opportunity and need to reduce costs as price increasingly changes from a qualifier to an order-winner. Multi-step delivery systems allow appropriate parts of the service to be allocated to staff with the relevant skill sets
Repeat high volume	Mass services	• Cash provision using ATMs • Voucher processing • Supermarkets	Services comprise standard offerings and the associated higher volumes provide the opportunity to reduce costs through system investment (from determining procedures to processing equipment) or the design of self-service delivery systems where customers participate in the creation of the service

Figure 4.9 Service delivery systems and their relationship to the service categories in Figure 4.5

maximized. In addition, the development and introduction of approaches and procedures help to further reduce costs where the role of price is changing from a qualifier to an order-winner.

High volume repeat delivery systems for mass services

As volumes increase and a service moves towards the high end of the volume scale, the opportunity and need to reduce costs becomes more pronounced. The increasingly standard nature of these services and their associated volumes justifies investment in various forms of systems from developing standard procedures through to a range of IT developments on the one hand and customer participation in service delivery by a growing use of self-service applications on the other, the purpose of which is to reduce costs. Often the service is delivered using a single-step system that simplifies the scheduling task, takes advantage of associated volumes and better matches staff skills to service requirements.

IT-based service delivery system designs

When designing delivery systems, many organizations have used developments in IT to rethink approaches. Such developments have not only reduced costs and lead times within systems and procedures, but also enabled organizations to redesign many of their delivery systems, as the following examples illustrate.

Automated banking

Banks are continuing to cut costs by automating more of their services. For example, ATMs are now the principal way to get cash from your bank account. Increasingly banks are adding video disc displays selling insurance, providing details on loans and screens offering share quotations. In parts of Europe and the US fully automated bank branches are replacing traditional set-ups, offering all the usual range of services but without bank tellers, and automated machines for depositing cash and cheques have become commonplace.

Teleworking

Since the early 1980s, companies have been extending the use of teleworking, the practice of using computers and telephone links to work away from the office. 'Home offices' are an established part of this growing trend while companies are making increasingly heavy use of telecommuting, a policy that allows employees to work in the office one or two days a week and spend the rest of the time with clients and working from home. Jack Nilles, the 'father of teleworking', coined the phrases 'teleworking' and 'telecommuting' in 1973 while leading a research project at the University of Southern California into the impact of IT at work.[4]

Teleworking brings benefits including productivity increases of 20 per cent or more, reduced office space requirements and lower staff turnover levels.[4] In addition, the benefits to a nation's economy are significant. It is estimated that traffic congestion costs the UK economy more than £100 billion in lost productivity while London commuters waste more than 10 hours per week going to work. In the US, clean air legislation is obliging large firms to reduce their commuter workforce. And by 2016, some 50 per cent of employees in the US worked part of their time remotely. Whereas in the late 1970s there were very few employees in this category, by the first part of this century this had grown to 30 million worldwide and was predicted to reach 200 million by 2017.

E-commerce

The internet has the capacity to personalize a service because it has the ability to tailor itself to every one of its millions of users. Similarly, benefits at the retail end of the spectrum have also been realized through company inter-trading that covers dealings with suppliers as well as customers. Corporate intranets can be linked in order to provide a safe, secure, manageable, business-to-business environment, with e-commerce becoming an integrated part of the customer/supplier partnership.

Dealing with customers and suppliers through e-commerce has profound implications for the way companies operate and, as more users gain access to the internet, the need for organizations to incorporate relevant technologies into the design of their delivery systems is crucial. Here are some examples of online service developments.

Travel booking – Since its early days, online travel booking has grown rapidly. The European online market is forecast to continue to grow by 20–30 per cent a year compared with single digit growth for the travel industry as a whole. Part of this growth has been boosted by the no-frills passenger airline phenomenon and the pressure by companies such as Ryanair and easyJet to force customers to book online and their success has encouraged more traditional airlines to move to increase online bookings.

Call centres – Whether the vendor is a PC manufacturer providing a help desk for users, a gas or electricity distribution company answering queries or a financial services company handling account and general enquiries through to mortgage and personal loan applications, a call centre has become the preferred solution.

The advances in computer telephony integration have enabled call centres to replace traditional service departments by linking the telephone to a computer that routes calls to the most appropriate agent, prompts the agent with caller data (known as 'screen popping') and leads the agent through a script to produce answers to thousands of different questions. Call centres cut staff costs compared to multi-site arrangements, in terms of both the number of staff required and the opportunity to locate centres in lower wage rate areas. With call centres, customers are offered free or low-rate calls to encourage their use, and international centres allow customers to call a local number while the system then transfers them to an overseas agent who speaks their own language.

In addition, some companies (for example Dell) transfer calls from one region to another (for example, mainland Europe to the UK or Ireland and then to the eastern seaboard of the US and so on) as a way of efficiently handling the times during a 24-hour period when the number of calls in a region are low. For example, bookings and enquiries for Radisson Hotels in Europe and the Middle East are handled by the group's call centre in Dublin from 7am to 7 pm. The operation handles more than 1,000 calls daily, with 22 incoming telephone lines (all free phones) operated by 25 staff speaking 11 different languages. From 7pm the service switches to operations in the US.

Grocery shopping – After its first tentative steps, online grocery shopping is gaining ground. Competitors in the field have, however, chosen different ways to provide this service. Ocado, the UK's first e-grocer, has taken a warehouse-based approach. Its dedicated picking and delivery system is based at its depot in Hatfield, north of London, which is the size of seven soccer pitches or about 20 average supermarkets. Others using the warehouse model include Simon Delivers in Minneapolis, Greengrocer.com in Australia and Carrefour, Europe's biggest retailer based in France.

Case 4.2 – Providing Personal Service Online at Garden Escape

Shopping for plants at the online nursery Garden Escape (www.burpee.com) offers many benefits. It is not just that the website offers unusual plants, but also because Garden Escape creates a personal 'store' just for regular customers. Greeted by name on your personal page each time you visit, you can make notes on a private online notepad, tinker with garden plans using the site's interactive design program, and get answers from the Garden Doctor. Given such a personalized service, many customers rarely go elsewhere.

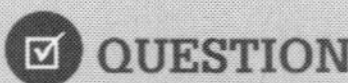

1 What are the advantages of shopping on the internet? Do you see any problems?

Tesco (the UK's largest supermarket), among others, has taken a different approach. It developed its own technology to enable it to use store-based picking – a low-investment route to this new type of shopping. This approach is now gaining ground in the US, with Safeway, California's biggest supermarket group, being one of the early adopters. In 2003 Tesco's internet food sales were close on £500 million. By 2008/9 food and non-food internet sales had risen to £1.9 billion, up 20 per cent from the previous year. Using this model, Tesco estimates that it can service up to £3 billion of sales through its existing stores. On the other hand, Sainsbury's (a large UK supermarket) has chosen a hybrid model, with a warehouse in north London but most sales done through store-based picking. In 2008/9 food-only sales exceeded £500 million with 100,000 orders per week. Now take a look at Case 4.2 for a further illustration.

FURTHER ASPECTS OF SERVICE DELIVERY

This section introduces some additional issues that organizations need to consider when developing the overall design of their service delivery systems.

ENHANCING SERVICES

Companies basing their approach on service differentiation employ several strategies to enhance the service they are providing. One way is to bring the intangible aspects of a service to the attention of a customer by making them tangible. By doing this, parts of a service package that may go unnoticed by the customer now become a visible part of the provision. Examples include the following.

- Maid service in a hotel bedroom can include collars placed on toilets with phrases such as 'Sanitized for your personal use', end-folded toilet paper and folding down the bed in the evening, with a personalized note and guest room checklist duly completed.

- Prompt service is also made tangible in one of several ways – many hotels guarantee an in-room breakfast that will be delivered within ten minutes of the requested time or it will be provided free of charge. Domino's Pizza promise to deliver an order to your home within 30 minutes (normal demand times) or 40 minutes (peak demand times) or it will be replaced or money refunded. In practice, this means that if a delivery is late, customers would be asked to pay for the pizza(s) but not, say, the soft drink(s) or dessert(s). Furthermore, if a delivery is considered very late (20-plus minutes), the whole order is offered free of charge. Domino's Pizza's replace or refund policy also applies to its quality guarantee.
- A car wash given free with a routine service or paper covers left inside the vehicle demonstrate to customers the level of care taken by the company when providing the core element of the service.

CUSTOMER PARTICIPATION IN SERVICE DELIVERY

When designing the delivery system organizations need to decide the extent to which customers will or will not participate in the creation of the service. The degree of customer involvement in the system affects many factors including the provision and management of capacity, service levels, staff training requirements and costs.

Employing the do-it-yourself concept in service delivery systems has been gaining ground over the last few decades. Examples of service industries increasingly using this approach include:

- **Supermarkets** control over 80 per cent of the gross retail market and sell principally on a self-service basis.
- **Fast-food outlets** form a growing part of overall restaurant provision.
- **Telephone services** are principally based on subscriber dialling, with almost all telephone calls now being made by customers.
- **Petrol stations** use self-service as the basis for providing fuel, screen washing, and oil, water and tyre pressure checks.
- **Online shopping** is a major provider in the retail industry. It requires a customer to complete the selection, application and payment parts of the procedure, with the business providing fast delivery once the transaction is fed into the service system.
- **Financial services** provide a growing range of products through self-service delivery systems from ATMs, general banking, insurance, mortgages and personal loans.

The reasons for the growth in these sectors vary. They include reduced costs, lower prices to customers, faster service and more customer control within the delivery system. Now take a look at Case 4.3 which provides an illustration.

Case 4.3 – Self-Scanning in Supermarkets

The downside of supermarket shopping is queuing to pay. To speed up this part of the delivery system, retailers are looking for ways to involve customers in this last step of the process. For some time now, the facility for self-scanning your purchases as you go and then paying at a designated checkout has been available. The way it works is that the system uses visual and voice commands to talk customers through the process. Bar codes are swiped in the normal way while, for loose items such as vegetables and fruit, price by weight details are stored on a database. If an item does not register properly the voice system asks the customer to scan it again.

Lack of pre-registering and being easy to use appeal to those who simply wish to shop and go! With the average person in the UK spending two hours in queues every week (even with internet banking and shopping), user-friendly forms of self-service are gaining ground.

QUESTIONS

1 Why are supermarkets introducing self-checkout systems?
2 Recently consumers ranked self-checkout technology second only to cash machines as the self-service they are most likely to use. Why?

POSITIONING YOURSELF ON THE SERVICE LADDER

Determining the markets in which to compete and how to compete in these markets is a prerequisite for developing a successful business. Research completed in a range of companies has resulted in developing the concept of viewing markets as being alternative steps on the 'service ladder'. To help position themselves vis-à-vis their competitors, companies first identify both their own position and that of their competitors on the ladder and then consider alternative strategic scenarios. This is undertaken by companies preparing a detailed comparison with competitors to clarify where they are and also where their competitors are before debating whether or not to move part or all of their business to an alternative step.

As shown in Figure 4.10, the ladder comprises four steps which are now explained.

Sell – competing on price with a basic, no-frills offering. Here, companies strip back the service specification to one that meets only a customer's basic needs, with price as a heavily weighted order-winner. Initially, customers pay for a low-priced, no-frills service to which they can add a limited range of extra features, each of which is priced separately. In that way customers only pay for the basic service plus any features they require. The basic service specification is then delivered through low-cost delivery systems typically involving a high number of self-service elements.

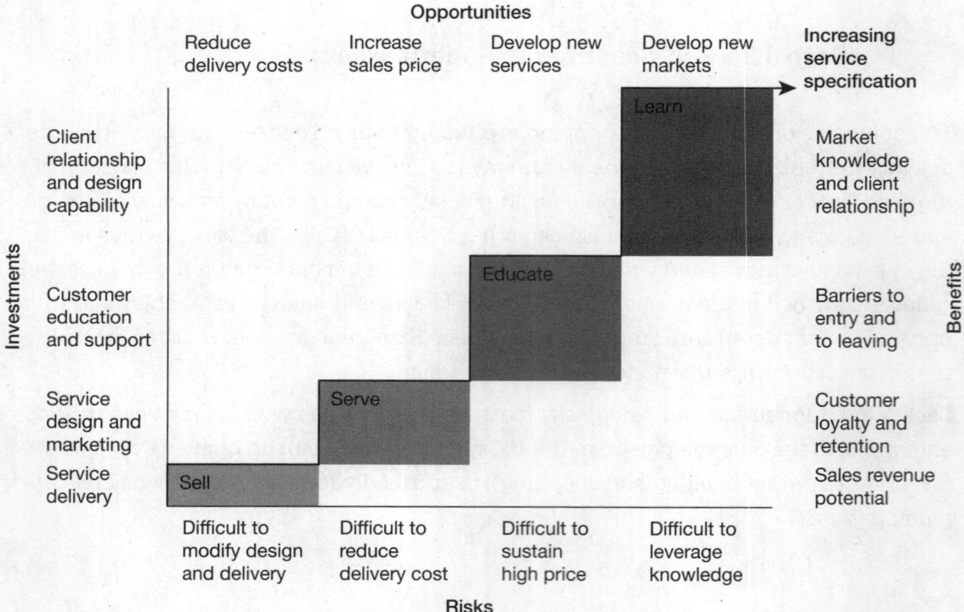

Note: Each step becomes greater as you move up the ladder due to the increasing level of investment, risk, benefit and opportunity involved.

Figure 4.10 Service ladder investments, risks, opportunities and benefits

Serve – competing on a mix of price and supplementary service features. Here, companies include in their offerings a number of non-essential features that form part of the standard package. In this segment, customers can modify the offering by selecting from a number of options at little or no extra cost.

Educate – helping customers to get the most from the service. Here companies provide customers with a premium-priced, high-specification offering that includes a wide range of non-essential, supplementary services at little or no extra cost. This enables customers to modify the offering and its delivery to better meet their own needs, thereby improving the value they get or helping potential customers to switch easily and quickly from competitors' offerings. Throughout, customers are encouraged to interact with the service delivery system through extensive, easily accessed before- and after-sales support provided by technically knowledgeable staff.

Learn – continuously learning with customers about their needs and designing tailor-made solutions to meet these requirements. Such companies sell expertise to clients at a premium price. To provide continuity and retain customer knowledge, the nucleus of the client team remains the same over time, using in-house or external specialists as required. The client team assesses a customer's requirements, designs a service to meet the diagnosed needs, monitors the delivery of the service and modifies the specification where necessary. The ongoing research, design, development and delivery process results in the provider learning together with clients about their needs and how best to meet them.

To illustrate how some companies have deliberately positioned themselves on a different step on the service ladder to that taken by typical competitors (the industry norm), Figure 4.11 provides some examples.

As markets continually change and become increasingly more competitive, companies need to continuously question their position on the service ladder in relation to their competitors. Such reviews provide important market insights and stimulate companies to assess whether they could move to a different step, whether such a decision would be supported by the market and be viable, how much of the current business should be moved, what changes to the current delivery systems would need to be made and what investments, risks, benefits and opportunities would be involved, bearing in mind, as noted in Figure 4.10 that these factors increase with each step.

REFLECTIONS

Although how a company chooses to meet the technical specification of its service offerings will impact delivery system design, operations managers must also ensure that those design decisions:

- are aligned to the order-winners and qualifiers of its chosen markets;
- reflect the internal requirements of the organization such as capacity utilization, control of costs, queue lengths and the interface with customers;
- incorporate IT and other development opportunities to help keep the business competitive and improve its ability to meet customer requirements.

This chapter has emphasized how businesses must recognize the key differences that exist between services and then incorporate these differences into delivery system design. Organizations first need to recognize the fundamental differences in approach that result (Figure 4.12), check the desired position on relevant factors and then incorporate these approaches into its delivery system designs.

What underpins the drive to develop delivery systems that meet the needs of customers is the impact this has on market share, retention and growth. Online retailers estimate that there is no overall profit on transactions until a customer has returned three or even four times. Similarly, keeping customers grows profit. Aligning delivery systems to markets is a key task, therefore, and requires sound corporate understanding on what is needed and how systems are to be developed.

Company		Market	Market norm	Breakthrough	When
Step chosen	Name				
Sell	McDonalds	Restaurant	Serve	Sell customers a limited, standard range of products with high level of self-service	1970s
	Dell	Personal computers	Serve	Sell products directly to customers over the telephone and through the internet	1980s
	Ryanair	European short haul airline	Serve	Sell transportation from one place to another and, similar to road and rail alternatives, require customers to self-serve and pay for any extra services	2000s
	ING Direct	Personal savings and banking	Serve	Sell high-interest savings products over the internet with limited telephone support; customers are asked to leave the bank if they call too often	2000s
Serve	Southwest Airlines	US short haul airline	Sell	Position itself as a budget airline with enhanced service, rather than a scheduled airline with low prices	1970s
Educate	Apple	Personal computers	Serve	Provide a range of inexpensive educational workshops to ensure customers get maximum benefit from its products	2000s
Learn	GE	Compressors and turbines	Serve	Learn with customers about their own power needs and then sell them power by the hour using products developed to best meet their needs	1980s
	Duke CE	Executive education	Educate	Learn with its clients about their development needs and how best to meet them through a continuous process of research, design review and development	2000s

Figure 4.11 Example: the norm and the breakthroughs that companies have made

Factors		Service delivery system design	
		Reactive	Proactive
Delivery system design	Objective	Streamlined and efficient	Customer-focused
	Structure	Rigid	Responsive
	Design premise	Events are consistent and unchanging	Change acknowledged and built into the design
	Approach to service failure	Prevention	Recovery
	Response to service failure	Not designed in the system	Integral part of system design
	Role of server in quality conformance provision	Procedures specify server behaviour	Proactive response expected
Achieving quality conformance	Systems design	Built into the system	Built into the staff
	Error handling	Refer to another level	Dealt with on the spot
	Level of recovery	Low and slow	High and immediate
	Response to failure	Back-office management	Frontline staff
	Quality objective	System has zero defects	Customer-centric
Staff	Attitude	Lack of involvement	Part of provision and solution
	Level of discretion	Low and not encouraged	High and encouraged
	Attitude to failure	Part of failure	Part of recovery solution and then part of success
	Level of motivation	Frustration leading to lack of interest	Part of service provision leading to becoming involved and motivated

Figure 4.12 Factors in reactive and proactive service delivery system design

Amazon

Jeff Bezos founded Amazon in 1994 with the aim of becoming the 'Earth's most customer-centric company where customers could easily find and buy anything they wanted at the lowest possible price'. He wanted a name for his company that began with 'A' so that it would appear early in any alphabetical listing. He began looking through the dictionary and chose the name Amazon because it seemed 'exotic and different' and is one of the biggest of its kind in the world, as he hoped his company would be.

Since then the company has grown rapidly and in 2015 had sales of $107 billion (see Case Figure 4.1) with websites all over the world (see Case Figure 4.2) selling billions of new, refurbished and used products through its different stores (see Case Figure 4.3).

As James Albright (financial analyst) explains, 'Amazon is no ordinary company and, if it was, investors would have given up years ago! Many people have criticized Bezos' focus on growth rather than profit, but his strategy seems to be working and his cute little startup internet business is now one of the world's largest retailers.'

HISTORY

In 1994, Bezos left his job in Wall Street as Vice President of D.E. Shaw and moved to Seattle to sell books through the internet at a time when no one else was doing this. He felt that books were the best products to sell online because an online bookstore could offer a wider range and reach more customers than a store in a physical location. With financial support from his relatives and friends, he spent a year designing and testing Amazon.com before launching it out of his garage in 1995.

From the beginning, Bezos has focused on six core values (see Case Figure 4.4), which he believed would persuade customers to start buying their books online.

He was right and after only six months he was selling more than 100 books a day. To keep costs low, he carried as little inventory as possible and relied on fast shipments from

$bn	2000	2004	2008	2010	2012	2013	2014	2015
Sales revenue	3	7	19	34	61	74	89	107
Operating profit	(1)	0	1	1	1	1	0	2
Net profit	(1)	1	1	1	(0)	0	(0)	1
Cash	1	1	3	4	6	8	9	15
Inventory	0	0	1	3	6	7	8	10
Stockholder equity	(1)	(0)	3	7	8	10	11	13

Case Figure 4.1 Amazon's financial performance

Date	Country
1995	US
1998	UK Germany
2000	France Japan
2002	Canada
2004	China
2010	Italy
2011	Spain
2012	Brazil
2013	India

Case Figure 4.2 Amazon websites by launch date

Date	Store
1995	Books
1998	Music, DVD/Video
1999	Consumer electronics Toy and games Home improvement Software Video games Gift ideas
2000	Kitchen
2001	Travel
2002	Apparel and accessories
2003	Gourmet food Health and personal care
2004	Jewellery Beauty
2006	Digital video download
2007	Digital music download

Case Figure 4.3 Amazon product stores on its websites by launch date

suppliers to meet customers' orders. To help increase sales, in 1996 Bezos launched the Amazon Associates Program that enables other businesses to promote Amazon products through their own websites (see Case Figure 4.5). Amazon then paid these businesses 15 per cent of the initial purchase and 5 per cent of any further purchases made by that customer through Amazon. This was a great success and by 2012 there were over 2 million associates on the programme.

On the back of Amazon's success competitors started to emerge: Book Stacks, BookZone and the Internet Book Shop. In 1997 Amazon decided to raise $54 million by going public, enabling it to improve its online presence through partnerships with America Online, Yahoo!, AltaVista, @Home, Excite, Netscape, GeoCities, and Prodigy.

Customer obsession – we start with the customer and work backward
Innovation – if you don't listen to your customers you will fail. But if you only listen to your customers you will also fail
Bias for action – we live in a time of unheralded revolution and insurmountable opportunity, provided we make every minute count
Ownership – ownership matters when you're building a great company. Owners think long-term, plead passionately for their projects and ideas and are empowered to respectfully challenge decisions
High hiring bar – when making a hiring decision, we ask ourselves, "Will I admire this person? Will I learn from this person? Is this person a superstar?"
Frugality – we spend money on things that really matter and believe that frugality breeds resourcefulness, self-sufficiency and invention!

Case Figure 4.4 Amazon's core values

Date	Service	Description
1996	Associates Program	Third parties can sell Amazon's products through their website and earn a referral fee (15% for initial purchase and 5% for subsequent purchases)
1997	Advantage Program	Third parties can sell products through Amazon.com
1999	Web Auctions	To compete with eBay, but closed that year
	zShops	Fixed-price marketplace where independent retailers can sell products through Amazon
2000	Marketplace	Replaced zShops
	Amazon Services	Third parties can sell Amazon's products through their own branded website for a fixed fee and Amazon would then fulfil these orders for a share of the sales revenue
2006	Fulfillment by Amazon Program	Sellers can send cartons of products to Amazon which then takes the orders online, delivers the products, answers any customer queries and processes any returns

Case Figure 4.5 Seller services by launch date

Later that year, it further improved the shopping experience on its website by introducing features such as 'customer reviews', 'online reviews', 'where's my stuff' and '1-click ordering' (see Case Figure 4.6).

It also introduced the Advantage Program, which enabled individuals and other businesses to sell their own products through Amazon (see Case Figure 4.5). As a result of these changes, customer accounts increased by almost 750 per cent to over 1.5 million, the repeat customers increased by 12 per cent to 58 per cent and sales revenue increased by over 800 per cent to $148 million in 1997.

The following year Amazon changed its mission to become 'Earth's biggest anything store' rather than just 'Earth's biggest bookstore' and launched its Music and DVD/video stores (see Case Figure 4.3). It also launched its websites in Germany and the UK (see Case Figure 4.2) and acquired a number of online service organizations, retailers and software developers (see Case Figure 4.7).

By 2000, Amazon was the world's largest e-tailer with sales of $2.7 billion, but it was still making a loss. To stop it from going bankrupt, Bezos decided to cut costs and change its business model. It closed two warehouses and one customer service centre, laid off 1,300 workers, stopped selling unprofitable products and started offering website developer services, enabling bricks-and-mortar retailers to use Amazon's e-commerce and customer service infrastructure to sell their products (see Case Figure 4.8). These changes turned the business around and in 2002 it made a profit of $64 million.

Over the next five years it continued to open new stores and launch new websites and new consumer, seller and website developer services. It also acquired, invested and partnered with other organizations to host and manage their website or enable them to sell products through Amazon (see Case Figure 4.9).

Date	Service	Description
1997	Customer reviews	Review products
	Online reviews	Amazon product reviews
	Where's my stuff	Track orders
	1-click ordering	Amazon retains customer delivery and payment details
1999	Purchase circles	Show popular items purchased by customers in a postcode
2000	Free shipping	For orders over $25
2001	Look inside the book	Browse through the pages of a book
2003	Search inside the book	Search key words inside a book
	Personalized recommendations	Amazon suggests products based on previous purchases, customer ratings and preferred authors
2004	Listmania	Customers list products that they like
2005	Amazon Prime	Free two-day shipping for $79 per year or upgrade to one-day overnight for $3.99
	Wedding List	Create wedding lists
	Gift wrapping	Gift wrap products
	Eye notification	Alerts customers when a new book on a favourite subject or by a favourite author comes into stock
2007	Amazon Vine	Review products to get free access to pre-releases
2008	Frustration-free packaging	Make packaging easier to open, use less and more recyclable materials, and fewer items shipped in oversized boxes
	iPhone app	Access certain Amazon.com features
	Online price comparisons	Take a photo of a product and find where to buy it online
2009	Instant order update	Tells customers if they have purchased a product before
	Amazon Wireless	Compare and purchase mobile phone service plans
	Gold box	Daily deals on specific products
	Kindle app	Buy and read Kindle books on iPhone or iPad
2010	iPad app	Access certain Amazon.com features
	Window Shop View	Using its iPad app, customers can browse for products as if they were looking through a shop window
2011	Cloud Drive	Manage and create music playlists
	Amazon Locker	Pick up and return goods from a locker
2012	Cloud Player app	Stream music from an Amazon Cloud account using an iPhone or iPad

Case Figure 4.6 Customer services by launch date

Date	Company	Location	Type
1998	PlanetAll	US	Service
	Junglee	US	Software developer
	Bookpages.co.uk	UK	Retailer
1999	IMDb	US	Service
	Alexa Internet	US	Service
	Accept.com	US	Retailer
	Exchange.com	US	Retailer
2003	CDNow	US	Retailer
2004	Joyo.com	China	Retailer
	Lab126	US	Hardware developer
2005	BookSurge	US	Retailer
	Mobipocket.com	US	Software developer
	CreateSpace.com	US	Retailer
2006	Shopbop	US	Retailer
2007	Dpreview.com	UK	Service
	Brilliance Audio	US	Publisher
	Endless.com	US	Retailer
2008	Audible.com	US	Retailer
	Fabric.com		Retailer
	Box Office Mojo	US	Service
	AbeBooks	Canada, Germany	Retailer
	Shelfari	US	Service
	Reflexive	US	Software developer
	Engine Yard	US	Service
2009	Zappos	US	Retailer
	Lexcycle	US	Software developer
	SnapTell	US	Service
	A9	US	Software developer
2010	Touchco	US	Software developer
	Woot	US	Retailer
	Quidsi	US	Retailer
	Buy VIP	Spain	Service
	Amie Street	US	Retailer, Service
	Living Social	US	Service
2011	LoveFilm	UK	Retailer
	Book Depository	UK	Retailer
	Pushbutton	UK	Software developer
	Yap	US	Service

2012	Kiva Systems	US	Software developer
	Teachstreet		Service
	Evi	UK	Software developer
2013	IVONA Software	Poland	Software developer
	GoodReads	US	Service

Case Figure 4.7 Acquisitions and investments

Date	Service	Description
2001	Amazon Enterprise Solutions	Other retailers can use Amazon's e-commerce and customer service infrastructure to sell their products
2002	Web Services	Developers can customize features in Amazon.com
2005	Amazon Mechanical Turk	Computer programs can coordinate the use of human intelligence to perform tasks that computers are unable to do
2006	Amazon Elastic Compute Cloud	Pay-per-usage services for developers
	Amazon Simple Storage Service	Data storage services
	Amazon Simple Queue Service	Stores messages as they travel between computers
2007	Amazon Flexible Payments Service	Other retailers can use Amazon's checkout experience
	Amazon SimpleDB	Creates and stores data sets and query data
2008	Amazon CloudFront	For developers and businesses to deliver content to end users
2012	Amazon Glacier	Cloud-based storage solution

Case Figure 4.8 Website developer services by launch date

In 2005, it launched its first own label product range and two years later it launched the first Amazon Kindle (see Case Figure 4.10).

By 2014, 73 per cent of Amazon's sales were electronics and general merchandise (see Case Figure 4.11), it employed 88,400 staff, had over 30 million customers and 40 per cent of its sales came from 1.3 million third-party sellers.

SERVING CUSTOMERS

'If there's one reason why Amazon have done better than their peers, it's because of its focus on the customer experience', comments Stuart Lee (financial analyst). 'Delivering a great customer experience is important for any business, but it is absolutely critical online where you live or die by what customers say about you. Amazon aims to be "Earth's most customer-centric

Date	Company	Location
1999	Sotheby's	US
2000	ToysRUs	US
2001	Borders	US
	Target	US
	Benefit	UK
	Sears	Canada
	Bebe	US
	Timex	US
	M&S	UK
	Mothercare	UK
	AOL	US
	Lacoste	France
	Edeals.com	UK
2011	DC Comics	US

Case Figure 4.9 Partnerships

company" and it constantly looks for ways to improve the experience for individuals who shop on its websites, merchants who sell through its websites and developers who use its infrastructure to create websites for other businesses' (see Case Figure 4.12).

Amazon continually tries to reduce its prices, increase its product range and make it easier for customers to find products and make more informed buying decisions. For example, multiple sellers offer the same product to help reduce prices and customers rate these sellers to help identify the ones with the best service. Customers can easily track orders, review estimated delivery dates and cancel

Date	Products	Description
2005	Pinzon	Own label textiles, kitchen, clothing, footwear, jewellery and household goods
2007	Kindle	eBook reader $399 to access 1 million books, newspapers, magazines and blogs
2009	Kindle 2	$359 text-to-speech and pdfs. Reduced to $259 in 2009 and $189 in 2010
	Kindle DX	Large screen eBook reader $489
	CreditCard	Co-branded with Chase Bank
2010	Kindle DX Graphite	$379
	Kindle 3	$139 wi-fi, $189 wi-fi/3G
2011	Kindle 4	$79 with ads, $109 without Kindle Touch screen, eBook reader wi-fi ($99 with ads, $139 without), wi-fi/3G ($149 with ads, $189 without)
	Kindle Fire	Tablet computer $199
2012	Kindle 5	$69 with ads, $89 without
	Kindle Paperwhite	Wi-fi ($119 with ads, $139 without), wi-fi/3G ($179 with ads, $199 without)
	Kindle Fire HD	$199 7-inch screen, $299 8.9-inch screen
2013	Kindle Fire HDX	$199 7-inch screen, $299 8.9-inch screen
	Kindle 6	$79 with ads, $109 without
2014	Fire TV	Set-top box $99
	Fire phone	$449 32 GB, $549 64 GB

Case Figure 4.10 Amazon products by launch date

$bn	2000	2004	2008	2010	2012	2013	2014	2015
By region								
US	2	4	10	19	35	45	55	64
International	0	3	9	15	26	30	34	36
By product group								
Electronics/general	0	2	8	18	39	49	61	76
Media	3	5	11	15	20	22	23	22
Other	0	0	1	1	3	4	0	1

Notes

1 Media includes books, music, DVDs, video, magazine subscriptions, digital downloads and video games.

2 Electronics includes computers, mobile devices and other electronic products.

3 General includes home, garden, groceries, apparel, jewellery, health, beauty, sports, outdoor, tools, auto and industrial.

Case Figure 4.11 Sales revenue

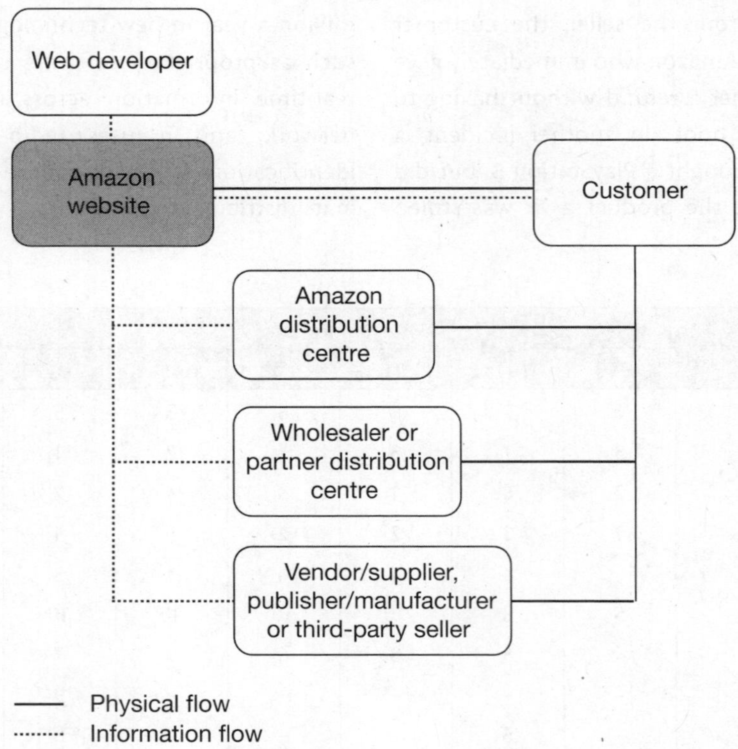

Case Figure 4.12 Amazon's supply network

unshipped items. Best sellers lists, personalized recommendations, customer reviews and online reviews are updated every hour to help customers find products they might want to buy. Customer behaviour is continually analysed and used to suggest products to customers that have been purchased by people searching for similar items.

As well as trying to provide the best service itself, it also works hard to make sure customers receive the best service from third-party sellers who use Amazon's email service. If there are problems with more than 1 per cent of the orders with a seller then it is no longer allowed to trade through Amazon. It also makes it clear to them that customers come first. For instance, a customer once purchased a 'like new' book from a seller that was actually nowhere close to new with many of the worksheets in the book already having been filled in. After getting no response from the seller, the customer contacted Amazon who immediately gave the customer a refund without having to return the book. In another incident, a customer bought a PlayStation 3, but did not receive the product as it was stolen after a neighbour had signed for the package and left it in the hallway. The customer contacted Amazon and a replacement was sent immediately, free of charge. Despite these tough performance standards, in 2015, Amazon was ranked at second for e-commerce marketplaces in an annual survey of third-party sellers (see Case Figure 4.13).

To ensure products are delivered quickly, reliably and at a low cost, Amazon has developed a supply chain that is viewed as one of the best in the world (see Case Figure 4.14) with a global network of fulfilment centres located near airports (see Case Figure 4.15). It also invests over $200 million a year in new technology systems such as proprietary software to provide real-time information across its supply network, and it uses radio-frequency identification (RFID) to manage inventory in its distribution centres.

Company	Rank						
	2010	2011	2012	2013	2014	2015	2016
eBay	6	9	5	5	3	5	1
Etsy	3	7	3	1	2	1	2
Amazon	2	6	1	3	4	2	3
Ruby Lane	1	3	2	2	5	4	4
Bonanza	–	4	4	4	1	3	5
eCrater	5	8	10	10	10	10	6
eBid	4	5	8	6	9	7	7
Pinterest	–	–	–	–	–	9	8
craigslist	–	6	–	–	7	6	9
Facebook	–	–	–	–	–	–	10

Note: Ranked on profitability (20%), customer service (20%), communication (20%), ease of use (20%) and whether respondents would recommend the website (20%)

Case Figure 4.13 Top 10 e-commerce marketplaces

Source: Based on a survey of 11,500 online third-party sellers by www.ecommercebytes.com.

Company	Rank										
	2005	2007	2008	2009	2010	2011	2012	2013	2014	2015	2016
Apple	–	2	1	1	1	1	1	1	1	1	1
Procter & Gamble	2	3	4	3	2	3	5	6	5	2	2
Unilever	–	–	–	–	–	–	10	4	4	5	3
McDonald's	–	–	–	–	–	8	3	2	2	4	4
Amazon	–	–	–	–	10	5	2	3	3	3	5
Intel	–	–	–	–	–	–	7	5	8	6	6
H&M	–	–	–	–	–	–	–	–	–	9	7
Inditex	–	–	–	–	–	–	–	–	–	7	8
Cisco Systems	–	–	8	5	3	6	8	7	7	8	9
Samsung	7	10	9	8	7	10	–	8	6	10	10

Note: Ranked on peer opinion (25%), research opinion (25%), return on assets (25%), inventory turns (15%) and revenue growth (10%).

Case Figure 4.14 Top 10 supply chain management companies

Source: Based on data from Gartner (previously AMR Research).

These investments have enabled it to stay ahead of the competition. It introduced Amazon Prime in 2005, offering customers free two-day shipping for $79 per year, which can be upgraded to one-day overnight for $3.99. Providing this service is expensive (see Case Figure 4.16), but the annual average spend per customer increased by 23 per cent in the year it was introduced.

As Stuart Lee comments, 'You can find just about any product you want on Amazon and you know it's going to be competitively priced and delivered quickly to your home with a simple click of the mouse. After a while, customers stop shopping around as it's simpler to just buy it from Amazon and you know this is probably the cheapest place to buy it anyway!' As a result, Amazon had the highest American Customer Satisfaction Index (ACSI) score of any online or physical retailer from 2000 to 2014 (see Case Figure 4.17).

THE FUTURE

'Other companies make strategic moves occasionally and in isolation', comments James Albright. 'But Amazon makes its moves continuously and seems to be able to think multiple moves ahead on several fronts at the same time. However, it risks spreading its resources too thinly across a wide range of industries where it is up against competitors with greater resources (eBay and Metro AG), longer histories (Barnes & Noble), more customers (Apple) and greater brand recognition (Google and iTunes). Unlike many of its competitors (such as Google and Apple), it has not invented a new product or service and the patents that it has (such as 1-click shopping) have proved difficult to leverage. The competitive advantage that it has gained from its low-cost warehouse and distribution capability is being eroded as more media products are being sold electronically and its delivery costs continue to rise' (see Case Figure 4.18).

Type	Continent	Country	Locations
Call centres	Africa	Morocco	1
	Asia	China	1
		Japan	1
		South Africa	1
		India	1
	Europe	Germany	1
		Italy	1
		Ireland	1
		UK	1
	Central America	Costa Rica	2
	North America	US	4
	South America	Uruguay	1
	Total		**16**
Distribution centres	Asia	China	3
		India	1
		Japan	8
	Europe	France	4
		Germany	7
		Italy	2
		Netherlands	1
		Slovakia	1
		Spain	1
		UK	11
	North America	Canada	2
		US	35
	Total		**76**
Software development centres	Africa	South Africa	1
	Asia	India	3
		Japan	1
		China	1
	Europe	Ireland	1
		UK	3
		Netherlands	1
		Romania	1
	North America	Canada	2
		US	9
	Total		**23**

Case Figure 4.15 Call, distribution and software development centres

$bn	2002	2004	2006	2008	2010	2012	2013	2014	2015
Revenue	0	0	1	1	1	2	3	4	7
Cost	0	1	1	1	3	5	7	9	12
Net cost	(0)	(0)	(0)	(1)	(1)	(3)	(4)	(4)	(5)

Case Figure 4.16 Amazon's delivery revenue and costs

Company	Rank										
	2000	2002	2004	2006	2008	2010	2012	2013	2014	2015	2016
Online											
Amazon	84	88	84	87	86	87	85	88	86	80	83
Newegg	–	–	–	–	88	84	84	83	81	79	83
eBay	80	82	80	80	78	81	83	80	79	75	81
Netflix	–	–	–	–	85	86	75	79	81	76	79
Overstock	–	–	–	–	82	78	82	79	77	73	79
Physical											
Dillard's	72	75	77	75	75	78	79	81	81	80	83
JC Penney	74	74	76	78	78	80	81	79	77	74	82
Nordstrom	–	–	–	–	80	82	84	83	86	82	80
Kohl's	–	84	79	80	80	81	81	81	80	77	79
Target	–	–	75	77	77	78	81	77	80	75	79
Macy's	–	–	–	71	74	76	78	76	79	73	79
Dollar General	–	–	–	71	75	80	78	80	–	74	78
Wal-Mart	73	74	73	72	70	73	71	71	68	66	72

Note: – = not available

Case Figure 4.17 Customer satisfaction for online and physical retailers

Source: Based on the American Customer Satisfaction Index (ACSI).

$bn	2000	2004	2008	2010	2012	2013	2014	2015
Cost of sales	4	5	15	27	46	54	63	72
Fulfillment	1	1	2	3	6	9	11	13
Technology and content	0	0	1	2	5	7	9	13
Marketing	0	0	0	1	2	3	4	5
General and admin	0	0	0	0	1	1	2	2
Total	5	6	18	33	60	74	89	105

Note: Shipping costs are included in Fulfillment.

Case Figure 4.18 Amazon's operating expenses

Albright continues, 'It's got some difficult decisions to make if it wants to stay ahead of its competitors. Can it continue to focus on growth at the expense of profit? Is it putting its customers before its shareholders? Should it focus on reducing costs in its supply chain or investing in high technology products to better compete with Apple, Samsung and Google? I'm not sure it has the resources to do everything.'

QUESTIONS

1 What is Amazon's business model?

2 How does it support the needs of its different customers?

3 How do its 'core values' help drive its business forward?

DISCUSSION QUESTIONS

1 Why do organizations complete some tasks in the front office and some in the back office? Give three examples to illustrate.

2 List the principal phases when developing the overall design of a service delivery system. Illustrate your answer with examples.

3 For a non-repeat, low-volume repeat and high-volume repeat service of your choice, explain how and why the following factors differ for each of the three types:
- service variety
- typical order-winner
- level of delivery flexibility
- ability of the delivery system to cope with new services and staff skill levels.

4 Give an example of both a single-step and multi-step service delivery system. Explain why each example was an appropriate choice.

5 What steps should an organization take when choosing the appropriate way to delivery its services?

6 What is the difference between a non-repeat and a repeat service? Give two examples to illustrate each category.

7 Explain a way to categorize services. How is this helpful? Why does it not translate into types of delivery systems?

NOTES AND REFERENCES

1 These concepts were first introduced by Sasser, W.E. Jr, Olsen, R.P. and Wyckoff, D.D. in *Management of Service Operations: Text, Cases and Readings*, Allyn & Bacon, 1978, pp. 10–11.

2 See also the approach to service delivery system design in Jeskett, J.L., Jones, T.O., Loveman, G.W., Sasser, W.E. Jr and Schlesinger, L.K. (1994) 'Putting the service-profit change to work', *Harvard Business Review*, March–April: 164–74.

3 See also Hart, C.W.L., Heskett, J.L. and Sasser, W.E. Jr (1990) 'The profitable art of service recovery', *Harvard Business Review*, July–August: 148–56; Reinartz, W. and Kumar, V. (2000) 'The mismanagement of customer loyalty', *Harvard Business Review*, July: 4–12.

4 Jack Nilles' books include *Managing Telework* (1998) John Wiley & Sons.

EXPLORING FURTHER

Arussy, L. (2002) 'Don't take calls, make contact', *Harvard Business Review*, 80(1): 16–18.

Brown, S., Bessant, J. and Lamming, R. (2013) *Strategic Operations Management*, 3rd edn, Routledge.

Brown, S., Blackmore, K., Cousins, P. and Maylor, H. (2011) *Operations Management: Policy, Practice and Performance Improvement*, Routledge.

Hollins, B. and Shinkins, S. (2006) *Managing Service Operations: Design and Implementation*, Sage.

Johnston, R. and Clark, G. (2008) *Service Operations Management: Improving Service Delivery*, 3rd edn, Pearson Education.

Moller, K., Rajala, R. and Westerland, M. (2008) 'Service innovation myopia? A new recipe for client-provider value creation', *California Management Review*, 50(3), 31–48.

Nunes, P.F. and Cespedes, E.V. (2003) 'The customer has escaped', *Harvard Business Review*, 81(11): 96–105.

Wright, J.N. and Race, P. (2004) *The Management of Service Operations*, 2nd edn, Thomson Learning.

5 PROCESS CHOICE

SUMMARY

The most significant decisions a manufacturing company has to make concern customers, products and the processes by which to make them. This chapter covers the task of deciding which operations process to use and addresses the following issues:

- **Factors involved in making products** – the category or type of product, the product complexity and the volumes involved are key factors in the task of making products.
- **Types of manufacturing process** – there are five generic types of manufacturing process: project, jobbing, batch, line and continuous processing. Each is distinct from the other. While project and continuous processing are product/industry type specific, the other three choices provide alternatives to a range of industries. Which one fits depends on the levels of volume and repetition involved.
- **Business implications of process choice** – products have both a technical and a business dimension. The former relates to the design, material and similar aspects, while the latter defines the business aspects (for example, volumes, order-winners and qualifiers). Operations concerns providing the business specification of its products and selecting the most appropriate process to provide these dimensions.
- **Hybrid processes** – to gain better fit between the business requirements and process characteristics, companies may choose a hybrid process (a mix of two generic types). Hybrids may or may not be IT-based.
- **Technology strategy** – advances in computer control have afforded fresh opportunities to compete in the manufacturing sector.

PROCESS CHOICE

When choosing the appropriate way in which to manufacture its products, a business will take the following steps:

1 Decide on how much to buy from outside the company, which in turn determines the make-in task or internal phase of the supply chain.

2 Identify the appropriate engineering-technology alternatives to make a product to its technical specification. This will concern bringing together the made-in components with the bought-out items to produce the final product specification at agreed levels of quality conformance.
3 Choose between alternative manufacturing approaches to completing the tasks embodied in providing the products involved. This will need to reflect the market in which a product competes and the volumes associated with those sales. The present processes in many existing factories may not be ideal because they were purchased some time in the past. Advances in technology on the one hand and changes in market volumes and requirements on the other often contribute to creating this position. This and other known items will be considered when the important insights into process choice have been covered.

The choice of process concerns Step 3 in this procedure. It will need to embody the decisions made in the other two steps and recognize any constraints imposed by them. The task then is to choose the most appropriate way to manufacture, given the market and associated volumes involved. In that way it addresses the internal phase of the supply chain with the external phase (suppliers and distributors), which is the subject of Chapter 9.

THE OPERATIONS FUNCTION

The principal function of the operations process is to take inputs (materials, labour and energy) and convert them into outputs (products) in line with agreed cost profiles and the needs of customers. To complete this, a business chooses between appropriate engineering/technology alternatives (Step 2 above) and operations alternatives (Step 3 above). The fundamental rationale for this latter decision concerns choosing a process that is best able to meet agreed cost structures and support a company competitively in its marketplace. Each choice of process will bring with it certain implications for a business in terms of response to its markets, operations characteristics, level of investment required, unit costs involved and the type of scheduling system and style of management that are appropriate. To help understand these, it is necessary to review the process choices available.

But first, let's look at the factors involved in making products that help determine the decision on which process to use.

FACTORS INVOLVED IN MAKING PRODUCTS

Categories of product

Figure 5.1 separates products into three categories and reflects the differences that need to be taken into account when designing the operations process. For example, it is clear that the process suited to making a Formula One/Indy racing car is, and needs to be, different from that used in a mass automobile plant because volumes, level of variety and degree of customization will all differ significantly, and the process needs to be able to cater for those differences.

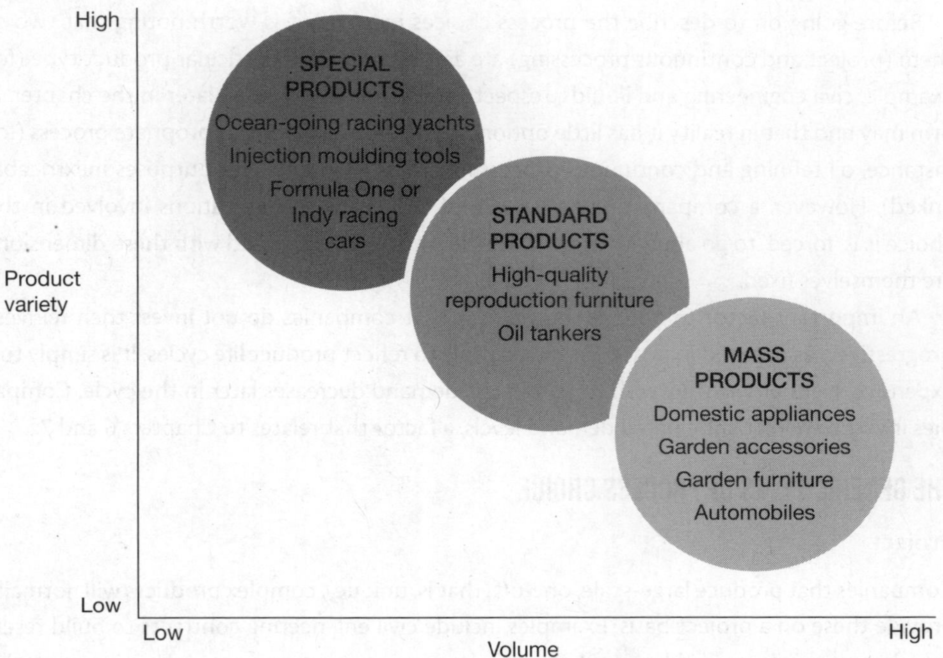

Figure 5.1 Categories of product

Source: Hill, A. and Hill, T. (2012) Operations Management, *3rd edn, Palgrave Macmillan.*

Product complexity

The complexity of a product varies. Compare engines for a lawn mower, automobile and Boeing 777 or Airbus 380 and the differences are marked. As the product complexity increases, the number of steps and different processes involved will also increase which, in turn, impacts process design.

Volumes

Figure 5.1 illustrates the important relationship between the three product categories and the levels of volume involved. The fundamental nature of this dimension is central to this chapter and the following section shows how it is reflected in the manufacturing process design.

TYPES OF MANUFACTURING PROCESS

There are five generic types of manufacturing process: project, jobbing, batch, line and continuous processing. However, in many situations, hybrids have been developed that blur the edges between one process and another. What these hybrids are, how they relate to the classic types and what they mean for a business will also be discussed.

Before going on to describe the process choices involved, it is worth noting that two of them (project and continuous processing) are associated with a particular product type (for example, civil engineering and liquids, respectively), a point addressed later in the chapter. A firm may find that in reality it has little option but to choose the one appropriate process (for instance, oil refining and continuous processing are to all intents and purposes inextricably linked). However, a company must be aware of the business implications involved in the choice it is 'forced' to go along with and that the trade-offs associated with these dimensions are themselves fixed.

An important factor to note at this point is that companies do not invest then reinvest progressively as demand increases, as for example to reflect product life cycles. It is simply too expensive. Neither will they wish to reinvest as demand decreases later in the cycle. Companies invest to reflect anticipated demand levels, a factor that relates to Chapters 6 and 7.[1]

THE GENERIC TYPES OF PROCESS CHOICE

Project

Companies that produce large-scale, one-off (that is, unique), complex products will normally provide these on a project basis. Examples include civil engineering contracts to build reservoir dams, tunnels and bridges, and aerospace programmes. A project process concerns the provision of a unique product requiring the coordination of large-scale inputs to achieve a customer's requirements. The resource inputs will normally be taken to where the product is to be built, since it is not feasible to move it once completed. All activities, including the necessary support functions, will usually be controlled by a total system for the duration of the project. Resources allocated to the project will be reallocated once their part of the task is complete or at the end of the project.

The selection of project as the appropriate process is based on one or both of the following features. First, the product is a one-off (that is, unique), customer-specified requirement; second, it is too large to be moved or simply cannot be moved once completed. This second criterion is such an overwhelming facet in this decision that products of this nature will always be made using the project process. However, businesses will also be concerned with determining how much of the product to make away from site and how best to provide the parts or sections that go into the structures made on site. Making on site is not an efficient way of working because resources have to be moved to and from the job as it progresses. This incurs costs and militates against achieving efficiencies. Hence, companies try to produce as much as possible of the product off site, which allows a more efficient process to be used. These parts of the total job will, in turn, be produced using a process other than project. Such decisions need to be based on other criteria, which will become clear in the descriptions of the other choices that follow.

Some confusion arises in the use of the word 'project'. It commonly refers to a one-off complex task and/or the managerial style used to control such an event. This needs to be distinguished from its use here, which identifies a distinct process of making a product, the characteristics of which (for example, moving resources to and from a site) are detailed in Figure 5.2.

Products	Made or produced on site as they are too large or too difficult to move after completion. Examples include building reservoir dams, tunnels, roads, bridges and houses
Process	Resources to make the product are brought to the site, allocated for the duration of the project and then reallocated once their part of the task is complete or at the end of the job

Figure 5.2 Project: key characteristics

Source: Hill, A. and Hill, T. (2012) Operations Management, *3rd edn, Palgrave Macmillan.*

Jobbing

Once products are transportable, companies look to another process to make them. The jobbing[2] process is designed to meet the one-off (that is, unique) requirements of customers where the product involved is of an individual nature and tends to be of a smaller size (and, therefore, transportable) than those produced using a project process. Product examples include ocean-going racing yachts, a purpose-built piece of equipment (for example, injection moulding tools), handmade; built-in furniture, customer-designed and specified control units and hand-crafted shoes. Such products require a supplier to interpret a customer's needs and/or design specification and apply relatively high-level skills in the conversion process. A large degree of this interpretation will normally be made by skilled employees, whose experience in this type of work is an essential facet of the process. Once the design has been specified, one skilled person – or possibly a small number of them if the task is time-consuming – is assigned the task and is responsible for deciding how best to complete and carry it out. This may also include a level of responsibility for scheduling, clarifying issues with the customer, liaison with other functions and some involvement with arrangements for the subcontracted phases, where necessary.

This one-off provision means that the product will not be required again in its exact form, or, if it is, the demand will tend to be irregular, with long time periods between orders. For this reason, investment in the operations process (for example, in jigs, fixtures and specialist plant) will not normally be warranted. Figure 5.3 provides a summary of the key characteristics of jobbing.

Products	Special (that is, will not be repeated) products. Examples include the design and installation of a control system, a purpose-built piece of equipment, handmade, built-in furniture and hand-crafted shoes and clothing
Process	One person or a small group of skilled people do everything, including interpreting the product specification, clarifying issues with the customer and ensuring that what is made meets the specification

Figure 5.3 Jobbing: key characteristics

Source: Hill, A. and Hill, T. (2012) Operations Management, *3rd edn, Palgrave Macmillan.*

Jobbing versus job shop

It is worth noting here that confusion often arises around the terms 'jobbing' and 'job shop'. While the former refers to the choice of process explained above, the latter is a commercial description of a type of business. For example, a small printing business may often be referred to as a 'job shop' or even a 'jobbing printer'. This is intended to convey the nature of the business involved or market served, that is, the printer undertakes work, typically low volume in nature, that meets the specific needs of a whole range of customers. However, printing is in fact a classic example of a batch process, which is explained in the next section. Thus, from a commercial standpoint, such a firm takes on low-volume orders (hence the term 'job') from its customers but, from a manufacturing perspective, uses a batch process to meet these requirements.

Special versus customized versus standard products

Finally, it is also important to distinguish between special, customized and standard products. The word 'special' is used to describe the one-off provision referred to earlier in this section – that is, the product will not again be required in its exact form or, if it is, the demand will be irregular, with long time periods between orders. The phrase 'standard product' means the opposite – the demand for the product is repeated (or the single customer order is of such a large volume) and thus warrants investment.

The word 'customized' refers to a product made to a customer's specification. However, the demand for a customized product can be either special (that is, not repeated) or standard (that is, repeated). An example of the latter is a container of a particular shape and size, as determined by a customer. Although customized, the demand for such a container (for example, Coca-Cola or other soft drink products) will be high and of a repeat nature. The appropriate choice of process will, therefore, be determined by volume and not the customized nature of the product.

Furthermore, some businesses are by their very nature the producers of customized products. The earlier example of the printing firm is such a case. Here products normally will be customized, in that the printed material may include the logo, company name, product name and other details of the customer in question. However, a printer will find a significant level of similarity between the demands placed on operations by the different customer orders. In fact, the differences will be in the printing plate containing the specific images and writing and the ink colours and paper size in question. To operations, therefore, customized jobs are not specials (as defined earlier) but standards. Thus, it will select a process other than jobbing to meet the requirements of the markets it serves. In the printing example, this would be batch, and the rationale for this and what is involved will become clear in the next section.

Batch

A company decides to manufacture using batch processes because it is providing similar items on a repeat basis and usually in larger volumes (quantity × work content) than associated with jobbing.[3] This type of process is chosen to cover a wide range of volumes, as represented in Figure 5.4 by the elongated shape of batch, compared to other processes. At the low-volume

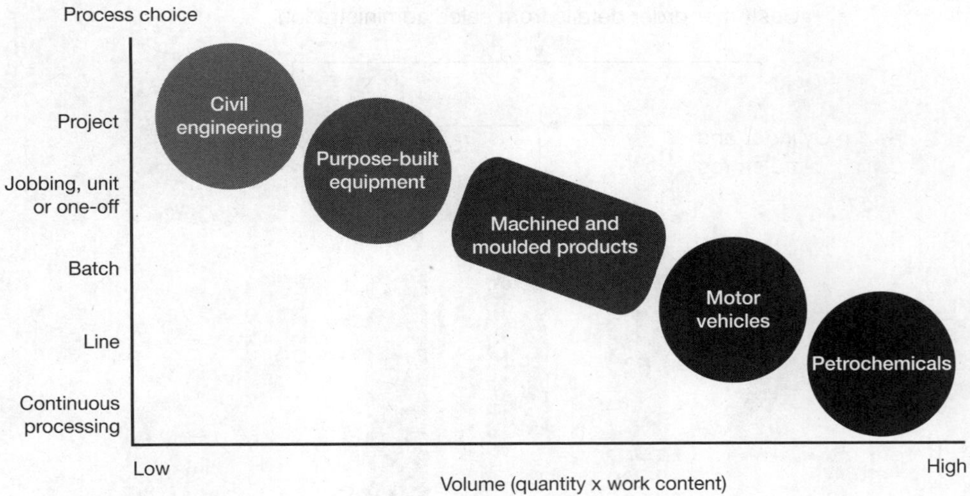

Figure 5.4 Process choice related to volumes

end, the repeat orders will be small and infrequent. In fact, some companies producing very large, one-off items will adopt a batch rather than a jobbing process for their manufacture. When this happens, the work content involved will be high in jobbing terms, while the order quantity is for a small number of the same but unique items. At the high-volume end, the order quantities may involve many hours, shifts, or even weeks of work for the same product at one or more stages in its designated manufacturing route.

The reason the batch process divides the operations task into a series of appropriate steps is simply to determine the most effective manufacturing route, so that the low-cost requirements of repeat, higher-volume markets can be best achieved. At this stage, suitable jigs, fixtures and equipment will typically be identified to help reduce the processing times involved, the investment in which is justified by the total product output over time.

When using a batch process, the first step is to divide the job into a number of steps. How many steps will depend, in part, on the complexity of the product involved. A product may be completed by a single batch process, with more complex products being completed using a number of steps. An example of such a multi-step batch process is shown in Figure 5.5.

Each order quantity is manufactured by setting up the step of the process that is necessary to complete the first operation for a particular product. The whole order quantity is completed at this stage. Then, the next operation in the process is made ready, the total order quantity is completed and so on, until all stages required to make a product are completed. Meanwhile, the process used to complete the first operation for the product is then reset to complete an operation for another product and so on. Thus, capacity at each stage in the process is used and reused to meet the different requirements of different orders.

A further illustration to the printing example given in Figure 5.5 is moulding. Here the mould to produce an item is put into a machine. The order for that component or

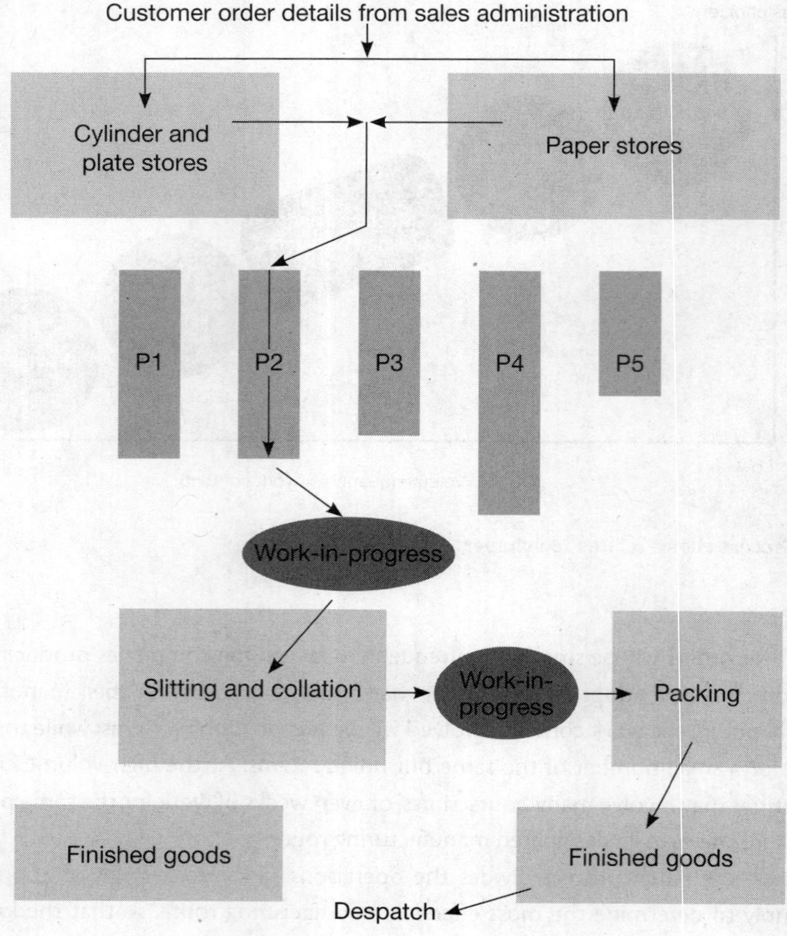

Notes
1 P1–P5 are printing machines
2 Arrows indicate the movement of a typical order

Figure 5.5 Printing: a multi-step batch process

product is then produced, the mould is taken off, the raw materials (type and/or colour) may have to be changed then a mould for another product is put into the machine and so on. Similarly in metal machining processes, a machine is set to complete the necessary metal-cutting operation for a product and the whole order quantity is processed. When finished, the machine in question is reset to do the required metal-cutting work on another item, while the order quantity of the first product goes on to its next stage, which is completed in another part of the process. At times, an order quantity may have more than one stage completed on the same machine. Here the same principle applies, with the process reset to perform the next operation through which the whole order quantity will be passed.

Figure 5.6 provides a summary of the key characteristics of batch.

Products	Standard, repeat products, the volume demand for which justifies the process investment. Examples include machined parts, injection mouldings and printing
Process	Having broken down the products into different operations, the order quantity is taken to the process where the first operation is to be undertaken. The process is made ready/set up and the whole order quantity is completed. The part-made product typically goes into work-in-progress inventory awaiting the next process that will complete the second operation. When available, the next process is made ready, the whole order quantity is processed and so on until the whole product is completed

Figure 5.6 Batch: key characteristics

Line

With further increases in volumes (quantity × work content), investment is made to provide a process dedicated to the needs of a single product or a given range of products. The cumulative volume of the product range underpins this investment, with the width of the product range being determined at the time of the investment. In a line process, products are passed through the same sequence of operations. The standard nature of the products allows for this, and in the process transfers the product from one step to the next. Workers or equipment complete the designated tasks at that stage of the process and then move the product on to the next step, and so on until the product is completed. However, changes outside the prescribed range of options (which can be very wide, for example, with motor vehicles) cannot be accommodated on the line itself.

As explained in a later section, it is important to recognize the fundamental differences in what constitutes volume. In a car assembly plant, for instance, customer order quantities are normally small. The eventual owner of a car orders in units of one, which a dealership passes on to the assembly plant as an order for a single car or cumulates it with one or more other orders for single units. In operations terms, however, all orders for single cars are handled by the production process as being the same product. Hence the order quantity of a car assembly plant comprises the cumulative volume of all orders over a given period. This constitutes the high-volume nature of this business, making line the appropriate process.

Normally, the wider the product range, the higher the investment required in the process to provide the degree of flexibility necessary to make these products. Where the options provided are very wide and the products involved are costly or bulky, the company is more likely to make them to order. For example, there will normally be a longer delay when purchasing an automobile (especially if several options are specified)[4] than, say, a domestic appliance. The underlying reason is the different degree of product standardization involved. The automobile will be made against a specific customer order and the domestic appliance to stock.

In summary, in a line process all products (irrespective of the options involved) are perceived to be standard. Thus the process does not have to be stopped and reset to meet the requirements of the range of products made on a line. However, in order to accommodate another product using a batch process (which, for example, may only involve a different colour), the process has to be stopped and reset.

Figure 5.7 provides a summary of the key characteristics of the line process.

Products	Standard, repeat, high-volume, mass products. Examples include motor vehicles and domestic appliances. Not widely found in manufacturing today, as the required volumes to justify the investment are not typical of current markets
Process	Products are separated into different operations. These are met by a series of sequential processes through which all items in a selected range pass. To the process, all the products are the same and, therefore, the line does not have to be stopped and reset to accommodate a change in requirement. However, the line can only cope with the predetermined range for which the process has been designed. To widen the existing range would require additional investment

Figure 5.7 Line: key characteristics

Source: Hill, A. and Hill, T. (2012) Operations Management, *3rd edn, Palgrave Macmillan.*

Continuous processing

With continuous processing, a basic material is passed through successive stages or operations and refined or processed into one or more products. Petrochemicals is an example. This choice of process is based on two features. The first is very high-volume demand; the second is that the materials involved can be moved easily from one part of the process to another, for example, fluids and gases.

The high volumes justify the very high investment involved. The processes are designed to run all day and every day with minimum shutdowns, due to the high (often prohibitive) costs of closing down and starting up. Normally the product range is narrow and often the products offered are purposely restricted in order to enhance volumes of all the products in the range. For example, oil companies have systematically restricted the range of fuel octanes offered and hence increased the volumes of all those grades provided. Another feature in continuous processing is the nature of the materials being processed. Whereas in line there are manual inputs into the manufacture of the products as they pass along, in continuous processing the materials will be transferred automatically from one part of the process to the next, with the process monitoring and often self-adjusting flow and quality conformance levels. The labour tasks in these situations predominantly involve monitoring, checking and some adjusting of the system but typically do not involve manual inputs into the process as they would on a line process.

Figure 5.8 shows an example of continuous processing. To close down and restart the plant would take several days because of the complex procedures and safety requirements involved. Figure 5.9 summarizes the key characteristics of continuous processing.

Figure 5.10 summarizes the previous section and also relates the different processes to the product categories introduced in Figure 5.1. You will see from this that the transition from special through to mass products given in Figure 5.1 relates, in general, to the types of process used. We now reflect on this link between product type, process type and volumes.

Figure 5.8 ExxonMobil's ethylene cracking plant, Fife, Scotland

Source: Hill, A. and Hill, T. (2012) Operations Management, *3rd edn, Palgrave Macmillan.*

Products	Standard, very high-volume (mass) products. Examples include oil refining and some petrochemicals
Process	Materials are processed through successive stages, with automatic transfer of the product from stage to stage. The costs of stopping and restarting are typically so high that the process is not stopped, hence the name 'continuous processing'

Figure 5.9 Continuous: key characteristics

Source: Hill, A. and Hill, T. (2012) Operations Management, *3rd edn, Palgrave Macmillan.*

1 Project for special and standard products

As shown in Figure 5.10, both special and standard products may choose project as the appropriate process. For example, a new estate of 120 houses comprising six designs would, for the builder, be a standard offering – that is, the house specifications would be known, the method of build would be decided ahead of time and any possible options to the vary the basic design would be fixed. However, the houses would need to be built on site as they cannot be moved. On the other hand, a large country house built to a unique design, although a special, would need to be built on site.

Process type	Product		Process description
	Category	Examples	
Project	Special	• Sydney Opera House • Oresund bridge connecting Denmark and Sweden • San Gottardo Tunnel in the Alps	Products that cannot be physically moved once completed use a project process. Resources (materials, equipment and people) are brought to the site where the product is to be built. These resources are allocated for the duration of the job and will be reallocated once their part of the task is completed or at the end of the job
	Standard	• Estate housing • Prefabricated industrial and warehouse units	
Jobbing	Special	• Ocean-going racing yachts • Injection moulding tools • Formula One and Indy racing cars • The design and installation of a process control system	Once a product can be moved, companies will choose to make it in house and then despatch it to the customer. Jobbing is the name of the process that is used for special (that is, unique) products that will typically not be repeated. Here, one person or a small group of skilled people will complete all of the product. Often the task requires the provider to install and commission the product as part of the job
Batch	Standard ↓ Mass	• Business cards • Golf tees • Packaging • Plastic bottles	The repeat and higher-volume nature of standard products requires a process designed to take advantage of these characteristics. Batch, line and continuous processing are the alternatives. Which one to use depends on the volumes involved and the nature of the products. Batch can be appropriately used for low through to high (mass) volumes. Because the method of making the product is known, the steps involved are predetermined and products move from step to step until complete. Batch is chosen for standard products with volumes insufficient to dedicate processes. Thus, different products share the same processes by setting and resetting each time. Consequences of this include waiting between steps and the prioritizing of jobs using the same process

Line	Mass	• Domestic appliances • Cans of Coca-Cola • Automobiles • Pet food • Mobile phones	Higher volumes mean that processes can be dedicated to the needs of a given range of products. Whereas in batch a process has to be reset each time a new product is to be made, in line the process does not have to stop as it has been designed to make the range of products required without being reset. As with batch, the products are standard. The steps to make them are sequentially laid out in line and a product goes from step to step until completed. Although the range of products will vary, to the process they can be made without stopping and resetting the line
Continuous processing	Mass	• Petrochemicals • Oil refineries • Some chemical plants	For some products, the high volumes involved are best handled by continuous processing. In addition to high volume, these products will need to be transferable through piping or in liquid form. Continuous processing is similar to line in that it handles mass products without being stopped and reset. Its distinguishing feature is, however, that to stop and restart the process is lengthy and expensive and consequently it is designed to be run continuously

Figure 5.10 Manufacturing processes and their relationship to the product categories in Figure 5.1

Source: Hill, A. and Hill, T. (2009) Managing Operations Strategy, *3rd edn, Palgrave Macmillan.*

2 Project and continuous processing are specific to certain product types

Typically, project would only be used when a product has to be built on site. Setting up and dismantling a site, moving equipment and people to and from a site increase costs and make the management task more difficult compared to making a product in house. As a consequence, project is typically only used where the product has to be made in situ.

Similarly, the use of continuous processing is limited. The products best suited to this process would be high volume, with the physical characteristics that allow them to be moved from step to step in the process using pipework, such as the refining of oil and the production of petrochemicals.

Hence, the appropriate use of project and continuous processing is restricted (as shown in Figure 5.11) and most organizations choose from jobbing, batch and line for their business needs.

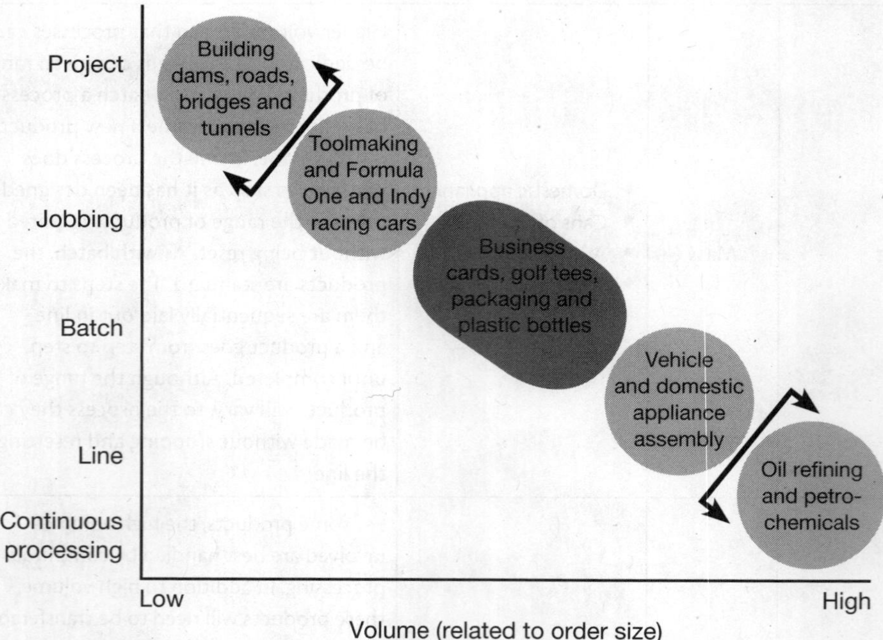

Figure 5.11 Process choices
Source: Hill, A. and Hill, T. (2012) Operations Management, *3rd edn, Palgrave Macmillan.*

3 Combinations of processes

Often companies will use more than one process type to meet the overall needs of their business. The reason is that one process best meets the different needs of a product or parts of a product. For example, building the 120 new houses in point 1 would use a combination of processes:

- *Project* would be needed to meet the overall requirements of bringing resources to and from the site, with one person having the overall management responsibility to undertake this task in line with the effective use of the resources and cost budgets involved.
- *Batch* would typically be used to meet several phases of the work. For example, once the footings have been completed on a number of houses, the concreting of the ground floor areas for these houses would be completed consecutively. In this way, one phase would be completed on one house and this same phase would be completed on the next house and so on until this task was completed for a number of houses. Other phases in the building of several houses would be similarly cumulated to enable them to be completed one after another (for example, roofing, glazing, electrics, plastering, bathroom fitting and kitchen installation). In this way, builders would take advantage of the increased volume associated with the repeat nature of each phase, thus enabling them to reduce costs and make the management task easier. As a consequence, all roofing tiles for several houses would be delivered to site at the same time, as well as the materials for the glazing, electrics and other phases. Also, contractors to complete

each phase would be less costly because they would undertake several consecutive days (even weeks) of work which, in turn, reduces their set-up costs on a job.

- *Jobbing* would be the appropriate process where specific alterations or additions to a standard design were requested and agreed. Here, skilled staff such as bricklayers and joiners would receive drawings, interpret them and be fully responsible for fulfilling the specification(s) and checking the results.

4 Jobbing, batch and line

These are the processes from which most companies choose and, again, they often choose more than one to best meet their needs, as illustrated in Figure 5.12. This shows that typically companies make components or parts in batch processes, while using line to assemble products. For example, the body panels for a Honda Civic will be made on a press. This will be set to make the left body panel, stopped and reset to make the right body panel and so on. However, Honda uses line to assemble the car.

5 What comprises volume?

Because volume is one of the fundamental factors in choosing appropriate processes, it is important to clarify the meaning of volume. When choosing an appropriate process, the following dimensions of volume are involved:

- Order quantity, that is, how many products are to be made at one time on the process. Because jobbing typically involves making an order quantity of one for each product ordered, the order quantity is low, whereas line is high because the order quantity comprises the total number of products made during the life of the process. In vehicle production, the order quantity is the total number of automobiles processed over the length of time the assembly line is in place. The order quantity, in reality, is the combined volumes over that time period.
- Volume is a combination of order quantity × unit time. The time taken to make the left body panel of the car is far less than to assemble the car itself, and so, although the quantity of left-hand body panels and cars is the same, the panel is lower volume than the car and hence more suited to batch.

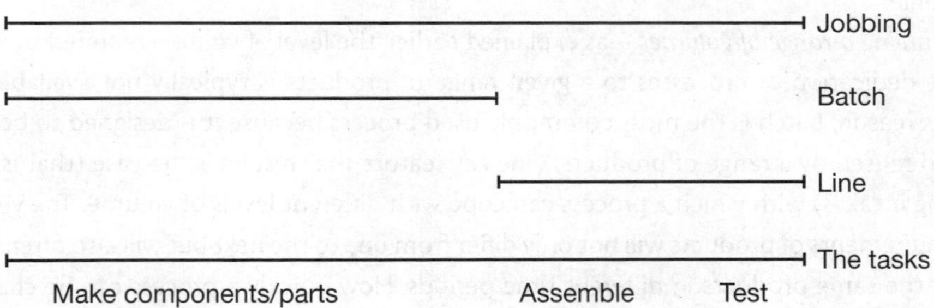

Figure 5.12 Tasks undertaken by jobbing, batch and line processes

Source: Hill, A. and Hill, T. (2012) Operations Management, *3rd edn, Palgrave Macmillan.*

6 Widening the product range to increase volumes

Several factors in today's markets have eroded demand for individual products and with it the volume to be processed by operations. Foremost among these factors is overcapacity within market sectors and the increasing difference rather than increasing similarity demanded by today's markets. One result is that companies have had to rethink process configurations, both in terms of the overall capacity (how many products in total a facility can produce) and the range of products that a process can make (the product range dimension of flexibility).

7 The dimensions of flexibility

One trend is to describe process capability as 'flexible' and 'agile'. Although these words capture the essence of the overall dimension being described, such descriptions embody several important distinctions. It is better, therefore, to set aside these single-word descriptions and use one that reflects the specific dimensions of process capability involved. As you will see from the list below, the dimensions differ markedly one from another, both in terms of their strategic relevance (the aspect of market advantage to which they relate) and how the investment spend would be directed. To achieve an improvement in any of the following aspects will result in more investment, so knowing the cost/benefit mix involved is an essential part of the decision.

In each of these dimensions of flexibility, companies need to assess how well a process can, and needs to, respond to the aspect of change involved, while recognizing that the flexibility factor will typically have both process and people skill implications:

- *Introduction of new products* – this aspect of flexibility concerns the ability of the operations process to handle new product introductions. These are vital to the long-term success of any business and operations is one of the functions that plays a key role in the overall process.
- *Handling a range of products* – most, if not all, companies produce a range of products and product options. Even Ford, with its Model T car and 'any colour as long as it's black' approach of the 1920s, was soon replaced by General Motors and its willingness to provide choice. The process flexibility to handle these dimensions is, in most markets, a key factor in the successful growth of a business because it reflects the nature of today's demand profile.
- *Handling a range of volumes* – as explained earlier, the level of volume required to justify the dedication of processes to a given range of products is typically not available. For this reason, batch is the most commonly used process because it is designed to be used and reused by a range of products. One key feature that results is the ease (that is, how long it takes) with which a process can cope with different levels of volume. The volume requirements of products will not only differ from one to the next but will also often differ for the same products in different time periods. How quickly a process can be changed from one product to another will directly impact on the loss of potential outputs while the process change is taking place – the shorter the changeovers, the more flexible the process.

- *Meeting demand peaks* – the demand for many products has a seasonality dimension. This aspect of flexibility concerns how easily the process can be ramped up to cope with sudden increases in demand.

Other non-process dimensions of being responsive (such as meeting changes in customer delivery schedules) are accomplished not through process investment but, in this example, through developing a system that can handle the rescheduling of delivery dates.

The key factors in managing the need for flexibility are to:

- Specify what dimension is involved – it brings clarity in analysis and prevents confusion in communication through a business.
- Identify where the investment needs to be made. This helps to ensure that the investment is appropriate to the need and that unnecessary investment is minimized.

8 The use of batch to best meet the requirements of most companies

As explained in points 2 and 4, for most companies the choice is between jobbing, batch and line and, of the three, batch is the most commonly used process. The reason is the nature of today's markets. Special products (using jobbing) and mass products (using line) are not commonplace. Demand for specials is limited, while the increasing level of difference required in today's markets has eroded volumes. For these reasons, batch is the most commonly used process because most companies make standard products, but not in volumes that would justify investing in line. Instead, companies invest in and develop processes that can be used and reused by a range of products. In this way, they are able to make a range of products whose volumes vary.

9 Unproductive and productive time

In batch processes and important insight when evaluating its use and fit is to recognize that as the process is stopped and reset for each different product, the use of the process capacity is categorized in three ways:

- *Unproductive time* – the utilization of the capacity is unproductive in nature. A classic example of this category is a machine breakdown.
- *Non-saleable productive time* – the capacity is being used in a productive way but the outcome is non-saleable. Examples here include making samples and resetting the process for the next product. The time spent on samples is a productive use of the resource but the output cannot be sold. Similarly, setting up a process for another product is productive (it has to be done) but again the outcome does not result in saleable output.
- *Saleable productive time* – completed products that will be sold to customers.

The non-saleable productive time element of this mix of outputs is a characteristic of batch since the process will need to be reset for each different product. Keeping the ratio between non-saleable and saleable productive time in balance is most important for a business. If the non-saleable percentage increases, saleable output goes down, which will have an adverse effect on sales and profits.

MARKETS AND PRODUCT VOLUMES

As emphasized throughout the preceding sections, the underlying factor in choosing which of the five processes is most appropriate to manufacturing a product is volume (that is, quantity × work content). It is important, therefore, to distinguish what is meant by volume.

Although companies express forecast sales in terms of a period (typically a year), operations does not make annual volumes – it makes order quantities. Thus contracts which are based on agreed total sales in a given period, but not the size of actual orders (or call-offs), can be very misleading. On the other hand, in order to enhance volume, operations often cumulates orders from different customers (using order backlog/forward load principles) or decides to make products to go into finished goods inventory to be sold in the future. The choice is restricted by the degree of customization of the product and factors such as current forward load, seasonality of sales and lead times in supplying customers' requirements. Hence, in Figure 5.4 (p. 161), process choice was plotted against order quantities or volumes placed on operations.

As explained earlier, the term 'flexibility' is used to describe several different requirements. One concerns the ability of a process to make different levels of volume at required levels of cost. In turn, cost considerations concern the relationship between set-up and process time. Thus, where a company experiences reducing order volumes but has already invested in a high-volume process designed to manufacture products at fast output speeds, it will need appropriate investment to ensure that it can keep set-up times sufficiently short to maintain the order quantity (number of hours to make) to set-up time (number of hours to complete) ratio at an acceptable level. Research work in many manufacturing companies provides numerous illustrations of where annual sales for a product may be similar to those in the past but actual order quantities (or call-offs) have reduced significantly. The link between this section and the previous one is fundamental in terms of process investment.

TECHNICAL SPECIFICATION VERSUS BUSINESS SPECIFICATION

As volumes increase, so the justification increases for investing in processes dedicated to making that product. High utilization of plant underpins this investment rationale. Similarly, if processes will not be highly utilized by one product, they need to be chosen so that they can meet the operations and business needs of other products. Therefore, when choosing processes, firms need to distinguish between the technology required to make a product and the way the product is made. On the one hand, the process technology choice concerns the engineering dimension of providing a process that will form, shape, cut and so forth a product to the size and tolerances required (the technical specification). On the other hand, the operations dimension concerns determining the best way to make a product. This decision needs to be based on volumes and relevant order-winners and qualifiers (the business specification) – see Figure 5.13. As volumes rise, the appropriate choice will change, as illustrated in Figure 5.4 (p. 161).

When companies invest in processes, they typically specify the technical requirements. This is recognized as fundamental, and appropriately so. On the other hand, they typically fail to specify the business requirements that the process investment has to meet – a factor crucial

Specification	Responsible function
Technical specification The fundamental requirements of a product including its physical dimensions	Research and development or engineering
Business specification The order quantities and relevant order-winners and qualifiers of the markets in which it competes	Operations

Figure 5.13 The constituents of customer orders when choosing processes and the function for their provision

to the success of a firm. In the past, operations has failed to develop these critical, strategic arguments and insights in part because it failed to recognize its role. The consequences for many companies have been serious, leading to premature reinvestment of a considerable size or even the closing down of parts of its business. Evaluating the choice of these investments against the single dimension of the technical specification has led to inappropriate decisions, based on the narrow base of technology. Operations management's failure to realize that it is the custodian of these decisions has indirectly supported this approach.

The choice of process needs to be understood, not in engineering terms (the technical specification), but in terms of operations constraints and other dimensions of the business specification. Understanding how well a process can support the order-winners of a product, the implications of the process for a company's infrastructure and other relevant investments is fundamental to this strategic decision. These issues are dealt with in the following section.

BUSINESS IMPLICATIONS OF PROCESS CHOICE

It has already been explained that market characteristics (order-winners and qualifiers) and product volumes are underlying factors in choosing the appropriate process. In addition, the nature of the product is also a factor in the decision regarding project and continuous processing, as shown in Figure 5.10.

With this in mind, let's now review the procedure to follow when selecting the appropriate manufacturing process:

1 The initial step reviews the technology/engineering alternatives to meet the technical requirements of the product.
2 At this juncture, the technology/engineering dimension finishes and the operations/business dimension starts. Phase 1 of the second step is to assess the market/volume dimension. This then forms the basis for choosing which process is appropriate to best meet the essential needs of the business. Using Figure 5.14 as an illustration, Phase 1 links volumes to the choice of process, while Phase 2 introduces the corresponding manufacturing and business implications of the many dimensions of process choice which are represented on

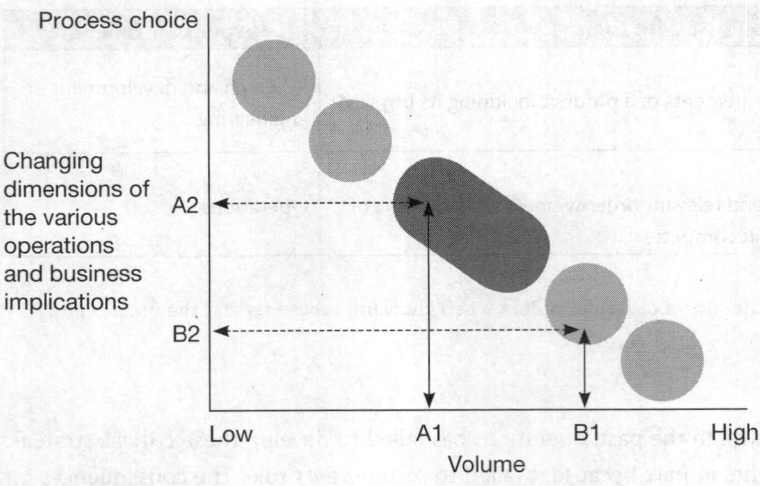

Phase 1 links the market/volume to the process choice.

Phase 2 picks up the corresponding operations and business implications of the many dimensions of process choice. The diagram shows volumes A1 and B1, the appropriate process choice and their corresponding points on the operations and business implications dimension, A2 and B2.

Figure 5.14 The operations and business dimension phases involved in process choice

the vertical axis. Figure 5.14 shows alternative volumes A1 and B1, the appropriate process choice and their corresponding points on the manufacturing and business implications, A2 and B2.

3 The final step is an iterative process that assesses the sets of dimensions and any constraints involved when deciding on the appropriate manufacturing process to use.

While companies incorporate the technical dimensions, most do not include the operations and business dimensions in such decisions. Engineering proposals currently underpin the major part of process investment decisions, which, in turn, are based on the forecast market volumes that form part of the corporate marketing strategy. The operations and business implications embodied in a proposal are typically given scant recognition. But it is these issues that bind operations and regulate its ability to respond to the needs of markets and customers. Once the investment is made, not only are the processes fixed but so also is the whole of the operations infrastructure. The result is that this decision dictates the extent to which operations can support the needs of the marketplace – an essential factor in the short- and long-term success of a business.

When Phase 1 in Figure 5.14 is completed, the choice of process is designated, while, by definition, it also stipulates the position on the vertical dimensions that will accrue as a result. Hence Phase 2 is inextricably tied to Phase 1. For this fundamental reason, decisions in Phase 1 cannot be taken in isolation. The choice has to embrace both Phase 1 and Phase 2. Only in this way will an organization avoid falling into the Cyclopean trap from which it may take years to extricate itself. Only in this way will a business take into account the short- and long-term implications that emanate from the decision to manufacture using one choice of process as opposed to another.

To help explain the business implications of process choice, Figure 5.15 separates the perspectives involved into four categories – products and markets, operations, investment and cost, and infrastructure. Furthermore, the issues for illustration and discussion have been chosen on the basis of their overall business importance. However, many other issues are equally important to understand, and these have distinct operational rather than strategic overtones.[5]

The critical issue embodied in Figure 5.15 is how each perspective changes between one choice of process and another. Thus, when a company decides to invest in a process, it will also have determined the corresponding point on each dimension within these four categories. It is necessary for companies to understand this and be aware of the trade-offs embodied in that choice.

Figure 5.15 contains many generalized statements that are intended to relate the usual requirements of one type of process to the other four. The reason for this approach is to help explain the implications of these choices and examine the consequences that will normally follow. In almost all instances, there is an arrow between jobbing and line. This is intended to indicate that, as a process moves from jobbing to low-volume batch to high-volume batch through to line, the particular characteristic will change from one form to the other.

Companies selling products typically made using the project process will need to make decisions on how much is made away from the site and transported in. For instance, many parts of a civil engineering structure are made off site by jobbing, batch or line processes, then brought in as required. Similarly, products with the fluid, semifluid or gaseous characteristics necessary to be suited to continuous processing may also be made on a batch process basis. Thus, the changing business characteristics displayed in Figure 5.15 illustrate the sets of alternatives embodied in these choices as well.

Finally, Figure 5.15 has been arranged to illustrate the linked relationship between jobbing, batch and line choices as opposed to the more distinct process–product relationship existing in project and continuous processing, described earlier. The section that follows adopts this division.

THE BUSINESS IMPLICATIONS IN MORE DETAIL

We will now further explain the implications of the dimensions provided in Figure 5.15. The four categories of products and markets, operations, investment and cost, and infrastructure are explained under each of the process choice headings, helping to link them. To emphasize the separate natures of project and continuous processing and the linked natures of jobbing, batch and line, we discuss project first, followed by jobbing, batch and line in one general section, and then continuous processing at the end. Despite their link, jobbing, batch and line differ from each other and so each is discussed in a separate subsection. However, since batch often links the change in dimensions between jobbing and line, these two processes are discussed before batch in order to describe batch within its overall perspective.

Aspects	Typical characteristics of process choice				
	Project	Jobbing	Batch	Line	Continuous processing
Products and markets					
Type of product	Specials/small range of standards	Specials	→	Standard products	Standard products
Product range	Wide	Wide	→	Narrow	Very narrow
Customer order size	Small	Small	→	Large	Very large
Level of product change required	High	High	→	Low and within agreed options	None
Rate of new product introductions	High	High	→	Low	Very low
What does a company sell?	Capability	Capability	→	Standard products/ commodities	Standard products/ commodities
How are orders won?					
Order-winners	Delivery speed/unique capability	Delivery speed/unique capability/repeat business	→	Price	Price
Qualifiers	Price/on-time delivery/ quality conformance	Price/on-time delivery/ quality conformance	On-time delivery/ quality conformance	On-time delivery/quality conformance	On-time delivery/quality conformance
Operations					
Nature of the process	Oriented towards general purpose	General purpose	→	Dedicated	Highly dedicated
Process flexibility	High	High	→	Low	Inflexible
Operations volumes	Low	Low	→	High	Very high
Dominant utilization	Mixed	Labour	→	Plant	Plant
Changes in capacity	Incremental	Incremental	→	Stepped change	New facility
Key operations task	To meet specification/ delivery schedules	Responsive to changes in specification/delivery date requirements and changes	→	Low-cost operations	Low-cost operations

Investment and cost					
Level of capital investment	Variable	Low	→	High	Very high
Level of inventory					
Components/raw materials	As required	As required/low	Often medium	Planned with buffer stocks/low	Planned with buffer stocks
Work-in-progress	High[1]	High[1]	Very high	Low	Low
Finished goods	Low	Low	→	High[2]	High[3]
Percentage of total costs					
Direct labour	Low	High	→	Low	Very low
Direct materials	High	Low	→	High	Very high
Site/plant overheads	Low	Low	→	High	High
Infrastructure					
Appropriate organizational					
Control	Decentralized/ centralized	Decentralized	→	Centralized	Centralized
Style	Entrepreneurial	Entrepreneurial	→	Bureaucratic	Bureaucratic
Most important operations management perspective	Technical know-how	Technical know-how	→	Business	Technology
Level of specialist support to operations	High	Low	→	High	Very high

Notes

1 *This would depend on stage payment arrangements.*
2 *However, many businesses here only make against customer schedules or on receipt of a customer order.*
3 *The finished goods inventory in, for instance, oil refining is stored in the post-processing stages of distribution and at the point of sale.*

Figure 5.15 Selected business implications of process choice

Project

Products and markets

Companies choosing project processes sell capability. They sell their experience, know-how and skills to provide for a customer's individual needs. Hence they are in a market that will require a high level of product change and new product introductions. Its product range will be wide, with low unit-sales volume. It will win orders on aspects such as unique design capability or delivery speed, with price normally acting as a qualifier rather than an order-winner. As a consequence of the competitive nature of today's markets, criteria such as quality conformance and on-time delivery have typically changed from being order-winners to qualifiers, as signalled by their presence in all types of market.

Operations

Oriented towards general purpose equipment, with specialist plant to meet particular product, design or structural features, project processes are highly flexible in coping with the low product volumes of the market and design changes that will occur during production. Changes in capacity mix, or in total, can be made incrementally, with the key tasks being on-time completion and meeting the specification as laid down by the customer.

Investment and cost

The capital investment in plant and other processes will tend to be low, but there will be some high-cost items that may be purchased or hired, depending on their potential usage, availability, costs and similar factors. Due to the opportunity to schedule materials, the inventory at this stage will be on an as-required basis. Work-in-progress levels will be high but normally much of this will be passed on to customers through stage payment agreements. In a make-to-order situation, finished goods inventory will be low, with immediate delivery on completion. The key cost will normally be materials, and sound purchasing arrangements, material usage and work-in-progress control are essential.

Infrastructure

Because of the uncertainties in the process and the need to respond quickly to any customer-derived changes, the organizational control should be decentralized and supported by an entrepreneurial, rather than a bureaucratic, style. In addition, once the business grows, the company must centrally control the key items of plant, internal specialist/engineering skills and other outsourced commodities or skills to ensure they are effectively scheduled by project and between projects. The operations manager must understand the relevant technology to appreciate and respond to unforeseen difficulties and problems, both technical and non-technical, and to use the local and centrally based specialist support effectively.

Jobbing

Products and markets

In essence, a jobbing business sells its capability to manufacture a customer's requirements. It is restricted only by the range of skills of its workforce or by its process capabilities. Thus it handles a wide product range, competing on aspects other than price. This does not mean that a business can charge any price it decides. But if the price is within what is reasonable for the market – and that includes provisions for post-contract changes such as shorter lead times and post-start modifications – then price is a qualifier rather than an order-winner.

Operations

As a consequence of the products it provides and markets it serves, the operations process must be flexible. Its major concern is the utilization of its high-skilled staff, with equipment being purchased to facilitate the skilled operator to complete the task. Changes in capacity can be achieved incrementally. The order backlog position that exists in make-to-order markets will allow operations to undertake any foreseen adjustments in capacity ahead of time. The key operations task is to complete the item to specification and on time, since normally this one-off item, as far as the customer is concerned, forms an integral part of some greater business whole.

Investment and cost

Although some of the equipment used in jobbing can be very expensive, generally this investment is low compared to batch and line. In addition, materials will tend to be purchased only when an order has been received, with material delivery forming part of the total operations lead time. Work-in-progress inventory will be high, with jobs typically involving long process lead times, while the make-to-order nature of its business means that products are dispatched once completed. There will tend to be few specialist and other support functions, which leads to a relatively low plant/site overhead cost. These specialist tasks will be largely part of the skilled worker's role which, together with the high labour content, normally makes this the highest portion of total costs. Material costs will tend to be low; any expensive materials involved will invariably be on a customer-supplied (free issue) basis.

Infrastructure

Organizational control and style need to be decentralized and entrepreneurial in nature, so as to respond quickly and effectively to meet the inherent flexibility requirements of this market. For this reason, the operations executives have to understand the technology involved because this forms an important part of their contribution to business decisions (for example, in accepting an order, agreeing estimated costs and resulting prices, confirming a delivery quotation, providing part of the specialist inputs into a business and agreeing customer-derived changes while estimating the additional costs and lead times involved).

Line

Products and markets

A line process reflects the other end of the spectrum to jobbing. The business sells standard products, associated with large customer orders or small orders from many customers for the same products and with price typically an order-winner. The level of product change afforded to a customer is usually prescribed within a list of options; outside this, the product is not normally available. Product design is determined at the outset to meet the perceived needs of the customer, with on-time delivery a qualifier in today's markets.

Operations

To provide low operations costs, the process is dedicated to a predetermined range of products. It is not geared to be flexible outside this range, due to the high costs of change. This provides the opportunity to maintain the necessary quality conformance levels throughout the process. Operations volumes need to be high to achieve the level of plant utilization necessary to justify the investment and to underpin the cost structures involved. As explained earlier, it is the cumulative volume of products made within a period that constitutes the volume dimension justifying investments. Output changes are more difficult to arrange, due to the stepped change nature of capacity alterations.

Investment and cost

The key to low operations costs is high process investment, which goes hand in hand with line. The volumes involved allow schedules of raw materials and components to be planned with associated buffer stocks to cover the uncertainty of supply. Work-in-progress inventory will be low. Although finished goods will tend to be high, many businesses, as part of a decision to keep inventory investment as low as possible, will only make standard products against customer schedules or on receipt of an order. Also, products offering many optional extras (such as motor vehicles) will tend to have a policy of only making to a specific order. Hence, even in times of relatively low sales, if the new car selected includes an unusual set of options and, consequently, is unlikely to have been built in anticipation of an early sale, delivery will be delayed. Finally, the high areas of cost tend to be in materials, bought-out components and site/plant overheads, with direct labour a relatively small part of the total.

Infrastructure

Since the choice of a line process represents a high-volume business, then a more centralized organization, controlled by systems, is more appropriate. On the operations side, the key operations executive task concerns the business aspects of the job, with specialist support providing the technical know-how for products and processes.

Batch

Products and markets

Batch comes between jobbing and line. This is chosen to cover a very wide range of volumes, as illustrated by the elongated shape depicted in, among others, Figures 5.4, 5.11 and 5.14. Batch links the low-volume/high-volume, special/standard products and make-to-order/make-to-stock businesses. In most instances, the choice of batch, rather than jobbing, as the appropriate way to manufacture products signals that operations volumes (that is, quantity × work content) have increased and are of a repeat nature but insufficient to dedicate processes solely to them, as would be the case in line. Some unique high-volume orders may also be done on a batch basis.

At the low-volume end of batch, the processes are able to cope with a high degree of product change and a high level of new product introductions. Here, the business is oriented towards selling capability, with price starting to become a more important order-winner, due to the volume and repeat nature of the products. At the high-volume end of batch, products have become increasingly standard, order sizes larger and product change lower, all of which illustrate the shift in product market characteristics toward line. As mentioned earlier, market pressures have typically changed quality conformance and on-time delivery from order-winners to qualifiers.

Operations

It can be deduced from the product/market features that batch processes usually have to cope with a wide range of products and operations volumes. To handle this task, these processes must be of a general nature, offering a high degree of flexibility. With some items of equipment, the utilization will be low; with others, equipment will have been purchased to meet the needs of a product or to offer distinct process advantages (for example, numerical control machines, machining centres and flexible manufacturing systems, each of which will be described in a later section). In these instances, high investment will normally be justified on a usage basis and the aim will be to utilize the capacity to the fullest.

To help underpin the total process investment, many companies adopt a deliberate policy of increasing the utilization of equipment in three ways:

1 Putting a wide range of products through the same set of processes.
2 Manufacturing many of the same products in a single order quantity or batch quantity (hence the name). In this way, the number of set-ups is reduced, which decreases the setting-up costs and increases effective capacity.
3 Making products wait for processes to become available. This policy, together with the order quantity decisions above, leads to a work-in-progress inventory investment that, in relation to the size of the business, tends to be very high compared to jobbing and, particularly, line.

Investment and cost

To be competitive in markets moving towards the high-volume end, a business will increasingly invest in its batch processes to achieve the low operations cost requirement of these markets. Many companies exploit this still further by putting more products through the same processes, thus increasing overall utilization. However, the major trade-off associated with this policy is the very high investment in work-in-progress inventory that typically results. The raw materials, components and finished goods inventory levels will in turn be associated with the make-to-order or make-to-stock decision adopted by the business. As with all companies in these mid-volume markets, the nearer it is to a make-to-order situation, the more the characteristics of that market will prevail and vice versa. The make-up of total costs is no exception.

Infrastructure

As a business moves away from the low-volume end of the continuum, centralized controls and a bureaucratic style become more appropriate. The increasing complexity of this growth will change the nature of the specialist functions, with design and production engineering becoming an ever-important support to manufacturing. The operations manager's role will be bound up with appreciating and recognizing the critical business issues involved, providing coordination throughout and spearheading the development of manufacturing systems.

At the low-volume end of batch, in many situations the characteristics, although not the same, will be more akin to those in jobbing. It is important, therefore, to recognize the extent and trends in these changes and make the necessary adjustments.

Continuous processing

Markets and products

At the other end of the volume spectrum, companies that choose continuous processing will sell a narrow range of standard products in markets where product change and the rate of product introductions are low. The company will sell standard products rather than capability and large customer orders will be won principally on price.

Operations

In a price-sensitive market, the key operations task will be low-cost production. To help keep costs low, processes will be highly dedicated, with the cost structure based on high production volumes, leading to a need to achieve high plant utilization. The fixed nature of capacity also creates restrictions when increases or decreases in output are required, with the decision based on whether or not to build a new facility on the one hand or how often to run the plant (known as 'campaigning') on the other.

Investment and cost

The high plant investment and high-volume output associated with continuous processing offers the opportunity to keep raw material inventory on a planned usage basis, with built-in buffer stocks to cover uncertainties. Work-in-progress will be relatively low, with inventory in finished goods high. This is because of the need to maintain output levels at all times against fluctuating sales patterns. In many cases, however, finished goods are held in the extensive distribution system of a business and sometimes at its own retail outlets (for example, petrol stations).

Owing to the high process investment, direct labour costs are small, with the highest cost usually in materials. Site/plant overheads in this process will be high owing to the need to support the process and handle the high output levels involved.

Infrastructure

The high-volume nature of these businesses lends itself to a centralized, bureaucratic organization control and style. Operations performance is measured against budgets, variance analysis is the order of the day and investment proposals are centrally monitored.

An understanding of the process and product technology is important when running a production unit, together with the ability to coordinate the high level of specialist support provided for operations.

AN OVERVIEW OF PROCESS CHOICE

To help clarify the issues involved in process choice, we now present an overview of how these alternatives link to one another. The first important fact to stress is that each of the choices embodies a totally different approach to manufacturing a product. Although described in some detail in the chapter, a short explanation of these differences will serve to reinforce this important point.

- **Project** – is used for one-off products that have to be built on site because it is difficult or impossible to move them once they have been made. Consequently, the resources involved need to be brought to the site and released for reuse elsewhere when they are no longer needed.
- **Jobbing** – for one-off products that can be moved once completed, jobbing is normally the preferred process. The responsibility for making the product is typically given to a skilled person, who decides how best to make it and then completes all or most of the operations involved, including checking quality conformance at each stage.
- **Batch** – with an increase in volumes and the repeat nature of products, companies select batch as the effective way to meet the requirements involved. Because the products are repeated, with a corresponding increase in volumes, companies can now invest at each of the manufacturing steps. This includes engineering time to decide how best to make a product, tooling to facilitate the completion of certain operations and equipment purchased with an eye to making these and other products with similar characteristics. However, the volumes involved do not warrant the purchase of dedicated equipment. The operations necessary to complete a product are, therefore, not linked and are said to be 'decoupled'.
- **Line** – when demand is sufficient to justify dedicating equipment solely to making a specified range of products, a line process is normally chosen. The operations necessary to complete a specified range of products are linked together so that each product goes from one operation directly to the next and so on. The operations necessary to complete a product in this instance are said to be 'coupled'. The operators involved will physically take part in assembling the products.
- **Continuous processing** – when the demand for a product is such that the volume required necessitates a process being used all day and every day, further investment is justified. The equipment in this instance is designed to automatically transfer the product from one stage to the next, check the quality conformance within the process and make adjustments where necessary. The investment associated with this is warranted by the volumes involved.

To emphasize these distinctions, Figure 5.16 shows the gap between the five choices. It also makes the point that, whereas there will sometimes be a transition from jobbing to low-volume batch, from low-volume to high-volume batch, from high-volume batch to line or from high-volume batch to continuous processing, the same will not apply between project and jobbing or from line to continuous processing. Similarly, when volumes reduce towards the end of a product's life cycle, the reverse movement may take place, but again it would only go as illustrated in Figure 5.16.

Some comments on Figure 5.16 may help to clarify. Transition refers to the fact that, as volumes increase or decrease, a business should ideally change its choice of operations to realign its process to the new levels of volume. The degree of transition is limited because many companies find themselves unable, or unwilling, to commit the fresh investment necessary to complete this realignment.[6] Thus, a motor vehicle manufacturer will use a jobbing process at the prototyping stage of product development but will invest just once to meet the commercial volumes of mainstream production. In the same way, a manufacturer of products that lend themselves to being produced using continuous processing (for example, fluids and gases), but with insufficient volumes to justify the high investment associated with this choice, will handle these requirements by using a high-volume batch process. Similarly, when demand falls for products currently made by continuous processing, the system will be managed on a high-volume batch basis by, say, running the process for three months, stopping it for three months, running it for three months and so on. This is known as 'campaigning' and is illustrated by the movement from D1 to D2 in Figure 5.16.

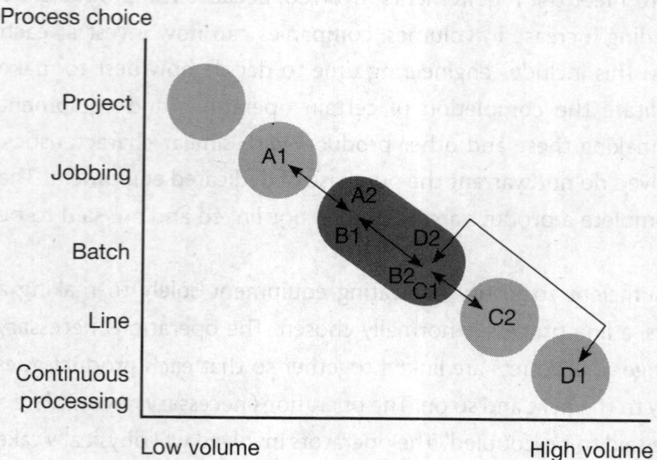

This shows four potential volume transitions that typically may face a business. The first example shows a move from one-off (unique), low-volume (A1) to repeat order, low-volume demand (A2) for a product or vice versa and the change in operations process that should ideally accompany this movement. Examples B1 to B2, C1 to C2 and D1 to D2 show similar demand changes at different points on the volume scale and require similar decisions concerning the realignment of the process choice.

Figure 5.16 Potential transitions between the different choices of process

HYBRID PROCESSES

As mentioned earlier, many companies have developed hybrid processes to enable them to better support the characteristics of their markets. Some comprise a mix of two of the five generic processes; while others are developments within an existing process type, often based on the use of numerical control (NC) machines. Some of the more important hybrid developments are now explained. Figure 5.17 shows their positions in relation to the generic processes. However, the list includes some (for example, machining centres) that have been generally applied and are provided as standard items[7] from a supplier's catalogue.

Batch-related hybrids

Numerical control (NC) machines

An NC system[8] is a process that automatically performs the required operations according to a detailed set of coded instructions. Since mathematical information is the base used, the system is called 'numerical control'. In reality, an NC machine is a development of a batch process; it is also low volume in nature. It is batch because the machine stops at the end of one process and is reset for a new job or stopped while a new program is being loaded. It is low volume because the set-up times are short, hence providing an acceptable ratio between set-up times and the length of the run before the next set-up. The position of NC machines on Figure 5.17 illustrates this.

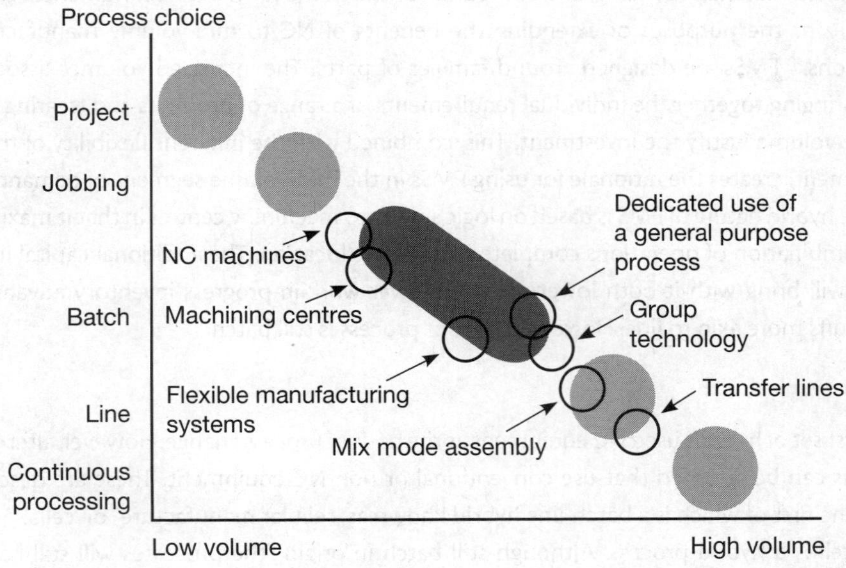

Figure 5.17 The position of some hybrid processes in relation to the five generic choices of process

Machining centres

Machining centres[13] combine the NC operations previously provided by different machines into one machine centre. Tool changing is automatically controlled by coded instructions and carousels hold the relevant range of tools. The appropriate tool is then selected and the particular operation completed. The hybrid nature of this process is that several operations are completed before the item of work is removed. Thus a machining centre completes many operations in sequence, without removing the item from the process. This reflects aspects of line within what is, in reality, still a batch process (that is, the process stops and resets itself not only between operations but between one item and the next).

Thus, machining centres are a hybrid between batch and line; as a consequence, the position on some trade-offs (see Figure 5.15) changes. For instance, work-in-progress inventory within the machining centre will decrease compared to completing the same operations at individual and unconnected work stations. Similarly, the relative level of investment will increase. As you will note, both these changes are more towards a line process, but the root process is still batch.

Flexible manufacturing systems

Whereas a machining centre is best suited to low volumes, a flexible manufacturing system (FMS) is appropriate to make mid-volume requirements – see Figure 5.17. This too is designed to complete a given number of operations on an item before it leaves the system. However, rather than the item being contained in a single centre, in an FMS the workpiece is automatically transferred from one process to the next.

Flexible manufacturing systems are a combination of standard and special NC machines, automated materials handling, and computer control in the form of direct numerical control (DNC)[9] for the purposes of extending the benefits of NC to mid-volume manufacturing situations.[10] FMSs are designed around families of parts. The increased volumes associated with bringing together the individual requirements of a range of products and treating these as one volume justify the investment. This, combined with the inherent flexibility of the NC equipment, creates the rationale for using FMSs in the mid-volume segment of demand.

The hybrid nature of FMS is based on logic similar to machining centres in that it maximizes the combination of operations completed at a single location. The additional capital investment will bring with it both lower cost and lower work-in-progress inventory advantages, trade-offs more akin to line. However, the root process is still batch.

Cells

The first set of hybrids used NC equipment as the basis of process change. However, alternative hybrids can be adopted that use conventional or non-NC equipment. These are described here, the first of which is a batch-line hybrid known as 'cellular manufacture', or 'cells'.

A cell is a hybrid process. Although still batch in origin (the processes will still have to be stopped and reset to handle a product change), they are in fact a mix of batch and line processes, offering changes on some key variables (see Figure 5.15). These include reduced lead times and lower work-in-progress inventory on the one hand and less flexible processes (it is more difficult to reuse any capacity that would become available if future demand were to reduce) and lower overall utilization of processes on the other.

Figure 5.18 shows the process or functional layout of the batch process (similar processes are grouped together in the same geographical area). The rationale underpinning cells is that grouping products together and treating them as being the same leads to an increase in volume (the volumes of all the products under consideration are added together and the aggregate is viewed as a whole) and hence justifies the allocation of processes to these products for their sole use. What happens, therefore, in cells is that the necessary processes, both in terms of capability and capacity, are allocated to the sole use of these products, with the 'dedication' being justified by the enhanced level of volume that results.

The approach involves separating out those processes that do not lend themselves to the application of cells because of factors such as the level of investment (where processes, in addition to those already available, would have to be purchased) and health considerations (for example, noise or process waste/fumes). The next step is to group together families of like products.

The third step is to determine the process configuration necessary to manufacture each product family involved and to lay out the cell to reflect the required manufacturing routings. The final stage is to complete a tooling analysis within each family, with a twofold aim. The first is to group together those parts within the family that can use the same tooling. This

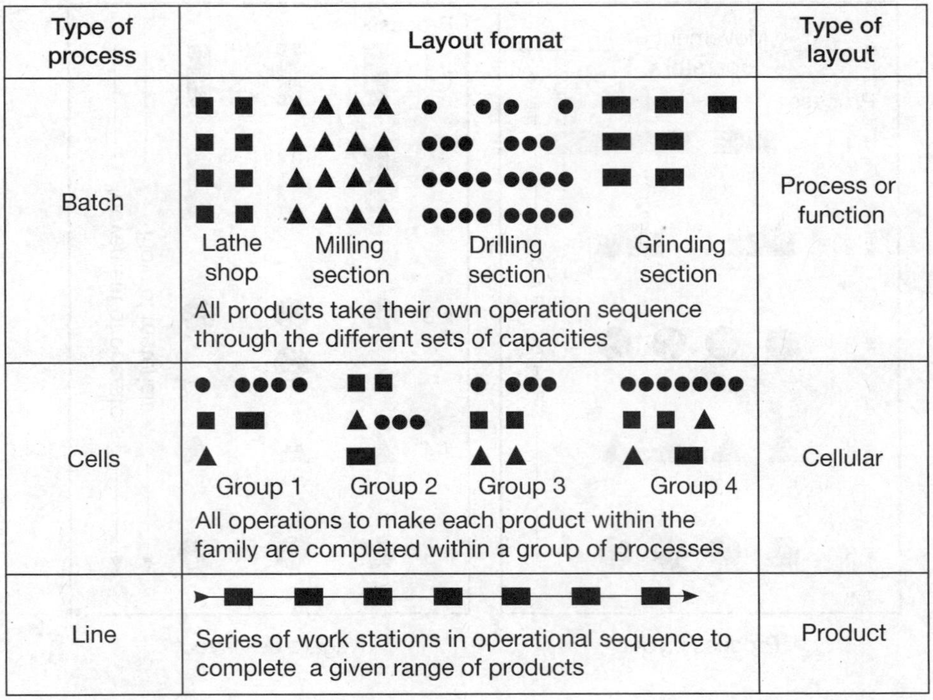

Type of process	Layout format	Type of layout
Batch	Lathe shop · Milling section · Drilling section · Grinding section All products take their own operation sequence through the different sets of capacities	Process or function
Cells	Group 1 · Group 2 · Group 3 · Group 4 All operations to make each product within the family are completed within a group of processes	Cellular
Line	Series of work stations in operational sequence to complete a given range of products	Product

Figure 5.18 Cellular layout and the transition from a functional (batch) to a product (line) layout

forms the basis for scheduling to reduce setting time. The second is to include this feature as part of the design prerequisites for future products.[11]

Nagare production system

The Nagare production system was developed within the disc brake division of Sumitomo Electric. The layout is a derivation of cells and, in the same way, provides an alternative to the process layout used in batch, as illustrated in Figure 5.19. The key differences between this system and cells are:

- The sequence of steps reflects the flow of materials in making the product.
- Operators move the part from step to step and hence complete a whole product.
- Operators typically produce to a JIT system using a Kanban-type arrangement.[12]
- The quantity of products produced at any one time is relatively small.
- The Nagare production system is ideally suited to making products that are similar to one another. This helps keep the level of change involved low and hence set-up times are reduced.

Linked batch

As with most of the developments discussed in this section, linked batch is a hybrid of batch and line. However, linked batch does not need to encompass a large number of processes, as is more typical in the previous examples. In some instances, only two or three sequential

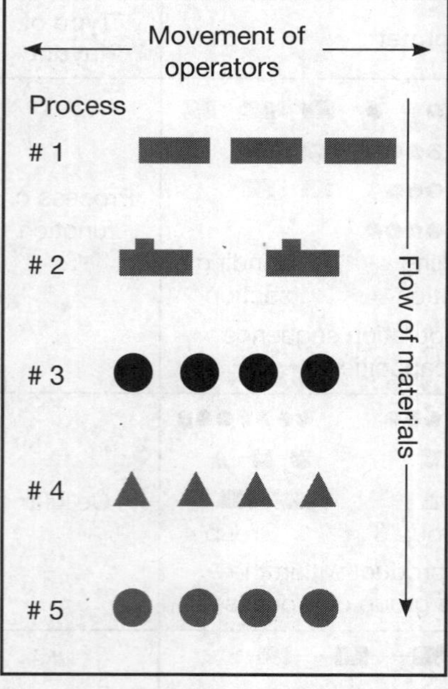

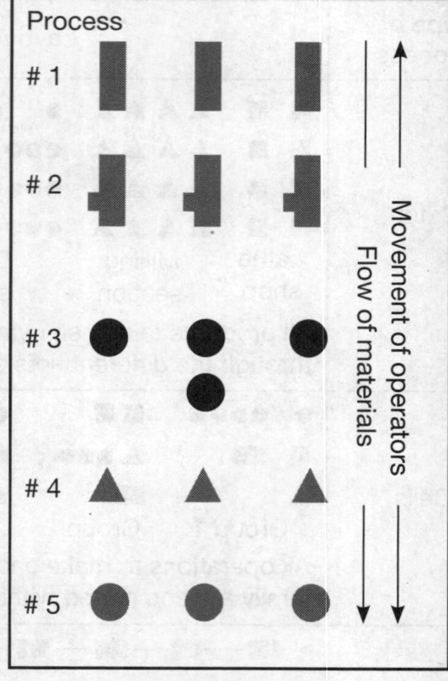

Figure 5.19 Changing from process to Nagare cell layout

Source: Hill, A. and Hill, T. (2012) Operations Management, *3rd edn, Palgrave Macmillan.*

processes may be linked; in others, for example, food packing, all of the filling and packing processes may be linked. Whereas in the other illustrations the investment decisions are typically made as part of a complete process review, linked batch is undertaken on a more piecemeal basis, with only two or three processes being linked. The sequential processes, although physically laid out in line (that is, one operation follows another), are run as a batch process (that is, when a product change is required, all the linked operations have to be stopped and reset to accommodate this change). Irrespective of the length of the set-up changes, the fact that the process has to be stopped and reset makes it a batch process.

Dedicated use of general purpose equipment

Where the volume of a specific part is sufficient, manufacturing can justify the allocation of a process to its sole use. This dedication is not in the plant itself but in the use of a general purpose process. Thus, the potential flexibility and other characteristics illustrated in Figure 5.15 of a general purpose process are retained and they will be reclaimed when volumes reduce. Characteristically, the process is not altered. Hence the process is still batch and, therefore, general purpose in nature.

Thus the hybrid stems from a change in use to reflect the high-volume demand for a product and not a physical change to the process itself. It remains a batch process, even though during the period in which its use is dedicated to the manufacture of a given product, it may be reset (for example, for colour changes) or may not be reset.

Line-related hybrids

Mix mode assembly lines

A line process can cope with a broad range of products without stopping, and, in reality, companies determine the product range to be handled when they make the process investment. However, the term 'mix mode' has been used to reflect processes in which companies have made systematic and purposeful investments to increase the product range involved. Typically this entails programming the line to make small quantities of different products in a predetermined sequence.

The origins of mix mode assembly lines are twofold. On the one hand, a reduction in demand for existing products releases capacity, which a company may wish to reuse. This, in turn, can lead to the adaptation of an existing line process to accommodate other products. On the other hand, a mix mode assembly line may be developed to handle a number of products currently completed in other ways (for example, using linked-batch processes). In this case, what makes the root a line process is that it does not have to be stopped and reset to accommodate the next product.

As can be deduced from this explanation, a mix mode assembly line is not technically a hybrid, in that the characteristics of another process have not been combined with those of line. Instead, it is a line process that can accommodate the requirements of a wider range of products than can typically be made on a classic line process. It has been included here to illustrate how process investment can change certain relevant trade-offs in a business.

Transfer lines

The last hybrid process to be discussed is transfer lines. Where the volume demand for products is very high, further investment is justified. Transfer line is a hybrid between line and continuous processing. However, its root process is still line because it can be stopped without major cost. The position of transfer lines on Figure 5.15 illustrates the features of this process. High volumes justify investment designed to reduce the manual inputs associated with a line process and to move more towards a process that automatically transfers a part from one station to the next, positions it, completes the task and then checks for quality conformance. Furthermore, deviations from the specified tolerances will be registered and automatic tooling adjustments and replacements will often be part of the procedure. To achieve this, the process is numerically controlled in part or in full, which provides the systems control afforded, in part at least, by the operator in the line process.

OPERATIONS' RESPONSES TO SIMILAR MARKETS

Different approaches are used in the same industry. Companies making similar products may choose similar processes yet manage the total operations task in significantly different ways. But, process choice, as shown in Figure 2.10, is only part of operations' strategic response. For example, providing support for the criterion of delivery speed necessitates reducing lead times throughout the supply chain and not just in the process elements of lead time (see Figure 3.12).

As explained earlier, Japanese car makers typically schedule their plants in accordance with sales forecasts and work on make-to-stock rather than on order backlog, make-to-order principles. Furthermore, given little order backlog, these companies are now offering to make and deliver a car to a customer's specifications in a much shorter time.

As stressed throughout, coherence between the many elements involved results in an integrated strategy. By raising the car specification, a company keeps options low and thereby reduces customer choice. This, in turn, leads to fewer schedule adjustments. In many instances, the automobile specified may be already planned or even in stock. Similarly, reducing lead times in all parts of the process is a significant factor (see Figure 5.20) in helping to achieve this difference.[14] Thus, recognizing the order-winners and qualifiers in relevant markets becomes the focus of activity and facilitates coherent functional support for key criteria.

TECHNOLOGY STRATEGY

Advances in computer control have brought fresh opportunities and the potential for innovation in operations is greater now than it has ever been. Advanced manufacturing technologies (AMT) have provided a viable option for sourcing manufactured components and products from other parts of the world. There is no doubt about the potential, and applications such as robotics, computer-aided design (CAD) and 3D imaging are growing at a pace year on year. The approach to the use of technology and ensuring the suitability of its application creates the most concern. Having tripped over engineering white elephants

Steps in the internal phase of the supply chain	Typical activities to reduce lead times
Customer order processing	Shorten administrative procedures
Material lead times	Purchasing-based negotiations to reduce lead times including consignment inventory arrangements
Order backlog/forward load	Adjusting short-term capacity to reduce the length of the order backlog or forward load
Process	Decreasing lead time through a combination of: • reducing set-ups • shortening process times • holding inventory to move increasingly towards an assemble-to-order and make-to-stock position
Post-process tasks	Reducing the overall time it takes to complete: • testing • packaging • despatch arrangements/documentation • delivery

Figure 5.20 Elements of operations lead time and typical actions to reduce the length of time involved

in the past should make companies understandably wary, not of technology improvements themselves, but of approaches that could lead to sizeable investments in inappropriate technologies. However, the preoccupation with the search for panaceas may well lead companies to duplicate yesterday's mistakes. Indeed, the case for a technology strategy in itself should sound warning bells. Articles advocating technology strategy comprise, for the most part, descriptions of the technologies and illustrations of specific applications and resulting improvements. However, they fail to explain how to select technological investments that best support a business to compete successfully in its markets. Without this conceptual base, companies are unable to make assessments and draw distinctions. As a result, they have to fall back on hunches or support the judgement of specialists who are invariably devotees of technological innovation and advantage, rather than business-oriented executives trying to ensure fit with the market and viewing process investment in a supportive role to this end.

To some extent, the emerging call for companies to develop technology strategies has its roots in process innovations and computer applications in operations. Historically, the clear link between operations and the marketplace, which developed in the postwar growth years, led to a well-understood operations strategy that was appropriately reflected in the activities and developments within the process, production and industrial engineering functions. Not only was the status of engineering clearly reinforced but its role also evolved so that engineers were perceived to be the custodians of determining appropriate process and investments.

FLEXIBILITY: A STRATEGIC COP-OUT?

For many businesses, past investments in dedicated processes have proved inappropriate for current markets. New investment requirements have been brought about, in part, by pressures of competition. But the response has often been to purchase new equipment with sufficient flexibility to make a wide range of products and to cope with low order-quantity requirements. However, decisions that are not based on assessments of the marketplace and evaluations of alternatives are tantamount to strategic cop-outs. 'If in doubt, resolve the doubt' has become 'if in doubt, buy flexibility'.

One company, after witnessing an overall decline in volumes throughout the parent group, committed itself to the purchase of flexible processes to cope with an environment of change. An analysis of processes, product life cycles and order-winners clearly showed that the purchase, in part, of dedicated plant would best meet these requirements. This eliminated a substantial investment on unnecessary flexibility. As another illustration, three companies, each manufacturing in different segments of engineering, were using expensive NC machines primarily on high-volume products. Discussions revealed failures in the companies to separate comparisons of the process capability necessary to hold tight tolerances (current technology versus 15- to 20-year-old machining) and the business needs of the process (low cost based on high volumes).

TECHNOLOGY PUSH VERSUS PULL STRATEGIES

Process investments can be used for either technology push or pull strategies. In a push strategy, the rationale for process investments comes from technology-based arguments; pull strategies reflect technology investments based on defined market needs. It is critical that companies with push strategies see arguments concerning the corporate potential to sell the spin-offs from the proposed technology investments as being only part of the evaluation. They must also be sure to evaluate such investments on their own merits.

OPERATIONS STRATEGY AND TECHNOLOGICAL OPPORTUNITIES

Current process innovations present an important opportunity for companies to compete effectively in world markets. However, committing scarce resources to investments based primarily on the perspectives of specialists or in search of a panacea to update and realign manufacturing presents enormous and unnecessary risks. It is essential that technology alternatives form part of operations strategy developments, as discussed in this and the previous chapter. A business must link investments with a well-argued understanding of its markets if it is to avoid inappropriate major capital expenditure.

Assessing the level of business fit when investing in processes

Assessing the level of mismatch between its current processes and current business, determining the adjustment it must or is able to achieve and making the appropriate choice of process for future products are difficult and critical operations management tasks. They are difficult, in that the decision is complex, and critical, in that the process investment will be substantial and changes will be expensive and time-consuming to implement.[15]

The nature of markets and operations

One of the core problems facing companies is that markets are inherently dynamic and operations' remit is inherently fixed. Markets are continually changing in response to internal initiatives and external pressures, while operations remains fixed in terms of the trade-offs embodied in its investments. Thus, whereas market change is an inherent outcome of time, operations will not change unless a conscious decision is made and additional investment is committed. A company that fails to regularly undertake these reviews and then commit to the outcomes will have an operations function that is less able to support its chosen markets.

Operations' strategic response

Companies have always recognized the need to embrace the engineering/technology dimension when choosing their manufacturing processes. But this is only part of the decision. The engineering input concerns providing alternative technical options that will enable a product to be manufactured to its technical specification. However, the choice of process concerns how the operations task is then completed to meet the needs of the market(s) served. Such choices need to involve the product/market, operations, investment/cost and infrastructure dimensions that were examined earlier in this chapter.

Engineering prescriptions, technology solutions seeking problems or the belief that panaceas are on hand can be instrumental, in part, for the uncompetitive position in which many manufacturing companies may find themselves. Couple this with a marketing-led strategy that may have overreached itself in some businesses or the universal impact of incremental marketing changes that, over time, have altered its business mix without a company recognizing the strategic consequences involved and the result is the erosion of its traditional markets by more responsive competitors. Other companies, persuaded by the apparent desirability of new markets or the short-term solution to get out of tough manufacturing industries, have also left the way clear in these high-volume, established markets. However, there is no long-term future in easy operations tasks. The short run may appear attractive but learning and relearning how to be competitive is essential to the long-term wellbeing of companies and nations.

Successful manufacturing nations have been systematically picking off many of the existing markets of long-established industrial nations by a combined marketing/operations strategy thus creating, at the expense of their competitors, a sound industrial base essential to a nation's long-term prosperity and growth. The Japanese have, in fact, built their manufacturing base on traditional smokestack industries. And, more recently emerging nations have been doing the same.

CASE STUDY

Cirque du Soleil

Cirque du Soleil is a phenomenal success story. Since the 1980s, it has redefined the circus industry, created its own market, toured all over the world, performed to over 100 million people and received numerous prizes and awards. By combining the traditional elements of circus and performance, it attracts people who normally go to the theatre and leaves them in awe. In 2016, it had sales of over $850 million and employed almost 5,000 people (see Case Figure 5.1).

HISTORY

Cirque du Soleil was founded in 1984 by three former street performers, Guy Laliberté, Gilles Ste-Croix and Daniel Gauthier. Laliberté chose the name 'soleil' (French for sun) because he saw it as a symbol of youth, energy, power and light. Since then, Cirque has grown from strength to strength, collaborating with organizations such as The Beatles, Elvis Presley Enterprises, The Michael Jackson Company, Live Nation, MGM and Walt Disney (see Case Figure 5.2) to create 31 shows (see Case Figure 5.3), 12 special events (see Case Figure 5.4) and 35 films, documentaries and TV series (see Case Figure 5.5).

While its shows become more sophisticated each year, Cirque has never strayed from its street performer roots. Rather than trying to create thrills using animals and star performers such as traditional 'three-ring' circuses, Cirque's rich and elegant shows tell a story using live music and artistry in glamorous tents with comfortable seating. As a result, it attracts adults who normally go to the theatre rather than children and families (the traditional circus customer).

Performance	2002	2004	2006	2008	2010	2012	2014	2016
Sales ($million)	452	503	618	733	846	943	852	862
Employees	2,397	2,934	3,236	4,822	5,020	5,234	4,834	4,836
Shows								
Residencies	3	4	6	10	11	11	10	9
Tent tours	5	5	6	7	6	7	6	7
Arena tours	–	–	1	1	4	4	4	5
Total	8	9	13	18	21	22	20	21
Tickets (million)								
Residencies	3	4	5	7	8	8	7	7
Tent tours	3	3	3	4	3	4	4	4
Arena tours	–	–	–	–	2	2	2	2
Total	6	7	8	11	13	14	13	13

Note: All figures in this case study are in US$.

Case Figure 5.1 Cirque's performance (2002–16)

Date	Development
1984	Founded by three former street performers, Guy Laliberté, Gilles Ste-Croix and Daniel Gauthier, using a grant from the Quebec government
1986	Toured Canada, but was a flop leaving it with $750,000 of debt. Gained additional grant from Quebec government
1987	Performed outside Canada at the Los Angeles Arts Festival. Columbia Pictures wished to make a movie about it, but Laliberté didn't want to lose artistic control
1990	The *Nouvelle Experience* show toured for 19 months across 13 cities in the US and Canada for four to five weeks at a time in 2,500-seat tent and tickets selling for $35. 1.3 million people saw the show
1991	Performed in Asia for the first time (sponsored by Fuji TV) and in Switzerland (partnered with Circus Knie)
1992	Entered a 12-month contract with Mirage Resorts Inc. to perform the *Nouvelle Experience* show at the Mirage Resort (Las Vegas)
1993	Entered a 10-year contract with Mirage Resorts Inc. to continue performing *Nouvelle Experience* at the Mirage Resort (Las Vegas) and develop the *Mystère* show for the Treasure Island Resort (Las Vegas). This provided Cirque with its first steady source of revenue
1995	Established its European headquarters in Amsterdam and started its first European tour with the *Saltimbanco* show
1997	Set up a $22 million 'Creation Studio' in Montreal for rehearsals, costume design and as its headquarters. Mirage Resorts Inc. built a theatre for Cirque at the Bellagio Resort (Las Vegas). Entered a contract with Disney who built them a theatre at Disney World (Florida)
1998	Laliberté bought out Gauthier's share of the business for $200 million (giving him 95% ownership). The *O* show opened at the Bellagio Resort (Las Vegas) and the *La Nouba* show at Disney World (Florida)
2000	MGM acquired Mirage Resorts Inc. and asked Cirque to develop the *KÀ* show for the MGM Grand resort (Las Vegas)
2004	Contracted with The Beatles to develop the *Love* show for the Mirage Resort (Las Vegas)
2006	Contracted with Live Nation to launch *Delirium* (its first arena tour) in venues with 8,000 to 12,000 seats
2008	Opened an office in Macau (China) and Laliberté sold 20% of Cirque to two Dubai investment groups for $600 million to fund a resident show in Dubai, but the project has been 'put on ice'
2010	Contracted with the Michael Jackson Co. to create the *Immortal* arena tour based on Jackson's music

Case Figure 5.2 Significant events in Cirque's history

Show	Location	Start	Finish
Cirque du Soleil	Tent Tour	1984	1984
La Magie Continue	Tent Tour	1986	1986
Le Cirque Réinventé	Tent Tour	1987	1987
Nouvelle Expérience	Tent Tour	1990	1992
	Las Vegas	1992	1993
Saltimbanco	Tent Tour	1992	2012
Mystere	Las Vegas	1993	
Alegria	Tent Tour	1994	2009
	Arena Tour	2009	2013
Quidam	Tent Tour	1996	2010
	Arena Tour	2010	2016
O	Las Vegas	1998	
La Nouba	Florida	1998	
Drailion	Tent Tour	1999	2010
	Arena Tour	2010	2015
Varekai	Tent Tour	2002	
	Arena Tour	2013	
Zumanity	Las Vegas	2003	
KA	Las Vegas	2005	
Corteo	Tent Tour	2005	2015
	Arena Tour	2017	
Delirium	Arena Tour	2006	2008
Love	Las Vegas	2006	

Show	Location	Start	Finish
Koozå	Tent Tour	2007	
Wintuk	New York	2007	2011
Zaia	China	2008	2012
Zed	Tokyo	2008	2011
Believe	Las Vegas	2008	2016
Ovo	Tent Tour	2009	2015
	Arena Tour	2016	
Banana Shpeel	Arena tour	2009	2010
Viva Elvis	Las Vegas	2009	2012
Totem	Tent Tour	2010	
Zarkana	Tent Tour	2011	2012
	Las Vegas	2012	2016
Iris	Los Angeles	2010	2013
Immortal	Arena Tour	2011	2014
Amaluna	Tent Tour	2012	
One	Las Vegas	2013	
Kurios	Tent Tour	2014	
Joya	Mexico	2014	
Toruk	Arena Tour	2015	
Paramour	New York	2016	2017
Luzia	Tent Tour	2016	
Septimo	Arena Tour	2017	
Volta	Tent Tour	2017	
Crystal	Arena Tour	2017	

Case Figure 5.3 Touring and resident shows

Date	Special event	Location	Duration
2002	7th Academy Awards	US	1 day
2004	Jazz Festival	Canada	1 day
	A Taste of Cirque	Celebrity Cruises	1 year
2005	World Aquatic Championships	Canada	1 day
2006	World Outgames	Canada	1 day

Case Figure 5.4 Special events

2007	One Day, One Game, One Dream	US	1 day
	Macau Opening	US	1 day
	Premio Craque	Brasil	1 day
2008	Awakening the Serpent	Spain	4 months
	400th Anniversary	Canada	1 day
	Dream of flying	Italy	
2009	Eurovision Song Contest	Rusia	1 day
	Les Chemins (Year 1)	Canada	1 day
2010	Canadian Pavilion	China	5 months
	FIBA World Championship	Turkey	1 day
	Electronic Entertainment Expo	US	1 day
	Les Chemins (Year 2)	Canada	1 day
2011	Les Chemins (Year 3)	Canada	1 day
2012	Les Chemins (Year 4)	Canada	1 day
	Super Bowl XLVI	US	1 day
	Fifa Women's World Cup	Azerbaijan	1 day
2013	Les Chemins Invisible (Year 5)		1 day
	Scalada (Year 1)	Andorra	2 months
2014	Scalada (Year 2)	Andorra	1 month
	30th Anniversary	Canada	1 day
2015	Allavita	Italy	1 day
	Scalada (Year 3)	Andorra	1 month
	Pan American Games	Canada	1 day
	Le Monde Est Fou	Canada	1 month
	Adiya Birla Awards	India	1 day
2016	Joel	Russia	1 week
	La Forge aux étoiles	France	1 year
	Tout excarbille	Canada	1 month
	Scalada (Year 4)	Andorra	1 month
2017	Reflekt	Russia	3 months
	Scalada (Year 5)	Andorra	1 month
	Stone	Canada	1 month

Case Figure 5.4 (Continued)

CREATING A NEW SHOW

All Cirque shows are built around two key elements: a unique theme and a unique soundtrack. These then guide the development of the acts, sets, equipment and costumes for each show. Cirque invests 40 per cent of its sales revenue each year into research and development, with each show taking 18 to 36 months to develop at a cost of up to $165 million, plus a new theatre if it

Date	Film
1988	*La Magie Continue*
1990	*Le Cirque Réinventé*
1991	*Quel Cirque*
1992	*Nouvelle Expérience* *Saltimbanco's Diary*
1994	*Saltimbanco* *Baroque Odyssey* *Truth of Illusion*
1996	*Full Circle*
1999	*Quidam* *Alegria* (the film)
2000	*Journey of Man* *Inside La Nouba*
2001	*Dralion* *Alegria*
2002	*Varekai* *Fire Within*
2003	*La Nouba*
2004	*Midnight Sun* *Solstorm*
2005	*KÀ Extreme*

Date	Film
2006	*Corteo* *Lovesick*
2007	*Flow* *Mystery of Mystere* *Thrilling Ride Through Kooza* *KÀ – Backstage*
2008	*Kooza* *Delirium* *All Together Now*
2010	*Zed in Tokyo* *Flowers in the Desert*
2011	*Crossroads in Macao*
2012	*Immortal* *Worlds Away*
2013	*Hatching* *Amaluna*
2015	*Le Grand Concert*
2016	*Toruk* *Luzia*
2017	*Kurios* *Volta*

Case Figure 5.5 Films, documentaries and TV series

is a resident show (see Case Figure 5.6). To help spread the financial risk, it uses sponsors such as American Electric Power, BMW and Fuji TV for tours and partners such as Disney and MGM for resident shows. For example, MGM invested $135 million in a 1,951 seat theatre for KÀ. Cirque and MGM then split the show's expenses (about $1.4

Start	Finish	Show	Location	Production cost ($M)	Theatre cost ($M)
1992	2012	*Saltimbanco*	Tent tour	2	–
1993	–	*Mystère*	Treasure Island (Las Vegas)	35	20
1994	2009	*Alegria*	Tent tour	3	–
1996	2010	*Quidam*	Tent tour	22	–
1998	–	*O*	Bellagio (Las Vegas)	92	70
1998	–	*La Nouba*	Walt Disney World (Florida)	70	52
1999	2010	*Dralion*	Tent tour	15	–
2002	–	*Varekai*	Tent tour	25	–
2003	–	*Zumanity*	New York New York (Las Vegas)	50	–
2005	–	*KÀ*	MGM Grand (Las Vegas)	165	135
2007	2011	*Wintuk*	Madison Square Garden (NY)	20	–
2011	2013	*Iris*	Dolby Theatre (LA)	70	30

Case Figure 5.6 Show production and theatre costs

million a week for costumes, 73 performers and 194 support staff) and revenues (up to $2 million per week for 10 shows averaging $110 per ticket) once it opened.

As James Vine (analyst) comments, 'There is no doubt that each show is expensive to develop and run, but with tickets selling for $40 to $195, between 2,000 and 3,000 seats per show and 10 shows per week, it doesn't take long to recoup this investment if they get it right!'

The creative process is driven by a team of artistic directors, costume designers, set designers and choreographers who are given an enormous amount of freedom to make their ideas a reality. Guy Laliberté (Chairman) and Daniel Lamarre (CEO) only intervene if they believe a production is not on track three months prior to its first show. Once a show is up and running, the 'creative team' are all given a sabbatical to help them recuperate. This could involve being asked to study competitor shows in different countries to understand what Cirque can learn from them or to determine how new material could be incorporated into existing Cirque performances.

The first step in creating a new show is to determine its core theme. For example, *Alegria* (Spanish for joy and jubilation) is about 'power' and 'contrast' and was inspired by an event in London discussed at a conceptual meeting by a set designer. Everyone was so moved by the story that they decided to make a show about it. As James Vine comments, 'Creativity is fostered in groups where people know and trust each other. Once you've got this, then a good idea can come from anywhere.'

After a theme has been identified, the soundtrack is developed using an eclectic mix of music styles to change the mood and theme during the show. Finally, the acts, sets, equipment and costumes are created to reflect the theme. For example, in *Alegria* a church dome symbolized 'power' and two staircases on either side of the dome created 'contrast'. In recent years, Cirque has outsourced the manufacture of some of its sets, but all equipment (such as a specialized trampoline and a double Russian swing) is still designed and made in-house at its 'creation studio' in Montreal.

FINDING THE RIGHT PEOPLE

It is a constant challenge to find the right artists for both Cirque's current productions and the ones they might put on in the future. Twelve full-time scouts travel the world looking for new talent to add to their database of over 20,000 potential recruits. Casting auditions are held twice a year at their 'creation studio' in Montréal and aspiring candidates can also submit video auditions. Each year, 50 to 60 performers are selected and enter 'basic training' where they spend four months being transformed from athletes into entertainers and taught how to use specific equipment such as the Russian swing (a rotating suspended platform). More than 50 per cent of its performers come from a gymnastic background (many are former Olympians) and this training helps them learn how to entertain an audience rather than win an athletic event.

A casting director can travel to over 20 countries to meet and hold auditions with local artists. However, they are careful about who they recruit. As one casting director explains, 'We have cast children who live on the streets of Brazil and changed their lives, but it can be hard growing up in Cirque without the support of friends and family. Recently, we went to some villages in Africa to look for talent and decided only to cast someone if we could take several equally talented people from the same village. Many people see us as a "dream-ticket", and we can be, but behind the magic of the show there is a lot of blood, sweat and tears! And you need to be ready for that too.'

Once in a show, performers are paid between $40,000 and $250,000 per year and given housing facilities and a 10 per cent profit share. They tend to stay with Cirque for three to six years, with 25 per cent leaving each year as they become too old to perform. They are paid per show and typically rehearse for 12 hours per week and perform for 20 hours per week (4 hours more than any Broadway show), which can become a strain after a while. To prevent 'burnout', Cirque only employs them for nine months a year, which gives performers time to explore other interests or take a break.

PUTTING ON A SHOW

To give each show a strong, uninterrupted storyline, performers move props and equipment on and off the stage and are guided by continuous live music that adapts to the performance. For example, if an act goes wrong then the tempo and volume of the music increase to move the show along. Cirque aims to create an unforgettable experience for its audiences and make them believe that anything's possible if you're prepared to play and have fun. For example, a lawyer in New York left his job after seeing a show saying, 'Cirque made me realize I was living the wrong life!'

Eighteen months before performing in a new city, Cirque sends a team of six people there to identify and work with local organizations to promote the show, find a location for setting up the tent and to arrange sponsorships and permits. They also perform stunts in bars and restaurants and challenge the locals to match them. This creates a buzz and excitement before opening night, which is a spectacular event attended by a number of influential people such as actors, critics and politicians.

Touring shows usually perform eight to ten times a week for six weeks in each city with tickets selling for up to $100 and VIP packages for more than $200 (which includes drinks in a VIP tent before, during and after the show, front-row seats and a gift package). Each show normally lasts for two hours and is performed by 50 to 80 artists, supported by 150 technicians, cooks, medical staff and teachers for children. The sets and equipment are transported in 50 to 75 trucks, which include a 2,500-seat blue and yellow Grand Chapiteau (big top) tent that can be ready for a performance in five or six days and takes three days to pack up. Shows normally premier in Montreal and then tour North America for five years before moving to Europe for three years, Asia for two, Australia for one, and South America for one. At this point, popular shows are then modified for touring in arenas or performing in a resident location.

Although touring shows all have different operating costs that vary by country, a performance typically needs 65 per cent of seats to be full to break even. Resident shows have higher operating costs because they need more support staff (up to 200), but have a lower break-even point at 60 per cent occupancy because they play for longer (48 weeks a year rather than 35 to 38 weeks for a touring show) and command a higher ticket price (up to $200). Shows also have a positive financial impact on the cities they visit or venue they perform in. For example, Santa Monica (California), estimated *Koozå* brought in $18 million extra revenue to the city and *Zumanity* increased the New York New York Resort's (Las Vegas) revenue by 31 per cent to $74 million in the first quarter after it opened.

Cirque uses a complex centralized information system to help keep track of its 5,000 multicultural staff (paid in different currencies for differing jobs and amounts of time), 15,000 costumes and 3,300 show instructions such as the make-up for each artist. Some interesting facts about its sets, costumes and performers are shown in Case Figure 5.7.

Sets and equipment

- *KÀ* at MGM Grand (Las Vegas):
  - A crane controls two moving platforms to rotate, lift and tilt them (up to 110°) to create its high energy action sequences. In one such sequence, the stage tilts at 12° per second and the artists are thrown 60 feet onto air bags below the stage
  - Each seat has two speakers placed near the ears to create surround sound
  - Infrared panels beneath the stage detect the location of an artist and change the video content accordingly
- *O* at Bellagio (Las Vegas):
  - This show is performed in an Olympic-sized swimming pool maintained at 31°C for the artists and at a lower air temperature for the audience and uses a virtual film to separate the two areas
  - Artists use an underwater communication system to talk to each other and air tanks to breathe
  - Musicians perform in glass enclosures in the pool

Costumes

- Over 4,500 costumes are worn every night by 1,300 performers worldwide
- The 'costume shop' employs over 300 people, produces 20,000 costumes, makes 3,000 pairs of shoes and uses over 150 km of fabric each year
- 80 per cent of the fabrics are treated and dyed in-house by the artisans of the textile design team
- 'Bibles' are used to catalogue and describe every costume used in a show, explaining how to dye, repair and fit it
- Before making a costume, each artist has to be measured from head to toe using a specially developed computer system and plaster casts are made of their heads so new wigs can be made for them while they are on tour
- In *Zarkana*, 225 body measurements were required to create the lead singer's costumes
- In *Alegria*, the hand-sewn costumes use1,600 yards of lace, 22 pounds of glitter, 2,500 yards of silk, 5,000 rhinestones and 400 pairs of shoes
- In *KÀ*, Diana's wig takes 4 weeks to make and has to be remade every 3 months
- In the Michael Jackson: Immortal World Tour, each costume in the Celestial/Human Nature scene has 275 blinking LED lights that change colour during the song to evoke star constellations

Case Figure 5.7 Some interesting Cirque facts

Performers
• Cirque has over 100 occupations and uses over 900 performers from over 50 countries speaking 25 different languages • Over 50 per cent have a gymnastics background (many former Olympians) with the rest from circus and theatre • They use translators and multilingual trainers with English and French language training provided to everyone

Case Figure 5.7 (Continued)

CREATING THE RIGHT CULTURE

Guy Laliberté has often stated that he wishes to pursue creativity instead of profit and make decisions that don't always make 'business sense'. He aims to create an environment in which people can develop their ideas to the fullest and create distinctive shows that take their creators, performers and spectators out of their comfort zone. To do this, he insists on retaining 100 per cent artistic control when entering a partnership, has never gone public and uses artistic vision rather than customer feedback to develop new shows. As James Vine comments, 'Creativity is at the heart of everything Cirque does. Shows are created out of personal experience, angst, joy and imagination. Surveying audiences to find out which acts they like goes against the whole ethos of the company.'

Cirque aims to be the most inspiring and creative company in the world and its artists are at the centre of this vision. They are among the best in the world at putting beauty, elegance, acrobatic skill, and aquatic talent together to challenge preconceived ideas and perceptions. To create the right environment for this to occur, it has a flat and organic structure, avoids using handbooks to prescribe employee behaviour, promotes cultural diversity throughout its organization and regularly holds parties for its employees.

As James Vine explains, 'The ethos of Cirque comes from a hippie, counterculture, artistic and Bohemian life. People who work at Cirque are a little bit crazy. It takes a certain kind of person who wants to run away to join the circus! As a result, Cirque is full of renegade, unconventional people who fight for their ideas. If you say "go left", then their response is "why not right?", just to challenge you to think differently.'

Recently when Guy Laliberté was walking through the headquarters in Montreal after not having been there for a couple months, he said, 'This place is boring. I can't stand it. I wouldn't work here. We have to do something crazy.' So he did a painting in the parking lot. When someone asked him, 'What's the purpose of that?', he said, 'There is no purpose. I want people to know that I'm still crazy and that they can be crazy. And that's what it's like to be part of Cirque!'

The offices in its Montreal headquarters are surrounded by training studios to create visual contact, to keep staff in touch with the artistic progress of each show and to ensure artists see the support they receive. Staff are also encouraged to be involved in the shows in any way possible. For example, they are used to raise the big top for all the opening nights in Montreal, were sent to see *Wintuk* at Madison Square Garden (New York) and were all asked to record a 'thank you' for a recent award ceremony. As one IT engineer comments, 'The closer you are to the ultimate show on stage, the more you feel the magic.'

THE FUTURE

There's no doubt that Cirque has been a phenomenal success, but times have been difficult since 2010. For the first time in 30 years, it received some bad reviews (*Believe*), closed shows early due to low attendance (*Banana Shpeel*, *ZED*, *Viva Elvis* and *Iris*) and lost $30 million on a film (*Worlds Away*). As a consequence, in 2014 it laid off 400 people (most at its Montreal headquarters) and closed four of its nineteen shows to reduce its high production costs.

As James Vine explained, 'Its global roster of shows is getting increasingly expensive to develop and manage, but the strong Canadian dollar hasn't helped. As 95 per cent of its expenses are incurred within Canada and 95 per cent of its revenue is generated outside Canada, a one-cent rise in the Canadian dollar reduces its bottom line by $3 million! Guy Laliberté's decision to keep tight ownership of the business has helped him maintain artistic control, but means they have little outside investment and support. Eighty-five per cent of its revenue still comes from its shows and over 50 per cent of this still comes from the US, which is becoming saturated. Its offering in Europe is not that original, Asia has not been that successful and Dubai is on hold.'

'In many ways, Cirque is a "luxury good" that only appeals to customers who can afford it. A recent study showed that 29 per cent of households in Portland, Oregon (US) earning over $50,000 went to see a Cirque show when it came to town. I can't see Cirque trying to create a trimmed-down, more affordable product to reach a mass market as this would require them scaling down its ambitions. If anything, it would rather spend more money and give the creative side more room to play. The recent changes in the business will help reduce its operating costs, but I'm not sure this will be enough. It might be that it has simply expanded too quickly and the market isn't big enough to support what it has created.'

QUESTIONS

1. Why has Cirque been so successful?
2. What are the issues described in the case study and how can it overcome them?
3. What can other organizations learn from Cirque?

DISCUSSION QUESTIONS

1 What steps should a business take in choosing the appropriate way to manufacture its products?
2 What is the difference between a technical and a business specification?
3 What are the five generic types of process? Define each and explain the key differences.
4 What comprises volume?
5 Project and continuous processing are specific to certain product types. Explain.
6 What are the several dimensions of flexibility? Illustrate your answers.
7 Why does the batch process best meet the requirements of most companies?
8 Select three product/market business implications and discuss how and why they differ across the generic processes.
9 Select three operations business implications and discuss how and why they differ across the generic processes.
10 Select three investment and cost business implications and discuss how and why they differ across the generic processes.
11 Select three infrastructure business implications and discuss how and why they differ across the generic processes.
12 What is a hybrid process? Select two and explain how they work and when they could be appropriate.

NOTES AND REFERENCES

1 This issue is specifically addressed by Hill, T.J., Menda, R. and Dilts, D.M. (1998) 'Using product profiling to illustrate manufacturing/marketing misalignment', *Interfaces*, 28(4): 42–63.

2 Also sometimes called 'unit' or 'one-off'.

3 Companies do manufacture order quantities of one on a batch basis. In this instance, what underlies their process decision is the repeat nature of a product, not the size of an order quantity.

4 Whereas this is typically the case in Western motor vehicle plants, Japanese car makers typically schedule their manufacturing plants on the basis of sales forecasts and make-to-stock rather than order backlog, make-to-order principles.

5 Many of these additional issues are illustrated and discussed in Hill, A. and Hill, T. (2012) *Operations Management*, 3rd edn, Palgrave Macmillan, Ch. 6.

6 A point examined in detail in Hill et al.'s *Interfaces* article, see note 1.

7 In reality, some customization may be offered but the substance of this equipment is standard.

8 NC systems use computer-based numerical control (CNC), which replaced the hard-wired control unit of the NC system with a stored program using a dedicated mini-computer. The memory storage makes the process more reliable and more flexible in program changes.

9 Direct numerical control (DNC) systems consist of a number of NC and/or CNC machines connected to a centralized computer. The centralized sources of information provided by DNC help in the control of manufacturing. Flexible manufacturing systems (FMS) combine the DNC principle together with the other features described in a later section.

10 Haas, P.R. (1973) 'Flexible manufacturing systems: a solution for the mid-volume, mid-variety parts manufacture', 2SME Technical Conference, Detroit, April; Hughes, J.J. et al. (1975) 'Flexible manufacturing systems for improved mid-volume productivity', Proceedings of the Third Annual AIEE Systems Engineering Conference, November.

11 A fuller explanation is given in Hill, A. and Hill, T. (2012) *Operations Management*, 3rd edn, Palgrave Macmillan, Ch. 6. Also refer to Edwards, G.A.B. (1971) *Readings in Group Technology*, Machinery Publishing Company; and Burbidge, J.L. (1975) *The Introduction of Group Technology*, Heinemann.

12 Both JIT Systems and Kanban-type arrangements are more fully explained in Hill, A. and Hill, T. (2012) *Operations Management*, 3rd edn, Palgrave Macmillan.

13 NC refers to the operation of machine tools from numerical data stored on paper or magnetic tape, punched cards, computer storage or direct information. The development of machining centres results from the concepts of NC. In a machining centre, a range of operations is provided using a carousel with up to 200 tools or more (that is, embodied in the centre) from which the program will select as required, with some taking place simultaneously as necessary. Consequently, a machining centre is not only able to cope with a wide range of product requirements, it can also be scheduled to complete one-offs in any sequence desired. More advanced NC systems include computer numerical control (CNC) systems using a dedicated minicomputer to perform NC functions and direct numerical control (DNC), which refers to a system having a computer controlling more than one machine tool. A DNC system includes both the hardware and software required to drive more than one NC machine simultaneously. To do this, DNC uses a computer, which may be a minicomputer, several minicomputers linked together, a minicomputer linked to a large computer, or a large computer on its own.

14 The lead time taken by typical US car makers from receipt of a dealer's order to the start of the manufacturing process is three times longer than the time taken by Toyota.

15 This issue is further highlighted in the pharmaceutical industry where the gamble on plant investment not only concerns the potential level of demand but also whether a drug will be accepted by the relevant drug authorities and which formulae will eventually be best received in the market.

EXPLORING FURTHER

Blois, K.J. (1980) 'Market concentration: challenge to corporate planning', *Long Range Planning*, 13: 56–62.

Bolwijn, P.T., Boorsma, J., van Breukelen, Q.H. et al. (1986) *Flexible Manufacturing: Integrating Technical and Social Innovations*, Elsevier.

Burbridge, J.L. (1980) 'The simplification of material flow systems', *International Journal of Production Research*, 20: 339–47.

Chakravorty, S.S. and Hales, D.N. (2004) 'Implications of cell design implementation: a case study and analysis', *European Journal of Operations Research*, 152: 602–14.

Fraser, K., Harris, H. and Luong, L. (2007) 'Improving the implementation effectiveness of cellular manufacturing: a comprehensive framework for practitioners', *International Journal of Production Research*, 45(24) pp: 5835–56.

Hyer, N.L. and Wemmerlöv, U. (2002) *Reorganising the Factory: Competing through Cellular Manufacturing*, Productivity Press.

Johnson, D.J. and Wemmerlöv, U. (2004) 'Why does cell implementation stop? Factors influencing cell penetration in manufacturing plants', *Production and Operations Management*, 13(3): 272–89.

Modrak, V. and Panchian, R.S. (eds) (2012) *Operations Management and Cellular Manufacturing Systems*, IGI Global.

Singh, N. and Rajamani, D. (2012) *Cellular Manufacturing Systems: Design, Planning and Control*, Springer Science and Business Media.

Sohal, A.S., Fitzpatrick, P. and Power, D. (2001) 'A longitudinal study of flexible manufacturing cell operation', *Integrated Manufacturing Systems*, 12(4): 236–45.

Suresh, N. and Kay, J.M. (2012) (eds) *Group Technology and Cellular Manufacturing*, Springer Science and Business Media.

Wang, H., Xu, X. and Tedford, J.D. (2007) 'An adaptable CNC system based on STEP-NC and function blocks', *International Journal of Production Research*, 45(17): 3809–29.

Wang, J.X. (2015) *Cellular Manufacturing: Mitigating Risk and Uncertainty*, CRC Press.

Wemmerlöv, U. and Johnson, D.J. (1997) 'Cellular manufacturing at 46 user plants: implementation experiences and performance improvements', *International Journal of Introduction Research*, 35(1): 29–49.

Yauch, C.A. and Steudel, H.J. (2002) 'Cellular manufacturing for small businesses: key cultural factors that impact the conversion process', *Journal of Operations Management*, 20(5): 593–617.

6 SERVICE/PRODUCT PROFILING

THIS CHAPTER DISCUSSES...

SUMMARY

With markets as the agenda and functions investing, developing and managing in line with their strategic role, a company needs to assess the level of fit between needs and provision and check the future level of fit in the light of changes. Service/product profiling provides such a checking mechanism and this chapter covers the following issues:

- The need to expand operations strategy's language base – to ensure that it makes an appropriate and full contribution to business strategy discussion and resolution, operations needs to explain its perspectives in such a way that other functions can relate to them within the context of the overall business.
- Service/product profiling – selecting relevant market and operations dimensions, then services/products/customers/markets can be assessed in terms of the level of fit between one and the other. The key here is to keep the number of dimensions small so that the role of profiling in discussing the level of fit between market requirements and operations characteristics is provided.
- Using service/product profiling – the outcomes of profiles are part of the way companies can assess current levels of alignment, the origins of any deterioration of fit or alert companies to alignment issues in the future.

For operations, the size of its delivery system and infrastructure investments and the timescales necessary to bring about change are such that companies need to be aware of any deteriorating alignment ahead of time. Chapters 4 and 5 discussed the implications of service delivery system and process choice, provided insights and, consequently, outlined some of the blocks on which to build operations' strategic decisions. Assessing how well existing delivery systems fit an organization's current market requirements and making appropriate choices of delivery system to meet future needs are critical operations responsibilities because of the high investment and timescales inherent in and associated with the outcomes of these decisions.

When investing in delivery systems and infrastructure, companies need to appreciate the business trade-offs embodied in these decisions (see Figures 4.8 and 5.15). Service/product profiling enables an organization to test the current or anticipated level of fit between the requirements of its market(s) and the characteristics of its existing or proposed delivery systems and infrastructure investments – the components of operations strategy (see Figure 2.10). The purpose of this assessment is twofold. First, it provides a way to evaluate and, where necessary, improve the fit between the way in which a company qualifies and wins orders in its markets and operations' ability to support these criteria (that is, operations' strategic response). Second, it helps a company move away from classic strategy building characterized by functional perspectives separately agreed, without adequate attempts to test the fit or reconcile different opinions of what is best for the business as a whole.

In many instances though, companies will be unable or unwilling to take the necessary steps to provide the degree of fit desired because of the level of investment, executive energy and timescales involved. However, sound strategy is not a case of having every facet correctly in place. It concerns improving the level of consciousness a company brings to bear on its corporate decisions. Living with existing mismatches or allowing the level of fit to deteriorate can be strategically sound if a company is aware of its position, makes these choices knowingly and adjusts its corporate expectations accordingly. Reality can constrain strategic decisions. In such circumstances, service/product profiling will help to increase corporate awareness and allow a conscious choice between alternatives. In the past, many companies have not aspired to this level of strategic alertness.

THE NEED TO EXPAND OPERATIONS STRATEGY LANGUAGE

Operations needs to express important perspectives in a manner that provides for corporate insight and discussion. Without this, other business functions will find difficulty in embracing the operations issues and choices on hand and, in turn, then being party to their resolution. Intuition, experience and gut feeling must give way to business-related concepts and explanations. This is not to imply that the former are of little value. On the contrary, they form an integral part of sound management practice. However, at the strategic level, they need to be explained in a way that other executives can understand, so allowing them to become part of the ongoing corporate debate and strategic outcomes. In fact, one of the key tests for the usefulness of management theory is whether or not it crystallizes the intuitive insights of experienced executives. Insights grounded in experience contribute to the essential intellectual nature of the management debate – intellectual not in the sense of theory but reflecting the complex and applied nature of the management task. Sound management is not about knowing things, it is about knowing what to do.

Each business will require its own approach and resolution. The examples described in the following sections met the specific needs of those businesses to which they relate. They should not be considered universally applicable. The conceptual base on which these analyses rest, however, can be transferred to other corporate scenarios and used to prepare similar analyses that will yield their own profiles.

TECHNICAL VERSUS BUSINESS DIMENSIONS OF SERVICES/PRODUCTS

As explained earlier (see Figure 2.12 on p. 34), when customers purchase a service or product they buy a combination of

- the service/product itself which has a specification (what it comprises);
- a number of related order-winners and qualifiers such as quality conformance, delivery speed, price and delivery reliability.

The former comprises the technical dimensions and the latter constitutes the business dimensions of the purchase. While the technical dimension is largely in the domain of functions other than operations (R&D/engineering for products and marketing/some technical function such as finance in the case of services), many (and often all) of the criteria making up the business dimensions are provided by operations.

Service/product profiling assesses the level of alignment of operations with its strategic task of meeting those elements of the business dimension for which it is solely or partly responsible.

SERVICE/PRODUCT PROFILING

Inconsistency between the market and the capability of operations' delivery systems and infrastructure to support the business specification of its services or products can be induced by changes in the market or delivery system and infrastructure investment decisions or a combination of these. In all instances, the mismatch results from the fact that while operations' investments are inherently large and fixed (once a company has purchased them it will typically have to live with them for better or for worse for many years), markets are inherently dynamic. In addition, corporate marketing decisions can often be relatively transient should a business so decide. The inherent changing nature of markets and a company's ability to alter the marketing function's perspectives to allow for change and repositioning are in opposition to operations decisions that bind a business for years ahead. A company must reconcile this, but to do so requires strategic awareness, recognition and action.

Service/product profiling is a way to ascertain the level of fit between the delivery system and infrastructure investment that have been or are proposed to be made and the order-winners and qualifiers of the services(s)/product(s) or customers under review. The sections that follow describe situations and, to some extent, different dimensions of the same problem.

LEVELS OF APPLICATION

Service/product profiling can be undertaken at either the level of the company or the level of a delivery system. Company-based applications provide an overview of the degree of fit between all or the significant parts of a business and existing operations facilities (delivery system and/or infrastructure) or its proposed operations investments and developments. Delivery system-based applications provide a check of the fit between the services/products that the delivery system under review is to provide.

PROCEDURE

The procedure used in service/product profiling is outlined below. We detail the basic steps to follow but the essential direction of the analysis needs to reflect the match/mismatch issues within the whole or parts of a business. Remember, the purpose of profiling is to draw a picture to help to identify the current or potential problem, allowing discussion of and agreement on what steps should be taken to improve a company's strategic position.

1 Select relevant aspects of services/products/markets, operations, investment/cost and infrastructure as outlined in Figures 4.8 and 5.15. This choice must meet two overriding requirements:
   - The selected criteria must relate to the issues on hand and reflect the strategic dimensions of relevant markets. Thus, additional dimensions to those given in Figures 4.8 and 5.15 will often be selected, as the examples that follow illustrate.
   - The number of criteria selected must be kept small enough to allow the picture illustrating the issues to show through. Choosing too large a list will blur the essential clarity required and detract from the facilitating role of this approach within strategic discussion and formulation.

2 Display the trade-offs of services delivery system/process choice (similar to those shown in Figures 4.8 and 5.15) that would be typical for each criterion chosen in Step 1. This provides the backdrop against which the service(s)/product(s) or customer(s) can be profiled.

3 The purpose of profiling is to provide comparison, so the next step is to profile the services/ products, services/ product groups, customers or companies involved. This is done by positioning the selected services(s)/product(s), group(s) of services/products or companies on each criterion selected. Remember, this is a comparative technique; therefore you are looking to show the relationship of one service/product or customer to another, to compare a company today with what it was (or would be) in a selected earlier (or later) period or to review one business against another. The purpose is to test the correlation between market requirements and operations' current or proposed response to their provision. Thus profiling (the position on each chosen dimension where what is being reviewed is placed) is to display a comparative picture and should not become an issue or concern of exactness.

4 The resulting profile illustrates the degree of consistency between the characteristics of the market(s) and the relative position of the delivery systems and infrastructure within operations. The more consistency that exists, the straighter the profile will be. Inconsistencies between the market and operations' inherent ability to meet these needs will result in a dog-leg-shaped profile.

   Remember throughout that the purpose of a profile is to display the issues relevant to a business and enable a company to review the degree of alignment that exists. This pictorial representation of the dimensions relevant to a business allows the executives responsible for strategic decisions to recognize the issues, their origins and the corrective action to take.

The examples that follow illustrate the points above and afford the opportunity to discuss particular applications.

COMPANY-BASED PROFILES

Inducing mismatch with delivery system investments

As emphasized in Chapter 5, all delivery system choices include fixed business trade-offs that can be changed only by further investment or development. Thus, a company investing in a delivery system that embodies trade-offs inconsistent with part or all of its markets would induce a mismatch. The degree of the mismatch so caused would correspond to the relative size and importance of the delivery system(s) involved and the associated level of reinvestment.

Let's take an example. A company producing a range of cartons decided to invest \$6m in part of its processes. These processes were core to a range of its products that accounted for some 30 per cent of total sales revenue. Based on the current level of activity, the investment had a pay back of 5.5 years. However, because the parent group's return on investment norm was four years, the company needed to increase the sales (and therefore the output) of these types of product by about 50 per cent.

For some time, the company's marketing strategy had been to position itself in the higher-specification end of all its markets. However, to gain the larger volumes necessary to justify this process investment, the company had to seek business won on price. Soon the company had almost 15 per cent of its total business with distinct low-cost needs, while having to meet the schedule change needs of a further 30 per cent of sales. The consequences were significant and the ramifications substantial. Within a short space of time, the process investment had introduced operations conflict in a large part of its total business.

Product profiling can highlight these sorts of mismatches by graphically representing key marketing and operations differences that the single set of processes had to accommodate (see Figure 6.1).

In the above example, the \$6m process investment was, in terms of its point on the jobbing-batch-line continuum in Figure 6.1, consistent with its existing processes and chosen to support its existing business. However, the additional price-sensitive business required different process and infrastructure support. The straight-line and dog-leg relationships in the figure reflect this.

A similar illustration is provide by a large utility company[1] supplying electricity to a wide range of customers classed as large companies, small and medium-sized enterprises (SMEs) and domestic consumers. (See also the details given for this example in Case 2.4.) In order to improve profits, the company undertook a number of decisions to reduce costs. Aimed at its large number of domestic customers (see Figure 6.2), these developments included a substantial IT investment to improve call centre service provision, changes in the service specification to standardize and simplify the services offered, the closure of many of its high street retail

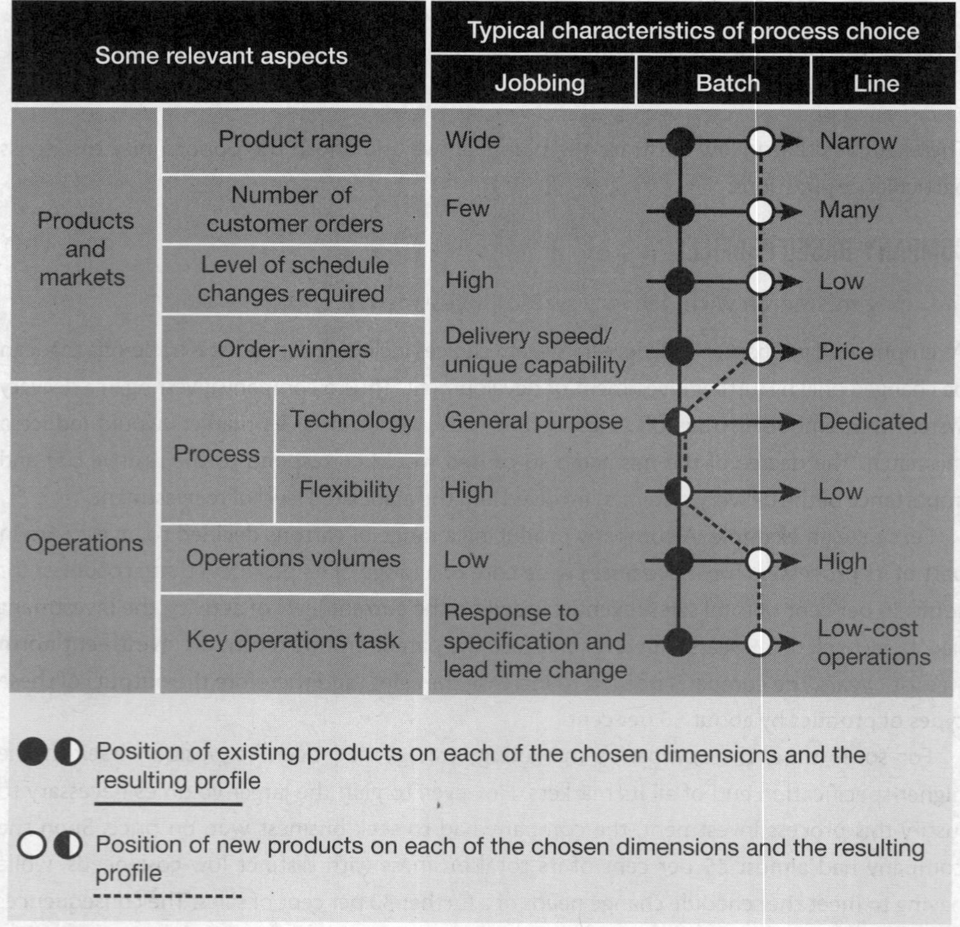

Figure 6.1 A product profile illustrating mismatch between the market and operations induced by process investment

Segment	% total	
	Sales	Customers
Large companies	42	2
SMEs	47	5
Domestic consumers	11	93

Figure 6.2 Utility company breakdown of sales revenue and customers

stores, a lower level of customer support and a move to more online service delivery. While the company recognized the needs of its relatively small number of large corporate customers and continued to provide key account managers as in the past, it now served the needs of its SME customers through its domestic consumers' delivery systems.

Some 18 months after these changes, a review of the total business confirmed the lower cost base in place to support its domestic and SME customers but lower sales revenue and overall profits in the SME segment. An additional review in each of its three segments highlighted SMEs as the highest margin part of its overall business and growing competition here had resulted in a loss of market share, reflecting the lower specification and less appropriate provision of the service offering. What became clear was that the support of SMEs' needs through a call centre and online provision and the closure of high street retail stores had alienated these customers and many had switched to other suppliers. The profiles in Figure 6.3 provided part of the review and facilitated recognition and discussion of the revised strategy. Whereas the needs of large companies

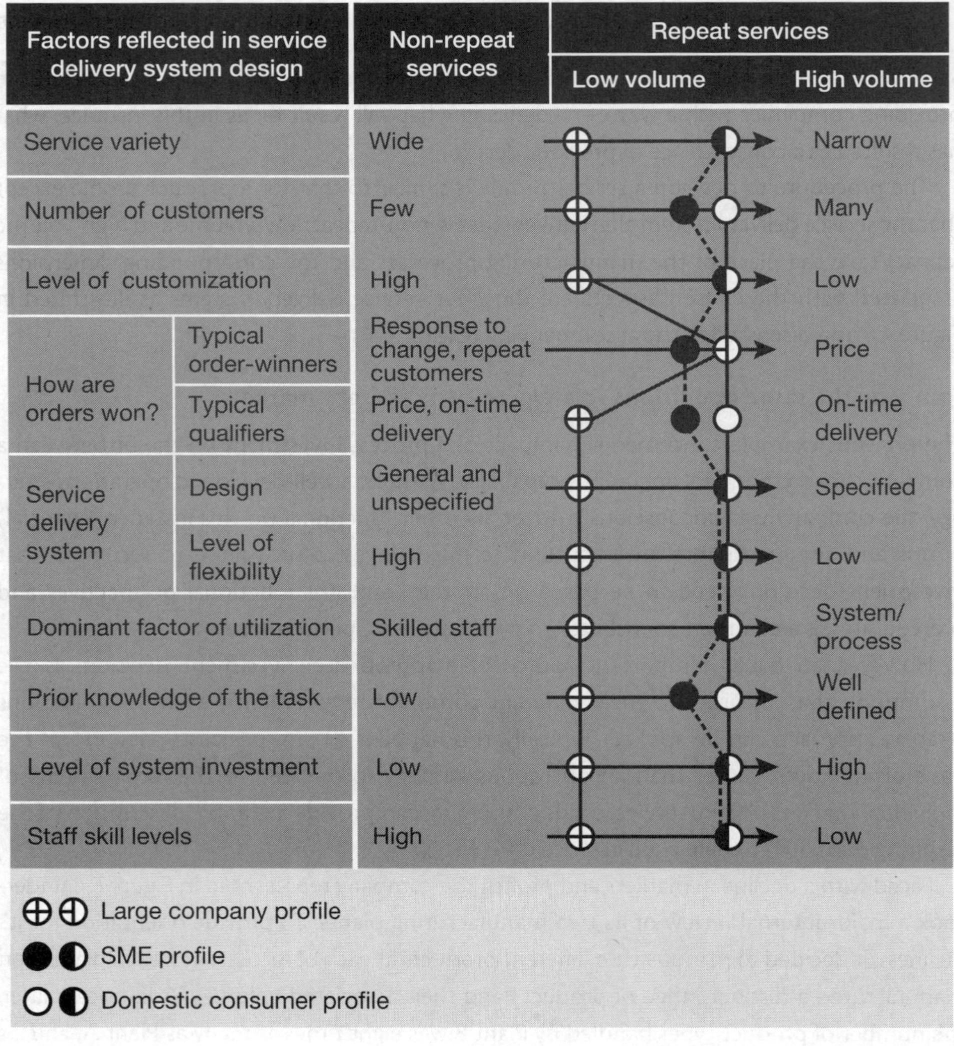

Figure 6.3 Service profiles for the utility company's large company, SME and domestic consumer segments

and domestic customers were aligned to their respective service delivery systems, SME customers were not.

Figure 6.2 gives the following information:

- Large company profile – the straight line illustrates the level of fit between the characteristics of the utility company's large customers and its ability to provide these. The pressure on price that such large customers can exert is shown in that price is the dominant factor in winning this business.
- Domestic consumer profile – the straight line illustrates the fit between these customers' requirements and the company's chosen service delivery systems. The investments in call centre and support provision are appropriate to meet these customers' needs.
- SME profile – the decision to meet these customers' needs by the low flexible custom design has resulted in the dog-leg shape of the profile representing aspects of misalignment.

Such visual representations of business decisions and their outcomes are most helpful in providing companies with a way of recognizing what will result or, as in this instance, what has resulted as a consequence of previous decisions.

The procedure to develop a service profile is similar to that for a product profile except that the service delivery system alternatives (that is, non-repeat, low-volume and high-volume repeat) take the place of the manufacturing processes and the corresponding dimensions associated with the chosen aspects are those for service delivery systems as illustrated in Figure 4.8 and discussed in the accompanying text (p. 126).

Applying the same operations strategy to two different markets

The previous example concerned the impact of a process investment on the fit between a company's markets and its operations capability. Without a well-developed operations strategy, the company was unconsciously driven by other functional (in this instance, financial) norms and arguments into an inappropriate major investment. Failure to recognize that investment decisions need to be based on strategy, and not functional perspectives and prerequisites, is a common contributor to poor corporate performance.

However, an equally important source of inappropriate investment decisions is the assumption that, in order to meet different corporate requirements, a similar operations strategy approach can be applied. Typically, this happens where specialists' views form the basis of initiatives, rather than an operations strategy formulated to the requirements of individual markets. Again, service/product profiling can provide a graphic description of the resulting mismatch to help explain these differences.

Faced with a decline in markets and profits, the company represented in Figure 6.4 undertook a major internal review of its two manufacturing plants. To provide orientation for its business, it decided to manufacture different products at each of its two sites; each plant then manufactured a distinct range of products and their associated volumes. A few years later, the number of product types handled by Plant B was eight times as many as Plant A, and, as one would expect, product volume changes were reflected in this position. While in Plant A, average volumes for individual products rose by 60 per cent, in Plant B they decreased by 40 per cent. In addition, to redress the decline in profits, the company also embarked on major operations investments at each plant, comprising identical process investments and infrastructure changes. Figure 6.4 illustrates how these changes fitted Plant A's markets, while they led to a significant mismatch for Plant B.

The review procedure followed is similar to the one outlined in the previous section. The first step is to describe, in conceptual terms, the characteristics of products/markets, operations, investment/cost and infrastructure features pertinent to the business. The dimensions selected for these two plants are detailed in Figure 6.4. First, the characteristics that reflect the change between jobbing, batch and line need to be described. Thus, the product range associated with jobbing is wide and becomes increasingly narrow as it moves through to line,

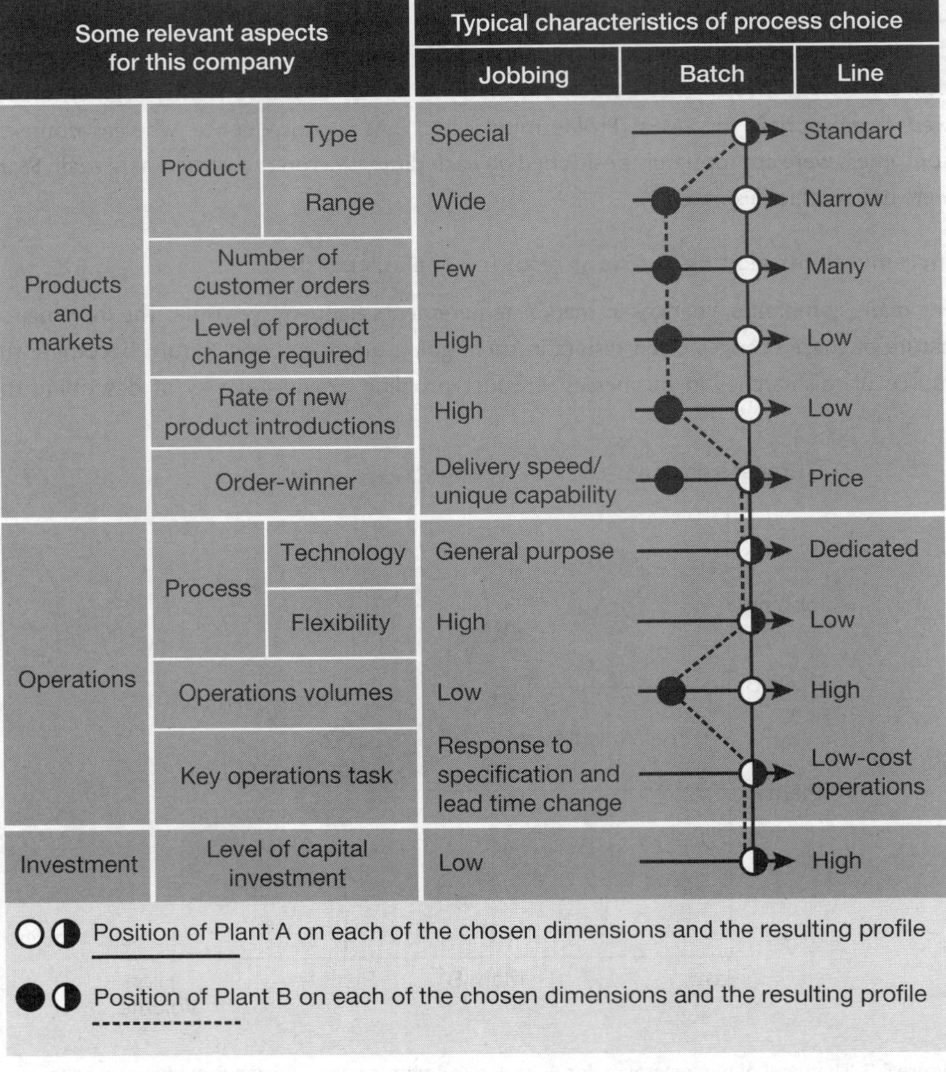

Figure 6.4 A product profile illustrating the level of match and mismatch between two plants and their respective markets induced by applying the same operations strategy to both plants

whereas the number of customer orders is few in jobbing and becomes increasingly more as it moves through to line and so on. These dimensions represent the classic characteristics of the trade-offs embodied in process choice. Plant A's profile shows a straight-line relationship between the products and markets and the operations and infrastructure provision. However, Plant B's profile shows a dog-leg shape due to the difference in markets compared to the similar process and infrastructure investments made in both plants.

Based on Figure 6.4, Figure 6.5 provides a further illustration and additional insights into the extent of the mismatch brought about by applying the same operations strategy to Plants A and B. Whereas Plant A had appropriate process investments in line with its product volumes, Plant B did not (Profile mismatch 1). As a consequence, whereas Plant A was appropriately positioned on each dimension on the vertical axis, again Plant B was not (Profile mismatch 2).

Figure 6.6 presents an illustration similar to that provided by Figure 6.5 for the SME and domestic customers profiled in Figure 6.3.

As in the example of two plants (see Figure 6.5), Figure 6.6 shows that, whereas the service delivery system investments were appropriate for the domestic consumer segments, they were inappropriate for SMEs (Profile mismatch 1). As a consequence, whereas domestic consumers were appropriately positioned on each dimension on the vertical axis, again SMEs were not (Profile mismatch 2).

Incremental marketing decisions resulting in a mismatch

For many companies, changes in market requirements happen over time. The incremental nature of these changes often results in them going unnoticed and in turn becoming the source of mismatches in businesses. Product profiling provides a way of describing the

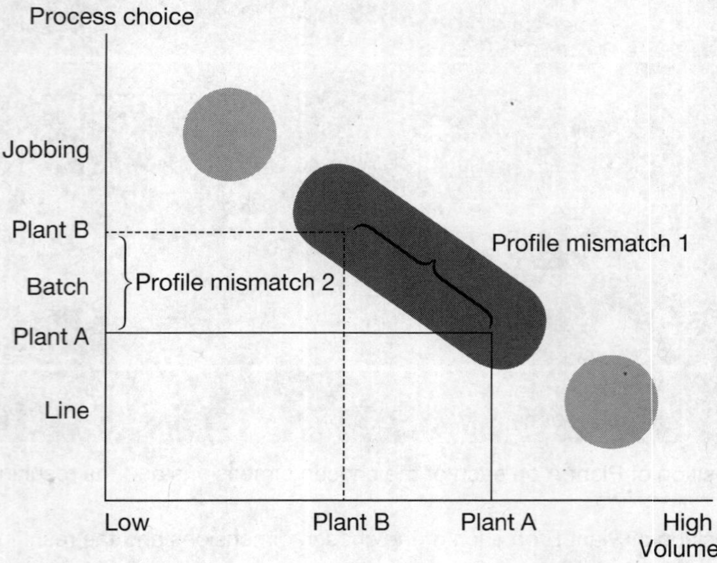

Figure 6.5 The level of inconsistency for Plant B at all points of the chosen dimensions on the vertical axis

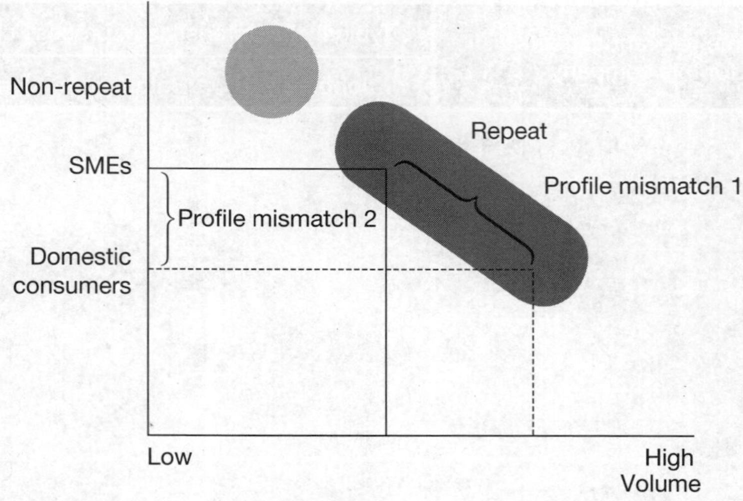

Figure 6.6 The level of inconsistency for SME customers on all points of the chosen dimensions on the vertical axis

resulting mismatch, as illustrated by the dog-leg profile in Figure 6.7, and its overall impact on a company.

As highlighted earlier, while markets are inherently dynamic, operations is inherently fixed. This is not, however, a result of either attitude or preference – markets will simply change over time whether or not a company so desires, whereas the operations investments will stay as they are unless deliberately changed by development or further investment.

Service/product profiling is a way of mapping the fit between the requirements of current markets and the characteristics of existing processes. The key to identifying these differences lies in a recognition that, while the needs of the market may have changed, the characteristics of manufacturing processes and infrastructure investment will not change without additional investment.

To illustrate, let us consider a US-based business that was under pressure from its parent company to grow sales and profits. Its response was to adopt a marketing strategy to broaden its product range. Process investments had already been updated and there was excess capacity over and above current sales levels. Supporting the required sales growth would consequently not require significant investment. As the strategy developed, the product range widened, while overall the trend saw an increase in demand for customer orders of a smaller size and a corresponding increase in the number of operations schedule changes. Several years into their marketing strategy, the company was experiencing problems in terms of operations' ability to support current markets and provide profit at required levels. To explain the causes of this problem it is necessary to compare the current year with the year in which the manufacturing process and infrastructure investments were made. This is because when a company invests in processes or infrastructure, it does so to reflect the characteristics of its markets as perceived at that time. As shown in Figure 6.7,

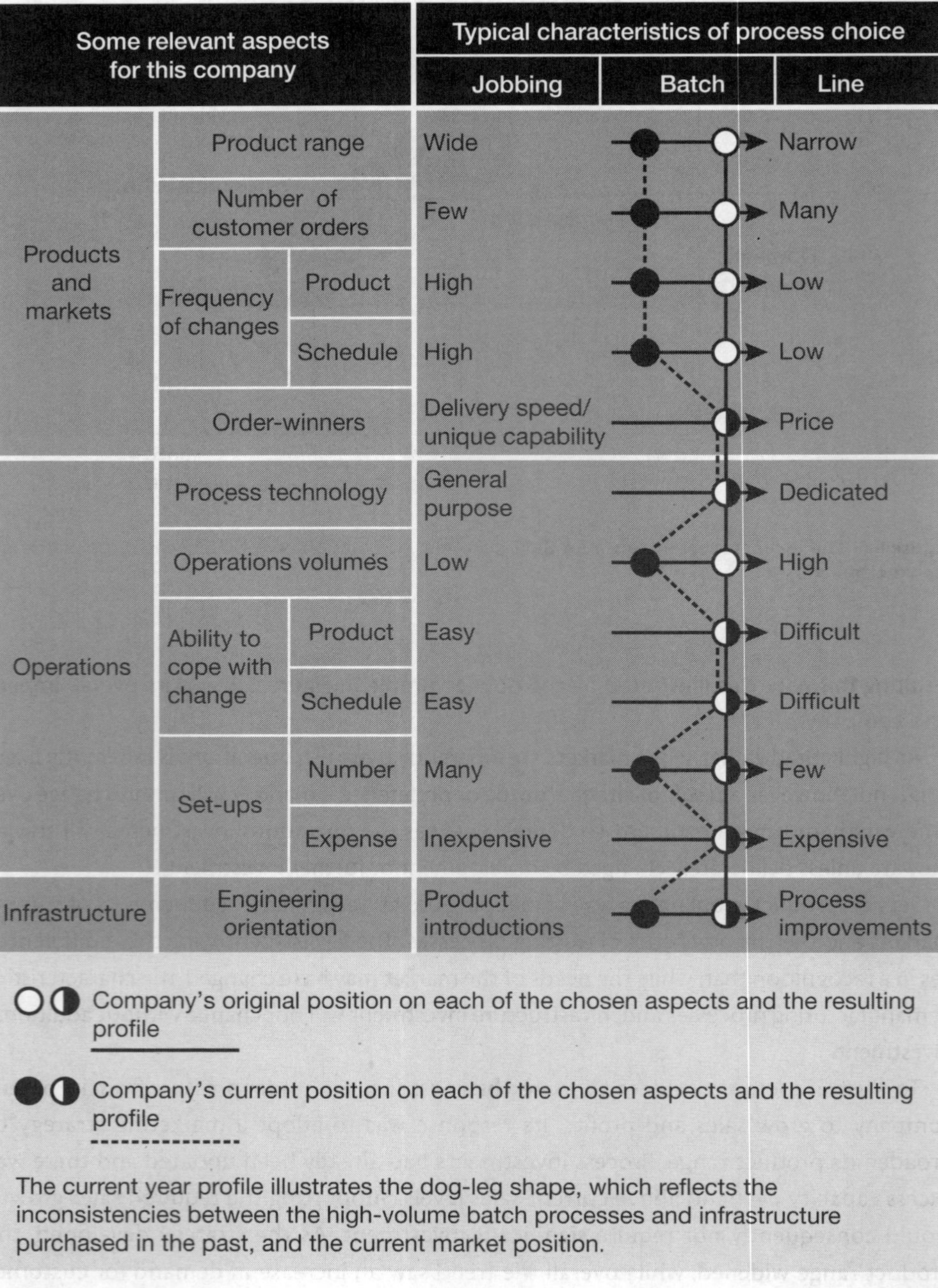

Figure 6.7 A product profile of a US-based business's mainstream products to illustrate the impact of incremental marketing decisions

at the time prior to the marketing strategy change, there was a match between the characteristics of the company's products and markets and the characteristics of its operations and infrastructure investments. The incremental marketing changes in the ensuing period had the cumulative effect of moving the company's position to the left on several, relevant product/market dimensions. The implications for operations of the incremental marketing changes in these years are revealed when drawing the equivalent profile for the current year. Again, the profile mismatch illustrates that operations has become increasingly less able to support the changing marketing trends, which the dog-leg profile in Figure 6.7 illustrates.

Reallocation of products due to downsizing

Companies faced with a reduction in overall demand often decide to downsize total operations capacity as a way of meeting future profit expectations. This decision would involve the reallocation of products from one plant to another, thereby enabling one plant to downsize or close while improving current machine utilization in the other. Decisions of this kind are typically evaluated against two criteria:

- A technical fit between the products to be made and the processes available to ensure that the processes on which there is spare capacity can physically make the product specifications to be transferred.
- The financial implications of the alternative decisions.

Often, however, companies fail to check whether the business specifications of the products to be transferred match the processes. Without this, companies can make decisions that, almost overnight, create alignment problems within a plant. The resulting profile is similar to that in Figure 6.4 but is due to stepped rather than incremental changes. It results from the failure to recognize that different units of capacity, although meeting similar technical specifications, do not have the same business specifications (see Figure 5.15).

Internal sourcing decisions based on unit costs

Within a group of companies the same product may be manufactured in two or more locations. Executives with profit responsibility for a region will understandably look to sourcing products as a major factor in profit performance. Where two or more plants make the same product, differences in unit price will attract some sister companies within the group to place their business with the least-cost company. For example, a North American multinational was under pressure to maintain its record of profit performance with the various parts of the business being required to match or even improve on their own current performances. The result was that executives switched their internal source of products on the basis of lowest cost as one way of maintaining or improving their own profit performance. Within a short time, however, the least-cost plant found that it could no longer maintain its previous cost levels. Attracting order volumes of differing (often lower) levels and being required to meet different market needs led to this 'once best' plant now underperforming. A product profile showed why, with reasons similar to those described in the previous two examples, although with different origins.

PROCESS-BASED PROFILES

Company-based profiles help reflect changes at the corporate level and identify the varying degrees of match or mismatch that exist or will exist if market needs and requirements are not reflected in operations. Process-based profiles provide similar insights but concern the review of a single process (or group of similar processes) in relation to the products produced on them. There can be more than one process-based profile completed within a single plant.

A prime reason why mismatches develop is that as demand for a product changes, capacity is released. Typically, companies will see this as an opportunity to allocate other products to that process so as to use the spare capacity that now exists. The explanation that is undertaken, however, is invariably restricted to a technical specification check with the equally essential business specification check neither recognized nor considered, and hence not undertaken. The products under review may be either new products or derivations of products already made on that process. In both instances the product range widens, overall individual order quantities decrease and the process stops and starts more often.

Consequently, a process will increasingly be required to support the business specification of products that have order-winners or other market characteristics that differ from one another. Profiles based on a format similar to those given earlier will help explain this to a business so that decisions are changed or expectations realigned.

A US-based pharmaceutical company located the manufacture of a major new product in its Kansas City plant. The initial sales of this product justified forecasts, and following this initial success, the company introduced new products and new variants to maximize total sales revenue. These variants took the form of dosage, package size and labels/leaflets in several languages. Sales continued to grow, and the company purchased further packaging equipment, similar to existing processes, to meet increased requirements. The introduction of new products and variants continued, and so did total sales growth. Although not competing on price (brand name and product patents were important factors for these products in winning orders), margins deteriorated. Furthermore, as competing products entered the market and price levels were revised, overall profit levels fell short of expectations.

The profile in Figure 6.8 explains why profit levels fell. A mismatch between market requirements and operations characteristics resulted because the engineering and operations task shifted away from exploiting the potential cost advantages associated with volumes towards that of handling the introduction of new products and new variants. The existing process and infrastructure investments in operations became increasingly misaligned to the needs of the market as the growth into lower volume products continued. As a result, profit margins fell short of the level necessary to support the high R&D expenditure essential to secure future growth and market penetration in pharmaceutical markets.[2]

USING SERVICE/PRODUCT PROFILING

The examples given in the previous sections illustrate the role service/product profiling can play in helping a company to check its existing service/product and delivery system relationship and allow, where relevant, comparisons to be made between similar applications or to

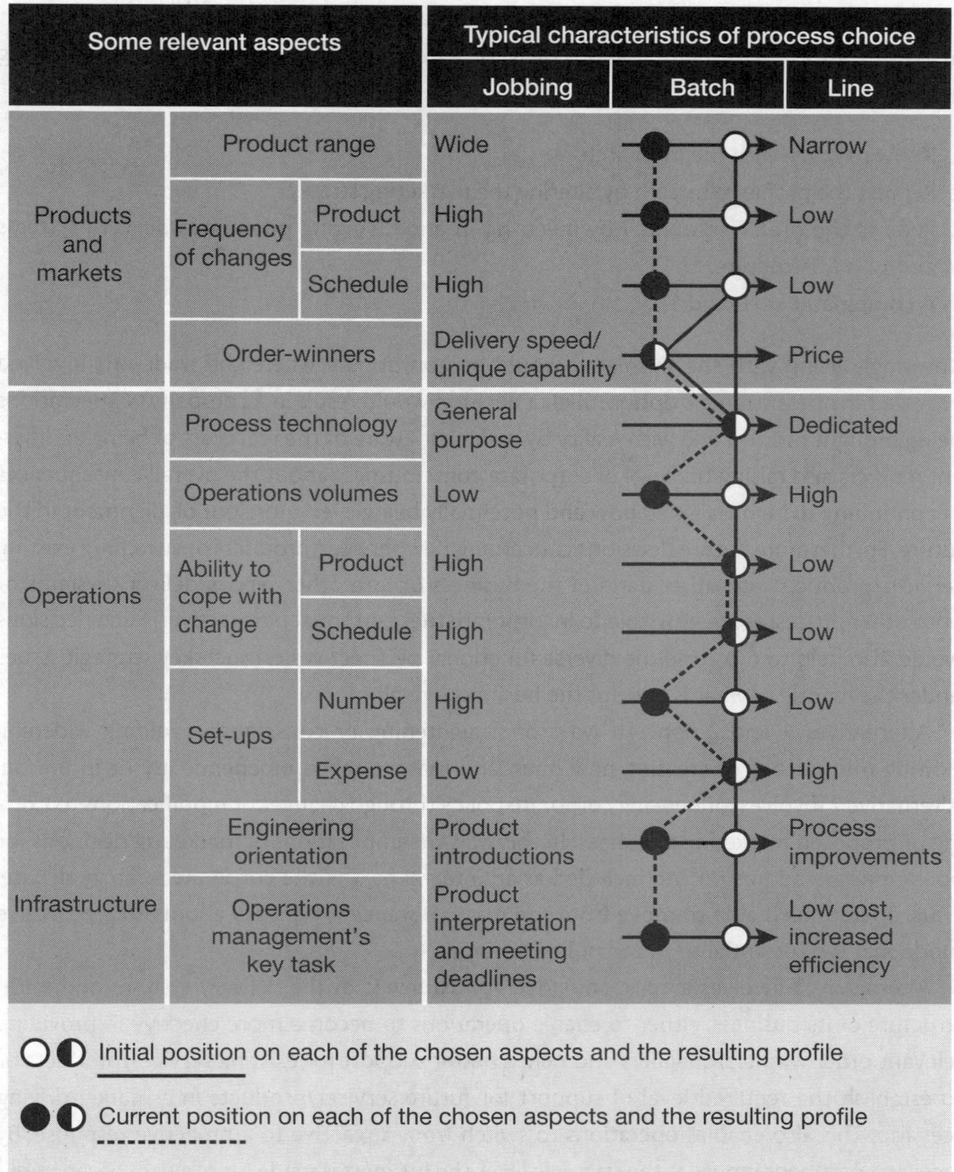

Figure 6.8 A profile of the product variants packed on a number of similar packaging lines

measure trends over time. Although these illustrations were based on hindsight and not on the essential forward-looking characteristic of strategy, service/product profiling is similarly useful to illustrate current positions and future alternatives because it helps in the discussion of options, to determine which strategic direction best meets the needs of the business or alerts an organization to any future deterioration in the essential alignment between market needs and operations provision.

Companies that are, for whatever reason, experiencing a mismatch between their current market needs and existing operations delivery system and infrastructure face the following choices:

1 Knowingly live with the mismatch.
2 Redress the profile mismatch by altering the marketing strategy.
3 Redress the profile mismatch by investing in and changing operations delivery systems and/or infrastructure.
4 A combination of 2 and 3.

Knowingly living with the mismatch would be appropriate where the trade-offs involved provided the best strategic option. Such a decision would result in a company's expectations being brought more in line with reality by making it aware of the real costs of being in different markets and raising the level of corporate consciousness about the overall consequences of continuing to be misaligned now and potentially being even more out of alignment in the future. Furthermore, future decisions concerning new services/products or switching existing services/products into other parts of the business or into other service delivery systems or onto other processes are now able to incorporate these essential perspectives. Such decisions would also help to reconcile the diverse functional perspectives on such key strategic issues under the mantle of what is best for the business overall.

Alternatives 2 and 3 concern ways of straightening or consciously avoiding widening existing mismatches or creating new ones, and may be taken independently or in unison. Alternative 2 involves influencing corporate policy through changes or modifications to existing or proposed marketing strategies. In this way, the implications of marketing decisions for operations are addressed and included as an integral part of the corporate strategy debate. Thus, operations is able to move from the reactive stance it typically adopts to a proactive mode that is so essential to sound policy decisions.

Alternative 3 involves a company's decision to invest in the delivery systems and infrastructure of its business, either to enable operations to become more effective in providing relevant order-winners/qualifiers and hence better support for existing services/products or to establish the required level of support for future services/products in a market-driving scenario. This also enables operations to switch from a reactive to a proactive response. By receiving pertinent inputs at the strategic level, the business is made more aware of the implications involved and is able to arrive at options based on the relevant and comprehensive inputs necessary to make sound strategic decisions.

Recognising the business dimensions of operations strategic contribution

The reasons companies fail to incorporate operations perspectives into the strategy debate are many. For one, operations is traditionally seen as a predominantly technical- or engineering-related function. This not only creates barriers to discussion, but also misrepresents the key operations perspectives that a company needs to recognize and incorporate in its strategy-making process. Operations is a business function that uses technology in its delivery systems to help provide the services or products in line with customer needs. A major thrust within operations strategy, therefore, is to reorient its contribution from being technical/engineering related to being business related. This widens the debate by introducing and highlighting the contribution made by operations in winning and retaining customers. This links operations with other functions by using the market as the common denominator. The result is business-based discussions leading to essential strategic outcomes.

Service/product profiling is one such development. By translating delivery system investments into business issues, companies are able to assess the fit between these major resources and the markets they are required to support. Being able to explain trends, mismatches and options in picture form enhances the power of the message and increases its role in corporate understanding and debate. It leads to sound strategy developments by enabling functions to explain themselves in corporate terms and provides a language to enhance essential discussion and agreement at the level of the business rather than at the level of functions.

Rumack Pharmaceuticals

'Of increasing concern is the difficulty we are having in meeting our schedules and the growing customer order backlog which is resulting. For many months now there has been pressure to maintain schedules and we have been trying hard to overcome these problems. But, it appears as though it may be a permanent feature needing a long-term solution. The part which is difficult to reconcile, however, is that on paper we should have more than sufficient packaging capacity to meet current sales levels. And, no doubt, the rest of the board will also have difficulty in understanding this apparent discrepancy.'

Pete Kovac, vice-president operations at Rumack Pharmaceuticals' plant in Bakersfield, California, was addressing the managers responsible for production, engineering and materials (see Case Figure 6.1) at the weekly meeting to review current issues and progress on agreed developments.

BACKGROUND

Nine years ago, Rumack Pharmaceuticals, needing to increase capacity, decided to build a new plant in Bakersfield, California to make and pack Restolvic, one of its successful stomach indigestion products. Within three years of making the decision, the plant was in full production and, six years later, it manufactures a wide range of derivatives under the Restolvic brand name together with some of its Hedanol products, one of Rumack's pain-killing preparations.

MARKETING

'Restolvic has proven to be one of the most successful products we have developed in the past decade. This is certainly so given the systematic way in which we have developed relevant variants in order to exploit the obvious sales potential. When the plant opened we had two identical lines for packing our solid products. At this

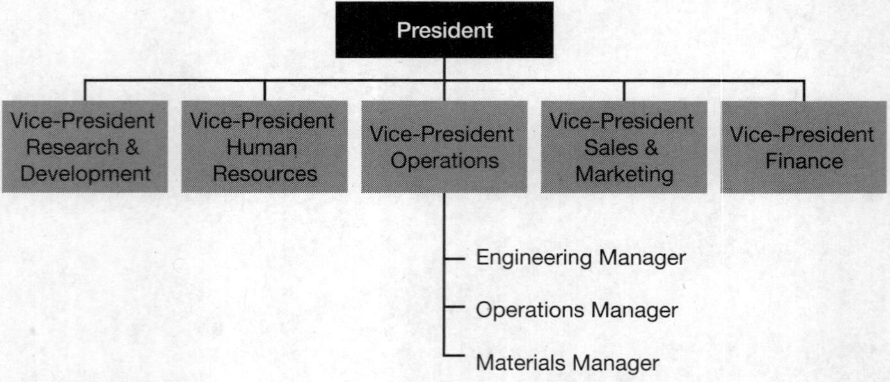

Case Figure 6.1 Part of the company's organization chart

time, we had more capacity than we needed and our task, therefore, has been to identify new opportunities to increase sales and hence overall profits. Initially, we explored additional dosage forms which met the particular needs of consumers. Later, recognizing the level of acceptance of Restolvic as a successful indigestion reliever for a wide cross-section of people, we decided to seek ways of capitalizing on the growing strength of its brand name. This led to adding further active ingredients in order to develop other OTC [over the counter] products such as Restolvic A (an anti-spasmodic preparation) and Restolvic E (an anti-emetic preparation). And the whole strategy has been highly successful.'

Jon Prynn, vice-president marketing gave further details of the way in which the product-line extensions and derivatives had been built on the Restolvic image and, in turn, had added to the whole, thus leading to specific gains of both an 'individual and synergistic' nature.

'All products make very high margins. In fact, some of those which target specific markets will often attract a premium price and consequently even higher margins. All in all, we are a highly profitable business both in terms of total profit and as a per cent of sales.'

OPERATIONS

'Since the opening of the plant some six years ago, we now make and pack OTC varieties of Restolvic, some Hedanol products and more recently prescription derivatives such as Restolvic A and Restolvic E. The latter were relocated here two years ago when the Rumack Group reassessed its overall capacity requirements in the US and decided to close one of its plants. The outcome was that the prescription Restolvic products were relocated and are now made and packed here.'

Jim Lawson, operations manager, explained that the manufacture of pharmaceutical dosage forms is divided into two major groups of activities – processing and packaging.

Processing concerns the conversion of powdered ingredients into bulk tablet or liquid preparations. Equipment is dedicated to a single operation such as granulation, blending, tablet compression, coating and liquid mixing. These products are manufactured in bulk, normally in quantities dictated by the capacity of the particular piece of processing equipment.

Filling bulk tablets and liquids produced in the processing phase of manufacturing takes place in packaging. Here tablets and liquids are bottled according to a range of sizes and on the relevant processes.

There are now four packaging lines at the plant with specific products allocated to each line.

'When we opened up the plant, we installed the relevant processing capability and also packing Lines 1 and 2, with Line 3 scheduled to come on stream 12 to 15 months later. From the start, Lines 1 and 2 worked well and this confirmed our decision to invest in three identical processes. Staying with tried and tested equipment is a significant plus point as well as the benefits for engineering support and maintenance.'

Jim continued:

> 'When the other US plant was closed, we transferred the prescription product range and the existing packaging equipment from that plant to here, then modified and added to the process in order to bring it up to the same specification as the other three lines. The prescription range is only made on Line 4.'

He added that when the Bakersfield plant was planned, sufficient floor space and facilities were allowed for in terms of future growth.

> 'The growth in demand for Restolvic has been rapid and this together with the transfer of products resulting from the plant closure has absorbed the excess floor space allowed for in the original plans.

The capacity problems we are experiencing do not concern the processing stage of manufacturing. Here we have sufficient capacity. The problems are in packaging.'

The discussion then turned to details on each of the packaging lines (see Case Figure 6.2 for an outline of the steps involved and Case Figure 6.3 for details of the four packaging lines).

The four packaging lines referred to in the case narrative have been developed to include both the filling and packaging stage of the process. The principal steps completed within a packaging line are outlined below:

1. Bottle unscrambling – bottles from outside suppliers are delivered and fed into a large hopper which unscrambles and delivers them correctly positioned onto the line.
2. Air cleaning – each bottle is cleaned in terms of dust by a jet of air.
3. Filling – the appropriate number of tablets/caplets are then put into each bottle.
4. Cotton insertion – a small quantity of cotton wool is placed into the empty head space of each bottle to prevent the tablets/caplets from moving. The amount of cotton reflects the space at the top of the bottle. This adjustment forms part of the set-up for each stock-keeping unit (SKU).
5. Capping – a cap is positioned and located on each bottle.
6. Induction sealing – the cap liner and bottle is then sealed, in part as a tamper-evident feature.
7. Labelling – the appropriate label is put on to the bottle.
8. Neck banding – a PVC band is heat shrunk around the neck/cap as a final seal and as another tamper-evident feature.
9. Cartoning – each bottle is placed into its own individual carton.
10. Packing – individual cartons are then placed in a case pack in predetermined quantities.

Note: Stock-keeping unit (SKU) is the phrase for any individual product specification that requires a manufacturing change including packaging.

Case Figure 6.2 Outline of the packaging process

Each line has a crew of seven, consisting of six operators and a mechanic. Three or four operators undertake the cleaning task which takes 3½ to 4 hours. The remainder work on carton and label changing, which takes about the same time as the cleaning element of the changeover. Without a bottle change, a product change would take between 3½ and 4 hours, increasing to 5 hours with a bottle size change. All the lines have the same crew make-up, and all crews work on changeovers that do not require a bottle size change.

Line 1

This line fills and packs both Restolvic and Hedanol products. The selection of these products was made on the basis of bottle size. All products packed on this line use the same bottle. In this way, set-up or changeover times are reduced. Even so, they are still lengthy. Each product change means that the filler has to be stripped, cleaned and reassembled. A typical changeover will take, at most, 4 hours. (Other details for this line are given in Case Figures 6.4, 6.5 and 6.6.)

Line 2

This line is designed to accommodate three different bottle sizes.[1] Over the past two years engineering has redesigned the bottles so that the only dimension which changes is the height. This was selected because it is the easiest form of size adjustment to make on a changeover. Nevertheless, this increases the overall changeover to 5 hours. Without a bottle change, a product change would take between 3½ and 4 hours as with Line 1.

Line 3

This line was installed 12 months after the plant was opened. It handles all liquid products for infants, children and adults. There are five bottle sizes and each bottle size change takes some 8 hours. Engineering has this set-up reduction as a priority given the enormous benefits reaped from the improvements that were made on Line 1 (see Case Figure 6.6). Contamination factors and resulting set-up times restrict, for all practical reasons, the use of this line for packing non-liquid products. The result is that only liquid products are made on this line.

Line 4

This line handles the 12 product types within the Restolvic prescription range. At present, there are five bottle sizes involved and typical set-up times for bottle and product changes are similar to those on Line 3. There is spare capacity, but if OTC products are to be packed on this line then they must meet the more exacting standards of prescription and associated costs. Furthermore, equipment will need to be added to provide the additional packaging formats which are required by OTC products.[2]

The current shift patterns allow the company to run three lines for 24 hours a day throughout all seven days of the week. Priority is given, wherever possible, to Lines 1 and 2 because the products on these two lines have the highest demand and, therefore, require maximum capacity to allow the company to meet current schedules. Lines 3 and 4 both have spare capacity and the company can meet current demand by running these for two shifts and one shift per day, respectively, plus additional times when crews have completed their part of a changeover on another line but the mechanic has other work to do (see Case Figure 6.7).

Changeovers on Lines 3 and 4 are scheduled to be completed at times when the process is not manned.

Notes

1 Bottle sizes differ, depending upon the two factors of tablet size and number of tablets involved.

2 Prescription products have simpler packaging specifications. For example, prescription products are bulk packed at the outer packaging stage where OTC products are individually packed. This additional equipment would require an investment of US$1.0 million.

Case Figure 6.3 **Details of the four packaging lines**

Product[1]	Annual volume in 000 bottles						
	Current year minus						Current year
	6	5	4	3	2	1	
AC Tablets (24)	1,148	1,755	1,906	2,773	3,844	3,896	4,597
AC Tablets (100)	631	907	1,179	1,053	1,180	1,304	1,666
AC Caplets (50)	145	163	402	210	326	409	341
AC Caplets (100)	226	127	172	277	306	440	498
IC Liquid (25 ml)	187	187	249	312	489	429	490
AC Liquid (75 ml)	262	112	158	234	325	294	388
CC Caplets (24)		232	674	977	1,038	1,356	1,457
AC Chewable (110)			438	485	281	480	509
IC Tablets (24)			109	145	254	331	265
CC Tablets (24)				151	151	165	127
IC Tablets (12)				504	432	720	832
CC Tablets (12)				138	311	248	204
AC Tablets (50)					208	256	243
AC Caplets (60)					96	240	262
AC Caplets (24)						65	470
Hedanol Tablets (24)						200	138
Hedanol Tablets (50)						150	42
Hedanol Caplets (24)						218	127
Chewable (20)							224
Chewable (12)							221
Total SKUs added[2]	17	20	22	35	37	45	51

Notes

1 Other than the three Hedanol products, the remainder are Restolvic.

2 SKU describes any differently packed item. Total SKUs are the number packed in each year. Thus, currently the company packs 34 more products than it did 6 years ago.

Case Figure 6.4 **Annual volumes for a number of representative products packed on Lines 1, 2 and 3**

Product	Number of production runs					
	Current year minus					Current year
	5	4	3	2	1	
AC Tablets (24)	10	17	24	33	35	41
CC Caplets (24)	4	10	16	20	22	24
IC Tablets (24)		4	6	9	10	10
CC Tablets (24)			7	6	7	7
CC Tablets (12)			6	9	8	8

AC Tablets (50)				8	9	8
AC Caplets (24)					3	12
Hedanol Tablets (50)					6	2
Hedanol Caplets (24)					4	5

Note: As explained in the case narrative, there are no bottle size changes on Line 1. Where the same product but not the same quantity of tablets is packed, padding is used as a filler.

Case Figure 6.5 **Number of production runs for some representative products on Line 1**

Products	Run size (bottles)	Average output (bottles/hour)
Chewable (24)	23,352	4,246
Chewable (24)	54,720	6,080
Chewable (12)	17,016	4,538
Chewable (12)	38,736	5,165
Chewable (24)	44,664	4,060
Chewable (24)	49,056	4,021
Chewable (24)	58,872	5,744
IC Caplets (24)	7,416	4,944
IC Caplets (24)	81,720	6,286
IC Tablets (30)	51,120	4,987
IC Tablets (30)	164,160	6,438
CC Tablets (12)	15,120	3,360
IC Tablets (24)	5,208	3,472
IC Tablets (24)	14,976	3,744
IC Tablets (24)	29,830	5,424
AC Caplets (24)	41,952	5,594
Hedanol Caplets (24)	31,176	4,454
Hedanol Tablets (50)	13,176	2,510
CC Caplets (24)	27,696	5,036
CC Caplets (24)	62,256	6,445
CC Caplets (24)	62,688	4,179
CC Caplets (24)	95,736	6,838
CC Caplets (24)	121,272	7,134
CC Caplets (50)	28,728	3,591
CC Caplets (50)	29,832	4,262
CC Tablets (24)	66,960	6,533

Case Figure 6.6 **Continued**

AC Tablets (24)	119,808	6,390
AC Tablets (24)	193,800	7,112
AC Tablets (24)	286,584	7,165
CC Tablets (24)	5,880	2,940
CC Tablets (24)	19,008	5,849
AC Tablets (30)	21,720	4,137

Case Figure 6.6 **Run size and output data for a number of representative products packed on Line 1 during the past six months**

The approach to completing the necessary set-ups/changeovers on the four packaging lines is explained below:

Line 1

Because there are no bottle size changes on this line, the product changes are undertaken by the line crew and mechanic who are on the line at the time. A product change requires the filler to be stripped down, cleaned and reassembled. This takes about 3½ to 4 hours using four members of the team. Meanwhile, the other members of the crew complete the labelling/carton changes with the mechanic providing support throughout.

Lines 2, 3 and 4

Product changes on these lines are undertaken in a way similar to that described for Line 1. However, where a bottle size change is also required then the packing crew would first complete the product change tasks, then move to another line which was ready but not being used. The mechanic would stay behind to complete the size change task. The length of time varies from line to line as shown below.

Line	Set-up (hours)		
	Product/packaging changes	Bottle size changes	Total for both bottle and product/packaging changes[1]
1	4	–	4[2]
2	4	5	5
3	4	8	8
4	4	8	8

Notes

1 Size changes and product changes are completed concurrently.

2 No bottle changes take place on Line 1.

Further set-up reductions are constrained in two ways:

- *The investment in a portable filling station and changes to existing lines to accommodate this arrangement total US$0.7 million per station.*
- *These changes would also require additional floor space equal to 50 per cent of the existing floor space required for each packaging line. At this time floor space is at a premium.*

Case Figure 6.7 **Set-up/changeover arrangements**

ENGINEERING

The engineering manager, Rob Chow, explained how the priority for his support group was to accommodate the continued growth in the new product derivations.

> 'We launch line extensions and new products on a regular basis in order to capitalize on the Restolvic image and brand name. And it continues to be a very successful strategy. Our contribution is, therefore, to ensure that we can make those new products in line with the agreed launch dates. The trade-off is that we allocate little or no time to process improvements per se. Also of late, the need to work on rationalizing bottle sizes on Line 3 and working on set-ups in general has been put on a back burner. We are aware of the need to address these issues but, at the moment and for the foreseeable future, they will have to take a low priority.'

THE FUTURE

Pete Kovac summed up:

> 'These are exciting times for our business. We have grown sales revenue and profits in line with, if not above, budget and the future looks equally promising. However, all this has been met only by making appropriate investments and the continued efforts of all concerned. The one issue of some concern is that of capacity in our packaging area. A new packaging line currently costs, including installation, some US$3.5 million with a lead time of 12 months from the placement of the order until it is commissioned and up to speed. The rationale for such an investment and the case to support such a proposal will need to be carefully thought through and will understandably be questioned by the rest of the executive group given our existing capacity projections.'

DISCUSSION QUESTIONS

1 Why is it necessary to check alignment between market requirements and operations characteristics?
2 What are the steps to take in service/product profiling?
3 What situations/circumstances can induce a mismatch between market requirements and operations investments?
4 How can a company use service/product profiling as part of its strategic response?

NOTES AND REFERENCES

1 This example is described and discussed more fully in Hill, A. and Cuthbertson, R. (2011) 'Fitness map: a classification of internal strategic fit in service organisations', *International Journal of Operations & Project Management*, 31(9): 991–1020.

2 Additional examples of the use of profiling to test or assess levels of alignment are provided in Hill, A. and Brown, S. (2007) 'Strategic profiling: a visual representation of internal strategic fit in service organisations', *International Journal of Operations & Project Management*, 27(12): 1333–61.

EXPLORING FURTHER

Day, G.S. (2003) 'Creating a superior customer relating capability', *Sloan Management Review*, 44(Spring): 77–83.

Galbraith, J.R. (2002) *Designing Organisations: An Executive Guide to Strategy, Structure and Process*, Jossey-Bass.

Ghosal, S. and Nohria, N. (1993) 'Horses for courses: organisational forms of multinational corporations', *Sloan Management Review*, Winter: 23–35.

Miller, D., Eisenstat, R. and Foote, N. (2002) 'Strategy from the inside out: building capability – creating organisations, *California Management Review*, 44(Spring): 37–54.

Zanon, C.J. et al. (2013) 'Alignment of operations strategy: exploring the marketing interface', *Browse Journals and Books, Industrial Management and Data Systems*, 113(2).

7 FOCUS: PRINCIPLES, CONCEPTS AND METHODOLOGY

THIS CHAPTER DISCUSSES...

SUMMARY

- The complexity of managing operations is a result of the number and interrelated nature of the aspects and issues involved in managing day-to-day operations and maintaining the necessary level of fit between the needs of the business and operations' strategic tasks.
- Operations tends to be arranged based on the principles of economies of scale and control through specialists. Facilities are usually large, with similar processes grouped together and infrastructure centralized into specialist functions.
- Focus creates a consistent set of management and strategic tasks that enables operations to better align service delivery systems/ manufacturing processes and infrastructure to business and market needs.
- Operations focus challenges the principles of economies of scale and control through specialists that allow wider service and product ranges and larger facility sizes to be managed but, in turn, create unclear strategic tasks.
- Business must consider the cost and competitive, management and strategic implications before focusing operations. A movement away from economies of scale brings management benefits, but potentially cost disadvantages.
- It is not necessary to focus all services, products and delivery systems. A combination of focused units and economies of scale may be more appropriate.
- Organizations can use an operation-within-an-operation arrangement to overcome the lower equipment utilization and investment costs that focus can create.
- Focus involves five main steps that tend to be iterative in nature. Initially, it must review staff and delivery systems/manufacturing processes to identify any that are too expensive to duplicate. Market order-winners and qualifiers are then identified. Based on these two reviews, a focus approach is selected. Services/products with similar order-winners are then grouped in the same unit. Staff, delivery systems/manufacturing processes and infrastructure are allocated and physically moved to each unit in line with their requirements.
- Maintaining focus must be a conscious strategic task. Focus does not occur naturally. In fact, corporate neglect and traditional views of what is best for a business tend to prevent it. The range of delivery services/products handled, markets served and delivery systems used must be continually reviewed.

Operations is a complex function and successfully managing this complexity is essential to ensure that operations fulfils its substantial role in the day-to-day running of a business while also making its strategic contribution to help retain and grow market share. This complexity in operations, however, does not come from the nature of the individual tasks that make up the job but rather from the number of aspects and issues involved in managing day-to-day operations, the interrelated nature of these aspects and issues and maintaining the necessary level of fit between the needs of a business's markets, operations' subsequent strategic tasks and its ability to provide these.[1]

In all but highly technical service/product market segments, it is not difficult for operations managers to cope with the technical dimensions of the job. Required technologies are typically purchased from outside with the necessary technical support provided for operations by specialist functions within. In that way, operations is not a technically related function but a business-related function whose role is to use these essential technologies to meet customer needs. Achieving the necessary fit between the competitive factors in a company's markets and its service delivery systems or manufacturing processes and infrastructure to provide them is an essential part of operations' strategic role. It uses technology to provide the needs of customers and, as discussed in the last chapter, this involves ensuring alignment between market order-winners and qualifiers and operations' ability to meet these while delivering the financial targets set by the business. Focus is one approach to organizing operations so that its strategic task can be best fulfilled.

FOCUS

Focus concerns linking operations to the appropriate competitive factors of the business so that it can gain greater control of its competitive position. One of the most difficult tasks in managing operations is responding to the different market demands made on its facilities. This is due to the typically wide and diverse market demands to be met (markets are increasingly different rather than increasingly similar) and the challenge of coordinating operations to meet what is often a conflicting set of requirements. Companies using focus to manage the range of strategic demands placed on operations find that conflicts in providing strategic priorities are reduced, a sense of direction is enhanced and strategic performance is improved.

When explaining focus, the words 'narrow' or 'narrowing' are often used. For example, Skinner, who was the first to talk about the benefits of focused plants, argues that 'a factor that focuses on a narrow product mix for a particular market niche will outperform the conventional plant, which attempts a broader mission.'[2] However, taken at face value, this argument can be misleading. Many companies do not have the narrow service/product mix alternative referred to here. The issue of focus, therefore, is more accurately explained in Skinner's fuller definition:

- **Management task** – learning to focus each plant on a limited, concise, manageable set of services/products, technologies, volumes, and markets.
- **Strategic task** – learning to structure basic policies and supporting services so that they focus on one explicit strategic task, instead of on many inconsistent, conflicting, implicit tasks.[3]

The emphasis here is on a consistent set of management and strategy tasks, which will often be far from the layman's definition of narrow. So, to avoid confusion, the dimension of narrowness should be set aside. It is the homogeneity of tasks and the repetition and experience involved in completing these that form the basis of focus. For example, take the two different scenarios of low and high volume. The characteristics of low-volume demand typically involve small quantities (by definition), multiple changes (as a consequence of low volumes) and fast response (demand forecasts are less predictable and making or preparing ahead of time is seldom a viable option). High volume, on the other hand, involves large quantities (by definition), few changes (as a consequence of high volumes) and more predictable demand forecasts that facilitate an operations' response to fulfilling these requirements.

Thus, focusing the demands placed on operations will enable resources, efforts and attention to be concentrated on a defined and homogeneous set of activities, allowing management to prioritize the key tasks necessary to achieve better performance. In most operations, however, focus is rarely understood. The factors that cause this are now discussed.

APPLYING THE PRINCIPLE OF ECONOMIES OF SCALE IN TODAY'S MARKETS

For many years it has been (and still is) argued that the principle of economies of scale is a sound and appropriate way of organizing and managing businesses. Relating to the cost advantage obtained due to size with unit costs decreasing as fixed costs are spread over more units of output, economies of scale, as an underlying approach, is highly attractive. However, for many organizations today this approach needs to be reassessed as the inherent benefits that can accrue from applying economies of scale are no longer being fully realized because the markets and necessary corporate response to and support for them have changed. While markets in the past were characterized by similarity, today's markets are characterized by difference.

Organizing operations based on economies of scale principles is most appropriate for and best applied to high-volume, steady-state markets (where similarity is the hallmark). However, for many companies these conditions no longer reflect the nature of their business. For many, these prerequisites are far from reality. In fact, if anything, the opposite applies. Their markets comprise lower volumes and are dynamic in nature (where difference is the hallmark). The key reasons why the conditions have changed are now explained.

Expanding service/product ranges

Marketing-led strategies are typically based on the premise of growth through extending service/product ranges. Invariably, new services/products (even those requiring new technologies) are provided, partly at least, using existing staff, service delivery systems or manufacturing processes and almost always within the same infrastructure. The logic for this is based on the principle of the economies derived from using an existing cost base to deliver increased sales. However, over time, the incremental nature of these marketing changes will invariably alter operations' strategic task(s). The results are greater complexity, more confusion and an organization that, because it is spun in many directions by a centrifugal force, lacks focus and an achievable strategic task.[4]

Increasing facility size

When faced with a shortage of capacity, companies often find the attractions of on-site expansion irresistible. The tangible arguments of cost and overhead advantages, plus the provision of a better hedge against future uncertainty, provide the basis against which companies measure the alternatives. However, they rarely take into account the costs of the associated increase in complexity, the bureaucracy that develops and the increased overhead costs that follow as facilities try to cope. These changes are further hidden or disguised by their piecemeal or incremental nature, as Schmenner concludes:

> Big plants usually have formidable bureaucratic structures. Relationships inevitably become formal, and the worker is separated from top executives by many layers of management. All too often, managers are shuffling the paperwork that formal systems have spawned ... Although there has to be some formality in plant operations, too much can wipe out the many informal procedures that keep plants nimble and able to adapt to change.[5]

Unclear strategic task

As well as the increased management task from the larger facility, in circumstances of incremental growth operations' strategic task will become less clearly defined. It will increasingly be required to meet multiple performance objectives that often change from one day to the next in line with the varying pressures placed on the business. The result is that operations will respond as best it can, independently deciding on the best corporate compromises or trade-offs involved. Invariably the result is reduced performance and lack of fit with overall business objectives and the market(s) it serves.

Utilizing staff, delivery systems and facilities

Embodied in the principle of economies of scale is the argument for continually increasing staff, delivery systems and facility utilization. Where capacity is released due to a fall-off in demand for existing services or products, companies typically reutilize the spare capacity by introducing new services or products. There is constant pressure on operations to fully utilize existing staff or delivery system/process capacity before any new investment can be made. However, when evaluating the suitability of existing staff or systems for new services or products, companies invariably only check that the technical specification of the new offering(s) will be met. They rarely check the consistency of the business requirement (its strategic task) for each of the new services or products involved. Furthermore, such business requirement checks are necessary not just for any new services or products, but must be made over time as the relevant order-winners for some existing services or products change.

Managing businesses using specialists

Businesses typically organize themselves into functional specialisms and appoint the individual with the highest specialist knowledge to manage each department.

> These professionals, quite naturally, seek to maximize their contributions and justify their positions. They have conventional views of success in each of their particular fields. Of course, these objectives are generally in conflict.[6]

This conflict often means that the close functional cooperation and understanding required to manage the business is missing. The failure of companies to clearly define the direction of their business exacerbates this problem. Without this direction, there is insufficient shared understanding of what is required. The result is that support systems, controls, information provision and other features of infrastructure are developed out of line with the appropriate total corporate need. The advantages and disadvantages of alternative strategies cannot be compared against a shared understanding of the business. Instead, they are assessed on the fragmented and uncoordinated specialist views based on what seems best at the time, rather than on an agreed strategic whole.

LOOKING FOR PANACEAS

Too often, strategy development is solution based rather than problem based. The belief is that success lies in simply finding the right solution, rather than understanding the problem a business faces and then developing an appropriate solution to address this. The result is that many firms spend their time searching for which of the many three-letter acronyms holds the key to success (see Figure 7.1). And most companies can, no doubt, recall their own range of redundant solutions. One example of a long line in operations is exhorting businesses to adopt the best system used elsewhere rather than analysing their own organization and developing their own approach or adopting approaches from elsewhere to fit their own requirements. Although such formulaic developments can contribute substantially to business success, they need to be derived from strategic discussion and in line with appropriate and agreed direction.

For strategic initiatives to be successful, they must fit the needs of the market and there must be sufficient time to develop and implement them. In Japan, systems such as just-in-time (JIT) and total quality management (TQM) were developed in response to requirements placed on their businesses, and it took some 30 years to perfect and carefully adapt these approaches to those needs. Western companies often take the ideas of these types of initiatives in a prescriptive form and expect to implement them in months rather than years. This approach results in inappropriate applications, unrealistic expectations and unsustainable

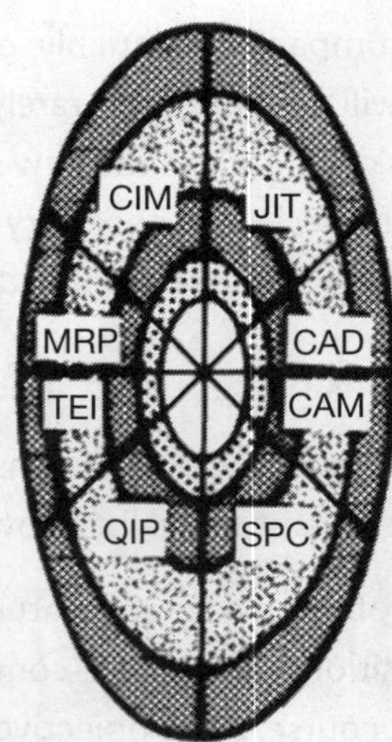

Figure 7.1 **In pursuit of a panacea: which three-letter acronym next?**
Source: Operations Institute, Johnson & Johnson, with permission.

developments. Worst of all, by continually searching for and trying to implement panacea approaches, managers are distracted from understanding and evaluating their own business requirements, and, more importantly, feel that there is no longer any need to be concerned as everything will be solved by the latest approach they have discovered and are implementing.

CONSTRAINTS TO FOCUSING OPERATIONS

While some operations facilities are purpose-built in line with known or anticipated profiles of demand, many evolve over time as organizations grow. With some purpose-built facilities, the characteristics of the demand profiles for which they were originally developed continue to be sufficiently similar over time that the level of fit remains intact. Where this level of fit in purpose-built facilities deteriorates as the characteristics and needs of the markets change, checking and restoring the level of fit is an essential strategic task that businesses need to undertake. Similar checks and changes need to be regularly made where organizations have and are continuing to grow. As you can envisage, new markets and customers will often bring different sets of demands that alter the strategic task which operations was originally set up to provide. Again, the need to check (and improve where necessary) the level of fit is required. However, there are several circumstances that may constrain businesses in their pursuit of focusing operations as a way of better meeting the needs of their markets. These constraints are now explained.

Excessive capital investment

Focusing the demands placed on operations allows resources, efforts and attention to be concentrated on a defined and homogeneous set of activities. Typically, such changes include allocating equipment as well as staff and other facilities to the specific use of a focused operations unit. Where such allocations would necessitate purchasing additional, expensive equipment then companies understandably need to assess the cost/benefit equation of such a decision in itself and compared to alternative investments.

Meeting regulatory requirements

In industries such as food and pharmaceuticals, regulations are in place to govern their manufacturing processes. The Food and Drug Administration in the US, the European Medicines Agency and the Medicines and Healthcare Products Regulatory Agency in the UK are typical of these arrangements. For a company to make such products, the processes and facilities to be used are first vetted and certificated on a plant-specific basis. Should a company wish to make the same products in another location or in the same location but using different equipment then the detailed vetting procedures have to be repeated. Given the timescales and costs involved, companies are reluctant to duplicate these arrangements, preferring to use any spare capacity on existing 'authorized' processes. Because food and pharmaceutical product packaging is specific to the country in which it is sold, then such products increase the range a process has to make. In turn this impacts on volumes, increases changeovers and extends process losses. Furthermore, when capacity is fully used, making low volume-demand products with their associated lower levels of productivity would further exacerbate these existing capacity constraints.

Servicing overseas markets

Companies, either by choice or in line with the requirements laid down by national agreements, set up local facilities in countries where they sell their goods and services. These decisions bring several benefits, including access to local knowledge and commercial contacts as well as more informed insights about markets and customers. However, such arrangements reduce the opportunity for operations to meet these requirements as part of the larger block of demand, thereby restricting options of how best to fulfil customers' orders.

Factoring in the costs of distribution

Companies that supply goods that are of low value but costly to distribute due to their size or weight typically build smaller facilities to meet customer demand. Such financially sound decisions provide better margins even though they limit operations' options on how best to meet the demand profiles of the total business.

FOCUSED FACILITIES

The approach to designing facilities using economies of scale principles reflects concerns about utilizing resources, whereas those designed using the principle of focus are built around the needs of markets. With the latter, services or products are allocated to a particular unit on the basis of the different market order-winners and qualifiers that operations supports. This approach creates a coherent strategic task in each unit that reflects the needs of the markets it serves. It is this factor that provides the basis for allocating services or products to a focused unit.

FOCUS – ADVANTAGES AND DISADVANTAGES

The alternative approaches to organizing operations facilities have advantages and disadvantages, as shown in Figure 7.2. When deciding on the appropriate approach, companies must consider the cost, management and strategic implications of such decisions.

Advantages and disadvantages		Alternatives to organizing operations using the principles of	
		Economies of scale	Focus
Basis		Resources	Markets
Advantages			
Cost	High utilization of facilities	✓	
	Minimize investment	✓	
	Minimize overhead costs	✓	
Managerial	Fewer services/products to provide		✓
	Less staff to manage		✓
	Better communications		✓
	Easier to control		✓
	Reduced range of		
	– Technologies		✓
	– Volumes		✓
Strategic	Coherent task(s)		✓
	High internal fit		✓
	High external fit		✓
Disadvantages			
Cost	Lower utilization of facilities		✓
	Higher overhead costs		✓
	System duplication		✓
Managerial	More services/products	✓	
	More staff to manage	✓	
	Larger area	✓	
	Poor communications	✓	
	Wider range of volumes	✓	
Strategic	Multiple and conflicting tasks	✓	
	Lower internal fit	✓	
	Lower external fit	✓	

Figure 7.2 The advantages and disadvantages of alternative approaches to organizing operations

The traditional approach of economies of scale has cost benefits in terms of higher equipment utilization, less investment and lower overheads. However, these arrangements are more difficult to manage and introduce multiple, conflicting strategic tasks that create low fit within operations and with markets. A move to focus brings the principal benefit of operations being able to harness its capabilities to better provide relevant order-winners and qualifiers. In other words, what operations needs to be good at is lined up with its strategic contribution. Additional benefits are also gained from reducing the size of the operation: it is easier to manage and control with smaller staff numbers, it covers a small area and involves a reduced range of technologies and volumes.

However, introducing the concept of focus into such decisions does not in any way imply only an either/or option. Understandably, the outcome is often a mix of economies of scale and focused approaches. Where a mixed arrangement is the appropriate way forward there will be additional benefits. The part of operations that remains unaltered will itself be simpler to manage (it is now smaller) and the mix of order-winners and qualifiers to be provided will be reduced.

Focusing operations is more difficult to understand

The principle of economies of scale is widely understood, in part because the phrase itself embodies the concept on which the principle is based. Similarly, splitting operations by service/product types or the delivery systems used in their provision can be more easily visualized than organizing operations based on how services or products compete within their markets. For example, services and products are often referred to as 'medical' or 'professional', or 'aerospace' or 'automotive' but never, for example, as 'price-sensitive' or 'delivery speed' services/products even when these are their agreed competitive criteria. One consequence is that businesses more readily support splitting operations facilities by service/product or delivery-system type, for example, than by order-winners and qualifiers.

Using a combination of approaches

As mentioned earlier, the economies of scale and focus approaches have different sets of advantages (see Figure 7.2). As such, it may not be, and often is not, appropriate to use the principle of focus to best organize operations. For example, a business supplies eight product groups where price is the principal order-winner for only product Group A. The other seven groups have a mix of order-winners and qualifiers such that there is no clear concentration. Here it would be appropriate to create separate operations facilities for product Group A that are designed principally to reduce costs, while continuing to supply the other seven product groups through the existing, economies of scale-based facility. Although these arrangements only use focused facilities to meet product Group A's requirements, the overall outcome also simplifies operations for the other seven product groups by 'removing' the conflicting demands of Group A's products from the overall task.

Equally, in some circumstances, an upstream process may be too expensive to duplicate whereas any additional investment in the subsequent steps in the process may be affordable. Here, the high investment process would continue to be centrally arranged and used to complete that step in the process for all products while subsequent processes can be split into sets of focused processes to meet the varying order-winners of the range of products made.

Operation-within-an-operation arrangements

As shown in Figure 7.2 and highlighted throughout the chapter, the principal disadvantage of focus concerns lower delivery-system utilization and the associated potential increase in investment and other additional overhead costs. A way to reduce this inherent disadvantage is to create an operation-within-an-operation (OWO) arrangement, thereby spreading several overhead costs across a number of focused facilities. Since many companies own existing sites with their sizeable investments of equipment, bricks and mortar, utilities and offices, then creating new facilities to accommodate separate, focused facilities is often not financially viable.

The way to provide focused facilities in these situations is to adopt an OWO configuration. This involves physically dividing offices or sites (often using partitions, different entrances and other facilities) into 'separate' operations units focused on different business needs. Each such unit is more manageable and strategically aligned to its markets than when a business tries to meet all its needs with a single operations facility. Although there are cost disadvantages from the apparent loss of economies of scale benefits, OWO provides the opportunity to review the overheads allocated to each unit. The improved clarity between business needs and overhead requirements often makes this review easier. By splitting the overheads down, the business is able to see clearly each aspect of the overhead provision, how much of each aspect is required and the business contribution each provides. As such, overhead costs better match requirements, a truer picture of the relative profitability of each service/product group can be calculated and the level of support provided by various overhead functions can be ascertained, better understood and appropriately allocated.

MAINTAINING FOCUS

Progression or regression in focus

Focused facilities are aimed at improving the link between market needs and operations' strategic role in providing those order-winners and qualifiers for which it is solely or jointly responsible. In this market/operations tie-up, whereas markets change independently as an integral part of their inherent characteristics, operations does not change unless as a result of a conscious business decision. Consequently, although operations can be designed on the basis of being focused, over time the degree of fit will regress as market needs (order-winners and qualifiers) and characteristics (such as volumes) change. For this reason, focused operations facilities need to be monitored to ensure that any regression is identified, what changes to make can be proactively discussed and agreed, and the level of strategic support for these changes can be adjusted.

Focus and the service/product life cycle

Figure 7.3 shows how volumes and strategic tasks change during a service/product's life cycle. In the early stages of growth, operations faces less predictable sales volumes, service/product and delivery-system modifications, customer orientation and varying levels of delivery speed.

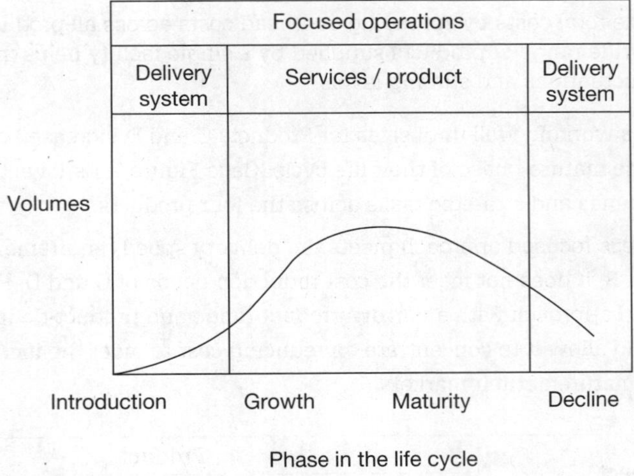

Figure 7.3 **A typical service/product life cycle and its relationship to focus**

Delivery system/process focus is usually most appropriate because it is flexible and technically capable of coping with these changes. As services/products mature, sales volumes increase, service/product and delivery system/process technologies are established and price becomes more sensitive. The narrow service/product range and service/product-dedicated delivery systems/processes of service/product focus allow operations to concentrate on reducing costs. As the service/product goes into decline, operations volumes decrease, become less stable and delivery speed tends to be more important. A delivery system/process-focused unit is better able to meet these demands.

Case 7.1 – Triplex Electronics

Telecommunications switchgear has evolved over a number of years from mechanical to electromechanical to electronic technology. Triplex Electronics has developed products to meet these changes (see Case Figure 7.1). Each product was launched before the end of the life of the previous one. As a result, original equipment and spares for various products are currently supplied.

Product A is based on a mechanical technology and sales are restricted to spares or replacement equipment for existing installations. The processes required to make this product were specific to this range and cannot be used to supply electronic technology products. Product B is also no longer sold, having been superseded by Products C and D which were introduced shortly after Product B due to rapid advances in product technology. The company chose to organize operations using a process-focused approach where Product A is supplied from one unit and Products B, C and D from another. The reasons for this were:

- To develop products within an existing facility and so avoid the need to use a new facility for each stage of a product's life.

- To minimize total costs by spreading overhead costs across all products.
- Having a wide range of products supplied by a single facility helps manage demand fluctuations and staffing levels.

Everything was working well until sales for Products C and D increased markedly as they entered the mature phase of their life cycle. Case Figure 7.1 shows the resulting changes in volumes and strategic tasks across the four products.

While the process-focused approach meets the delivery speed requirements of Products A and B, it does not meet the cost reduction needs of C and D. Here, a product-focused approach with a narrow product range and product-dedicated processes would allow it to concentrate on reducing cost to meet the increasingly price-sensitive nature of their markets.

Aspect		Product			
		A	B	C	D
Production volumes	Current	Low	Low	High	Low/medium
	In 2–3 years	Stable	Decreasing	Decreasing	Increasing
Key strategic task	Current	Delivery speed	Delivery speed	Cost reduction	Quality conformance and on-time delivery
	In 2–3 years	Delivery speed	Delivery speed	Cost reduction	Cost reduction

Case Figure 7.1 Changes over time in production volumes and strategic task

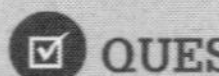

QUESTIONS

1 How would you focus operations at Triplex Electronics?
2 What would be the benefits of the approach you proposed?

Functional pressure to regress

Achieving and maintaining focus must be a conscious strategic decision. Focus does not occur naturally. In fact, corporate neglect or traditional views of what is best for a business often tend to prevent it, as discussed below.

- **Marketing** often stimulates the desire to create and maintain a broad service or product line. This is typically an integral part of its strategy with sales revenue an important measure of its performance.
- **Sales** understandably believe it is easier to sell a broad service/product line. They argue that a wide service/product range allows them to appeal to a broader market and smooth out seasonal or cyclical demand patterns. Sales revenue is typically the most important measure of its performance with the use of sales value-based commission schemes reinforcing this emphasis.

- **Operations** may resist focus because of the high cost of purchasing equipment, moving or retraining/relocating staff and uncertain benefits.
- **Accounting and finance** often place an overriding emphasis on short-term earnings that restricts capital investment. Also the practices used to monitor and evaluate operating costs may distort reality. For example, the typical accounting practice of absorbing overhead costs across a wide range of services/products often means that the actual profit for a single product and the actual financial impact of providing a wide range of services or products are both unknown.
- **Strategy development** is often, if not typically, dominated by the perspectives of a single function. The relative importance given to the various insights brought to strategy discussions and the outcomes and decisions taken are, therefore, often imbalanced and based on a too narrow set of views and perspectives. As sales revenue growth is often high on the strategic agenda, then unless the discussions and decisions include due weight to ascertaining the impact on operations' ability to support the growing set of market needs (and subsequent impact on profit margins) then the inherent tendency to regress will be accelerated and unchecked.

APPROACH TO FOCUSING OPERATIONS

The principles and concepts underpinning focus were outlined in the previous sections. We now turn our attention to the steps to take when focusing operations. The idea of focus is to arrange operations so there is a consistent task within each unit. Before outlining the steps to focus facilities, it is important to bear in mind the following.

- Using a combination of approaches – Focus should not be seen as the preferred dogma on which to base operations arrangements. Replacing one dogma with another replaces one set of advantages and disadvantages with another set. Often businesses are better served by a combination of economies of scale principles with those of focus. Since combinations often yield the best overall results, companies need to be pragmatic rather than dogmatic in these developments.
- Improving business and market support – the principle of applying focus is to improve on what currently exists. Focusing parts of a business not only leads to gains within these parts but also simplifies that which remains unchanged, thus facilitating business activities throughout.
- Making incremental changes – it is often best to rearrange a business one part at a time and enlarge the scope of change one phase at a time. Choosing areas where the rationale is clearest helps to improve the rate of success, reduce the size of the task, maintain acceptable timescales and allow everyone to learn.

The underlying reasoning when focusing a business is to be pragmatic. Thus, if focus does not bring overall cost, managerial or strategic benefits, it should not be applied. In most businesses, a combination of approaches will often result in the best overall improvement. Companies must have the desire to change and overcome the inertia and resistance that exists in many organizations. Furthermore, the process of change needs to be ongoing. As markets continually change, so must operations' response. In the past, many companies failed to question existing approaches because there was no viable, well-argued and well-articulated alternative. Focus provides another approach to organizing arrangements to better exploit a company's resources and market opportunities.

FOCUSING OPERATIONS[7]

This section outlines the steps to be followed when focusing operations (see Figure 7.4). As with most strategy developments, it is iterative in nature and needs adequate time to work through the issues involved.

1 Review staff and service delivery systems/manufacturing processes

The first task is to review the existing operations to identify any staff, service delivery systems or manufacturing processes that are too expensive to duplicate.[8] Examples of these differ from one business or industry to another and include specialist staff (for example, specialized market analysts and actuaries), specialist processes (for example, heat treatment) and specialized facilities (for example, clean-rooms). These types of staff or delivery systems/processes are best managed centrally using economies of scale principles so that these resources can be best exploited. Staff delivery systems or processes that are not too expensive to duplicate will be arranged to exploit market opportunities. In some companies, services or products are tied to given staff, delivery systems or processes. Any rearrangement of such capabilities would therefore lead directly to staff, delivery system or process duplication with potentially high additional investment. In manufacturing, upstream processes will often fall into this category. On the other hand, downstream processes (for example, packing) are normally less likely to be affected by this constraint because of the lower levels of investment typically involved.

2 Identify order-winners and qualifiers

The next step is to identify the operations-related order-winners and qualifiers for the services or products provided. The outcome will determine how best to arrange resources, given

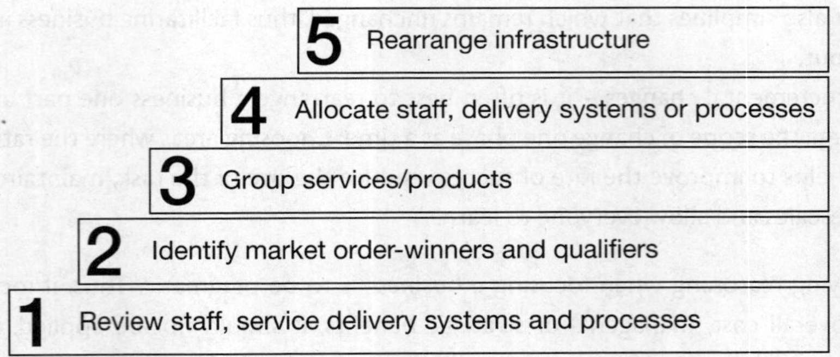

Figure 7.4 Methodology: the five steps

the constraints identified in the staff/delivery system/process review. It may be that some services or products have different order-winners depending on the nature of the customer order received. For example, an automotive component may be supplied to an original equipment manufacturer where orders would typically be won on price. However, spares orders for similar components are also supplied and here delivery speed would typically be more important. Although some supermarkets launched their online service initially using in-store pickers, many (for example Tesco in the UK) are now building out-of-store facilities to process this growing element of their business as a way to handle higher demand and control costs.

3 Group services or products

At this point, services or products are grouped by the order-winners and qualifiers identified in Step 2. In some instances, it may make sense for a service/product to be supplied by two alternative units depending on the nature of the order received. Taking the examples used in Step 2, the automotive component business might decide to set up a separate low cost-focused unit and a delivery speed-focused unit to meet the different order-winners of its markets. The same component may then be supplied from two different units depending on the requirement of the customer order received.

Ideally, a similar set of order-winners and qualifiers within each customer group should be created and thereby a coherent strategic task set for each unit. In the Tesco example, setting up a separate facility created a delivery system specific to its online business while removing the growing complexity in its high street stores as the online part of its business continued to grow.

However, the constraints of reality and what is best for the business need to be considered when making this decision. Once the split is agreed, then services/products, delivery systems/processes and infrastructure can be allocated to each unit.

4 Allocate staff and service delivery systems/manufacturing processes

Once service/product groups have been agreed, staff and service delivery systems/manufacturing processes are allocated and physically moved to each unit to meet their capability and capacity requirements. As identified in Step 1, some staff, systems or processes may remain central because they are too expensive to duplicate. These would be managed using economies of scale principles to serve the varying needs of each unit.

5 Rearrange infrastructure

The final step is to review and allocate the infrastructure required by each unit. As with allocating staff and delivery systems/processes, it is important to review activities and assess whether they should be allocated to a unit or remain central, serving all units. Significant benefits can often be achieved because:

- Overheads are typically a large part of the total cost and capability base of an organization. Aligning them to support the varying market needs will help it maintain and improve its support for customers. The total overhead costs across a business are also often reduced because the appropriate level of resources to support each market can be more clearly assessed and unnecessary provision identified.

- Reshaping and repositioning overheads is usually not restricted by the same issues (such as investment) as are service delivery systems or manufacturing processes. Therefore, there are often more opportunities and gains to be made than when allocating service delivery systems and manufacturing processes.

In reviewing and allocating infrastructure, two key principles must be considered:

- **Review activities not functions** – identify those activities that are better allocated to a unit and those which should remain central. In many instances, this will involve splitting existing functional activities, as shown in Figure 7.5.
- **Locate activities in the unit** – the overhead resources must be physically allocated to a unit and moved to the relevant site. This ensures that the unit is responsible for the level of resources required and how they should be managed. In this way, their prime focus reflects the operational and strategic needs and tasks of a unit.

MAINTAINING FOCUS

Since markets are inherently dynamic (they will change whether or not you want them to) and operations is inherently fixed (it will not change unless you deliberately change it), businesses will naturally become unfocused over time. Focusing operations is, therefore, not a one-off task and companies must continually review their markets and align operations to support their needs. A service's or product's order-winners and qualifiers will change over time as it goes through its life cycle and the nature of the market in which it competes will also change. Very often the best response is to move the service or product to another unit that is oriented to its new strategic task, but new units may need to be developed.

Function	Activities typically best allocated to a	
	Central function	Focused unit
Quality	Quality assurance – agree sampling and other routines, laboratory testing and establish checking procedures	Quality control – undertake quality conformance checking procedures such as inspection
Operations planning control and scheduling	Long-term tasks such as capacity planning	Day-to-day scheduling and control of operations
Purchasing	Vendor selection and negotiating supply contracts	Arrange for call-offs of bought-out materials, components and other items in line with the operations schedule

Figure 7.5 Examples of the activities typically best allocated to a central function or focused unit

Case 7.2 – Maintaining focus in maturing markets

A major supplier of components and products to the private, commercial and off-highway vehicle markets was reviewing one of its operations facilities. Product range widening, volume changes and the growing original equipment/spares mix in recent years had created a very complex business. As a result, the facility was difficult to manage, had high work-in-progress inventory and was increasingly unable to meet customers' delivery lead times or earn a satisfactory level of return on its investment.

To reduce the management task of the operation, the company decided to create several product/market-focused units. It hoped these would better reflect customers' needs and reduce work-in-progress inventory. To test the validity of the approach, the company initially took the smallest manufacturing unit within the product/market split and relocated the necessary processes and infrastructure to an unused part of the existing site. A review of this decision showed a series of gains resulting from the smaller unit being easier to manage. However, more testing showed that market support had not been improved. The level of order-winners demanded was still not being adequately met. The company had merely created a smaller version of the original facility with the same strategic problems. The high-volume original equipment and low-volume spares demanded different order-winners. The appropriate split would have been to create order-winner-focused units. Aligning operations with its markets would have generated both management and strategic benefits.

 **QUESTIONS**

1 Why was the initial smaller unit 'easier to manage' but 'market support had not been improved'?
2 In principle, what alternative facilities split would you recommend?

FOCUS EXAMPLES

This section provides examples of alternative focus approaches and how they meet different business needs.

Case 7.3 – Refocusing as products mature and diversify

A US-based pharmaceutical company reviewed its European operations in order to reduce costs and better align facilities to the markets served. At the time, the company had five product-focused units that supported all sales in Europe as well as the Middle East and Africa. Units 1 and 2 were much larger than the other three and supplied a range of products at varying stages in their life cycles. As a consequence there were instances of high-volume demand for products from large national economies (for example, France, Germany and the UK) as well as low-volume demand for the same products from smaller countries, as well as for other products in the latter stages of their life cycle. Units 3 and 4 also had similar mixed volumes, while all the products supplied by Unit 5 were at the end of their life cycles and of low volume. The review identified very high levels of excess capacity across the five units and so it decided to close Units 1 and 2 and refocus the three remaining facilities. A market review showed that, because price was not an order-winner for any of the pharmaceutical products, the key strategic task for operations was to ensure that products were available for customers to purchase when they needed to. Not meeting this requirement had previously resulted in lost sales and customers moving their loyalty to other brands. The decision was made to focus Units 3 and 4 to make and pack the high-volume end of product demand and Unit 5 to make and pack all low-volume products. This allowed Units 3 and 4 to orient their priorities around process-throughput speeds, meeting growing customer demand and always delivering on time, while Unit 5 prioritized reducing set-up times to better handle its low-volume demand and developing a fast-response capability for urgent orders. The overall result was a cost saving from the closure of the two facilities and a strategic benefit from the improved alignment of the three remaining facilities with their markets.

 **QUESTIONS**

1 What was the rationale underpinning the focusing decisions regarding Units 3, 4 and 5?
2 Explain the improved alignment that resulted.

Case 7.4 – Strategic review resulting from increased demand for a product group

A large European electronics manufacturer was deciding where to locate its thick-film operation. It had two facilities in geographically separate sites but it needed to double its overall capacity in the near future to meet the anticipated growth in thick-film applications. The alternatives were to meet the increase either by using existing spare capacity in both sites or by reviewing existing demand in both facilities and transferring work to create space in one site. An assessment of the situation identified two issues. There was a need to achieve higher levels of quality conformance in the new market for which an increase in engineering and development infrastructure support would be required.

Secondly, a review of the market order-winners and qualifiers of its products showed that they fell into two groups. One group had exacting product specifications, comprised low volumes, and required both a high level of development activity and a high calibre of engineering and specialist support. The other group of products involved lower specifications but higher volumes. The decision was made to create two order-winner-focused units to support these two product groups. The availability and likelihood of attracting highly skilled engineering and specialist staff was higher at one facility than the other. This latter site was, therefore, chosen to make the low-volume products with their more exacting specifications and it was at this site that the new thick-film capability was allocated.

In this example, an increase in demand for a product group had initiated a strategic review of the whole business. There were no management benefits from the restructure because the units were still the same size as before, but there were strategic benefits from the improved alignment between operations and the markets served.

 **QUESTIONS**

1 Detail the changes outlined in the case.
2 Explain the strategic benefits that resulted from these changes.

Case 7.5 – Benefits of allocating infrastructure

A large food company grew its business while staying at the same operations site. The facility was sufficiently large to meet the increases in demand and well placed to access the local labour pool and relevant distribution channels. Although the company enjoyed good profits and steady sales growth, it continually questioned its cost base and the appropriateness of its organizational structure. While it had managed to keep up with demand, its overheads had grown significantly. It decided to review them to see if they could be reduced and also to check whether operations could be better aligned to its markets.

The first step was to review the processes. The technical requirements of the product groups that the company makes means that they can only be made by certain processes. This prevented any opportunity to cross-link different products by markets or order-winners because the investment required to purchase additional equipment could not be justified. However, the company next reviewed its infrastructure and found that the centralized specialist and other overhead functions were not aware of the differences within its markets and the varying strategic tasks that resulted.

It was found that the support and other overhead functions were not aligned to the company's different sets of market requirements. To rectify this, the company chose to reallocate support staff to each of the different manufacturing units which allowed it to provide support that was tailored to the particular needs of its various markets. The outcome was a significant reduction in overhead costs through removing unnecessary duplication of procedures, systems and support staff. There were also strategic benefits because the remaining overhead resource was better aligned to its markets.

QUESTIONS

1 Where did the benefits arise from the decision to reallocate support staff to the different manufacturing units?
2 Why would these changes result in a reduction in overhead costs?

Case 7.6 – Creating an operation-within-an-operation arrangement

A multinational packaging company has several operations in Europe and North America that cover a wide range of products from labels through to injection-moulded parts. A strategic review in one of its Canadian facilities concluded that the most appropriate way to support its diverse markets was to move to an operation-within-an-operation arrangement[9] where each unit would support a different set of market needs. Before the change, the processes and infrastructure were functionally organized in a similar way to that shown in Case Figure 7.2. The new layout is shown in Case Figure 7.3. Each of the three units contains the necessary capability and capacity of processes and infrastructure to support the needs of its market. However, some activities remained central – for example, vendor selection, negotiating supply contracts, goods receiving and shipping. The company found that allocating some activities to the unit and keeping others central enabled it to better serve its markets without increasing costs.

QUESTIONS

1 Explain, using this case, the operation-within-an-operation arrangement.
2 Why would the arrangement of allocating some activities to the unit while keeping others centrally work well?

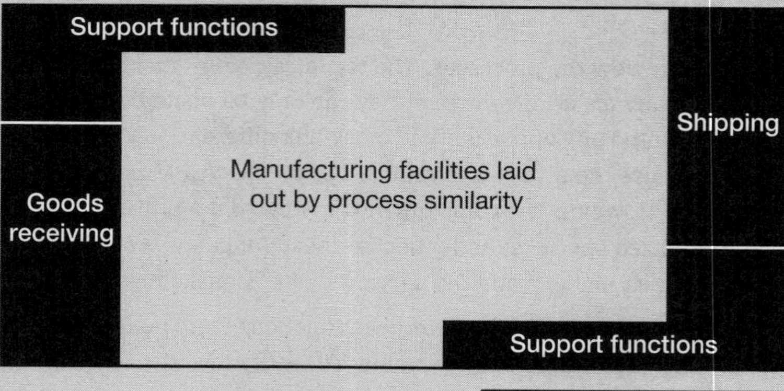

Case Figure 7.2 Layout of existing plant based on economies of scale principles (not to scale)

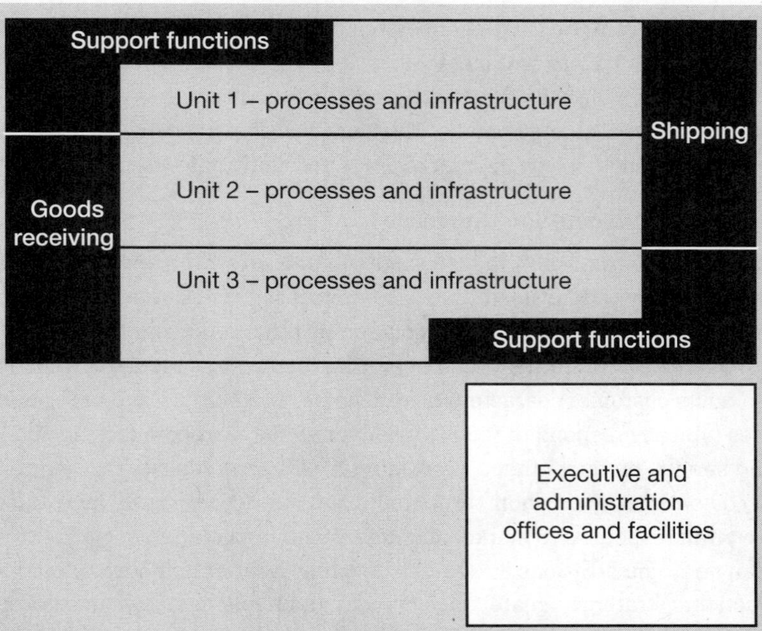

Support functions
Unit 1 – processes and infrastructure
Shipping
Goods receiving
Unit 2 – processes and infrastructure
Unit 3 – processes and infrastructure
Support functions
Executive and administration offices and facilities

Case Figure 7.3 Operation-within-an-operation arrangement (not to scale)

REFLECTIONS

Supporting markets with differing requirements

Businesses create problems by failing to understand how well their delivery system(s) and infrastructure support their current and future needs. By unquestioningly using economies of scale as a rationale for their organizational set-up, companies too often find that they are not able to compete effectively in today's markets. However, simply substituting economies of scale with focus is not the answer. Businesses must choose the approach to best exploit their resources and market opportunities. Markets are becoming increasingly different from one another and firms must learn to compete effectively in several markets at the one time. Selecting the right approach to organizing resources is a key strategic decision that directly affects these outcomes. Each method has varying cost, managerial and strategic advantages and disadvantages. The appropriate approach for an organization will reflect the resources it possesses and the requirements of its current and future markets.

Being able to fashion operations facilities and support activities to the needs of various markets enables companies to compete more effectively. An approach based on reducing or eliminating diversity within corporate sales portfolios is often a weak strategy. Advocates of these policies are turning their backs on the reality of business today and the opportunities it presents. A company must learn to compete effectively in different types of markets and the principle of focus needs to be part of its approach to achieving this.

Many companies need to review their operations provision with some urgency. Splitting out those parts of a business that more readily lend themselves to focus is a key place to start. However, avoiding the dogmatic use of these approaches is essential in order to gain substantial and lasting benefits. The dynamics of markets will necessitate continuous review and revision in order to avoid becoming unfocused.

Halting the drift into deteriorating focus

Focus does not occur naturally. In fact, there are pressures from marketing, sales, finance and even operations itself to become unfocused. These pressures arise, in part, from strategic decisions made in isolation by other functions or the outcome of a drive to reduce costs rather than supporting markets. As markets change and evolve, so do its customer characteristics, customer preferences and order-winners. Companies typically respond to this by using a number of approaches, including expanding service/product ranges, increasing facility size, reusing staff/equipment, reducing costs, focusing on short-term profits and restricting capital investment. These are often responses to market changes and/or declining financial performance rather than strategic decisions and tend to occur as a set of independent actions. Cross-functional strategic debate, development and implementation must occur to prevent this from happening. Whether strategy is planned or emergent and market led or resources based, it must be built around key elements. The starting point is to identify the existing core of the business, in which it has a clear competitive advantage. Once this is understood, then a business can start to identify its current and future markets, how it will compete and the appropriate corporate and functional strategies to develop and implement. In this way, functions will be pointing in the same strategic direction and thereby better able to meet overall corporate objectives. Financial decisions must be based on short-term and long-term strategic objectives and the reporting systems modified to provide data giving insight into these objectives and monitoring whether they are being met. This is not a one-off exercise, but an ongoing process. Markets must be continually assessed to ensure changes are identified and understood so they can be appropriately reflected in services/products, delivery systems/processes and infrastructure. Even if a business chooses not to respond to changes, this must be a conscious, cross-functional, strategic decision based on and supported by appropriate analysis.

M2

'The recent growth of our bespoke service (see Case Figure 7.4) means we're now running out of space', explained Tom Naismith, M2 CEO and co-owner. 'We need to work out how much more space to rent, how long we should commit to renting it and which parts of the business we should relocate to the new premises?'

M2 Communications was established ten years previously to provide information to online databases such as Factivia and Lexis Nexis edited from company press releases and third party reports. It receives a share of the fee users (typically accountancy, banking, law and blue chip companies) are charged when they access this information for research, credit and fraud and risk assessments, with 95% of the revenue coming from the articles added in that year. The business is run by a small team of people who work from home producing over 15,000 articles per year (see Case Figure 7.5) on a range of topics, as shown in Case Figure 7.6. Three people are based in the UK (two full-time and one part-time), three in Asia and M2 also has a US supplier which is contracted to produce 120 articles per day. As Tom Naismith explained, 'Our communications team work very well together and require little support from the rest of the business, which enables me to focus on developing our bespoke business.'

£000s	Year			
	−3	−2	−1	Current
Sales revenue				
Communications	1,332	1,350	1,353	1,280
Bespoke	101	335	744	1,140
Total	1,433	1,685	2,097	2,420
Direct costs				
Communications	399	420	526	541
Bespoke	29	101	238	388
Total	428	521	764	929
Overheads				
Management and sales	273	328	299	318
Rent	36	36	36	36
Total	309	364	335	354

Case Figure 7.4 Sales revenue and costs (£000s)

Year	No. of press releases
Current	15,897
−1	10,668
−2	14,319
−3	29,660
−4	28,731

Note: 3.245 million M2 articles are currently available through third-party online databases.

Case Figure 7.5 **Articles added to databases each year**

Topics	No. of editorials
Mergers & acquisitions	70
Equities	74
Pharmaceuticals	22
Banking & financial news	18
Other	10

Case Figure 7.6 **Article topics covered in a typical day**

M2 set up its bespoke business three years ago as companies started using 'content' rather than 'banners' and 'native' methods to advertise on the internet (see Case Figure 7.7). It currently offers four bespoke services (see Case Figure 7.8) to help clients increase their ranking in search engines (such as Google, Bing and Yahoo), increase the traffic (number of visitors) to their website, increase sales or enable them to sell higher margin services or products. The locations of its current 'features' clients are shown in Case Figure 7.9 and typical 'news', 'features' and 'thought leadership' monthly contracts are shown in Case Figure 7.10.

As Tom explains. 'Our in-house writers are assigned to different clients so they get to know them and understand what they are looking for. They work with clients to identify topics they want us to research and

Type	Description
Banners	Image and text at the top or side of a web page
Native	Image and text within the content in a web page matching the style and format of the page on which it appears
Content	Editorials and articles published in the news or through social media to create interest in a service/product or position an organization as a 'thought leader' in a particular area

Case Figure 7.7 **Types of internet advertising**

Service	Description
News	M2 develops 150 relatively short (less than 300 words) articles a week for over 50 clients on agreed topics (such as the benefits of motoring for car insurance companies or recent product developments for online computer retailers) on specified days and times each week (for example, MISCO requires four articles every day whereas Hastings Direct requires one article every Monday, Wednesday and Friday). These articles are then published by its clients on their website, blog or through social media

Service	Description
Features	35 more in-depth (typically 600 to 800 words) articles are produced per week and used by over 60 clients. To position themselves as experts in a number of different topics, M2's writers work with clients to understand how they want to position themselves and what articles M2 should develop to help them do this. These articles often have to be researched, written and edited in less than 48 hours (x% articles) to give an insight or commentary on a recent market trend or development
Thought leadership	10 in-depth insights or commentaries (1,000 to 1,250 words) are produced per week that help build a client's reputation as a 'thought leader' in a particular area. M2 currently works with clients to identify these topics and then subcontracts the research and writing of them to experienced analysts and researchers with different areas of expertise
Social media	As well as producing articles, M2 also offers to publish them through social media networks (such as Facebook, Twitter and LinkedIn), search for and re-post articles published by other people, develop a social network (such as a LinkedIn group) and/or position the client as a 'thought leader' within that network. It currently provides this service to 30 clients

Case Figure 7.8 Bespoke services

Location	% sales revenue
UK	60
US	20
Europe	12
Middle East and Asia	8

Case Figure 7.9 Location and percentage sales revenue of 'features' clients

write articles about before writing them and sharing them with the other M2 writers who help edit and develop them. Writers start by working on "news" items as these are simpler and typically involve editing and reformatting news articles that have been published by someone else. We use our more experienced and higher-skilled staff for "features" as they require a deeper understanding of client needs and take longer to research and write. "Thought leadership" articles are our most in-depth pieces, which involve creating new material (rather than editing existing

Contract	Revenue (£s)	Direct costs (£s)
1	240	57
2	1,000	520
3	325	143
4	860	520
5	500	286
1	390	110
2	480	80
3	375	91
4	1,135	264
5	1,440	792
1	625	240
2	300	120
3	1,140	760
4	800	480
5	520	320

Notes: Direct costs include staff salaries and other costs associated with each client contract.

Case Figure 7.10 Typical news, features and thought leadership monthly contracts

material published by other people) to give a fresh perspective on a topic and position a client as someone who is challenging existing ideas and creating new ones. We currently subcontract these articles to experienced analysts and researchers with different areas of expertise.'

'We also started providing a social media service last year (see Case Figure 7.11). Initially, this started as simply distributing content through social media networks (such as Facebook, Twitter and LinkedIn), but we now also help clients grow their network (typically to around 500,000 people) and position them as an 'expert' within it. This normally takes 3 to 6 months with clients charged per hour or per transaction (as shown in Case Figure 7.12) depending on the agreed brief and contract. Once their profile has been raised, we then target someone else in the group we have developed, explain what we have achieved for our client and offer to do the same for them.'

'We have always tried to keep overheads as low as possible with just myself, my partner and our Business Manager', explained Tom. 'However, we've had to take on sales staff over the last three years to help grow our

Sales revenue (£000s)	Year			
	−3	−2	−1	Current
News	101	181	252	224
Features	–	141	373	649
Thought leadership	–	13	82	107
Social media	–	–	37	160
Total	101	335	744	1,140

Case Figure 7.11 Sales revenue for different bespoke services

Contract	Revenue (£s)	Direct costs (£s)
1	1,500	408
2	1,050	380
3	400	190
4	1,478	304
5	104	33

Case Figure 7.12 Typical social media monthly contracts

bespoke business as the communications market has matured and become more competitive. We're planning to grow this further next year by offering a search engine optimization (SEO) service to help improve clients' ranking in searches on engines such as Google, Bing and Yahoo. This means we could then offer a "one stop shop" for all their digital marketing needs.'

'Our success to date has been built on creating and delivering content that improves how our clients are perceived, increases traffic to their website and increases sales of more sophisticated higher margin services and products. We now have some good case studies showing how we have managed to do this and the impact we have had. We could start using them to attract new clients, but I'm still not sure which services we should grow and what capabilities we should develop to do this.'

QUESTIONS

1. How is M2 currently performing?
2. Which parts of its business should it focus on developing in the future?
3. What investments should it make to help do this?

DISCUSSION QUESTIONS

1. Explain why the complexity of managing operations results from the size of its management and strategic task. Use examples other than those described in this chapter.
2. What has been the historical rationale for organizing operations using the principles of economies of scale and control through specialists? What has been the impact of these decisions?
3. Explain how focus moves away from the principles of economies of scale and control through specialists. What are the advantages and disadvantages of these approaches to organizing operations?
4. 'Businesses can choose to focus their operation around resources or markets.' Explain this statement using examples other than those described in this chapter. What are the advantages and disadvantages of alternative focus approaches?
5. 'Order-winner focus is the only approach with strategic benefits.' Explain this statement using examples other than those described in this chapter.
6. Once focus has been achieved, what steps need to be taken to maintain it?
7. 'When focusing operations, the optimal solution often involves a combination of approaches and all services/products and service/delivery systems/processes may not be focused.' Explain this statement using examples other than those described in this chapter.
8. Outline the main steps involved in focusing operations. Why do these tend to be iterative in nature? What are the main issues to consider at each stage? Give examples of how companies can overcome these issues.
9. Explain why maintaining focus needs to be a conscious strategic decision.

NOTES AND REFERENCES

1. Brought to prominence in Schumacher, E.F. (1975) *Small is Beautiful: Economics as if People Mattered*, Harper & Row.
2. Skinner, W. (1974) 'The focused factory', *Harvard Business Review*, May–June: 113–21.
3. Based on Skinner, 'The focused factory', p. 114.
4. Skinner, 'The focused factory', p. 118.
5. Schmenner, W. (1983) 'Every factory has a life cycle' *Harvard Business Review*, March–April, p. 123.
6. Skinner, 'The focused factory', p. 115.
7. In his book *The Strategy Quest* (1998, AMD Publishing), Terry Hill depicts the procedures and concerns that characterize the development of an operations-within-an-operations business. Written as a novel, it is intended to help overcome the marked and understandable misgivings and questions raised when this issue is considered by any organization. While the style of the book is unusual, the issues addressed and debates pursued are commonplace.

8 In some instances, there may be other factors, for example space constraints, but often these also constitute cost-related reasons for not duplicating existing capabilities.

9 This is described in detail in *The Strategy Quest*, 1998. Email: amdpublishinguk@gmail.com.

EXPLORING FURTHER

Berman, R. (2002) 'Should your firm adopt a mass customisation strategy?', *Business Horizons*, July/August, 45(4): 51–60.

Berry, W., Bozarth, C., Hill, T. and Klompmaker, J. (1991) 'Factory focus: segmenting markets from an operations perspective', *Journal of Operations Management*, 10(3): 363–88.

Bozarth, C.C. (1993) 'A conceptual model of manufacturing focus', *International Journal of Operations & Production Management*, 13(1): 81–92.

Bozarth, C.C. and Edwards, S. (1997) 'The impact of market requirements focus and manufacturing characteristics focus on plant performance', *Journal of Operations Management*, 15(3): 161–80.

Brush, T.H. and Karnani, A. (1996) 'Impact of plant size and focus on productivity: an empirical study', *Management Science*, 42(7): 1065–81.

Casalino, L.P., Devers, K.J. and Brewster, L.R. (2003) 'Focused factories? Physician-owned specialty facilities', *Health Affairs*, 22(6): 56–61.

Davidow, W.H. and Uttal, B. (1989) 'Service companies: focus or falter?', *Harvard Business Review*, July–August: 77–85.

Devers, K.J., Brewster, L.R. and Ginsburg, P.B. (2003) 'Specialty hospitals: focused factories or cream skimmers?', Center for Studying Health System Change, Washington.

Hayes, R.H. and Schemenner, R.W. (1978) 'How should you organise manufacturing?', *Harvard Business Review*, 56(1): 105–19.

Hayes, R.H., Pisano, G.P., Upton, D.M. and Wheelwright, S.C. (2005) *Operations, Strategy, and Technology: Pursuing the Competitive Edge*, Wiley.

Hill, A. (2007) 'How to organise operations: focusing or splitting?', *International Journal of Production Economics*, doi:10.1016/j.ijpe.2007.06.002.

Ketokivi, M. and Jokinen, M. (2006) 'Strategy, uncertainty and the focused factory in international process manufacturing', *Journal of Operations Management*, 24(3): 250–70.

Kimes, S.E. and Johnston, R. (1990) 'The application of focused manufacturing in the hospitality sector', Proceedings of the Manufacturing Strategy Conference of the Operations Management Association UK, University of Warwick.

New, C.C. and Szwejczewski, M. (1995) 'Performance measurement and the focused factory: empirical evidence', *International Journal of Operations & Production Management*, 15(4): 63–79.

Pesch, M.J. (1996) 'Defining and understanding the focused factory: a Delphi survey', *Production and Inventory Management Journal*, 38(2): 32–6.

Pesch, M.J. and Schroeder, R.G. (1996) 'Measuring factory focus: an empirical study', *Production and Operations Management*, 5(3): 234–54.

Schniederjans, M.M. and Cao, Q. (2009) 'Alignment of operations strategy, information strategic orientation and performance: an empirical study', *International Journal of Production Research*, 47(10): 2535–63.

Skinner, W. (1974) 'The focused factory', *Harvard Business Review*, May–June: 113–21.

Skinner, W. (1996) 'Manufacturing strategy on the "S" curve', *Production and Operations Management*, 5(1): 3–14.

Van der Vaart, T. and Van Donk, D.P. (2004) 'Buyer focus: evaluation of a new concept for supply chain integration', *International Journal of Production Economics*, 92: 21–30.

Van der Vaart, T. and Wijngaard, J. (2007) 'The contribution of focus in collaborative planning for make-to-order production situation with large set-up times', *International Journal of Production Economics*, doi:10.1016/j.ijpe.2006.12.053.

Van Dierdonck, R. and Brandt, G. (1988) 'The focused factory in service industry', *International Journal of Operations & Production Management*, 8(3): 31–8.

Vokurka, R.J. and Davis, R.A. (2000) 'Focused factories: empirical study of structural and performance differences', *Production and Inventory Management Journal*, 41(1): 44–55.

8 MAKE OR BUY AND MANAGING THE SUPPLY CHAIN

THIS CHAPTER DISCUSSES...

SUMMARY

This chapter looks initially at the make-or-buy decision that organizations need to address and then how to manage the supply chain that results. In particular it looks at:

- The factors and concerns to take into account when choosing whether to make or buy
- The dimensions involved when developing supply chains
- The origins and evolution of supply chains
- Factors in globalization and offshoring
- The dimensions involved in managing supply chains
- Ways of managing stability in the internal and external phases of supply chains

Companies rarely, if ever, own the resources, facilities, activities and skills necessary to provide a service or make a product from start to finish including delivery to customers. The decision on what to provide or make in-house and what to buy and the task of managing the supply chain that results are key strategic issues within a company, and ones that fall within the remit of operations. They concern the width of the internal phase of the supply chain (how much of a service or product is provided in-house), the degree and direction of vertical integration alternatives and the links and relationships at either end of the spectrum with suppliers, distributors and customers (the external phase of the supply chain).

Both the make-or-buy decision and the task of managing the supply chain have major ramifications for a business. They impact growth and level of success and are crucial to survival. The corporate stance and response on both these key issues need to be the result of business-based discussions set in an appropriate strategic context and involving sufficient recognition of the integrated nature of the resources, capabilities and skills that forge a company's ability to compete.

What a company decides to make or buy will impact its potential to be successful in its current markets, while restricting or facilitating its ability to change direction in the future. Having made a decision, a company needs to appreciate that the various elements involved will invariably impact many of the order-winners and qualifiers in its own markets today and in the future. Corporate approaches, however, often fail to recognize the integrated nature of the whole and the need to proactively manage all elements in line with the company's own market needs. Developing cooperation and improving coordination are not just good things to do but are essential if a company is to compete successfully now and in the future. In the past, the activities comprising the supply of skills and materials through to the distribution of services/products to customers, although financially significant, were considered strategically peripheral. Now companies are recognizing that the ownership of activities and capabilities is not what matters but rather the ability to manage these in support of their markets.

WHAT IS A SUPPLY CHAIN?

The series of steps between the origin of a service or product and its use or consumption is known as a 'supply chain'. Organizations will undertake some of these steps themselves – known as the 'level of vertical integration' and the 'internal phase of the supply chain' – while buying in earlier steps in the form of materials and services and contracting other organizations to undertake the later stages, for example distribution – known as 'outsourcing' and the 'external phase(s) of the supply chain'. There will be a varying number of tiers of suppliers and customers, depending on the complexity of the service or product, and a varying number of suppliers and customers in each tier, reflecting not only the complexity factor but also how much of a service or product is provided in the internal phase, how much is bought from outside and the steps in the route to market, as illustrated in Figure 8.1.

CHOOSING WHETHER TO MAKE OR BUY

Although in theory every item can be made or bought, in reality the choice is far more restricted. In some instances, companies may have no alternative other than to subcontract the provision of a skill capability or the making of a material, component, subassembly or even final assembly due to technical, financial or other barriers to entry. Similarly, while making an initial buy decision or changing from a make to a buy decision are not, in theory, once-and-for-all in nature, in reality they often are. The difficulties of reversing such decisions at a future date can be overwhelming due to similar barriers to entry that have evolved. However, when they consider their current make-or-buy positions, few businesses find that they were reached according to a well-considered and consistent set of criteria that were developed initially and readdressed over time.

In the past, companies competed on the basis of the assets and resources they owned. Being vertically integrated was the underlying rationale on how best to become and remain competitive. Since the 1980s, many, if not most, companies have reconsidered their competitive positions and increasingly migrated from the vertically integrated model. For instance, a

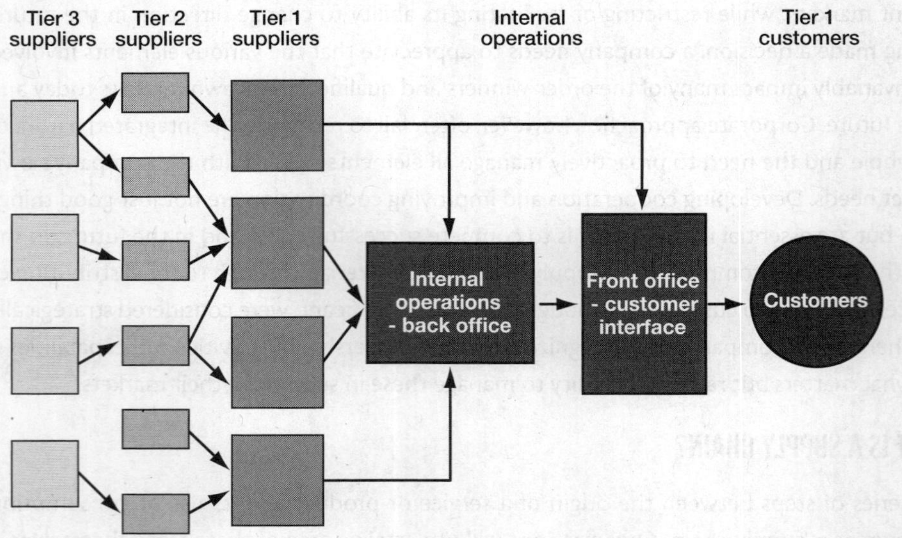

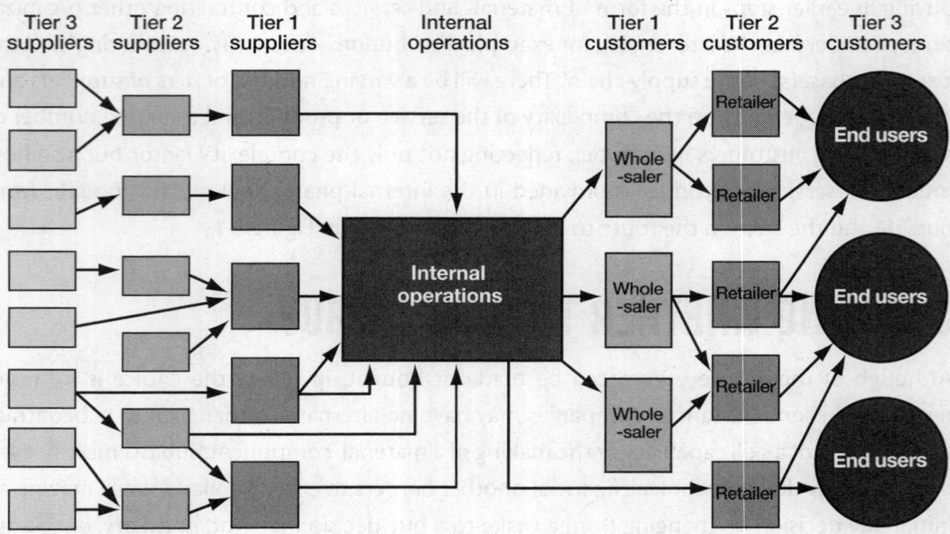

Note: The above diagrams are not to scale, and the number of customers and suppliers are illustrative.

Figure 8.1 Supply chains for a high street sandwich bar and a manufacturer of consumer goods

2005 survey of large and medium-sized companies reported that 82 per cent of large firms in Europe, Asia and North America had outsourcing arrangements of some kind and 51 per cent used offshore providers.[1] Similarly, in 2010 the 100 biggest US manufacturers spent 50 cents out of every dollar of sales to buy materials and components compared with 43 cents in 1996.[2]

Given these trends, the next section outlines the advantages and disadvantages of choosing whether to make or buy before reviewing some of the factors affecting this decision and some of the consequences and concerns that result.

THE BENEFITS AND DISADVANTAGES OF THE MAKE-OR-BUY DECISION

Until more recently, for many businesses changes in make-or-buy decisions were associated principally with a preference for widening rather than narrowing the internal phase of the supply chain. However, the increasingly global nature of business, the growth of non-Western economies such as China and India and the availability of skilled people and lower staff costs in many regions around the world have created the opportunity and increased the rationale for buying in a range of skills, services or products. Well-received arguments about identifying core competences and shedding other non-core investments and system capabilities have further accelerated such transitions.

This section now discusses the benefits and disadvantages inherent in the choice of whether to make or buy.

Benefits of providing/making in-house

All make-or-buy decisions bring a mix of internal and external benefits and costs. For example, providing/making in-house offers firms a range of potential advantages linked to greater knowledge of markets and technology, improved control over its environment and increased opportunity to support the characteristics of its markets. These include:

- **Support for markets in one's own hands** – having in-house the sets of staff skills, delivery systems/processes and capabilities that directly support the order-winners and qualifiers within a company's markets results in corporate ownership of those aspects of a business that are essential to the successful application of its chosen strategy. In this way, the link between investment priorities and strategic needs is in one's own hands.
- **Improved market and technological intelligence** – increases the ability to more accurately forecast trends concerning key aspects of a business from demand patterns to technology and cost changes. It further provides guarantees for suppliers and markets which, in turn, strengthens a firm against known and opportunistic competitors.
- **More readily available technological innovations and options** – leads to a greater opportunity to share in the benefits from technology initiatives and their outcomes. Furthermore, it enables companies to transfer experience, so helping to reduce some areas of uncertainty.
- **Creates control over aspects of a firm's competitive environment** – these opportunities can take the form of backward integration to reduce dependence on suppliers and forward integration to help gain market penetration or acceptance. Instances of forward integration range from overcoming strong entry (even monopolistic) barriers to gaining acceptance of new services or products. For example, St-Gobain, a French glass-maker, purchased the UK-based glass processor and merchant, Solaglass, as a way of entering the UK glass market, which at the time was dominated by Pilkington Glass. In the nineteenth and early twentieth centuries, the advent of both aluminium and rayon provides examples

of the way vertical integration facilitated the acceptance of the use of these new materials as substitutes in existing markets.

- **The provision of low-cost opportunities** – internal demand contributes to the high volumes that underpin low-cost operations. For example, in the semiconductor market, Japanese companies such as Fujitsu, Hitachi, Mitsubishi, NEC and Toshiba have progressively outcompeted their US rivals, partly through the high level of integration that characterizes their businesses. Since the invention of semiconductors in the 1950s, accelerating growth has created a worldwide industry of over \$130 billion, more than four times what it was in the mid-1980s. However, the highly integrated Japanese semiconductor manufacturers are able to make their products at increasingly lower costs than their competitors throughout the rest of the world. A substantial part of this is the result of the high-volume base created by internal, corporate demand. Giant Japanese zaibatsus (conglomerates) make semiconductors along with everything else from robots to cars and satellites. The result is that Japan has over 50 per cent of the world semiconductor market in 2017.
- **More ability to differentiate services or products** – this occurs in all aspects of operations from service/product customization to the availability and use of new, alternative materials to meet a service/product's technical, cost and other requirements.

Benefits of outsourcing

On the flip side of this key decision are the benefits to be gained from outsourcing. These primarily concern cash, costs and technology and include the following:

- **Freed resources** – buy decisions reduce or more often eliminate the associated resources necessary to provide the service or make the component, or those involved in subassembly or final assembly. One outcome is that resources are freed, making funds available to be used elsewhere in a business.
- **Reduced operating costs** – with less being made internally, the staff skill sets, process technology requirements and associated support are reduced, together with the management and control tasks that typically accompany these aspects of operations.
- **Easier-to-control costs** – with buy decisions, the dimension of cost control is simplified to one of a supplier's unit price. Although contract negotiations demand their own set of skills, the task of cost control for the bought-out skills, materials, components, subassemblies or assemblies involved is simplified.
- **Access to world-class capabilities** – purchasing from selected vendors creates the opportunity to source from potentially world-class capabilities. It gives access to the technologies and expertise that make up a provider's primary business.
- **Increased focus on own core tasks** – the reverse side of the last point, it allows a company to increase its attention, in terms of development time and investment, on its own primary business and associated core tasks – the underlying advantage of the strategy alternative known as 'core competence'.[3]
- **Reduced new service/product lead times** – outsourcing parts of a new service or product enables a company to access the capacity of suppliers. In turn, this can enable the business to reduce the overall lead times in bringing new services/products to market.

Disadvantages of making in-house

These next two sections address the disadvantages of make in-house and outsourcing, respectively, and are, in part, the inverse of the previous two sections that discussed the benefits of these alternatives. The disadvantages include:

- **Constraints on business development** – a lack of critical mass in some processes, systems and skill sets may result in insufficient volumes and range of activities to:
  - attract and retain skilled staff. Skilled staff typically and understandably seek career opportunities that will help them to improve and develop their personal capabilities and provide tasks that are at the cutting edge of their skill sets and expose them to the current developments within their respective areas of expertise.
  - support the case for investment and reinvestment as technologies develop, leading to the possibility of falling behind competitors' offerings.
  - justify allocating resources to refine systems and processes to lower costs, meet more demanding design specifications or reduce lead times.
- **Resources on non-core activities being tied up** – all activities absorb resources and a decision to keep non-core activities in-house absorbs resources that could otherwise be available to support and develop the core activities of the business.
- **Deteriorating company performance in the long term** – insufficient time and attention given to non-core/non-key activities, processes or delivery systems leads to potential neglect, the subsequent, gradual deterioration of these resources and its impact on levels of quality conformance, lead times and costs as well as restrictions on its capability to meet its customers' changing needs.
- **Inability to take full advantage of the technical developments and investments being made by potential suppliers.**

Disadvantages of outsourcing

As mentioned under the disadvantages of making in-house, to some extent the disadvantages of outsourcing are their inverse, and supplement the benefits of making in-house. They include:

- **Loss of control over important capabilities** – outsourcing brings with it the possibility of losing control of key capabilities. For example, dimensions such as quality conformance, delivery speed and delivery reliability are now, in part, within the processes and delivery systems of suppliers. Managing the whole supply chain, as discussed later, becomes increasingly important.
- **Loss of control over the supply of key materials** – the decision to outsource brings with it less control over the supply of materials. While sound supplier relationships help to mitigate possible supply problems, exposure to potential material shortages goes hand in hand with the decision to outsource. For example, in late 2004, Nissan Motors was forced to stop production at three of its four car assembly plants in Japan for five working days after running out of steel, with the loss of 25,000 vehicles. It is expected that the growth of the manufacturing sectors in China, India and South Korea will continue to put Asian steel suppliers under pressure to meet the demand for steel in the period ending 2020. In the meantime, steel prices have risen sharply, bumping up companies' costs and eating into profits.

- **Loss of control over intellectual property** – one concern for companies that outsource from offshore is the rigorousness of the intellectual property rights protection regime within the countries where the suppliers are based, with China as the country where these concerns are highest. In 2005, General Motors and Honda both sued Chery Automobile in the Shanghai courts concerning unauthorized use of trade secrets and breaches of competition laws.[4]

  Between 2002 and 2014, Novartis AG, the world's fourth largest pharmaceutical company, was engaged in a high-profile battle with the Indian government over Glivec, a popular cancer drug. India has denied Novartis a patent for Glivec (known as Gleevac in the US), alleging that it does not offer 'improved efficacy' over its predecessor. Novartis, which has obtained patents for Glivec in more than 40 countries, including China, insists that India's stringent requirements for 'novelty' violate international intellectual property treaties.[5]
- **Creating your own competition** – outsourcing, no matter what form it takes, presents a new risk to companies. Sensitive information needs to be shared on the one hand, while providing the opportunity for new entrants to gain expertise presents a risk on the other For example, it is important for firms to look long and hard before turning to suppliers for systems help. If the technical dimension in all its forms is part of a company's competitive advantage, giving it away means having less of an edge in the marketplace. In today's competitive environment, this could be a significant, long-term disadvantage. As illustrated in Case 8.1, examples from the past illustrate the consequences, while more recent ones point to the potential involved.[6]
- **Irreversibility** – the decision to subcontract is invariably irreversible. This is due, in part, to a reluctance to reconsider and then change direction on previous outsourcing decisions, coupled with the stepped nature of such a change in terms of buying in technical capability and expertise from a zero base.
- **Need for new management skills** – managing a supply chain requires different skills from those needed to handle in-house operations. Often, and particularly in the past, purchasing and related functions within a business have been allocated 'Cinderella' status, with corresponding levels of resource and management talent. Integrating the essential links within a supply network requires skills of a high order to secure the essential contribution to ensure that the needs of a firm's markets are met.[7]

Case 8.1 – How to create your own competition

Outsourcing risks

- In the 1960s, the then-dominant US television industry gave the technology to build picture tubes to low-cost Asian suppliers. Some time later, Asian companies began making entire TV sets and the US industry nearly went out of business.

- In an interview, Hisashi Sakamaki, who at the time oversaw all Canon's (the Japanese photo and printer giant) operations, recalled the important lessons learned from US companies' mistakes, as described by the MIT Commission on Industrial Productivity. He said: 'The key for us has been to figure out how to benefit from production overseas without losing our capacity to develop production at home. Most American firms rushed abroad and lost that knowledge.'[8]
- Boeing's outsourcing of some 90 per cent by value of the 787 provides a more recent example, with Airbus following suit in producing the A350. Critics of Boeing's decision argued that the company was giving away intellectual property in return for capital. In that way, it was helping suppliers in China and Japan to develop technologies that they would use to make their own aircraft. Since the 1980s, Boeing has let Japanese suppliers get close to fuselage design practices on wide body jets. Boeing has long advocated partnerships as a way of controlling the Japanese but there is growing concern that such practices will help to stimulate an Asian aircraft industry. Given Japanese engineering prowess in other sectors, aerospace is a ready-made extension of their expertise.
- IBM essentially created the PC industry, but by 2008 the company's nameplate was no longer to be seen on PCs because IBM had left this sector, except for its joint venture with Lenovo. Formed in 1984 as a distributor of IBM's and other companies' equipment in China, Lenovo now makes its own PCs and is the fourth largest PC manufacturer in the world. The same story is repeated with Sanmina-SCI that makes IBM's PCs and in 2005/6 acquired some of IBM's own factories. Originally distributors of well-known brand names, Lenovo and Sanmina moved into assembly and now design and engineer custom electronic products.

Questions

1 Analyse the US television, Boeing/Airbus and IBM examples and identify the commonality between them.

2 How did Canon differ in its approach?

The rationale for outsourcing is well articulated. Too often it is not set adequately within the strategic context of a business in terms of its own long-term position and how it needs to manage those relationships to ensure it controls the overall scenario to its own desired advantage. Reducing labour costs and freeing up capital, on the one hand, and allowing the original equipment manufacturer (OEM) to concentrate on its strengths – R&D, design, marketing and product launches – on the other, have been well articulated in the past. However, such decisions are a two-edged sword. A company's access to an OEM's intellectual property, its exposure to developments in the range of companies it serves and its growing manufacturing prowess provide sufficient advantages and strengths to integrate forward and bite the hand that feeds it. Taking the easy option of subcontracting the difficult manufacturing tasks in support of reducing profit margins, on the one hand, and facilitating support for short service or product life cycles and speed to market of new services and products, on the other, looks good on paper and points to immediate success and a pain-free resolution of its immediate difficulties.

The counter-argument is that this is the way the world is, and without doubt outsourcing is a growing trend. Identifying what should be the preferred supply chain mix between the internal and external phases is one that companies need to address and readdress with care.

Once the decision is made to outsource, the decision is virtually irreversible, and may result in losing out altogether. The Bowmar/TI example given later in this chapter is one of many, and yet lessons from history continue to be disregarded.

FACTORS AND CONCERNS AFFECTING MAKE-OR-BUY DECISIONS

Given the trend by Western companies to increasingly subcontract elements of their businesses, this section discusses the factors to be considered when deciding whether to make or buy, while highlighting some of the actual reasons that underpin such decisions, some concerns to recognize and address, and some alternatives to be considered.

Retaining core technologies

Most companies choose to keep in-house those skills, systems or processes that represent the core, technically related elements of their business. For instance, a management consultancy company specializing in human resources management would retain in-house sufficient staff in the relevant skill areas to meet current and future demand. The reasons, in addition to the prime task of matching its clients' current and future needs, include meeting the lead-time requirements of its clients and ensuring that it maximizes the likelihood of repeat business from existing customers. Similarly, a company that makes its own products will, as a minimum, invariably retain the assembly-onward end of the operations process. The reasons include the wish to retain immediate control of product identities, design security, final product quality (conformance to design specification) and the ultimate link with its customers.

In the same way, companies will seek to protect aspects of their services or products that reflect advantage. Design security has already been highlighted and, in the same way, retaining control over core staff skills and process technology developments will invariably lead to that stage being retained in-house.

Strategy considerations

Make-or-buy decisions need to be made within the strategic context of a business and take into account both the short- and longer-term competitive environment in which a company will need to compete. In the short and medium term, the order-winners and qualifiers that relate to a company's markets and that make-or-buy decisions affect need to be reflected in such choices and their outcomes. In the longer term, such decisions must be set within the scenario of future markets and the competitive forces that will likely prevail. For example, in its early years, Dell Computer Corporation's ability to assemble personal computers quickly in response to customers' orders was constrained by components suppliers' long lead times.

However, companies that are alert to key market-related issues incorporate these into their make-or-buy and sourcing decisions. For example, in the clothing industry, whereas the make-or-buy decision chosen by many, if not most, companies is to outsource manufacturing to low-cost suppliers in Asia Pacific, Central America or Eastern Europe, Benetton and Zara based their make-or-buy decision on strategic rather than cost-alone factors. The decision to retain local (Italian and Spanish, respectively) suppliers was made in order to create a supply chain that would meet the fast response needs of their fashion-based market places[9] and to help them outperform competitors in terms of being able to support a greater number of designs as well as being better able to respond more quickly to the demand for those designs and colours that customers preferred post-launch.

Overall though, there has been a growing trend in many sectors towards outsourcing and away from making in-house. For example, the roll-out of the Boeing 787 Dreamliner marked a strategic success for the company through its decision to build a fuel-saving, medium-sized passenger jet rather than go head to head with Airbus's giant A380. But the 787 is remarkable in another way – the degree to which Boeing has outsourced production around the globe (see Case 8.1). This was for a number of reasons, including the ability to tap into technical expertise and capacity elsewhere in the world and thereby avail itself of state-of-the-art technology while securing essential lead times and also reducing costs. The outcome is that Boeing itself is now only responsible for about 10 per cent by value of the 787 – the tail fin and final assembly. The rest is done by 40 partners. For example, the wings are built in Japan, the carbon composite fuselage in Italy, the landing gear in France and a variety of components in China and elsewhere.

Similar scenarios have been evolving in many, if not most, other sectors and not only fuelled by the attraction of lower-cost labour, as in the cases, for example, of call centres, textiles, footwear, publishing, design, technical drawing, graphics, technical support services and white goods. The continuing development of technical capability and accompanying skills has widened the opportunity to outsource in sectors ranging from heavy industries such as steel and shipbuilding through to IT, banking, pharmaceuticals and semiconductors while, in turn, the activities being subcontracted range from design through to final assembly. Couple this with overseas government subsidies and the attraction to relocate with associated lower costs are both substantial and available. For example, in 2007 the Indian government announced a package of measures to attract chip and electronics factories and to create 10 million additional jobs in the following seven to eight years. It estimated that the demand for semiconductors in India would increase to $40 billion by 2017 from $3.25 billion in 2006, due to an expanding electronics goods manufacturing sector. The package of measures included interest-free loans and subsidies of up to 25 per cent of the capital needed where companies invested a minimum of $25 billion in semiconductor plants and $250 million for plants manufacturing other products. Similarly, China offers preferential tax rates if companies locate factories within a technology park or a special economic zone.

As the examples below illustrate, the combination of lower costs and technical capability offers a sound strategic option which many companies are choosing.

- 2005 Advanced Micro Devices (AMD), the world's second biggest maker of PC processors, agreed a joint venture with SemIndia and the Indian government to build a $3 billion factory in India to make chips for wireless phones and computers and a year later began building its first plant in India. AMD now has research, development and design facilities in Bangalore and Hyderabad.

- 2007 STMicroelectronics, Europe's largest semiconductor manufacturer, launched its first designed-in-India chip and announced plans to double its workforce in India to 3,000 to take advantage of lower salaries, estimated to be as little as one-sixth of those in the USA.
- 2007 Infineon Technologies, one of Europe's largest makers of semiconductors, licensed Hindustan Semiconductor Manufacturing to make products in two plants, involving a $4.5 billion investment.
- 2008 STMicroelectronics began building its first assembly plant in China.

Whether or not a company makes in-house, supply chain performance regarding relevant order-winners and qualifiers in its markets will directly impact a company's ability to retain customers, grow share and be profitable. The issues involved will be addressed in detail in the later section on managing the supply chain, where the fundamental nature of this decision is clearly highlighted, fully discussed and appropriately illustrated.

Service, product and system technologies and the internal phase of the supply chain

An earlier section highlighted make-or-buy positions that reflected a company's decision to retain core service, product and system technologies. In situations where there is a significant stepped change in these technology developments, the very opposite can happen. Take the case where a company applies new technology developments to its existing services or products or on the introduction of new services or products and finds itself without the in-house technical skills or capabilities to meet these new requirements. For a manufacturing company, one option is to buy in the technology as components. Normally, this narrowing of the internal phase of the supply chain takes place in the upstream stages of a process, where the new technology developments are the most radical; the later downstream processes are kept in-house because the technology associated with these is more in line with existing manufacturing expertise and is also closer to the final product itself.

The IT sector provides a classic example of this. With the rapid rate of component development, IT companies often have no alternative other than to buy in the technology from outside in the form of chips and other parts in order to keep pace with competition and changing technical developments. The examples of semiconductor and chip plants reflect this trend. As Figure 8.2 illustrates, although such companies may have had a wide internal span of process for their earlier products, this is correspondingly reduced with technology developments.

In Figure 8.2, when producing only product range A, a company had developed in-house much of the process technology to make the products involved. The advent of product range B and, later, product range C heralded a distinct technology change. Not having the manufacturing process capabilities to provide these new requirements, the company bought them in from outside in the form of components.

In such situations, when and by how much to widen the internal phase of the supply chain, after the initial narrowing, is a significant strategic decision, which in practice is often treated

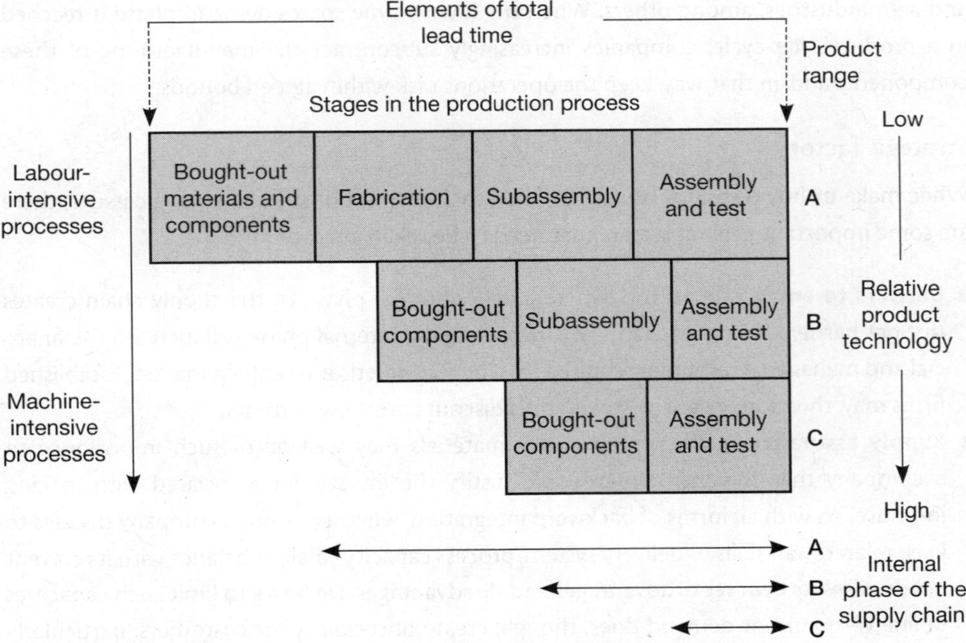

Figure 8.2 The reduction in the internal phase of the supply chain where more advanced technology is incorporated into a product (not to scale)

as an operational issue. A classic example of this was provided in the 1970s in the hand-held calculator market. Bowmar, the one-time market leader, failed to integrate backwards into integrated circuit production and eventually withdrew from the business, while Texas Instruments (TI) successfully integrated forwards into calculators and took over the market leadership. One major reason for TI eventually displacing Bowmar was that its comparative process position gave it more opportunity to reduce costs and exploit potential experience curve gains, and that is what it did. Bowmar, restricted to assembly cost gains, was constrained by its suppliers' price reductions for a large part of its costs. TI, on the other hand, had no such limitations.

Since the 1980s, the dominance of the Intel Corporation in PC design and the supply of chips, such as microprocessors, has redressed, if not revised, the supplier/customer relations within the IT sector. Intel's increasingly powerful position as a supplier of chips has strengthened its opening position vis-à-vis customers and greatly changed the nature and results of subsequent negotiations within the board sector of the IT industry.

Handling mixed volumes

Companies faced with the task of providing high and low volumes can adopt an operation-within-an-operation alternative, as reviewed in Chapter 7. Similarly, a company may also consider buying out those services or products with a low-volume demand. Examples of such decisions are typical in component-making companies in the automobile, truck and aero industries, among others. When the low-volume spares demand phase is reached in a product's life cycle, companies increasingly subcontract the manufacturing of these components and, in that way, keep the operations task within agreed bounds.

Strategic factors

While make-or-buy decisions usually embody their own set of specific strategic issues, there are some important general factors that need to be taken into account.

- **Barriers to entry** – in sectors where a wide internal phase of the supply chain creates distinct barriers to entry advantages, increasing the internal phase will increase the financial and managerial resources required for a new competitor to enter a market. Established firms may, therefore, raise the stakes, thus discouraging new entrants.
- **Supply assurance** – the supply of key materials may well be of such importance to a company that this gain alone would justify the investment associated with making in-house. As with all forms of backward integration, whether or not a company decides to keep related staff skills or delivery system/process capacity solely in balance with its current needs raises its own set of advantages and disadvantages. Deciding to limit such capacities in line with current demand does, though, create uncertainty for customers, particularly regarding any planned future growth they themselves may have.
- **Secured outlets** – as supply can be assured by integrating backwards, securing outlets can result by integrating forwards. Additional advantages also accrue with this move – improved customer feedback leads to a position of being more aware of demand changes and provides an opportunity to increase the accuracy of forecasts.

THE REALITY OF MAKE-OR-BUY DECISIONS

The previous section identified some of the principal reasons that may form the basis of make-or-buy decisions. In reality, many companies approach this critical task and base the strategic decision involved on reasons that are less rational and seldom sound. The more common of these are now discussed.

Continuing yesterday's decisions

Make-or-buy decisions taken at one moment in time are often not proactively reconsidered at a later date. Inertia, a reluctance to add additional executive tasks and the avoidance of possible short-term problems militate against taking appropriate reviews. Once made, make-or-buy decisions often remain unchallenged.

Since the 1970s, a reduction in service/product life cycles, rapid changes in technologies and growing world competition have increased the size and difficulty of the overall management task. One result has been that executives, while responding to changes that require immediate attention, have deferred addressing other key, longer-term issues. This can result in companies taking their eye off the ball and failing to undertake periodic reviews within reasonable timescales. In key areas such as the make-or-buy decision, the corporate impact, especially in times of accelerating change, can be damaging, if not irreparable.

Supply problems – delays in awareness and response

Relating in part to the last point, the reluctance of suppliers to alert customers to potential or ongoing problems and customers' tendency not to proactively undertake systematic, in-depth and regular reviews of suppliers will invariably contribute to the length of delay between the time when a supply problem starts and the time when the customer becomes aware that a supply problem exists.

Suppliers will typically wish to contain supply problems in-house. Where suppliers are unable to resolve the problem then further time will be lost because delays in finding alternative sources of supply can be lengthy. Even where there are multiple suppliers, negotiating for one or more of these to take on the additional volumes will invariably incur delays.

Supply problems – uncertainty

With globalization, supply chains have become elongated and exposed to growing uncertainties. As Figure 8.3 shows, there are a range of business risks that go hand-in-hand with sourcing overseas.

At the extremes, companies face an array of potential issues from human rights violations, illegal use of child labour, the emergence of counterfeit goods, inadequate and unsafe working conditions for workers and the impact of natural disasters. For example:

- In 2012 the weather in India and Mexico severely affected the international supply of vanilla resulting in a steep price rise in 2013 and a great deal of dependence on the Madagascan crop, a country beset with political instability.
- The factory fire of November 2012 in Dhaka, Bangladesh resulted in over 200 deaths. The factory was a supplier of t-shirts, polo shirts and jackets to major customers including Walmart, Carrefour and Ikea. This and other similar events have since led to reforms in workers' rights and safety laws in Bangladesh.

Factors	Percentage of businesses identifying a particular risk (%)
Raw material price fluctuations	53
Currency fluctuations	47
Market changes	41
Energy/fuel-price volatility	38
Environmental catastrophes	34
Raw material scarcity	28
Rising labour costs	26

Figure 8.3 Business risks in the supply chain

Source: PwC/MIT Forum for Supply Chain Innovation (2013).

The dominance of cost and technology arguments

The format used to address the question of whether to make or buy typically centres around issues of technology and cost. The initial consideration is whether or not a company has the skill base to undertake the work or the process technology to make a component or product. Where the technical capability is not already in-house, to buy from outside is often an automatic response.

Where process technology is not a barrier, the next consideration is the cost of provision. While a most important dimension in itself, decisions made on this dimension alone and without addressing the requirements of markets and relevant order-winners and qualifiers (such as delivery speed, quality conformance, ability to ramp up and delivery on time) will invariably lead to inappropriate decisions, with a potentially damaging impact on a firm's short-term let alone long-term strategic position, as illustrated in Case 8.2.

Shedding difficult operations tasks

Over recent years companies have tended to shed difficult operations tasks by subcontracting or divestment. Many firms approach this decision with an eye more on the difficulties embodied in the task, which may range from technical advances similar to those highlighted in the last section, reinvestments to update processes or replace them due to wear

Case 8.2 – The dominance of the cost argument

Part of a large US-based conglomerate, Rawlins Industries (RI) manufactures and assembles pumps to meet a wide range of industrial requirements in the chemical, oil refining and mining sectors, for example. Three years ago, RI split its UK-based facility into a number of focused units to reflect the industries in which its customers competed. Since that time the company has arrested the decline in overall sales by increasing its market share in all sectors. Each focused unit is responsible for sourcing its own material requirements including castings, motors, seals and shafts.

The Group had set up a casting plant in Asia to avail itself of lower unit costs. All Group subsidiaries were encouraged to make use of this opportunity and 12 months ago the focused units within RI made the switch. However, while previously its casting supplier provided a 4-week lead time, the Group's Asian casting plant offered lead times of between 16 and 20 weeks using fixed production schedules as a prerequisite to reducing manufacturing costs. With its own customers looking for lead times of 6 weeks, RI found it was no longer able to meet these requirements. In order to avoid losing sales, RI decided to hold casting inventories and also guarantee placing orders with its casting supplier equivalent to an agreed level of capacity within which it could decide on the actual castings it required. In this way, it brought its own operations lead time to 6 weeks and was now able to meet its customers on timescales.

However, RI now faces Group pressure to reduce its inventory levels.

and tear, or enhancing staff capabilities. Short-term gains, taken on their own, look most attractive as well as being easier to make by not giving adequate weight to appropriate strategic issues. Surrendering ownership of costs, lead times, response to growth and issues around quality conformance are one set of strategic issues. The accompanying loss of skills, operations' know-how and other factors that form the essential infrastructure from which to launch future changes in direction can also limit future options. Proponents of such business decisions often base their analysis on short-term figures rather than long-term consequences.

The accompanying loss of skill, essential operations know-how and infrastructure may limit a company's ability to respond in the future. A maxim to bear in mind is: 'If the operations task is easy, any company can do it.' The key to operations success is to resolve the difficult operations issues because this is where high margins are to be made.

Furthermore, when evaluating these decisions, some companies omit related costs and investments and so distort the picture. For example, a large manufacturing company established an offshore operations capability to avail itself of the low-cost opportunities inherent in that decision. In a subsequent review of the decision the company discovered that the initial analysis had not allocated appropriate costs and inventory investment to the offshore site. In the original analysis all rework costs and pipeline inventory had been charged against the home-based plant. These distorted figures reinforced the buy option that had been taken and this initial decision to offshore had encouraged later similar decisions to be made. However, when the accounting rules were changed, future offshore options became less attractive.

Political pressure

Within the context of the continuing movement of jobs to lower-cost countries, some companies face growing pressure from workers to stem or even reverse this trend. One such example is Volkswagen. In 2007, VW factories had been running at about 70 per cent capacity for some time. As part of its manufacturing agreement with IG Metals, the trade union representing 97 per cent of VW workers, employees' hours increased from 28.8 to 33 hours a week for the same pay (representing a reduction in labour costs per hour of almost 15 per cent), for which VW agreed to certain minimum production levels. The outcome was that VW cut thousands of jobs at its Spanish, Portuguese and Belgian factories. With labour costs per hour at VW's Portuguese plants one-third that of the company's West German factories, the restructuring gains would be more than cancelled out. In the long term, 'you can still argue [that] this is a company with too much production in Germany and too many decisions made by Germans', reflected one VW executive.[10]

SOME CONCERNS

Since the 1980s, faced with increasing pressure to reduce costs, many companies turned to the option of sourcing skills, services and products from countries with a lower cost base. Over time, the selection of this alternative became a somewhat routine decision on the basis that it was clearly the right way to go – a 'follow the leader' frame of mind.

This section highlights some concerns that need to be fully addressed when decisions to buy rather than make are being evaluated.

The numbers

When repositioning the internal/external phases of a supply chain, a business must fully assess the issues involved. In particular, it needs to ensure that the estimated process and infrastructure costs, investments and savings are realistic. All too often the costs are understated and benefits fail to measure up to expectations. Additional sizeable investments are often incurred after the event, which, although not included in the original decision, form an integral part of securing the benefits. Ensuring that the numbers underpinning such decisions are robust is all too often undertaken with insufficient rigour. While estimates will remain estimates, analysing past decisions after the event enables companies to check the accuracy of its assumptions (of benefit, as well as costs) and so leads to more realistic (and thereby accurate) assumptions being used in future analyses. The increase or decrease in overhead costs provides a classic example of the difficultly of making estimates and the value of past analysis to check estimates against corporate reality. While direct costs (those costs concerned with providing the service or making the product and the physical handling of materials through the process including material purchase) can be fairly accurately ascertained, some aspects of cost, although sizeable, are more difficult. These include:

- Coordination between the home-based operations and the outsourced skills, services and products.
- Combining similar associated overhead tasks. Where a decision is made to change from a make to a buy provision, the overhead cost reduction typically claimed and included in the evaluation is invariably difficult to identify and even more difficult to bring about. Known as 'vertical slicing', Figure 8.4 depicts those costs.

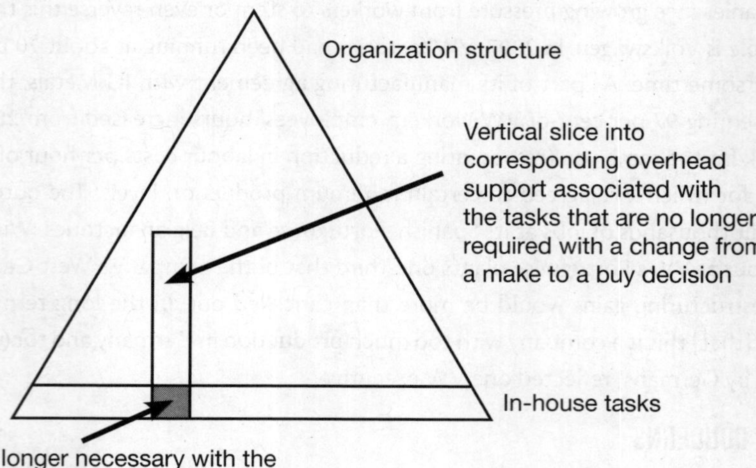

Figure 8.4 The anticipated reduction in overheads (represented by the vertical slice into organizational support and associated costs) that accompanies a decision to buy rather than make part of the operations tasks

- Controls, procedures and other infrastructure requirements (such as external training) to support the buy decision. While the tangible costs of systems and equipment can be readily identified, evaluated and agreed, the costs of less tangible areas that support such investments are not as apparent nor as easily quantified. Because everyone has a view, the projected costs of less tangible areas are often scrutinized in great detail. This interrogation invariably leads to lowering estimates of requirements and costs, even to the point that the existing infrastructure is believed to be able to cope or will just have to do so. While the numbers are made to look better at the time, because reality has not changed the costs invariably resurface in the future. Post-analysis to check what really happens and to inform future decisions is, therefore, a key task to undertake.

The management task

Changes in make-or-buy decisions invariably lead to changes in the make-up of the management task within a business, for which many executives are unprepared. What makes the management task complex is not a technical dimension as with, say, nuclear physics but the number of factors involved in the issues to be handled, that these factors all interrelate and that they are constantly changing. In the make-or-buy scenario, the complexity of the management task that accompanies the growing role of supply chains in meeting the day-to-day and strategic needs of companies changes the mix of issues to be understood and addressed and often outweighs any simplifying gains from shedding tasks. Such factors need to be part of any discussions on changing the make-or-buy status quo, while the changes in perspective and scope that follow then need to be embraced.

The hollow corporation and creating your own competition

As highlighted previously, in the 1980s and 1990s many Western corporations began outsourcing manufacturing to boost efficiency, take out costs and focus their energies. At the time these companies insisted that all of the important research and development activities would always remain in-house. Today, the likes of Dell, Motorola and Philips are buying complete designs of some digital devices from Asian developers, tweaking them to their own specification, attaching a label and selling them as their own. But the downside of getting the balance wrong can be game changing as illustrated by the example given in Case 8.3.

Such developments illustrate an increasing recognition of and growing concern about a phenomenon referred to as the 'hollow corporation'. Where companies have considered the question of how operations should best be organized to meet the dynamics of their markets, many have shied away from addressing and incorporating the operations dimension within the debate concerning the appropriate short-term and long-term strategies for a business. The attraction of low-cost opportunities in the Asia Pacific region, Eastern Europe and Mexico lured many European and North American manufacturers to subcontract substantial parts of their existing processes without regard for, adequate understanding of, or sufficient in-depth debate about the long-term implications of these critical and often irreversible decisions. The simplistic rationale of problem avoidance has such siren-like qualities as to make the decision difficult to argue against.

Case 8.3 – Suppliers that grow to be competitors

One of the damaging downsides of outsourcing is the danger of fostering new competitors. For example, Motorola hired Taiwan's Ben Q Corporation to design and manufacture millions of mobile phones. However, in 2006, Ben Q began selling phones in China under its own brand name. As a result, there was a new and powerful competitor in the market and Motorola, having cancelled its contract with Ben Q, then had to source mobile phones from another supplier.

Ben Q is just one example of the emerging Taiwanese 'original design manufacturers' (ODMs) – so named because they both design and make products for others – that are now strong competitors in every digital device on the market. For example, ODMs make almost 30 per cent of all mobile phones, over 30 per cent of digital cameras, nearly 70 per cent of MP3 players and 70 per cent of personal digital assistants (PDAs). And, Taiwan's ODMs recognize themselves as major players in these markets. As the President of HTC, one of Taiwan's many large ODMs, reflected 'We know our products a lot better than our customers do and have the capability to integrate all the latest technologies.'

The long-term consequences of low-cost outsourcing decisions to companies and nations need to be fully recognized and adequately assessed. Such decisions bring the instant rewards of solution and profit. For many organizations, moving offshore becomes a last resort to offset sizeable structural disadvantages, but usually the impact of this short-term thinking has not been fully assessed. The alternative is to become competitive in the relevant dimensions such as design, price, quality conformance and delivery performance. To the nation as a whole, there is an increasing dependence on imports, compounded by a loss of technological know-how and ownership, which will invariably lead to being driven out of some businesses altogether. Companies pursuing this rationale rarely do so as a way of buying time to enable them to strategically regroup. For most, it is a comprehensive solution in its own right, with an apparent disregard for the long-term implications and inherent constraints imposed on future strategic options. Furthermore, the ripple effect means that for every $1 billion of imports, there is a further substantial loss to a nation's economy as a whole.[11] In addition, as time goes on, these offshore plants will draw the service jobs that surround manufacturing and at a company level, the effects are similar: once skills have been transferred out, that know-how will be lost to the company.

The trend towards outsourcing on a larger scale has gathered momentum partly on the back of increased corporate moves towards downsizing that took a strong hold on business strategy direction from the mid-1980s. Bolstered by doctrines such as core competence, the benefits and rewards offered by solution-based approaches have a unique appeal to unquestioning recipients. The attraction of such offerings as fixed asset freedom, cash infusion, capital fund availability and lower overhead cost structures was and still is much heeded at the economic altar of financial markets.

The decision on whether or not to outsource is a sound one to address. What are of concern are the bandwagon consequences of panacea solutions, the failure to review the decisions within the context of the overall business and to assess the strategic impact over appropriate timescales.

At the extreme, the post-industrial company could be vertically disaggregated, relying on other companies for manufacturing and many essential business functions. It would become an industrial, corporate shell. And there are strong forces pushing companies that way. In the short term, these decisions offer fixed asset freedom and dynamic networking, both arguably suited to meeting the characteristics of today's markets. Such arrangements allow companies to respond quickly to exploit new markets and new technologies. The organizations become more agile, flexible and responsive. Typically, firms need less capital, carry lower overhead costs and can better tap into outside technology. In essence, they are more entrepreneurial.

One outcome of this is that manufacturing companies of a new kind are evolving – those that do little manufacturing. They import components and assemble them or import the products themselves and sell them. The result is a hollowing of once-powerful manufacturing companies. Following a strategy of this kind, companies become trapped in a position where their ability to compete is increasingly undermined by their own and their competitors' actions. Unchecked, this will invariably lead to the abandonment of their status as strong industrial companies and the retardation of their capacity for innovation and productivity improvement. The erosion of a nation's wealth-creating activity is the aggregate effect of these policies, which in the end reduces the standard of living enjoyed by its people.

Onshoring

As developing economies such as China and India continue to grow then pressure on labour rates within these countries will increase. For example, between 2010 and 2015 China's average yearly wages in manufacturing increased by 16 per cent every year. If such increases continue year on year, the low-cost advantage over developed economies will continually be eroded. Coupled with quality conformance problems, longer, fixed delivery lead times and higher freight costs, many companies are having second thoughts about outsourcing and are bringing operations back home – the phenomenon of 'reshoring' or 'onshoring'.

For example, by 2002 Hornby (the UK-based Scalextric and Airfix model maker) had relocated its entire production to China as the Group took part in the mass migration of manufacturing to the Far East. Having already returned products of its Humbrol paint to the UK in 2009, Hornby has continued its onshoring decisions – a glueless range of Airfix model aircraft is now made at an injection-moulding plant in Sussex, England. The rationale is to create a shorter lead time for these new models so that the company can adjust quickly to demand. Products from China or India take 6 or more weeks to arrive.

The reasons for these sourcing decisions are central to the way companies compete. The Engineering Employers Federation (the trade body for UK manufacturers) confirms that onshoring is a phenomenon that has become increasingly common since 2010. The reasons for this include growing labour and transport costs, levels of quality conformance and long lead times.

Technology developments

Developments in technology can and will alter future make-or-buy decisions. 3D printing is one such development. Whereas the traditional machining processes such as drilling and boring work by cutting away the unwanted material to make a part, with 3D printing, layers of material are instead gradually deposited to build parts from plastic or metal. In that way, 3D printing uses only the material it needs, thereby minimizing waste. Each layer is formed and bound together by computer-controlled lasers that melt the material which then cools and hardens, and thus the need to make casts or other tooling is eliminated. The outcome is that anything can be made anywhere, which enables manufacturing to be on site or closer to the end user, thereby reducing investment, costs and lead times. Designs can be sent and downloaded with no large tools and equipment, no manufacturing processes, little labour and less space. Making in-house becomes a viable alternative.

ALTERNATIVES TO MAKING IN-HOUSE

The discussion so far has implied that the choices companies face involve only an ownership or non-ownership option. Either a company invests in the skills and systems/processes through ownership or it buys out its requirements from suppliers. For companies where being reliant on suppliers is not a feasible option but where greater control is necessary, alternatives to widening the internal span of process may well be a better option. The alternatives below are based on an appropriately high degree of liaison between those involved. Some involve legal agreements or arrangements of some kind. Others attempt to exploit opportunities with links that are beneficial to all concerned.

Joint ventures

Where companies have similar needs and both can benefit from combining, a joint venture is a sensible alternative. This is particularly the case in areas such as applied technology and research.

Joint ventures are separate entities sponsored by two or more actively involved firms. Because joint ventures draw on the strengths of their owners, they have the potential to tap the synergy inherent in such a relationship and the improved competitive abilities that should accrue. Since the late 1970s, joint ventures have increased substantially in Europe and the USA, particularly in sectors such as communications systems, IT and services. As Figure 8.5 shows, most companies see joint ventures as a viable alternative and one that, in most businesses, will increase.

Joint ventures have become an important way of improving the strengths and reducing the weaknesses of cooperating businesses. Companies willing to undertake the necessary high degree of commitment and cooperation can exploit opportunities from which they previously would have been debarred, due to investment or lead-time barriers.

However, joint ventures should not be seen as a convenient means of hiding weaknesses. If used prudently, such arrangements can create internal strengths. They can

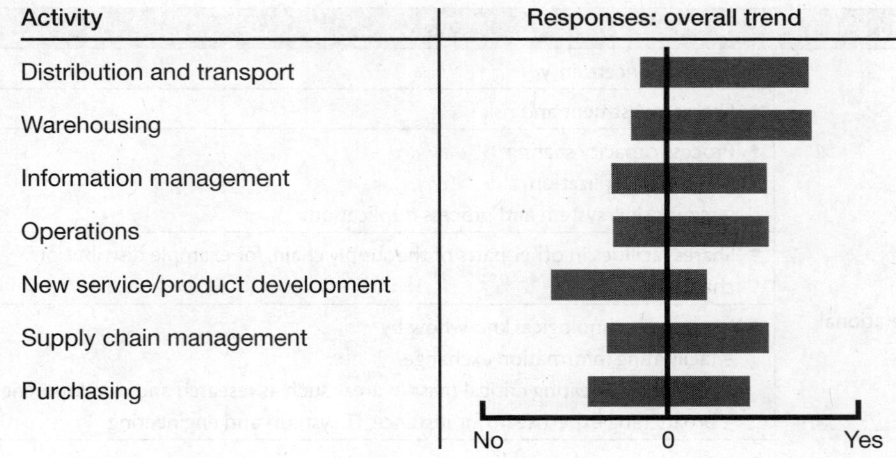

Figure 8.5 Responses to the question: 'Are joint ventures a viable alternative?'

Source: Hill, A. and Hill, T. (2012) Operations Management, *3rd edn, Palgrave Macmillan.*

be resource-aggregating and resource-sharing mechanisms, allowing sponsoring firms to concentrate resources where they possess the greatest strengths. Figure 8.6 provides a comprehensive list of reasons for forming joint ventures, classified into operational and strategic uses.

Joint ventures, therefore, not only share investment but, often more importantly, also provide direction and make fresh opportunities possible. Identifying the areas on which to focus attention, with the knowledge that the developments will have a commercial outlet, can give substance to such decisions. Reducing risk while also limiting the investments required to bring the activity to fruition may provide an ideal solution. In this way, a joint venture is a sensible alternative to the owner/non-owner option.

<table>
<tr><th colspan="2">Advantages</th></tr>
<tr><td rowspan="3">Strategic</td><td>• Strengthens current strategic position by
– pioneering developments into new segments
– rationalizing existing segments
– reducing competitive volatility</td></tr>
<tr><td>• Pre-empts competitors
– facilitates access to new markets and customers
– supports growth in market share
– strengthens negotiating positions
– gains access to global markets</td></tr>
<tr><td>• Augments strategic position
– creates and develops synergies
– facilitates technology and skill transfers</td></tr>
</table>

Figure 8.6 Reasons for forming joint ventures

	Advantages
Operational	• Reduces uncertainty
	• Shares investment and risk
	• Process capacity sharing – increases utilization – avoids skill, system and process duplication
	• Shares facilities in other parts of the supply chain, for example distribution channels
	• Increases technological know-how by – facilitating information exchange – potentially creating critical mass in areas such as research and development – broadening expertise in, for instance, IT systems and engineering
	• Strengthens market intelligence
	• Helps retain key staff – increased job scope – better career opportunities

Figure 8.6 (Continued)

Non-equity-based collaboration

Companies unwilling or unable to cope with joint venture arrangements can resort to an appropriate form of non-equity-based collaboration to meet their needs. These mechanisms provide the means of establishing cooperative working arrangements that need a long-term base if the collaboration is to yield meaningful and useful results. Such arrangements include:

- Research and development consortia to enhance innovation and the exploitation of results.
- Cross-hyphen marketing agreements to provide opportunities, such as utilizing by-products, widening service/product lines and sharing distribution channels.
- Cross-operations agreements to avoid duplication of skills and facilities, provide vertical integration opportunities and transfer technical know-how.
- Joint purchasing activities to enhance buying power in terms of price gains and increased supplier allegiance.

DEVELOPING THE SUPPLY CHAIN

The goal of supply chain management is to link the market, distribution channel, operations system/process and supplier base such that customers' needs are better met at lower costs and in line with customers' expected lead times. While many companies began fixing their operations problems from the early to mid-1980s, few addressed the total cost of ownership. By the early 1990s, progressive companies had begun to realize the need to refocus from 'fixing' operations to addressing how to better manage their supply chains, a fact confirmed by a 1996 European-based survey. This identified that 88 per cent of the companies reviewed had been carrying out significant overhauls of supply chains and saw supply chain management as the focus for improvement in their overall performance.[12] However, we should have learned from history that little ever changes. In 1929, Ralph Borsodi observed that in the

> 50 years between 1870 and 1920 the cost of distributing necessities and luxuries had nearly trebled while production costs had come down by one-fifth... what we are saving in production we are losing in distribution.[13]

A similar scenario exists today.

ORIGINS AND EVOLUTION OF SUPPLY CHAINS

As emphasized earlier when discussing the concept of focus (Chapter 7), the origin of organizations in the twenty-first century is rooted in functional management and control, with the subsequent result of split responsibilities. The classic outcome was a fragmented supply chain emphasizing vertical rather than horizontal processes, as illustrated in Figure 8.7 for a typical manufacturing company. Figure 8.8 shows similar relationships for a typical service company.

For most companies, developing a supply chain is a multi-phase task. Phase 1 is the initial position and the second phase starts with integrating the steps within the internal phase of the supply chain, as illustrated in Figure 8.9. This internal coordination emphasizes the horizontal nature of the systems and processes inherent in the basic tasks of procurement through to supplying the service or product. It forges cooperation within and between the steps to create an integrated whole and the opportunity to reduce costs and delays on the one hand and improve responsiveness to customer needs on the other.

The next phase concerns coordinating activities between businesses. As shown in Figure 8.10, this stage involves recognizing additional facets within the supply chain (for example Tier 1 and Tier 2 suppliers and stages in the distribution channel) in order to ensure that these form part of the collaborative development between supply chain partners.

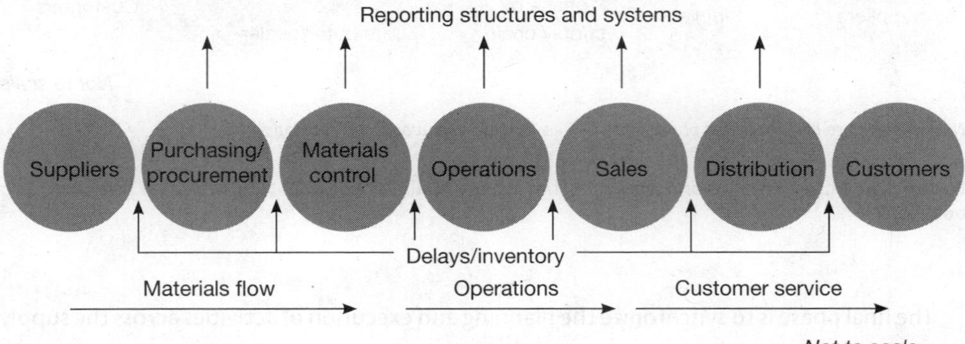

Figure 8.7 Manufacturing company Phase 1: typical initial position of functionally fragmented supply chains with built-in delays/inventory, vertical reporting structures and systems and the separation of suppliers, operations and customers

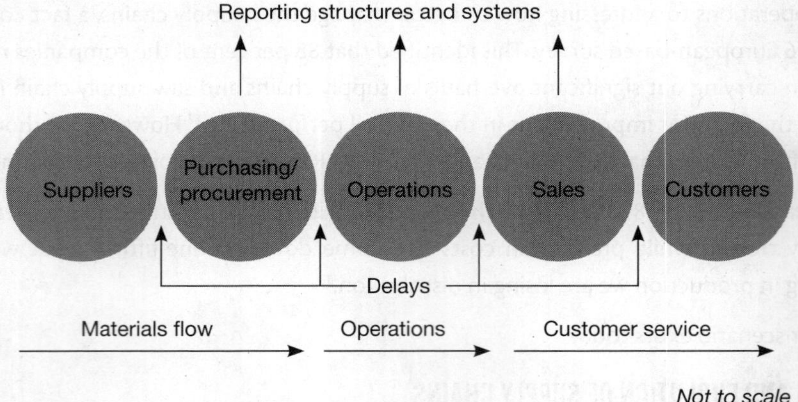

Figure 8.8 Service company Phase 1: typical initial position of functionally fragmented supply chains with built-in delays/inventory, vertical reporting structures and systems and the separation of suppliers, operations and customers

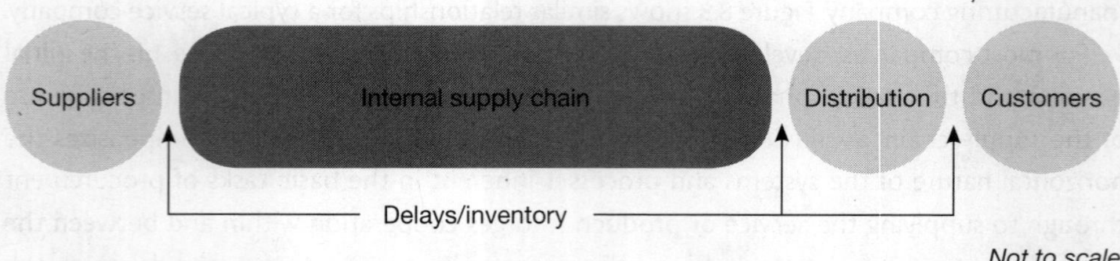

Note: This figure illustrates this phase for both a service and manufacturing company.

Figure 8.9 Phase 2: integration of the supply chain activities within a business

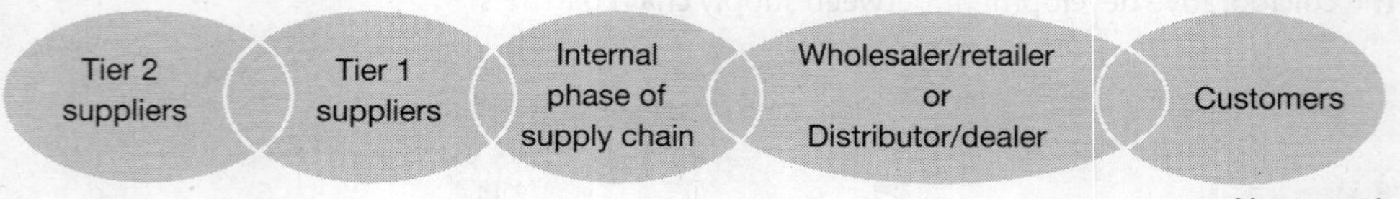

Note: This figure illustrates this phase for both a service and manufacturing company.

Figure 8.10 Phase 3: collaboration across the supply chain by coordinating activities between businesses

The final phase is to synchronize the planning and execution of activities across the supply chain, as shown in Figure 8.11. This requires partnership and strategic alliance arrangements that will include the transfer and access of data between businesses from design through to order fulfilment, call-offs and delivery schedules. Traditional roles and responsibilities will change markedly, with suppliers at times taking responsibility for design through to

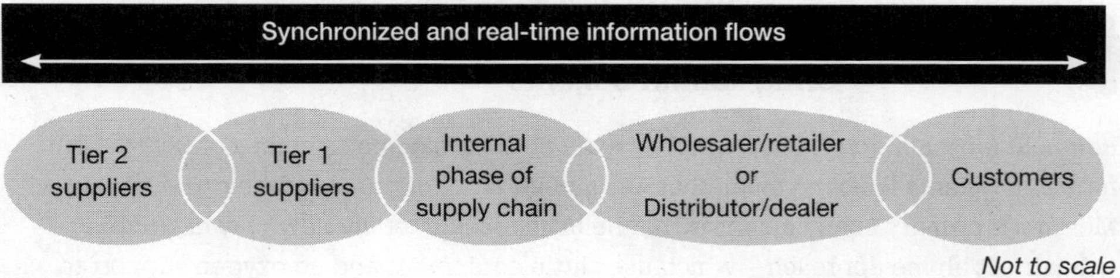

Note: This figure illustrates this phase for both a service and manufacturing company.

Figure 8.11 Phase 4: synchronized and real-time planning and execution of activities across the supply chain

the internal phase of the supply chain and deciding how much and when to ship goods to customers at other times.

The principles underlying these changes have their origins in a recognition that the whole, and not solely the internal phase, of a supply chain is the basis for today's competition. Given the extent and nature of the support for markets that is provided by operations, then aligning the supply chain provision with the requirements of the agreed market has to be a central feature of strategy implementation. Key issues that result include:

- **Overcoming the barriers to integration** – functions within organizations and organizations themselves create barriers to integration. Viewing the supply chain as a whole is a prerequisite for rethinking how best to provide market support through the entire supply chain and for overcoming any inherent obstacles.
- **Responding to short lead times** – delivery speed is an order-winner or qualifier in many of today's markets. Customers are seeking to reduce lead times and suppliers need to match these quick response demands. To do this reliably requires developing lean logistics and managing the supply chain as an integrated whole.
- **Eliminating costs** – an integrated approach lowers costs by reducing inventory, simplifying procedures, eliminating duplication and other non-value-added activities together with associated overheads. Viewing the supply chain as a whole enables systems, processes and procedures to be structured with the associated gains of reduced time and cost.
- **Moving information, not inventory and delays** – non-integrated approaches have built-in delays comprising time and inventory. By moving information, delays are reduced and subsequent parts of the chain can match real-time needs rather than using inventory to protect against uncertainty and the unknown.

One parallel to lean supply chain management is provided by the revolutionary changes brought to high-peak climbing by Reinhold Messner. As Case 8.4 explains, the 'direct alpine approach' he introduced changed the 'conventional mountaineering strategy' (one based on 'massive amounts of support including extra oxygen') to one using 'little equipment and no oxygen support to reach the top'. Messner argued that under the conventional approach, the slowest man sets the pace, whereas his goal was 'speed of execution' – the final assault was made 'by himself, or with one other person, in a single day'.[14]

Case 8.4 – Lean supply chain concepts work elsewhere and bring similar benefits

Reinhold Messner, the Italian climber, is one of the great sports heroes of Europe, but his claim to fame is not so much that he climbed all 14 of the world's highest peaks. Messner's primary achievement is that he introduced a totally new way of climbing – the direct alpine approach – which uses little equipment and no oxygen support to reach the top.

Conventional mountaineering strategy is based on massive amounts of support, including extra oxygen, which was thought to be essential for climbs over 25,000 feet. Men such as Sir Edmund Hillary and Chris Bonington relied on hundreds of guides who carried food, oxygen and other supplies; for example, an American expedition to climb Everest in 1963 included 900 porters trudging up the mountain with 300 tonnes of equipment. Messner argues that under this strategy, the slowest man sets the pace. His goal is speed of execution.

Although assisted by guides up the base of a mountain, Messner usually makes the final assault by himself, or with one other person, in a single day. He scaled the north face of Everest solo, without oxygen – one of the most severe mountaineering challenges ever attempted.

When Hillary and Tenzing became the first mountaineers to climb Everest in 1953, they took seven weeks. On 22 May 2004, Pemba Dorji Shelpa took 8 hours and 10 minutes using the direct alpine approach.

GLOBALIZATION

With trade barriers easing and markets opening up, the globalization of business activity has accelerated. Two key issues result from this – a widening choice of offshore suppliers and the need to manage the global supply chain that emerges.

The growing operations base (from IT design and support to light and heavy manufactured goods) of regions and countries such as Asia Pacific, Eastern Europe, Mexico and South America has received high exposure, in part, if not exclusively, due to the low-cost operations provision they offer. While for some companies low cost is consistent with their market needs, it is essential that market requirement and not unit cost drives choice. Low cost is often not the strategic priority for a business that historically it was thought to be, and companies are clearly beginning to recognize this. For example, many banks are repatriating their call-centre provision, recognizing that customers are better served by local staff.

There is an increasing emphasis on global capability. In order to take full advantage of this opportunity, companies need to manage the processes and interfaces involved. It is essential to avoid the scenario of gaining advantage in one phase of a supply chain and losing the benefits in the next. Key to this is globalizing total customer relations from design through logistics to the end user.

DOMESTIC VERSUS OFFSHORE SOURCING OPTIONS AND STRATEGIC FIT

As highlighted in the last section, companies across all sectors are taking advantage of lower-priced goods and services offered by offshore suppliers. The advantage of lower labour costs means that they are able to undercut domestic competitors. But outsourcing decisions include an offshore as well as a domestic option. So, what are the trade-offs involved in this choice, particularly regarding strategic fit?

Research on retail companies in the US and the UK and the sourcing of goods from both domestic and overseas suppliers highlighted many of the trade-offs involved. As the results in Figure 8.12 show, not only do the domestic versus offshore alternatives differ but so do the offshore regions involved. The trade-off between high discounts and low latitude for change is clearly evident for Central American and Asian suppliers versus alternatives. Because the whole supply chain needs to support the needs of a company's chosen market, both the external and internal phases of the chain need to support the relevant order-winners and qualifiers of these markets – the concept of strategic fit.

OFFSHORE MANUFACTURING PLANTS

Offshore manufacturing plants are typically established for the classic benefits of tariff and trade concessions, lower labour costs, subsidies and reduced logistic costs. As a consequence, they are often assigned a limited range of tasks and responsibilities that reflect the prime reason for which they were built. Companies are now reviewing this classic perspective and broadening their expectations of offshore plants and the way they manage and measure them. It is important for companies to exploit these opportunities and Figure 8.13[15] lists some potential roles for offshore factories, while Figure 8.14 gives examples of companies assigning additional roles to offshore plants.

Percentage		Supplier location				
		Asia	Central America	Europe	US	UK
Percentage discount	US retailer	20–30	20–25	5–10	0	–
	UK retailer	25–35	–	10–15	1–5	0
Percentage of suppliers not allowing any changes once order placed[1]	Order volume	66	41	29	16	9
	Order mix	70	46	37	21	21

Figure 8.12 Percentage discount by supplier location agreed with US and UK retailers, and percentage of suppliers not allowing any changes to order volume and order mix once order placed

[1] *Figures before season starts. As you would expect, the percentage of suppliers not allowing any changes to order volume/mix increased once the season has started.*

Source: Based on data from Lowson, R.H. (2001) 'Offshore sourcing: an optimal operational strategy?' Business Horizons, *44(6), Nov–Dec, pp. 61–6.*

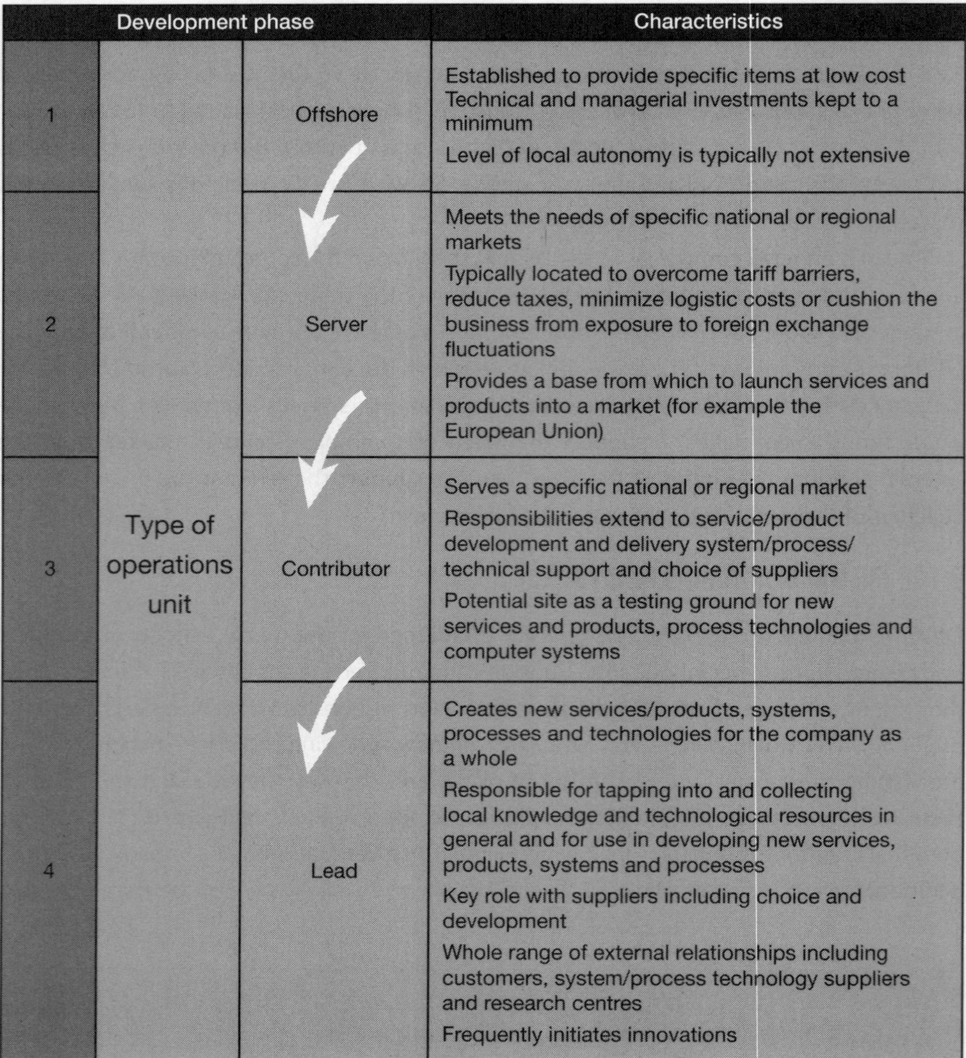

Development phase			Characteristics
1	Type of operations unit	Offshore	Established to provide specific items at low cost Technical and managerial investments kept to a minimum Level of local autonomy is typically not extensive
2		Server	Meets the needs of specific national or regional markets Typically located to overcome tariff barriers, reduce taxes, minimize logistic costs or cushion the business from exposure to foreign exchange fluctuations Provides a base from which to launch services and products into a market (for example the European Union)
3		Contributor	Serves a specific national or regional market Responsibilities extend to service/product development and delivery system/process/technical support and choice of suppliers Potential site as a testing ground for new services and products, process technologies and computer systems
4		Lead	Creates new services/products, systems, processes and technologies for the company as a whole Responsible for tapping into and collecting local knowledge and technological resources in general and for use in developing new services, products, systems and processes Key role with suppliers including choice and development Whole range of external relationships including customers, system/process technology suppliers and research centres Frequently initiates innovations

Figure 8.13 Progressive roles of offshore facilities

LOGISTICS COSTS

It is estimated that US companies spend almost 11 per cent of GDP (in 2016 the GDP of the US was estimated to be $18.46 trillion) to wrap, bundle, load, unload, sort, reload and move goods around. With figures like these, the cost of making products is not necessarily the area in which to seek savings. A typical box of cereal in the US is estimated to spend 140 days getting from factory to supermarket shelf. It goes through a procession of stages, each of which has a warehouse, resulting in inefficiencies and high logistic costs.

Company	Location	Tasks
Hewlett-Packard	Guadalajara (Mexico)	• Assembles computers • Designs memory boards
3M	Bangalore (India)	• Manufactures software • Writes software
Motorola	Singapore	• Manufactures pagers • Designs pagers

Figure 8.14 Examples of companies seeking and gaining additional roles from offshore plants

When developing their supply chains, companies need to take into account location choices and associated costs. The lack of attention paid to supply chain development in the past and the growing size of logistics in terms of costs and lead times make the potential benefits attractive and should be high on most companies' priority list.

ASPECTS OF CHANGE

Underpinning the developments set out in the last section are a number of changes that need to be secured if the desired supply chain benefits are to be realized. The most important of these are now discussed.

Efficient customer response

There is more to supply chain development than hard-nosed procurement and securing tight controls over inventory levels. While efficient supply chains concern eliminating delays and reducing resources along the way, the orientation of such developments needs to be towards more efficient customer response where market requirements and not traditional dimensions such as cost reduction underpin priorities and direction.

More efficient customer response combines a company's own internal orientation with seeking changes in all of the external elements of the supply chain. These range from suppliers shouldering some or all of the associated development costs to smaller, more frequent deliveries, necessitating suppliers to hold inventory or produce more often in smaller lot sizes. For most companies, there is little choice but to seek more from suppliers because their own customers are exacting the same pressure on short lead times and the sharing of risk.

The result fosters closer relations with fewer suppliers. The greatest challenge is developing both the internal and external phases of the supply chain to meet the needs of agreed markets. One key to making this happen is information.

Increasing use of IT

Since the early 1960s, four major IT developments have transformed the way in which companies conduct business, and each wave of technology has radically altered the supply chain that links suppliers through to end users.

1. The initial phase of IT application was based on mainframe computers. It began in the early 1960s and continued to be the dominant technology for the next 10–15 years. Business applications included material requirements planning and manufacturing resource planning (MRP and MRPII, respectively). These enabled companies to standardize and systemize the day-to-day tasks in operations and parts of the supply chain. As a result, companies developed functional expertise supported by systems designed around tasks of relevant functions.
2. The second phase was based on PCs and began in the 1970s, continuing well into the 1980s. PC applications such as word processors, spreadsheets and presentation software facilitated communication across functional boundaries. PCs also put the power of computing into the hands of employees, and businesses built on this opportunity by focusing on the development of cross-functional processes that brought both functional and overall business benefits.
3. The third phase of IT applications was based on network computing. Starting in the mid-1980s, it continues to be a dominant influence on how companies are managed and business is conducted. Network computing, customer/supplier applications, electronic data interchange (EDI), point-of-sale (POS) response and other forms of electronic mail are reducing the costs of handling information and transactions, while speeding up information exchange that allows real-time systems and responses to be developed while leveraging the efficiencies of functional expertise (phase 1) and cross-functional business processes (phase 2).
4. The fourth phase is based on the internet and the World Wide Web. Providing a universal infrastructure, the internet facilitates the interchange of information between businesses by not only reinforcing existing trends of cooperation but also helping companies to consider their supply chains as a whole and their role to manage and orchestrate priorities and performance. By fostering better communication and interchange of information between companies, this phase enables fully integrated systems between businesses, not only customers to suppliers but also between suppliers.

One of the lasting effects of these technology applications is that they have facilitated the breakdown of barriers from cross-individuals to cross-corporations (see Figure 8.15).

The rapid growth of e-commerce has, however, brought with it some concerns that originate from both the mechanisms that underpin these delivery systems and the speed of its use within commercial activities and transactions.

- **Fraud** – in 2016 fraud was estimated to cost the UK economy £193 billion while cybercrime (any crime involving a computer or a network) is estimated to cost $450 billion globally, based on financial losses and time lost.[16]

Phase	Aspects of change
1 Cross-individuals	Broke down barriers between functional experts themselves and between this group and the executives responsible for managing core parts of a business, particularly operations
2 Cross-functions	Facilitated links between functions by requiring and helping the interchange between different parts of the same business
3 Cross-businesses	Impacted the way companies conducted business by removing barriers within an organization and between parts of the immediate supply chain
4 Cross-corporations	Continued the cross-corporate changes by facilitating cooperation of businesses within a supply chain including Tier 2 suppliers

Figure 8.15 The evolving role of IT in managing a supply chain

- **Vulnerability** – the level and nature of vulnerable outcomes inherent in the growing use of the internet are being highlighted in a series of incidents throughout the world, from bomb-making to arranging and managing gang violence.

Focusing on non-value-added activities

Increasingly, companies have focused attention on minimizing non-value-added activities while providing information and communication tools that allow employees to focus on the value-added and strategic activities within the business. As firms reduce non-value-added activity, they redirect those newly released resources to the value-added and strategic dimensions of their business. For example, companies are increasingly using electronic intranet catalogues that enable office staff (the consumers) to order non-operations services and goods (for example, office supplies and computer software) directly from agreed suppliers. Not only does this break down barriers but it also eliminates non-value-added activities such as data re-entry and checking, thus allowing more time for purchasing staff to focus on their value-added activities such as developing supplier relations and contract negotiations.

E-procurement

Within these supply-chain management developments is the role of e-procurement. While supply-chain management addresses the core activities within a business, e-procurement extends electronic applications into the wide range of indirect goods and services that are bought by staff at all levels in an organization. As with the purchase of direct services and goods in the past, the procurement of indirect services and products has received little attention, while the size of spend is considerable. For example, in the UK, annual public procurement totals £200 billion. Similarly, at the corporate level, it is estimated that companies can spend up to 15–20 per cent of sales revenue on indirect services and products.

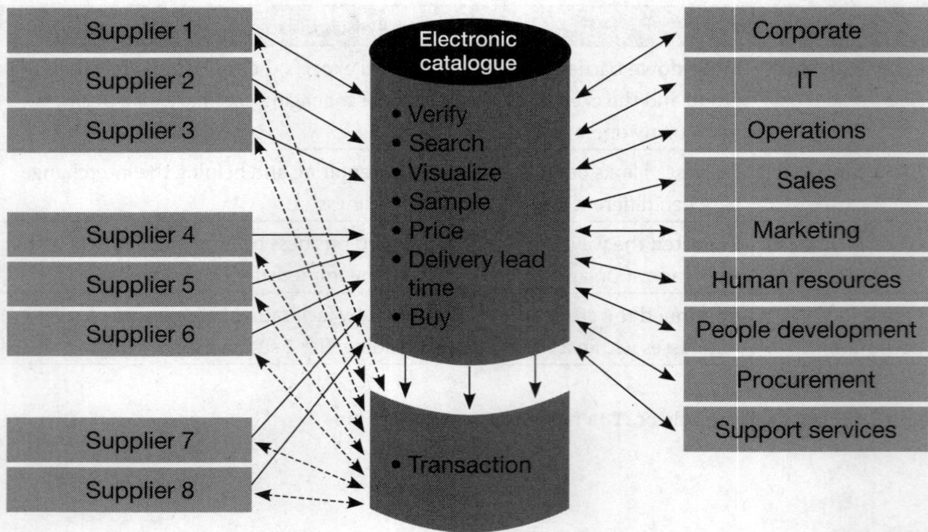

Figure 8.16 E-procurement system

Source: Hill, A. and Hill, T. (2012) Operations Management, *3rd edn, Palgrave Macmillan.*

While the IT investment required to move to e-procurement systems has to be made, the change is more cultural than technological. Many organizations have already taken on board electronic catalogues but the necessary cultural changes do not stop there. Online procurement is not a new tool for the purchasing function but a new way of working for the whole organization. With e-purchasing, everyone in the organization is now empowered to buy online. For this transition to take place, a leap of faith is required. Gone is the system based on forms, counter-forms and authorizations. This is replaced by checks and controls embodied in the software. It is not a case of computerizing the old manual process but of re-engineering the system itself. Now repetitive ordering can be devolved through the organization in a controlled manner.

As illustrated in Figure 8.16, electronic catalogues are at the heart of this development. These can be managed by the purchasing company or a third party such as British Telecommunications Group and Commerce One, a USA-based provider. Goods are purchased by anyone in the organization by completing an electronic purchasing application. The system checks the specification, searches, visualizes the requirements, offers checks on price and delivery dates and then places the order. Progress of an order is then monitored electronically. The electronic catalogue is updated by supplier information and the growing needs of the organization itself. Estimates suggest that companies can save up to 11 per cent of indirect purchasing costs by introducing e-purchasing systems for dealing with the procurement of indirect services and products.

Online procurement has arrived and the challenge for companies is how to turn its potential to best organizational advantage. The principal benefits awaiting these developments include:

1 **Increase in contract compliance** – typically this benefit comprises the largest element of the e-procurement development, bringing with it:

- increased use of preferred suppliers;
- reduced off-contract spending;
- reduced processing errors.

2 **Leveraging the purchasing spend** – e-procurement brings together the disparate purchasing transactions that characterize most organizations' traditional approach to purchasing indirect services and products. In so doing, it allows companies to improve the potential leverage of these purchases through:

- providing greater oversight of the purchasing spending;
- recording details of the actual spend by supplier and service/product category;
- allowing full purchasing power to be leveraged when negotiating discounts, with more services and goods ultimately purchased at lower prices.

3 **Lower processing costs** – the business, staff and system costs involved in procurement will be reduced as a result of several factors including:

- faster processing times;
- lower number of emails/telephone calls;
- reduced error rates.

Cisco Systems, for example, has reduced the cost of procurement from an average of $130 per order to $40 – its target is to lower the cost to $25 per order.

4 **Increased involvement of people** – being able to purchase online takes delays out of the procurement process. The result is that staff feel more involved, with an increased sense of responsibility for their own sphere of work. The controls built into the system are further enhanced by an individual's ability to seek alternatives and the increased personalization of the system, both of which enhance the search for good value.

5 **Optimizing corporate tax savings** – locating the purchasing function in a low tax economy can enable a company to attribute cost savings (that is, profit) there.

6 **Offers a sure route to an early e-business success** – the low-risk nature of these developments in what are non-business critical systems makes these developments a good place to start. Furthermore, the measurable objectives of e-procurement investment proposals result in a clear and persuasive business case, offering a short financial payback.

Online procurement offers the opportunity to break down departmental and intercompany trading barriers that opens the way to reducing costs and time in the purchase of indirect goods and services. The organization-wide nature of these changes requires a top-down process in order for an organization to grasp the potential of the e-procurement opportunity. While the technology base of these developments is not in itself complex, the cultural change within the organization should not be underestimated.

MANAGING THE SUPPLY CHAIN

The make-or-buy decision is not only critical in itself but it also governs the mix between the internal and external phases of the whole supply chain and thereby the nature of the operations task in managing these resources.

Whether a company makes or buys, effective management of the whole supply chain has increasingly been recognized as a key executive role and one that directly impacts on a company's ability to compete in its chosen markets. The task of managing the in-house or internal phase of the chain is addressed throughout this book. This section deals with the key issues and approaches that relate to managing the external phase(s) of a supply chain.

The concept of a totally integrated supply chain – from service or material producer through to end customer – is bringing great changes to the way businesses operate. Increasingly, companies no longer compete just with each other but they also compete through their supply chains (see Figure 8.17). To bring this about, companies need a supply chain that is managed as an integrated whole in line with market needs and corporate objectives and underpinned by responsive and adaptive systems, procedures and attitudes. This, in turn, requires meaningful collaboration and fuller relationships with suppliers to provide the essential basis for cooperation and joint developments.

SUPPLY CHAIN MANAGEMENT ISSUES

In the 1980s, companies turned their attention to fixing their operations problems but few addressed total supply-chain costs. By the early 1990s, firms started to realize the need to shift emphasis. With shortening service/product life cycles, more customer choice and reducing lead times set within the context of growing world competition, it became essential to review the whole supply chain, identify opportunities and manage these requirements. Because most companies have been outsourcing more and more in recent years and future trends point the same way, the need to manage the supply chain effectively should continue to be high on the corporate agenda. Whether you make or buy, the responsibility for managing the whole chain can no longer be ignored as it was in the past. Some of the key management issues involved are now discussed.

Changes in attitude

Historically, in relationships with suppliers, cooperation was not the way in which many customers behaved. Pitting suppliers against each other and ruling by threat and fear are

Period	Basis of competition
Yesterday	A company versus another company
Today	A company and its supply chain versus another company and its supply chain

Figure 8.17 The changing basis of competition

being abandoned in favour of long-term relationships, often with single suppliers. Companies are also bringing suppliers on board much earlier in the design process, seeking technical help and contributions, and even inviting suppliers to help in identifying future services and products.

To underpin these changes, customers are reviewing the way they manage suppliers and the level of cooperation involved. The trend towards greater cooperation goes hand in hand with a more proactive style, as illustrated in Figure 8.18.

Reflecting on the earlier discussion on 'creating your own competition', whatever type of relationship a company has with its suppliers, proactive collaboration on all aspects of

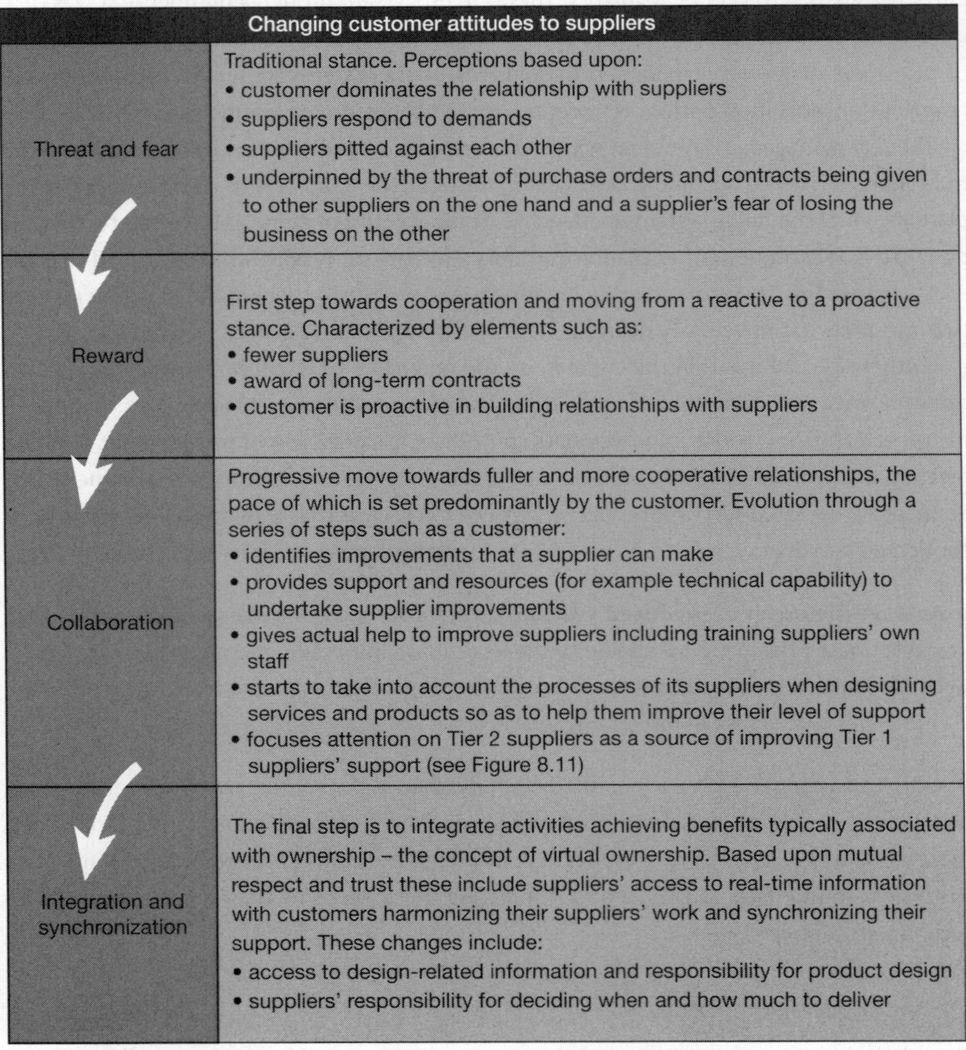

Changing customer attitudes to suppliers	
Threat and fear	Traditional stance. Perceptions based upon: • customer dominates the relationship with suppliers • suppliers respond to demands • suppliers pitted against each other • underpinned by the threat of purchase orders and contracts being given to other suppliers on the one hand and a supplier's fear of losing the business on the other
Reward	First step towards cooperation and moving from a reactive to a proactive stance. Characterized by elements such as: • fewer suppliers • award of long-term contracts • customer is proactive in building relationships with suppliers
Collaboration	Progressive move towards fuller and more cooperative relationships, the pace of which is set predominantly by the customer. Evolution through a series of steps such as a customer: • identifies improvements that a supplier can make • provides support and resources (for example technical capability) to undertake supplier improvements • gives actual help to improve suppliers including training suppliers' own staff • starts to take into account the processes of its suppliers when designing services and products so as to help them improve their level of support • focuses attention on Tier 2 suppliers as a source of improving Tier 1 suppliers' support (see Figure 8.11)
Integration and synchronization	The final step is to integrate activities achieving benefits typically associated with ownership – the concept of virtual ownership. Based upon mutual respect and trust these include suppliers' access to real-time information with customers harmonizing their suppliers' work and synchronizing their support. These changes include: • access to design-related information and responsibility for product design • suppliers' responsibility for deciding when and how much to deliver

Figure 8.18 Phases in changing customer attitudes to suppliers

supplier relations needs to underpin its supply-chain management style. While content and level of trust need to reflect the company's short- and long-term strategies, the style used to manage suppliers needs to be driven by a recognition that they form an integral part of the total capability essential to remaining competitive in today's markets.

Incorporating uncertainty

Today's markets are characterized by shortening service/product life cycles and stiffening requirements for all aspects of customer service. Against this background, large companies are characterized by complexity, as clearly illustrated by a review of the steps through the delivery systems within the operations functions. Multiple suppliers provide services and parts/materials with varying regularity. These are processed through a number of stages that, in turn, are characterized by uncertainty. Finished services and products then go to a range of customers, often with varying sets of demands. These patterns are further confused by the range of transportation options to meet the spread of customers around the world.

The real management problem within this complex network is, however, the uncertainty that characterizes it. But many companies still treat this task as if it was predictable. The planning and scheduling systems inadequately take account of demand uncertainty. They are designed as if certainty rather than uncertainty was the reality with which they had to cope. And, because the situation today is increasingly less predictable than in the past, this leads to circumstances of unnecessary delays, inventory and high obsolescence.

Furthermore, all this is in the context, on the one hand, of IT developments such as electronic POS scanners that provide up-to-the-minute data on customer buying patterns and, on the other hand, operations improvements concerning the provision of smaller order sizes and meeting shorter lead times. At the same time, the drive to meet customer requirements has dramatically widened service/product ranges, even in sectors that traditionally have not been considered fashion driven. But new service/product introductions have two adverse side effects:

- **Average life cycles are reduced** – this, in turn, shortens the relative duration of the more stable phase of demand in relation to the less certain initial and end phases.
- **Total demand is spread over more stock-keeping units**[17] – the more items on offer, the more difficult the task of forecasting sales.

Overall, the result is a growing unpredictability that increases the need to manage each phase of the supply chain and the interface between them. As highlighted earlier, Dell, having shortened its own assembly lead times in response to the delivery speed requirements of its customers, found itself constrained from meeting these needs by the long lead times of its component suppliers.

Customer/supplier dependence

The relationship between customers and suppliers is influenced by the level of dependence of the one on the other – see Figure 8.19. Where customers and suppliers are positioned will impact potential relationship options, as explained in the next section.

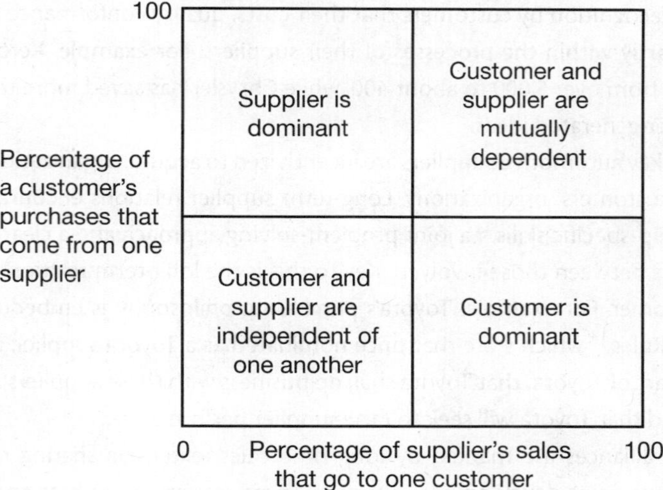

Figure 8.19 Customer/supplier dependence

Types of supplier relations

Part of managing the make-or-buy decision is how best to structure relationships with suppliers. Customers can position themselves in a number of ways within the constraints of dimensions such as the 'dependence factor' introduced above. The characteristics of these different types of supplier relationships are now reviewed. A company's choice needs to reflect the characteristics of the services or materials or components involved and the marketplace in which it operates.

- **Trawling the market** – here suppliers are held at arm's length with a growing amount of business completed using computerized interaction. For example, General Electric (GE) in the US increasingly purchases components over the internet where it posts details of parts, and prequalified vendors then quote for the contract. Here, there is little face-to-face interaction and the key order-winner is price. Delivery on time and quality conformance are qualifiers and form part of the listing prerequisites. Benefits also include reduced processing costs, for example GE quotes a 90 per cent reduction compared to traditional paperwork procedures. Finally, this phase may entail placing a significant amount of business with competitors.
- **Ongoing relationships** – these involve establishing medium-term contracts with suppliers and developing relations in terms of information sharing, and require sound management by customers.
- **Partnerships** – involve long-term contracts characterized by the extensive sharing of information and increased trust. For example, since 1988 the US car maker Chrysler's average contract length with suppliers has more than doubled.
- **Strategic alliances** – the trend in sourcing is towards strategic alliances that are characterized by the increased depth and breadth of the whole customer/supplier relationship. A prerequisite of more cooperative relationships is a dramatic reduction in the supplier

base and a recognition by customers that their costs, quality conformance levels and lead times are partly within the processes of their suppliers. For example, Xerox has reduced its suppliers from over 5,000 to about 400, while Chrysler has saved more than $0.5 billion from supplier-generated ideas.

In Japan, key automotive suppliers are incentivized to acquire organizational capabilities from their customers' organizations. Long-term supplier relations encourage investment in relationship-specific skills,[18] a joint problem-solving approach and a clear set of rules for sharing gains between those involved. Key to this is the long-term relationship developed by the customer. For example, Toyota's purchasing philosophy is embedded in its 1939 Purchasing Rules,[19] which state that once nominated as a Toyota supplier, they should be treated as part of Toyota, that Toyota shall do business with these suppliers and not switch to others and that Toyota will seek to raise supplier performance.

Strategic alliances are marked by long timescales, extensive sharing of information, increased trust, joint development of services, products and processes and the intent to work together over an extended period. Boeing has strategic alliances with GE and Rolls-Royce, partly to reduce the financial risk of new aeroplane programmes and partly to cope with the complex technical interfaces between engines and airframes that have to be designed in conjunction with each other.

- **Backward integration** – the final step is to change from relationship to ownership. This leads to the full sharing of information and the transfer of goals and culture. To illustrate the nature and extent of partnering arrangements and supplier developments, Figure 8.20 provides examples of relationship developments in a range of industries.

STRATEGIC PARTNERING

Building on from the last section, the need to be more competitive has led some companies to partner others in the supply chain. As highlighted earlier, customer/supplier relations

End customer	Customer/supplier developments
Hitachi (VCR equipment)	• Six-monthly supplier meetings where Hitachi's CEO provides details of aggregate plans and policies to suppliers' top executives • Suppliers arranged into groups by categories of parts – cosmetic, electronic, mechanical and assembly. Each group has bimonthly two-day meetings to resolve quality conformance, technical and delivery reliability issues
Volvo (cars)	• 75 per cent of every car is made outside Sweden • Volvo collects parts from suppliers and ships them to Gothenburg • Suppliers required to maintain two to four weeks of stock • Pallets of parts not opened until moved to the assembly area, necessitating a guarantee on quality conformance and quantity • Volvo provides a 12-month forecast: first six weeks are firm, next 12 weeks can vary but Volvo accepts responsibility for materials and work-in-progress inventory

Boeing (passenger aircraft)	• Design-build teams used on the 777 passenger airliner • First plane off the assembly line – parts were so accurate that the nose-to-tail measurement was less than 23/1000 of an inch (0.6 mm) from design specification • Success built on computer-based design and the design-build teams used that included suppliers. Core to this success was the mutual respect and trust built up within the teams
UK-based motor manufacturers	• Forum established comprising experts from General Motors, Honda, Nissan, Toyota and Volkswagen • Purpose is for these major competitors to cooperate in educating and improving tier 2 supplier base to the auto industry
Canon (photocopiers and printers)	• Sent own engineers to Daisho Denshi (a $0.25 billion maker of circuit boards and other parts) at a time when it was on the verge of bankruptcy • Improvements in efficiency, quality conformance and on-time delivery resulted • Led to Daisho Denshi cutting prices to Canon by 10 per cent

Figure 8.20 Examples of customer/supplier relationship developments in a range of industrial sectors

continue to undergo major changes where the goal is to synchronize activities to the point where virtual integration is achieved (see Figure 8.18).

Strategic partnering involves:

> a long-term relationship between an organization and its suppliers. It is designed to leverage the strategic and operational capabilities of individual participating organizations to help them advance significant, ongoing benefits.[20]

Such developments concern the extent to which critical and even proprietary information is communicated within the partnership. How far this can be secured is not only constrained by the parties involved but also by the stage in a sector's evolution. For example, in the early days of the computing industry, the major players had no option but to build the infrastructure that would enable them to produce all the components and parts to build a computer. They had little choice. As the industry grew, more specialised companies developed to produce specific components. This allowed new entrants a choice. As Michael Dell (founder of Dell Computers) explained:

> As a new start-up, Dell couldn't afford to create every piece of the value chain. But more to the point, why should we want to? We concluded we'd be better off leveraging the investments others have made and focusing on delivering solutions and systems to customers ... It's a pretty simple strategy ... but at the time it went against the dominant 'engineering-centric' view of the industry. Companies such as IBM, Compaq and HP subscribed to a 'we-have-to-develop-everything' view of the world. If you weren't doing component assembly, you weren't a real computer company.[21]

Strategic partnering is based on a conscious decision that sees its ultimate goal as virtual integration. This seeks to incorporate other parts of the supply chain as if they are part of one's own business. On the delivery end of the chain, companies work with their customers to better understand their needs. In some partnerships, retail stores are sharing POS data to help suppliers better meet market trends and changes. On the sourcing end of the chain, suppliers are delivering more frequently, keeping consignment inventory in a customer's warehouse (and only invoicing on use) and managing the replenishment cycle to reflect usage that also helps them to optimize their own schedules. While the customer frees up resources, the supplier has longer-term customer commitment, a barrier from competition that reduces sales and marketing effort and firm data on which to plan and schedule operations and its own suppliers.

However, partnerships must deliver value and should not be entered into for their own sake. They are costly to implement, require additional management costs to develop, coordinate and maintain, together with an attendant increase in the level of risk sharing. They can only be justified if they yield substantially better results than a firm would achieve without partnering, with the added check that the results could not be achieved without a partnership in place.[22]

SUPPLY CLUSTERS

At the heart of Toyota's supply chain lies the concept of clustering. Of Toyota's 15 plants in Japan, 12 (along with the manufacturing facilities of most of its suppliers) are located around Toyota City (once the mill town of Koromo), situated less than an hour's drive from Nagoya. This organizational arrangement in the sourcing and operations phases of a supply network is called a 'supply cluster' – a geographically close group of interconnected companies and associated businesses in a particular sector(s) including end product manufacturers, component suppliers and supporting firms.[23] Senior executives in Toyota 'believe that the cluster not only has allowed the company to use its just-in-time system but has also shaped Toyota's culture. They plan to create similar clusters overseas.'[24]

While the above example relates to a corporate cluster, industrial clusters represent a collection of many interrelated supply chains (or supply networks). These industrial clusters comprise many levels of independent suppliers and manufacturers, with different companies possibly supplying the same manufacturers as well as different manufacturers ordering from the same supplier.[25] This supply-cluster concept, for example, forms the basic structure by which almost all manufacturing in China is conducted.

There are two principal types of supply clusters used in China.[26] The first is known as 'hub and spoke'. Here a large manufacturer (often a state-owned enterprise or joint venture) is surrounded by many suppliers and support firms. The hub company is typically highly regulated and limited to certain capital-intensive industries such as chemicals, energy and steel. The second type of cluster comprises a large number of small and medium enterprises (SMEs) that have developed into the equivalent of large revenue-generating conglomerates, which again are surrounded by many related suppliers and support firms. The companies making up these clusters are a mix of domestic and foreign-owned.

By 2015, there were well over 1,500 such supply clusters covering almost all major export products, with most of these configurations located in China's most developed economic regions, including the eastern provinces of Guangdong, Fujian, Zhejiang and Jiangsu and large metropolitan areas such as Shanghai, Beijing and Tranjin. Examples include:

- The Nanhai district of Foshan in Guangdong province comprises some 18 townships, each specializing in an aspect of manufacturing such as ceramics, textiles, ferrous metal processing, electrical appliances, underwear and toys. The township of Dali, for instance, accounts for 40 per cent of China's output of aluminium products by volume.
- The Donman township in Guangdong province has 13 factories employing 18,000 workers producing cell phones, game consoles, PCs and other electrical hardware. Within two hours of these factories are thousands of suppliers, resulting in component costs that are less than 20 per cent of those for similar products made in the USA.[27]
- In Zhejiang province, there are hundreds of industrial clusters, each generating annual sales revenues of between $150 million and $2.5 billion. For example, some 5,000 companies in the Zhili township produce children's garments, while the combined annual output of companies in the Datang township exceeds six billion pairs of socks.

The impact of clustering enhances supply-chain performance for both customers and suppliers and is derived from a range of benefits.

1 **Material and component supply**
   - facilitates the sourcing of material and components;
   - increased purchasing power for raw materials and components lowers costs;
   - simplifies the flow of inventories, facilitating just-in-time provision.
2 **Capacity-related benefits**
   - capacity pooling to better handle uncertain demand, including outsourcing customer orders in times of high demand and supplementing the level of activity of another supplier experiencing a short-term dip in sales;
   - spreading the investment costs of facilities that can be shared, for example treatment plants for the dyeing and printing sectors and warehousing.
3 **Operational costs**
   - lowers costs for both inbound and outbound transportation;
   - spreads infrastructure development investment;
   - shares process improvements and technical know-how;
   - increased purchasing power for both support services and equipment lowers costs.
4 **Information-related benefits**
   - sharing of hardware and software facilities and capabilities in information transmission – many SMEs do not have their own means (investment and skilled staff) to develop and maintain effective IT systems;
   - facilitates the collection and flow of market, technical and competitive information.

5 **Working relationships**
  - helps create and maintain personal relationships, strengthens community ties and fosters trust in working relationships between suppliers and between suppliers and customers.

6 **Regional benefits**
  - regions develop a reputation for expertise in a particular sector, so helping to maintain current and increase future levels of activity with existing customers while attracting new business;
  - arranging joint marketing activities such as trade fairs;
  - creates local competition so enhancing the drive for continuous improvement and helping a cluster to remain competitive.

MANAGING STABILITY IN THE INTERNAL PHASE OF THE SUPPLY CHAIN

In most companies, operations is responsible for managing the major portion of costs and investments to maximize profit and cash flow. Stabilizing delivery systems is an essential element of achieving this, especially given the growing reliance on suppliers as companies outsource more goods and services and the task of better managing the external phase of the supply chain that results. Various researchers[28] have highlighted the role of inventory, order backlog and capacity in managing the variation between an operations delivery system and its markets. Their findings support Hopp and Spearman's conclusion that 'while there is no question that variability will degrade performance, we have a choice of how it will do so. Different strategies for coping with variability make sense in different business environments.'[29,30]

Just as the concepts underpinning the choice of delivery system respond to different market characteristics and mix of qualifiers and order-winners (see Chapters 4 and 5), then the underlying characteristics of supply chains will need to exhibit similar characteristics and appropriate outputs.

While markets are inherently unstable, an operations delivery system needs to be stable (the level of which will vary depending on the characteristics of the market it is designed to support). Consequently, a company must decide how best to cushion its delivery system from the instability inherent in its markets. As shown in Figure 8.21, there are three categories of mechanisms (and choices within each category) by which to cushion the operations delivery system and these are now outlined.

Basic category

One fundamental decision that companies make concerns whether to make-to-order (resulting in a backlog of orders waiting to be processed) or make-to-stock (making all or part of a service/product ahead of demand with customer orders met from inventory). Some companies use a mix of these by initially building up a backlog of orders and then make sufficient products to meet all outstanding orders plus a quantity that go into inventory. Future orders are then met from this inventory holding and when it is used up, further orders go into order backlog and the cycle repeats.

Alternatively, companies that experience seasonal demand may decide to make inventory in low-demand periods, thereby absorbing capacity in one time period and transferring it forward to be sold in a future time period. Where this occurs, companies may choose to make work-in-progress or finished goods inventory, taking into account future demand forecasts and the labour-hour-to-value-of-inventory ratio.

Strategically, these alternatives embody trade-offs concerning operations lead time and delivery speed requirements versus issues of cost and cash flow.

Secondary category

Companies can also choose from a range of secondary mechanisms to help provide the cushioning role. As illustrated in Figure 8.21 these include demand management, forecasting, scheduling and process improvement. You will see from these that while the first two help make demand more stable, the latter two help the operations delivery system to better meet demand with the actual capacity on hand.

Within this basic category there is also the mechanism of 'planned capacity'. This provision can take several forms including planned overtime or additional shifts in peak demand periods, employing temporary versus permanent staff, annualized hours and including an element of non-direct activity in the work mix of direct employees which can be switched into direct activity should the need arise.

Such decisions as these need to be assessed and made well ahead of time and will form a more permanent element in the capacity provision within operations.

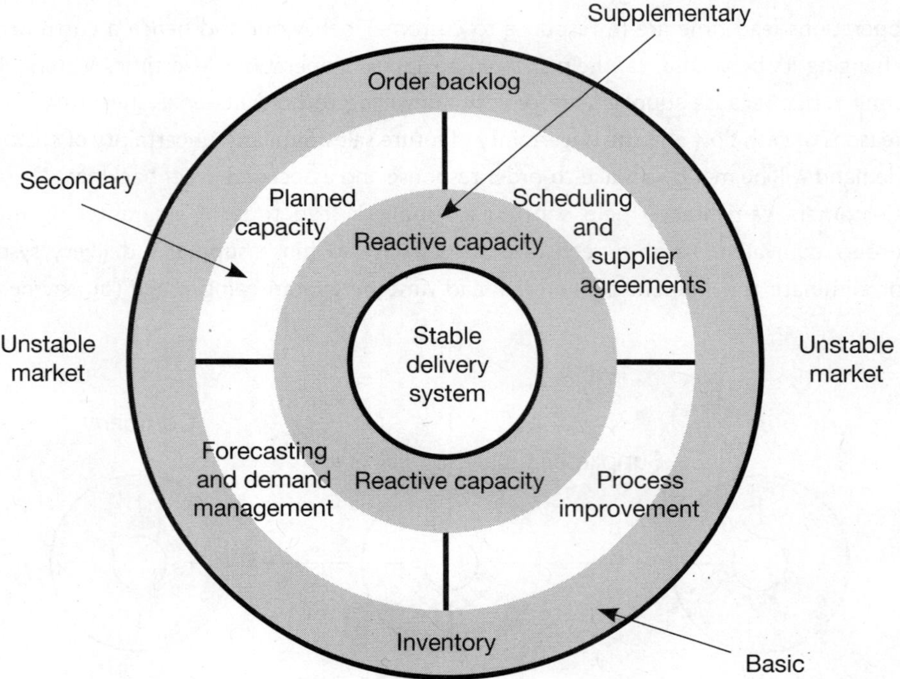

Figure 8.21 Cushioning the delivery system – categories and options

Supplementary category

The final category of cushioning mechanisms is the option of providing additional capacity through overtime working. It is intended to be used as a short-term temporary measure, arranged on an as-needed basis. Referred to as 'reactive capacity' (to distinguish it from planned capacity), it is an option used somewhat as a last resort.

MANAGING STABILITY IN THE EXTERNAL PHASE OF THE SUPPLY CHAIN

A key aspect of managing a supply chain is to recognize that a company's suppliers also wish to cushion their own delivery systems and do so by choosing from the same options within the basic, secondary and supplementary categories described above and overviewed in Figure 8.22. Helping suppliers to handle this requirement becomes an integral part of a company's approach to managing its supply chain. Key to a company understanding the task and helping suppliers are the following factors:

1 The instability of a company's suppliers' markets is generated by the company itself.
2 A supplier's choice of basic mechanisms is in response to the company's own behaviours. Uncertainty of demand will be met by make-to-order responses, associated order backlogs and a corresponding increase in a supplier's operations lead times.
3 As a supplier's operations lead time comprises the same elements as its customers (see Figure 8.23), the way for a customer to help shorten a supplier's lead time response is to remove or reduce the cushioning mechanisms a supplier has chosen to use that have a lead-time element. A look at Figure 8.23 shows that two of the elements making up a supplier's operations lead time are in response to customer behaviour and hence a customer, by changing its behaviour, can help shorten a supplier's operations lead time. Material lead time exists because suppliers are typically unwilling to hold materials inventory due to reasons of cash flow and the uncertainty of future sales. Similarly, uncertainty of customer demand will be met by a make-to-order response and associated order backlogs.
4 Customers can directly help shorten a supplier's lead time by guaranteeing future orders equivalent to an agreed level of capacity within a supplier's delivery system, or eliminate the element of material lead time by guaranteeing usage (or payment if

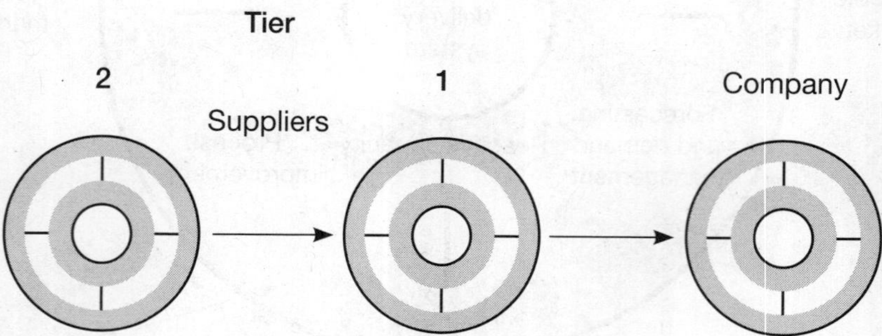

Note: In this example the 'Company' is the customer of the 'Tier 1 Supplier'.

Figure 8.22 The cushioning requirements at each step in the supply chain

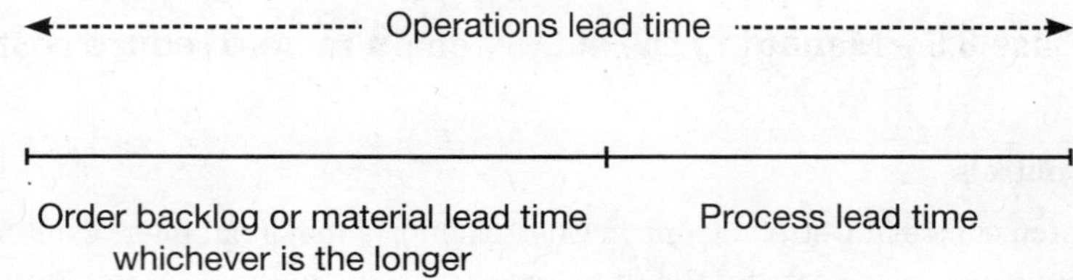

Figure 8.23 Components of operations lead time

material inventory is unused) of an agreed amount of material, or both. In this way, a supplier's operations lead time could be so reduced as to comprise only the process lead time element – see Figure 8.24. Shorter material lead times from suppliers will, in turn, reduce this element in a customer's own operations lead time – see Figure 8.24. In this way, companies can begin to better manage their supply chains to create a more responsive operations system of their own, while helping suppliers to better manage their own delivery systems.

BENEFITS OF SUPPLY CHAINS

While some supply chain developments attract specific sets of gains, there are several benefit clusters that are invariably present, in full or in part, in all such developments. This section summarizes these sets of general gains as a way of reflecting on the issues discussed in the previous sections, while highlighting the potential benefits involved.

REDUCING COSTS

Companies are becoming increasingly aware of an obvious truth, at least in hindsight – the maker of a part should be more able to design and make it at a lower cost than its customer. The expertise base, the experience curve benefits associated with cumulative volume (Chapter 4) and continuing transfer of ideas from one solution to another should always lead to lower cost applications.

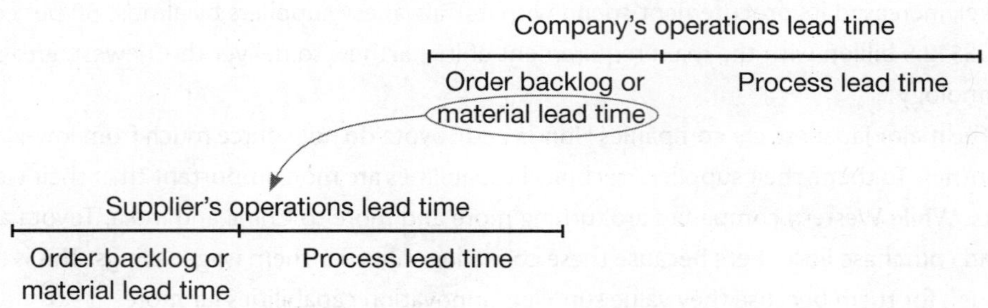

Figure 8.24 A company's material lead time equates to a supplier's operations lead time

Case 8.5 – Managing the supply chain to help reduce costs

Johnson Controls

In its research centre in Detroit, Johnson Controls Inc. (a major supplier of automotive seats) designs and tests seats for the principal car makers in the USA and Europe. Different teams are allocated to meet the seating needs of a range of competing companies. As a supplier that sells parts to an entire industry, the system is a way of transferring new techniques from one manufacturer to another, with the result that, as a maker of a part, Johnson Controls is able to conceive a new seating requirement more cheaply than a final assembler responsible for the whole product.

Airbus

In 2007, Airbus, the European aircraft maker, began the task of shedding more than four-fifths of its suppliers as part of a cost-cutting programme. At the time, Airbus had been badly hit by costly delays to its A380 superjumbo and announced its decision to reduce the number of suppliers from 3,000 to 500 as part of its drive to cut €350 million from its annual costs. By whittling down its supplier base it could then force down the price by buying in greater bulk.

A.T. Kearney Inc., a Chicago consulting firm, estimates that, where manufacturers properly incorporate suppliers into their product development process, they can cut their purchased parts and services costs by as much as 30 per cent. Working with suppliers can lead to cost reductions other than from the more traditional sources. Encouraging suppliers to come up with cost-cutting ideas and design innovations can lead to potentially large savings.

ACCESSING TECHNICAL EXPERTISE

The cost gains associated with cumulative volume can be similarly secured on the dimension of expertise. The application of a supplier's technical capabilities to similar design requirements, together with the transfer of solutions to and from other applications, enhances technical insights and accelerates design improvements. Many companies recognize these benefits and such gains can drive supplier choice. For example, Dell, the world's largest PC maker, increased its procurement spend with its Taiwanese suppliers by almost 50 per cent to US$12.5 billion with the main requirement of its partners to deliver the 'newest, greatest technology'.

The major Japanese car companies Honda and Toyota do not source much from low-wage countries. To them, their suppliers' technical capabilities are more important than their wage costs. While Western companies are turning more and more to China and India, Toyota and Honda purchase little there because these countries only offer them wage savings. This is not enough for them because they value suppliers' innovation capabilities far more.

SHORTENING LEAD TIMES

The importance of recognizing the value-creating potential of the supply chain is central to successful strategies in today's competitive environment. For many companies, this translates into the opportunities available in each phase – suppliers, internal supply chain, logistics and customers – and their roles in bringing about these gains. One key competitive dimension is lead-time reduction.

In 2016, IKEA, the Swedish home furnishings retailer, had more than 390 stores in 48 countries, 1,200 suppliers in over 55 countries and its website contained over 12,000 products. The company's insistence on low cost from its suppliers has two key implications. First, sourcing is widely dispersed and parts of finished items may be purchased from different locations. Second, items must be bought in large volumes. Both factors require an efficient system for ordering parts, integrating them into products and delivering them to stores, while keeping inventory levels low and meeting demand quickly. This is achieved by building on long-term supplier relations and a sophisticated logistics system, the centrepiece of which is IKEA's network of warehouses. Point-of-sale information at each retail outlet provides online sales data to the nearest warehouse and the operational head office in Almhult where information systems analyse sales patterns worldwide. In turn, the warehouses act as logistics control points and consolidate requirements. As transit hubs, they work with retail stores to anticipate demand and eliminate shortages while keeping inventory (and corresponding floor space) low. Underpinning all this is the need for short lead-time provision. Working with suppliers as well as in-house supply chain developments has enabled IKEA to meet the delivery-speed needs of the fashion market it serves.

Reducing lead times is also at the centre of the supply strategy of A.W. Chesterton Co. (a family-owned seal, pump and packing manufacturer in Massachusetts). Key to the substantial but essential improvements that were required is the company's management of its supply chain. This is well illustrated by the reduction of its suppliers from 1,300 to 125 and its approach to evaluating which supplier to partner, allocating delivery reliability, short lead times and quality conformance twice as much importance as price. For Chesterton, the demands of its own markets require putting pressure on its own suppliers. A decade ago, delivery time for mechanical seal parts was 12–16 weeks. Today, it is down to days or even hours. To facilitate this, the company installed computer systems that allow customers to transmit drawings and engineering specifications directly to the plant floor where new process investments help reduce process lead times.

However, the lead times of other aspects of a business are equally critical to overall success. The emphasis is on getting suppliers to become more than just parts providers. One key area is to participate in and contribute to new designs, particularly with regard to cutting costs and reducing development lead time. Dana Corporation, a major supplier of truck axles, has an entire 60-engineer laboratory near Toledo dedicated to U-joints. Using a computer-aided design (CAD) system, Dana can design new products cheaply and quickly – in fact, prototypes for customers can be built in a few hours.

The Taiwanese Acer Corporation, with other PC makers, has had to reduce lead times in line with the short product life cycles of its market. The company works on a ten-month product life cycle, with three months allowed for product development and modifications, six months for sales of the product and one month to sell old inventory before the next cycle begins.

LOWER INVENTORIES

The classic, uncoordinated approach to managing a supply chain typically results in each stage having enough material (or its equivalent) inventory not to run out and sufficient finished goods (or its equivalent) to ensure that customers' requirements could be met. One result of each stage adopting these positions is excess inventory; and the longer the lead time, the greater the likelihood of these inefficiencies occurring in the process. Managing the supply chain as a whole means stitching together an entire business, with external providers being treated as partners as if they were inside the company. Figure 8.25 provides a simple illustration of the 'one-firm concept' designed to eliminate the interfaces between the external and internal phases of the supply chain that results in an integrated system. Some examples of how lower inventories result now follow.

Eastman Chemical's processes call for 1,500 different raw materials provided by 850 suppliers. To make sure that as little inventory as possible sits idle, Eastman devised what

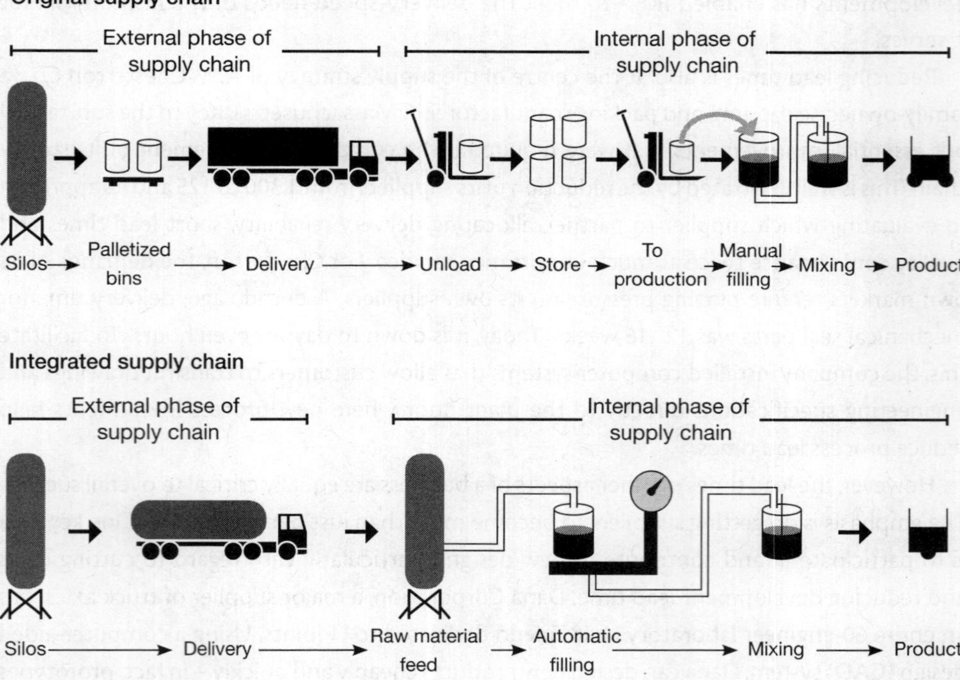

Figure 8.25 Integrated supply chain: the one-firm concept

it calls 'stream inventory management'. This requires treating the whole supply chain as a pipeline. When a customer order is received, Eastman uses one pound of product, with the raw material function working with the supplier to put another pound in at the other end of the pipeline in order to achieve continuous flow. And stream inventory management has paid off. Eastman can now monitor inventory while at its suppliers which, combined with more accurate operations forecasts, means that there is no longer the need to hold excess inventory that sits idle, just in case it is needed. Examples of its dramatic inventory reductions include:

- Wood pulp stock down from three months' supply to nine days with the next target set at four days.
- Twenty-five years ago the company kept 18 million pounds of paraxylene, a material for polyethylene terephthalate (PET) plastic soda bottles, to support 520 million pounds a year of PET production in the USA. Today, Eastman holds only 14 million pounds of paraxylene to support three times the volume of PET production.
- In 2006, total inventory had fallen to 9 per cent of sales revenue and by 2013 to less than 5 per cent.

Michael Dell began his business in 1984 with a simple insight: to sell direct to customers on a make-to-order basis. Thus, in one swoop, he eliminated the reseller's mark-up and the costs and risks associated with finished goods inventory. The 'direct business model', as it is known, gave Dell Computer Corporation a substantial cost advantage and directly contributed to growing a $55 billion company by 2016.

To achieve this, Dell uses technologies and information to blur the traditional boundaries in the supply chain from suppliers through to customers. In so doing, Dell is moving towards 'virtual integration' (as Michael Dell describes it) that combines individual strategies such as customer focus, supplier partnerships and just-in-time operations into a coordinated whole. Virtual integration harnesses the economies-of-scale benefits of two traditional business models. On the one hand, it taps into the benefits of a coordinated supply chain that are traditionally only available through vertical integration while, on the other hand, it taps into the benefits of specialization where companies (in Dell's case, its suppliers) focus on what they are good at with the associated gains from volumes and technology investment.

There are many challenges facing Dell Inc. to realize this potential and establish these collaborations. One key driver is monitoring low inventories. In the fast-changing technology business, inventory carries more risk than in many other sectors. The dimensions of risk in computing concern the response time to launching product developments and protection from falling material prices. As Michael Dell explains:

- If I've got 11 days of inventory and my competitor has 80, and Intel comes out with a new chip, that means I'm going to get to market 69 days sooner.
- If the cost of materials goes down 50 per cent a year and you have two or three months of inventory versus 11 days, you've got a big cost disadvantage. And you're vulnerable to product transitions, when you can get stuck with obsolete inventory.

For these reasons, Dell works closely with its suppliers to keep reducing inventory and increasing speed, as its arrangements with Sony exemplify. With Sony (considered a reliable supplier with defect rates on monitors of less than two per million), Dell collects monitors daily in the quantities needed to meet its own customer orders and then ships direct. The result is reduced lead times and no finished monitor inventory. Similarly, Dell has agreed with Airborne Express and United Parcel Services (UPS) to collect a fixed number of computers a day and the same quantity of monitors from Sony's plant in Mexico. Then they match the one with the other and deliver them directly to Dell's customers. To do this, Dell has developed real-time information on its own demand profile and links this into its suppliers, sometimes every few hours. With this insight and certainty, suppliers can meet Dell's five or six days of lead time. 'The greatest challenge in working with suppliers is getting them in sync with the fast pace we have to maintain. The key to making it work is information', explained Kevin Rollins, vice-chairman of Dell Computer Corporation.

Efficient customer response (ECR) combines the concepts of just-in-time and partnership sourcing. Its central doctrine is that many practices that make good business sense to individual parts of the supply chain may add cost and complexity from the perspective of the chain as a whole. One central theme of ECR is co-managed inventory. Instead of sending out orders to suppliers as stock gets low, customers hand over to suppliers the task of generating orders. Both parties agree forecasts and suppliers take over the responsibility for replenishment using up-to-date sales information from the customer.

VOAC, the Swedish-based division of the US manufacturer Parker Hannifin, makes mobile hydraulic equipment. Originally the company had its head office and factories in Sweden and eight sales offices across Europe. All had their own warehouses and distribution set-ups. Inventories were high, the level of customer delivery performance was variable, lead times were long and logistics costs were substantial. Its partner in changing the logistics organization was UPS Worldwide Logistics. VOAC now has one European distribution centre in the Netherlands, online connections for all offices and direct order input. Electronically processed orders are then tracked from beginning to end, with UPS providing vendor-managed inventory facilities that take into account future demand forecasts, operations lead times and existing inventory levels. Improved supply-chain management has extended the customer order cut-off point during a working day from 3 pm to 6 pm and resulted in shorter delivery lead times and inventory reductions of 60 per cent.

Whether to make or buy needs careful assessment and the factors that substantiate these decisions need to be clearly understood. In the past, carried on the winds of growth and believing that they could provide anything, as a matter of course, many companies decided to make rather than to buy without an adequate understanding of strategic fit and the tactical consequences involved. Also, early entrants into new technology markets such as IT had little option at the time but to make the components involved. In recent times, subcontracting has been in vogue. What often characterizes these trends is the flavour-of-the-month approach rather than issues of strategic fit. It is essential when deciding whether to make or buy that companies undertake strategic and tactical analyses while being careful to avoid the lure of short-term gains without considering long-term, strategic outcomes.

When changing make-or-buy decisions, companies need to establish the true extent of the costs and benefits involved. Understatement of costs and overstatement of benefits are all too often the basis on which companies make decisions and evaluate outcomes. However, such make-or-buy decisions are not only substantial but often final, at least within commercial timescales – when a company closes an outlet or plant, it will never reopen it. The make-or-buy decision invariably commits a company for years ahead and consequentially is critical to the strategic positioning of a company.

The make-or-buy decision is the first part of a two-phased task. The second is that companies have to recognize the need to manage both the internal and external phases of the supply chain. And this typically requires a company to make a fundamental shift in approach and thinking, as summarized in Figure 8.26.

The format of the joint cooperation that is a core feature of strategic alliance developments is moving at a pace, as the following illustrations highlight.

Other examples serve to illustrate the developments in supplier/customer relations that are changing the mindsets of those involved. TNT (Europe's biggest freight and logistics company) launched its internet service, known as Quickshipper, to enable its customers to track orders from beginning to end directly through the TNT website. After planning their order, customers can then use the site to follow its progress to the point of delivery. Quicker order processing also means faster deliveries.

As response time becomes a more important factor than low labour costs in keeping major customers, offshore manufacturers of everything from PCs to garments need to

<table>
<tr><th colspan="2" rowspan="2">Dimensions</th><th colspan="2">Approach</th></tr>
<tr><th>From</th><th>To</th></tr>
<tr><td colspan="2">Customers and suppliers</td><td>Contractual relationships</td><td>Harness the power of partnerships</td></tr>
<tr><td colspan="2">Basis for competition</td><td>A company</td><td>A company and its supply chain</td></tr>
<tr><td colspan="2">Organization relationships</td><td>Functional/corporate orientation</td><td>Cooperation</td></tr>
<tr><td colspan="2">Focus</td><td>Individual contract</td><td>Relationship</td></tr>
<tr><td colspan="2">Communication</td><td>Primarily one way</td><td>Two way and balanced</td></tr>
<tr><td rowspan="3">Performance measures</td><td>Focus</td><td>Individual parties</td><td>Partnership</td></tr>
<tr><td>Development</td><td>Independently</td><td>Jointly</td></tr>
<tr><td>Results</td><td>Might be shared</td><td>Joint performance</td></tr>
<tr><td colspan="2">Risk/reward evaluation</td><td>By transaction</td><td>Over the life of the relationship</td></tr>
</table>

Figure 8.26 Changing approach to managing supply chains

Case 8.6 – Evolving roles and relationships between companies and their suppliers

Volkswagen

Components account for some 60 per cent of the cost of a new car, yet the component makers have traditionally shared relatively few of the risks of a new launch. The car makers, on the other hand, have to meet large fixed investments, such as factories and capital equipment, in what are increasingly uncertain markets. Part of the move to strategic alliances is now based on shared costs, shared uncertainty and shared benefits. When Volkswagen (VW) built its bus and truck plant in Resende (some 150 km from Rio de Janeiro, Brazil), about 35 per cent of the fixed costs were met by component suppliers. Resende was then also co-managed by VW and its suppliers under a profit-sharing consortium. As of 2009, the plant has been under the ownership of MAN Latin America.

Mercedes-Benz

The Hambach plant in eastern France, which builds the two-seater Mercedes-Benz sports car, provides another example of the changing relationships within strategic alliance developments. Ten suppliers preassemble important sections. For example, steel bodies come from Magna International, the Canadian group; VDO, a German automotive electronics maker, builds fully assembled cockpits, including the instruments; while Ymos (a German component specialist) makes complete door assemblies, including trim, window winders and glass. But that is not all. The ten suppliers invested almost $300 million in the project.

Skoda

The assembly plant for Skoda's Octavia saloon is designed with six zones adjacent to the production line. The zones are also positioned on an outside wall so that the suppliers involved have direct truck access. The component suppliers are responsible for supporting the production schedule that includes the preassembly of parts just before they are required to go onto the car.

embrace e-commerce developments. Take as an example Lite-on Technology Corporation, the Taiwanese manufacturer of computer hardware. In the late 1990s, it typically had one month to execute orders from IBM, Compaq Computers and other overseas customers. Since then the required lead times have shrunk dramatically (see Figure 8.27). Lite-on achieves this

Item	Lead time to fill a US order
Colour monitors	2 days
Notebook computers	1 day
CD-ROM drives	4 hours

Figure 8.27 The short lead-time requirements of customers

by integrating its customers, factories, warehouses, accounting functions and parts suppliers into a single digital supply chain. This cuts lead times in all phases of the procedure from order taking, operations scheduling, suppliers' deliveries and shipping.

With today's markets becoming more global and competitive in nature, companies need to rethink their responses. Because support for many order-winners and qualifiers is the responsibility of the operations function, how it manages these responses is a key strategic task. But to do this effectively, it needs to manage the internal phase of the supply chain as well as the external elements, including a proactive relationship with customers. In this way, a coordinated response that harnesses the potential of the whole supply chain will be looked for, identified and delivered. Without it, strategic advantage will be surrendered and the growth and prosperity of a company will be undermined.

CASE STUDY

Lego

Founded by Ole Kirk Christiansen (a Danish carpenter) in 1932, the Lego Group is still privately owned. It focuses on developing children's imagination and creativity through fun products and experiences that teach them how to care for the world around them (see Case Figure 8.1) and has developed a loyal community of customers who also believe that 'good play enriches a child's life and its subsequent adulthood'. But over diversification and a loss of focus on its core markets meant that it made a loss for the first time in 1998 and then almost went bankrupt in 2004 (see Case Figure 8.2).

As Douglas Skinner, Financial Analyst, commented, 'Lego lost its way for a while and forgot who it was and why people love it. The 2004 crisis forced it to go back to basics and re-establish the values and principles that had made it successful in the past.' This helped turn the business around and it is

Value	Description
Imagination	Curiosity asks 'why?' and imagines explanations or possibilities. Playfulness asks 'what if?' and imagines how the ordinary can be extraordinary. Children develop their imagination through 'free play' – the foundation for creativity
Creativity	Creativity is the ability to come up with ideas and things that are new, surprising and valuable. Systematic creativity combines logic and reasoning with playfulness and imagination
Fun	Fun is the happiness experienced when fully engaged in something that requires mastery (hard fun), when challenge and ability are in balance and progress is being made. Fun is in the doing and the completing of a task. Fun is the thrill of adventure, the joy of enthusiasm and the delight of what you can create
Learning	Learning is about experimenting, improvising and discovering. It expands our thinking and doing (hands-on, minds-on) and helps us to see and appreciate multiple perspectives
Caring	Caring is wanting to make a positive difference to the world around us, going the extra mile for others not because we have to, but because it feels right and we want to. Caring is about humility, thinking of ourselves less, but not less of ourselves
Quality	Quality means continuously improving what you do to create the best toys for children and their development, and being the best for your partners and the community around you

Case Figure 8.1 Lego's core values.

Source: Based on www.lego.com.

Billion DKK	1998	2000	2002	2004	2006	2008	2010	2012	2014	2016
Sales revenue	7.7	9.5	11.4	6.3	7.8	9.5	16.0	23.1	28.6	37.9
Operating profit	(0.2)	(1.0)	0.8	(1.2)	1.4	2.1	5.0	7.6	9.7	12.4
R&D	N/A	N/A	N/A	N/A	0.2	0.2	0.3	0.4	0.4	0.6
Cash	(0.7)	(0.8)	(0.2)	0.1	0.3	2.0	1.1	0.5	0.5	0.9
Inventory	N/A	N/A	1.5	0.7	0.9	0.9	1.3	1.7	2.2	3.0
Equity	5.8	5.7	6.5	0.4	1.2	2.1	5.5	9.9	12.8	20.0
Employees (000s)	9.1	7.9	8.3	6.6	4.9	5.4	8.4	10.4	12.6	17.8

Notes
1 Research and development (R&D) figures not available before 2006.
2 Inventory figures not available before 2002.
3 Employees are full-time equivalents.

Case Figure 8.2 Lego's performance (1998–2016)

now the second largest toy manufacturer in the world. Mattel is currently the largest with 2016 sales of $5.5 billion and operating profits of $0.5 billion compared with Lego's 2016 sales of $5.2 billion and operating profits of $1.9 billion. In 1998 Mattel had sales of $ 4.8 billion compared to Lego's 1998 sales of $1.5 billion.

STARTING THE BUSINESS

In 1916, Ole Kirk Kristiansen bought a workshop in Billund (Denmark), wrote 'Only the best is good enough' on the wall and started making furniture and houses for local farmers. Sixteen years later, he made his first wooden toy and called it Lego after the Danish words 'leg godt' meaning 'play well'. Some of the key events in Lego's history are shown in Case Figure 8.3.

In 1947, Ole Kristiansen bought the first plastic injection-moulding machine in Denmark and two years later made his first plastic brick. Eight years later, Godtfred (Ole's son) developed the Lego 'system of play' with 28 sets and 8 vehicles after a retailer complained that his toy department was a mess and lacked organization. Then, in 1960 after a fire destroyed their factory, Ole and Godtfred decided to stop making wooden toys and focus solely on plastic bricks. They were convinced that they were onto something because you could build anything out of them, keep adding to what you already have and make a new toy every day that doesn't fall apart when it's thrown around.

In 1963, Godtfred developed Lego's 'principles of play' to guide future product development (see Case Figure 8.4). This sparked a period of rapid innovation and by 1969 Lego produced 218 bricks with different colours and shapes, which were all compatible with each other.

It then looked for ways to enhance the overall customer experience and opened its first Legoland in Billund (Denmark) in 1968, introduced larger Duplo bricks for children under five in 1969 and Lego Technic for teenagers in 1977. By 1980, it was estimated that over 70 per cent of families in Western

Date	Event
1932	Ole Kirk Christiansen founded a toy factory with the motto 'Only the best is good enough'
1934	Introduced Lego name from Danish for 'play well'
1947	Purchased first plastic injection-moulding machine
1955	Launched Lego System of play (28 bricks and 8 vehicles)
1958	Launched Lego Brick that is still used today Godfrey Kirk Christiansen appointed CEO
1960	Concentrated on the Lego System after fire in the factory
1963	Introduced 'good play' principles for product development
1968	Opened Legoland in Billund (Denmark)
1969	Launched Lego Duplo (big bricks for small hands) for children under five
1973	Kjeld Kirk Kristiansen (Godfrey's son) appointed MD of Swiss production companies
1978	Split production into product ranges and lines Launched Lego Minifigure, Lego City and Lego Technic Kjeld Kirk Christiansen appointed CEO
1986	Developed Lego Technic Computer Control in partnership with MIT, Boston (US)
1996	Launched www.lego.com Opened Legoland in Windsor (UK) Set up Lego Media in London (UK) to develop movies, video games, TV shows and books
1998	Launched Lego Mindstorms programmable bricks Lost money for the first time in its history
1999	Announced restructuring programme Moved design responsibilities from Billund (Denmark) to Global Centres in London, Milan and San Francisco Launched online shop and opened Retail Stores in Europe and the US Launched Lego Star Wars (licensed from Lucas Films) and Lego Winnie the Pooh (licensed from Disney) Opened Legoland in California (US)
2001	Launched Lego Bionicle with toys and action themes Launched Lego Harry Potter (licensed from Warner Bros)
2002	Repositioned Lego Duplo on learning and development Opened Legoland in Gunzberg (Germany)
2003	Launched Lego Clikits for girls
2004	Suffered its worst financial loss in history Jorgen Vig Knudstorp appointed CEO Published new 'shared vision' and recovery plan
2005	Sold Legoland, but kept 22% equity in the new operator Relaunched Lego City, Duplo and Mindstorms Shut down Lego Video Games and Clikits

2006	Outsourced production of Lego Duplo and System to Flextronics (Hungary) Relocated production of Lego Technic and Lego Bionicle to factory in Czech Republic (for European market) Relocated US factory to Mexico (for US market) Closed factories in Korea, Switzerland and the US Outsourced control of factories in Czech Republic and Mexico to Flextronics
2007	Outsourced distribution to Exel (Texas) for North American market and to DHL (Czech Republic) for the rest of the world Opened first Legoland Discovery Centre in Berlin (Germany)
2008	Stopped partnership with Flextronics and brought production back in house
2010	Opened Legoland Discovery Centres in Manchester (UK) and Chicago (US)
2011	Opened Legoland in Florida (US) Opened Legoland Discovery Centre in Atlanta (US)
2012	Opened Legoland in Malaysia Opened Legoland Discovery Centres in Tokyo (Japan) and Kansas City (US)
2013	Opened Legoland Discovery Centres in Toronto (Canada), Oberhausen (Germany), New York (USA) and Dallas (US)

Case Figure 8.3 Key events in Lego's history (1932–2014)

1.	Unlimited play potential
2.	For girls and for boys
3.	Fun for every age
4.	Year-round play
5.	Healthy, quiet play
6.	Long hours of play
7.	Development, imagination, creativity
8.	The more Lego, the greater the value
9.	Extra sets available
10.	Quality in every detail

Case Figure 8.4 Lego's 'principles of play'

Europe with children under five years owned a Lego product.

In 1973, Godtfred appointed his son, Kjeld, as Managing Director of Lego's Swiss manufacturing facilities and five years later he focused Lego's production units around different product groups (called 'factories within a factory'). This triggered another intensive period of product development, although the overall product range was still tightly controlled by Godtfred, with no new brick or colour introduced without his approval. For example, it took ten years to convince him to make a green brick!

In 1986, Lego launched their first programmable brick, Lego Technic Computer Control, in collaboration with the Massachusetts Institute of Technology (MIT) in Boston (USA). Sales continued to grow and by 1992 Lego was one of the largest toy manufacturers in the world. However, the market suddenly changed as birth rates in North America and Western Europe declined, electronic toys emerged, retail channels consolidated and its main competitors (Mattel and Hasbro) dropped their prices after setting up low-cost manufacturing facilities in Asia.

DIVERSIFYING THE BUSINESS

As demand for Lego's traditional products started to decline, Kjeld looked for ways to grow sales by tailoring products to different retailer and customer needs. For example, he introduced chunkier and more complex Lego bricks (such as the lower and upper side of a car), launched a range of children's wear made under licence by Kabooki, set up Lego Media in London (UK) to develop movies, video games, TV shows and books and launched the Lego Mindstorms range of programmable bricks and robots. But sales didn't grow overall and in 1998 the company made a loss for the first time.

To help turn the business around Kjeld brought in Poul Plougmann as Chief Financial Officer. He soon became Chief Operations Officer and took over the day-to-day management of the business. In an attempt to reduce costs by DDK 1 billion (US$140 million) Plougmann cut the workforce by 1,000, reduced the number of layers in the organization, restructured the business around its key customers and markets and looked for ways to streamline operations. When he announced these drastic measures, employees stood up and applauded!

Design responsibilities were moved from the rural village of Billund (Denmark) to Global Product Development centres in London, Milan and San Francisco. Several tool-making factories were sold, where possible production processes were automated and all manual processes were moved to Lego's new factory in the Czech Republic. Sales were consolidated from 25 countries to 5 regions, incentives were linked to the accuracy of sales forecasts and global back-office functions were created to serve all parts of the business. To develop the capability to lead this new organization they recruited externally, moved managers every 6 to 12 months and promoted people based on their leadership abilities rather than how long they had worked at Lego.

In 1999, the company started selling products directly to customers through its website, www.lego.com, and opened its own retail stores in Europe and the US to showcase the entire Lego product range, help to build the brand and avoid the large discounts demanded by its increasingly powerful third-party retailers. It also launched Lego Star Wars (licensed from Lucas Films) to help children tell stories using Lego products. This proved a huge success and soon accounted for 35 per cent of all Lego's sales. Off the back of this, it launched Lego Winnie the Pooh (licensed from Disney) and Lego Harry Potter (licensed from Warner Bros).

Douglas Skinner, financial analyst, commented that:

> All seemed to be going well as between 1998 and 2002 sales increased by almost 50 per cent ... However, its cost base was spiralling out of control! The decision to launch a new product was based on the cost of the extra tooling rather than the total impact across the supply chain and, as a result, the actual production costs for different products were not known. Furthermore, it had over 11,000 suppliers at this time, on-time delivery was between 5 and 70 per cent and inventory obsolescence

was increasing. To get the support they needed, retailers increasingly had to 'buck the system' and call friends working in production to order more products or allocate products to their existing orders.

It was only later in 2004 when the company stopped and analysed why it had all gone wrong did it realize that since 1993 its product range had doubled to a point that there were 10,900 different products (157 colours and 3,560 shapes) and up to 675 different products in a set [see Case Figure 8.5].

Although customers liked the Lego retail stores, the company struggled to run them efficiently and managers started blaming poor sales on factors outside their control. For example, one manager claimed that sales had declined because of a recent spell of good weather! The company was also increasingly dependent on its licensed Star Wars and Harry Potter products, which now accounted for over half its sales. On the other hand, it had dramatically increased product variety and demand variability while cannibalizing its more profitable core brick products.

CUTTING PRODUCTS

It was clear that the changes were not working and in 2003 the business was almost bankrupt. Kjeld fired Plougmann and four of his 14-person management team, invested in the company himself to keep it afloat and promoted Jorgen Vig Knudstorp (a former McKinsey consultant who joined Lego in 2001) from Director of Strategic Development to CEO. Soon after his appointment, Jorgen published a seven-year plan to restructure the business around three core principles:

- Create value for customers and sales channels;
- Refocus on the value we offer customers; and
- Increase operational excellence.

The plan had three stages:

1 Manage for cash (2004–2005)
2 Manage for value (2006–2008)
3 Manage for growth (2009 onwards)

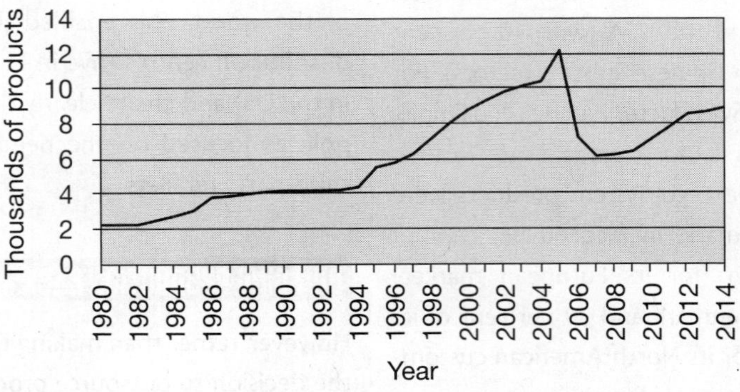

Note: Each product has a unique colour and shape combination.

Case Figure 8.5 Number of Lego products (1980–2014)

The first step was to refocus Lego back on its brick products, the unique 'system of play' and their loyal customer community. It shut down Lego Video Games, discontinued Lego Clikits, returned Lego Duplo to its original market position and relaunched new and improved versions of Lego City and Lego Mindstorms. To pay off some of their outstanding debt, the Legoland theme parks were sold to Blackstone for €375 million, but 22 per cent equity was retained in the new operator (Merlin Entertainment) to provide some control over the brand. These changes helped the company back into profit in 2005, although 50 per cent of this pretax profit came from the sale of its assets. To help recreate the original family-like culture of the business, Knudstorp made sure he constantly talked to everyone to help them understand why the changes were taking place and where he saw the business going in the future.

OUTSOURCING PRODUCTION

The next step was to fix Lego's supply chain. At the time, 90 per cent of its products were made in-house at its product-based factories in the Czech Republic, Denmark, South Korea, Switzerland and the USA (with 10 per cent outsourced to Chinese subcontractors). For example, one Swiss factory made Lego Duplo, another Swiss factory made Lego Technic products while Lego System products were made in Denmark. In fact, 60 per cent of its production (for its European market) occurred in Denmark and 30 per cent of its production (for its North American customers) occurred in its US factory.

To reduce costs and fixed assets, it aimed to outsource 80 per cent of its production by 2006. First it outsourced the high volume Lego Duplo and Lego System production for its European customers to Flextronics who were keen to grow their plastics manufacturing capability and had set up a factory in Hungary specifically to produce Lego components. At the time, Flextronics had $30 billion annual sales and facilities in 30 countries on four different continents with 27 million ft^2 capacity and 160,000 employees (120,000 in Asia of which 90,000 were in China).

It then downsized production in Denmark to focus just on Lego Technic and Lego Bionicle products, transferred the remaining production for its European market to its factory in the Czech Republic and closed its factories in Switzerland and South Korea. It also closed its US factory and moved production for its North American market to Mexico. Then, at the end of 2006, it outsourced control of its factories in the Czech Republic and Mexico to Flextronics and signed a five-year fixed price contract with them.

To further reduce costs, in 2007 it outsourced distribution for its North American customers to Exel in Texas (US) and to DHL in Prague (Czech Republic) to supply the rest of the world. This enabled it to close its distribution centres (five in Europe and one in the US) and create clearly defined service policies focused on the needs of its large third-party retailers.

BRINGING PRODUCTION BACK IN HOUSE

However, rather than making things simpler, the decision to outsource production made things worse. Although its overall operating costs reduced, production costs actually increased (see Case Figure 8.6). Lego's seasonal demand (60 per cent in the last

Operating costs (billion DKK)	2004	2006	2008	2010	2012	2014	2016
Production	2.7	2.8	3.2	4.4	6.8	8.1	10.7
Sales & distribution	2.9	2.6	3.0	4.6	6.2	7.8	10.6
Administrative	0.6	0.6	0.6	0.9	1.3	1.4	2.3
Restructuring	0.7	0.3	(0.1)	0.1	–	–	–
Other	0.6	0.1	0.7	0.9	1.2	1.6	1.9
Total	7.5	6.4	7.4	11.0	15.5	18.9	25.5

Case Figure 8.6 Lego's operating costs

four months of the year), short product life cycle (16 to 18 months) and unpredictable demand (fluctuations of plus or minus 30 per cent within a month) did not fit with Flextronics' low-cost, high-volume and stable production capability.

It was difficult to get Flextronics to understand Lego's needs, its 12-week production lead times made it impossible to respond to changing customer demands and the Lego factory in Billund (Denmark) facility was still more efficient than the Flextronics facilities, even three years into production. For example, in Billund, two or three people could run 64 moulding machines at the same time whereas Flextronics often had one person for three or four machines. Also, Flextronics would purchase individual boxes for each product whereas Lego would order large volumes of boxes and then customize them for different products or customers.

In 2008, Lego announced it would bring production back in house and cancelled the outsourcing arrangement with Flextronics. First, it took back control of the factory in the Czech Republic, then it took over the facility in Hungary and the following year it closed the factory in Juárez (Mexico) and moved it to Monterrey (also in Mexico).

'At first glance, the decision to outsource to Flextronics looks like it was a complete disaster!', commented John Kerr, financial analyst. 'However, Lego learnt some important lessons along the way. It now realizes that outsourcing is not always the right solution and often doesn't yield the benefits it's meant to. Also, it's important to select suppliers that can support your market needs rather than ones who can simply make your products. It also helped Lego to better understand the needs of its own market, the type of production capability required to support it, provided the stimulus for restructuring its supply chain and helped it develop low-cost factories in the Czech Republic, Hungary and Mexico. Its new structure of market-based (rather than product-based) factories has made it much easier to benchmark performance between them as each factory has similar processes and products.

This has helped it understand the true profitability of both its products and customers and identify ways to reduce cost and shorten delivery lead times.'

Working with Flextronics also forced Lego to standardize its way of thinking (mindset, values and attitudes), processes and procedures (management and operations) and the hardware used to make products (production machines, lines and layouts). As a result, Lego halved the number of products it used from 12,000 in 2004 to 6,000 in 2008 (see Case Figure 8.5). For example, there are now only four different Lego policemen (rather than 16) and 70 per cent of the bricks in new sets are also used in other sets.

Lego also had to improve the level of transparency and control across its supply chain. For example, a sales and operations planning process was introduced to monitor and coordinate the different roles, responsibilities and capacities across the supply chain. Sales forecasts were also disconnected from sales incentives to improve their accuracy and scenario planning was used to estimate the potential impact of certain events. For example, what would be the impact on demand of a Star Wars event in Los Angeles? Or, where would demand fall if a particular product range became popular? This process was maintained after the break-up with Flextronics and is now considered a key strength within the organization.

USING CUSTOMERS TO DRIVE INNOVATION

Lego users have a long tradition of developing new ideas and sharing them with others through unofficial Lego conventions, clubs and websites. For example, 300,000 Lego creations and 4.5 million photos, drawings and instructions have been uploaded to www.mocpages.com and thousands of Lego-inspired movies have been shared on YouTube, with the top five movies viewed more than 64 million times.

In 2005, Knudstorp told fans at a US Lego convention that he wanted to work more closely with them. This marked the beginning of a more open and collaborative relationship and a realization that its fans might be a great source of innovation. Later that year, it launched the Ambassador Programme to increase communication between Lego and its customers. This exposed Lego to a wide range of new ideas, technologies and partnerships.

It started to realize that not everything had to be developed in house and allowed fans to start influencing Lego's strategic direction. Some examples of how Lego has engaged with its customers and used them to drive innovation are shown in Case Figures 8.7 and 8.8.

Lego designers and developers also became better at analysing customer data and using it to create new products that enhanced the overall Lego playing experience. They adopted a more disciplined approach to innovation. For example, before a new product would be considered, a one-page document had to be produced explaining the designs of the bricks to be used and the proportion that did not require new shapes or colours. At least 70 per cent of bricks within a new set had to be ones that were, or could be, used in other sets. It was found that ideas improved with the new objectives and constraints and the average time to develop a new product reduced from three years to less than twelve months.

New innovations were identified and managed by designers worked in four groups (see Case Figure 8.9) within eight areas (see Case Figure 8.10) and at three different levels (see Case Figure 8.11).

Although they were organized into separate groups, all designers were encouraged to work together. For example, a member from each group attended all the meetings in the

Activity	Description
Ambassador Programme	Created in 2005 to increase the level of communication between Lego and its customers. By 2009, it had 44 members from 27 different countries
Conventions	To find ideas and test new products. In 2010, 11,000 people attended the Lego Convention in Seattle (US)
User groups	To help develop and test new products. By 2012, it had 150 known user groups with 100,000 members and collaborated with them on 80 projects from arranging events to developing and testing new products
Families	Test new products in their homes and give feedback on how they work and what could be improved
Live with customers	Product designers and developers are sent to live with and observe consumers for weeks at a time
Lego.com	Brings customers together through games, stories, activities and experiences. In 2009, it was voted the best family and children's website with 3.2 million members
Cuusoo.com	For customers to create ideas, share them and see what other people think. If an idea gets 10,000 votes it is reviewed by Lego. If it then goes into production, the inventor gets 1 per cent of its total net sales. A limited-edition Japanese deep sea submersible received 10,000 votes and went on sale in 2011

Case Figure 8.7 Examples of how Lego uses customers to drive innovation

Innovation	Description
Ldraw.org	Freeware computer-aided design program, was developed by a Lego fan in 1995 for users to develop, test, render and document Lego model designs before making them and share these designs with other users
Bricklink.com	Set up by a Lego fan in 2000 as a marketplace for customers (usually adults) to buy and sell large quantities of Lego pieces. It now has 200,000 members and offers more than 134 million different products
Mindstorms NXT	Partnered with a company owned by a customer to increase the number of sensors on its programmable robotics sets, which significantly expanded its capability over previous models
Architecture	Worked with Adam Reed Tucker (Chicago architect and Lego fan) to develop sets for architecturally significant buildings that are sold in museums and souvenir shops
Minifigures	Partnered with customers to develop Minifigures better matched to their interests and other Lego products

Case Figure 8.8 Examples of customer-driven innovations

Group	Roles and responsibilities
Product and Marketing Development	100 designers look for ways to extend existing product lines. They come up with 200 to 250 new products each year, 80 per cent of their proposals are accepted and 95 per cent of current Lego sales come from these products
The Concept Lab	Developers invent new products and physical play concepts. Typically, less than 2 per cent of their proposals are accepted
Community, Education and Direct	2,000 employees develop, manage and support digital products and online play experiences for school projects, online experiences, consumer communities, retailers and online stores
New Business Group	Develop new business models with limited sales potential. Given freedom to experiment with small ideas

Case Figure 8.9 Lego innovation groups

Area	Type	Description
Business 'How do consumers buy Lego's products and experiences?'	Sales channel	Retailers, direct-to-consumers and alliances
	Business model	Revenue model, value chain structure and partnerships
Product 'What products and experiences do consumers buy from Lego?'	Product offering	Model and element, function and technology, packaging, build instructions and software
	Platform	Element, technology, packaging and digital platforms
Communication 'How do consumers communicate with Lego?'	Messaging	Campaigns, point of sales, websites, packaging and catalogues
	Interaction	Communities, events and customer service
Processes 'How does Lego deliver its products and experiences?'	Core processes	Innovation, development, production, purchasing and delivery
	Enabling processes	Strategy, research and organization

Case Figure 8.10 Lego's areas and types of innovation

Level	Description
Redefined innovation	Analyse long-term social, cultural and industry trends to create propositions that haven't been seen before
Reconfigured innovation	Analyse customer needs, industry trends and market forces to create better solutions for known propositions
Adjusted innovation	Use customer experience and insight to optimize existing solutions

Case Figure 8.11 Levels of innovation identified by Lego

early phase of a new project and each project was reviewed annually to see if it could be better handled by another group. By 2011, 50 per cent of the products sold in that year had been developed in the previous two years and accounted for 60 to 70 per cent of its sales. A summary of Lego's current key business areas is shown in Case Figure 8.12, and Case Figure 8.13 shows how its range of play materials, robotics sets and board games have evolved over the years.

SUPPORTING RETAILERS

Lego also started looking for ways to customize products and services to the needs of different retailers. For example, Wal-Mart was very cost focused, whereas ToysR'Us was more concerned about offering customers a wide product range. Lego also worked hard to increase stock availability by decoupling moulding from packaging, which enabled them to hold component (rather than finished goods) inventory and assemble sets to order as required. As a result, moulding factories now only make-to-order 60 to 70 per cent of the time, making production easier to plan and improving on-time delivery reliability. As a result, third-party retailers increased their margins on Lego products from 19 per cent in 2004 to 30 per cent in 2009 and turned inventory five times in

Business	Description
Play materials	Lego's core business includes Lego Baby (0 to 24 months), Lego Duplo (18 months to 5 years), Lego System sets (5 to 11 years), Lego Technic (11 to 13 years) and Lego Mindstorms (11 to 13 years)
Theme parks	First one opened in Denmark in 1968 and there are now six Legolands worldwide. In 2007, opened its first Discovery Centre in Berlin (a smaller version of Legoland) and there are now eight worldwide
Clothing	In 1993, Lego clothing (0 to 12 years) was first produced and marketed by Kabooki under licence from Lego
Video games	Has developed a number of games since 1997 including Island, Creator, Racers, Star Wars and Indiana Jones
Robotics sets	Launched Mindstorms in 1998, enabling users to program 'intelligent' bricks with light and sound sensors
Books and magazines	Released its first book in 1999 and has published many others since, as well as comics and graphic novels
Business consultancy	Set up Lego Serious Play in 2000 to help other organizations foster creative thinking using Lego products
Retail stores	Opened its first store in 2000 in Cologne (Germany) and now has 46 worldwide. Each opening involves a 'master model builder' who creates a huge Lego statue with the help of local children that is then displayed in the store
Board games	Launched in 2009, players build boards out of Lego bricks, play with Lego-style players and a Lego dice
Films and TV	Launched its first computer-animated movie on DVD in 2010 and its first TV series in 2011

Case Figure 8.12 Lego's current business areas

Range	From	To	Range	From	To
City	1966	–	Ninja	1998	2000
Homemaker	1971	1982	Znap	1998	1999
Dacta	1972	–	Roboriders	1999	1999
Racers	1975	–	Rock raiders	1999	2000
Castle	1978	1979	Slizer/Throwbots	1999	2000
	1983	2000	Star Wars	1999	–
	2003	–	Winnie the Pooh	1999	2011
Technic	1977	–	Mickey Mouse	2000	2002
Space	1978	1993	Sports	2000	2006
	1998	1998	Studios	2000	2004
	2011	–	Alpha team	2001	2005
Fabuland	1979	1989	Bionicle	2001	2010
Scala	1979	1980	Harry Potter	2001	2007
	1997	2001		2010	2011
Duplo	1981	1990	Island Xtreme	2001	2003
	1992	1993	Jack Stone	2001	2002
	1996	–	Gladiator	2002	2002
Baby	1983	2005	Spider-Man	2002	2004
Model team	1986	2006	Williams F1	2002	2003
Mindstorms	1989	–	4+	2003	2004
Pirates	1989	2010	Clikitis	2003	2006
Belville	1994	2009	Creator	2003	–
Aquazone	1995	1998	Discovery	2003	2003
Time travels	1996	1997	Inventor	2003	2003
Wild West	1996	1997	Spybotics	2003	2003
	2002	2002	Quatro	2004	2006
Adventures	1998	2000	Dino attack	2005	2005
	2003	2003	Vikings	2005	2007
Thomas the Tank Engine	2005	2009	Hero factory	2010	–
Batman	2006	2009	Minifigures	2010	–
	2012	–	Pharaoh's quest	2010	2011
Avatar	2006	2006	Prince of Persia	2010	2010
Exo-Force	2006	2008	World racers	2010	2010
SpongeBob	2006	2012	Ninjago	2011	–
Aqua raiders	2007	2007	Pirates of the Caribbean	2011	2011
Mars mission	2007	2009	Dino	2012	2012

Modular horses	2007	–	Friends	2012	–
Agents	2008	2009	Lord of the Rings	2012	–
Architecture	2008	–	Minecraft	2012	–
Indiana Jones	2008	2009	Monster fighters	2012	–
Speed racer	2008	2008	The Hobbit	2012	–
Games	2009	–	Super heroes	2012	–
Power miners	2009	2010	Legends of China	2013	–
Toy Story	2009	2010	Mutant Ninja Turtles	2013	–
Atlantis	2010	2011	The Lone Ranger	2013	–
Ben 10	2010	2011			

Case Figure 8.13 Lego's range of play materials, robotics sets and board games (1966–2013)

2009 compared with only twice in 2004. The increased attractiveness of Lego products has led to the average shelf space allocated to its products increasing from 9 feet in 2004 to 30 feet in 2009.

THE FUTURE

'Reduced product variety and increased commonality across Lego sets has increased product compatibility, increased stock availability, reduced delivery lead times and lowered production costs', commented John Keer, financial analyst. 'However, product variety is creeping back up! And I can't see how it's going to come back down as each new set requires 200 to 300 new products and the more complex ones create the highest sales growth. The question is when will this diversity start to tip it back into bankruptcy? All looks good at the moment, but I'm worried there might be some underlying problems we haven't seen yet.'

QUESTIONS

1 Why did Lego almost go bankrupt in 2004?

2 How has Lego turned the business around?

3 Why did Lego bring production back in house?

4 What can other organizations learn from Lego's journey?

DISCUSSION QUESTIONS

1. What factors should be taken into account when choosing whether to make or buy?
2. What are the principal benefits of making in house?
3. What are the principal benefits of outsourcing?
4. What are the principal disadvantages of outsourcing?
5. What is meant by a hollow corporation? What is the significance of this phenomenon?
6. What are the key factors to assess when deciding whether to source from domestic or offshore providers?
7. What is e-procurement? Explain its increasing use in companies.
8. What types of supplier relations can be used?
9. What is strategic partnering?
10. What are supply clusters? Explain their evolution and the benefits that may accrue.
11. How can companies cushion the operations process/delivery system from the inherent instability of its markets? How do these approaches extend into the management of the supply chain?

NOTES AND REFERENCES

1 Gottfredson, M., Puryear, R. and Philips, S. (2005) 'Strategic sourcing: from periphery to core', *Harvard Business Review,* 83(2): 132–9.

2 Institute for Supply Management (formerly US National Association of Purchasing Management), Tempre AZ, USA.

3 Hamel, G. and Prahalad, C. (1994) *Competing for the Future,* Harvard Business School Press.

4 For example, see Norman, P.M. (2001) 'Are your secrets safe? Knowledge protection in strategic alliances', *Business Horizons,* 44(6): 51–60.

5 Mehta, N. (2009) 'Novartis to challenge IPAB's patent decision on Glivec', *The Economic Times of India,* 20 July.

6 For example, see Arruñada, B. and Vázquez, X.H. (2006) 'When your contract manufacturer becomes your competitor', *Harvard Business Review,* 84(9): 135–59.

7 For example, see Slone, R.E., Mentzer, J.T. and Dittmann, J.P. (2007) 'Are you the weakest link in your company's supply chain?', *Harvard Business Review,* September: 116–18.

8 Quoted in Kano, C. (1998) 'Can Canon keep clicking? The Japanese photo and printer giant is on a roll. But it must find new ways to compete in a wired world', http://archive.fortune.com/magazines/fortune/fortune_archive/1998/02/02/237194/index.htm (accessed 6 June 2017).

9 Also, see Tait, N. (1997) 'Handling the sourcing decisions: lowest cost is not always the answer', *Financial Times,* 15 October: 13.

10 Milne, R. (2006) 'Volkswagen chooses to swim against the current', *Financial Times,* 7 October: 28.

11 It is estimated that for each $1 billion of foreign-made consumables, up to a further 50 per cent is the total cost to a nation including other manufacturing, wholesale and retail margins, transportation, plant construction, other new materials, mining, financial and insurance.

12 Economist Intelligence Unit and KPMG management consultants' 1996 report entitled *Supply Chain Management: Europe's New Competitive Battleground.*

13 Borsodi, R. (1929) *The Distribution Age*, D. Appleton & Co.

14 Blecke, J.A. (1989) 'Peak strategies', *McKinsey Quarterly*, Spring.

15 Adapted from Ferdows, K. (1997) 'Making the most of foreign factories', *Harvard Business Review*, March–April: 73–88.

16 *Hiscox Cyber Readiness Report 2017*: report based on a survey of 3,000 executives, IT managers and other key professionals in the US, UK and Germany. Available at https://www.hiscox.co.uk/cyber-readiness-report/ (accessed 6 June 2017).

17 Products that are different from any other product in any way (including, for example, the number of units in an outer packing case) will have a unique company code number and are referred to as stock-keeping units (SKUs).

18 Asanuma, B. (1989) 'Manufacture–supplier relationships in Japan and the concept of relation-specific skill', *Journal of Japanese and International Economies*, 3: 1–30.

19 Toyota Motor Corporation (1988) 'Toyota: a history of the first 50 years', TMC.

20 Li, S., Ragu-Nathan, B., Ragu-Nathan, T. and Subba, S. (2006) 'The impact of supply chain management practices on competitive advantage and organisational performance', *OMEGA, International Journal of Management Science*, 34: 110.

21 Margretta, J. (1998) 'The power of virtual integration: an interview with Dell Computer's Michael Dell', *Harvard Business Review*, March–April: 72–83.

22 Lambert, D.M. and Knemeyer, A.M. (2004) 'We're in this together', *Harvard Business Review*, December: 114–22.

23 Porter, M. (1988) 'Clusters and the new economics of competition', *Harvard Business Review*, November–December: 77–90.

24 Steward, T. and Raman, A. (2007) 'The HBR interview with Katsuaki Watanabe: lessons from Toyota's long drive', *Harvard Business Review*, July–August: 74–83.

25 Wu, L., Yue, X. and Sim, T. (2006) 'Supply clusters: a key to China's cost advantage', *Supply Chain Management Review*, March: 46–51.

26 Wu et al., 'Supply clusters', p. 48.

27 Wu et al., 'Supply clusters', p. 49.

28 For example, Newman, W., Hanna, R. and Maffei, M.J. (1993) 'Dealing with the uncertainties of manufacturing, flexibility, buffers and integration', *International Journal of Operations & Production Management*, 13(1): 19–34; and Caputo, M. (1996) 'Uncertainty, flexibility and buffers in the management of a firm's operating system', *Production Planning and Control*, 7(5): 518–28.

29 Hopp, W.J. and Spearman, M.L. (2000) *Factory Physics: Foundations of Manufacturing Management*, 2nd edn, Irwin/McGraw-Hill.

30 See also Fisher, M., Hammond, J., Obermeyer, W. and Raman, A. (1997) 'Configuring a supply chain to reduce the cost of uncertainty', *Production and Operations Management*, 6(3): 211–25. In this, they highlight the different supply chain requirements for innovative and 'functional' products, which they term 'responsive' and 'efficient' respectively.

EXPLORING FURTHER

Barnes-Schuster, D., Bassock, Y. and Anupindi, R. (2002) 'Coordination and flexibility in supply contracts with options', *Manufacturing and Service Operations Management*, 4(3): 171–207.

Blois, K.J. (1972) 'Vertical quasi-integration', *Journal of Industrial Economics*, 20(3): 253–72.

Boyer, K., Hult, G. and Tomas, M. (2005) 'Extending the supply chain: integrating operations and marketing in the online grocery industry', *Journal of Operations Management*, 23(6): 642–61.

Buzznell, R.D. (1983) 'Is vertical integration profitable?', *Harvard Business Review*, January–February: 92–102. This offers an analysis based on the profit impact of market strategies (PIMS) data to assess a number of relationships, including vertical integration and profitability, vertical integration, investment intensity and return on investments, and vertical integration, relative market share and profitability.

Carranza Torres, O.A. and Villegas Moràn, F.A. (eds) (2006) *The Bullwhip Effect in Supply Chains: A Review of Methods, Components and Cases*, Palgrave Macmillan.

Child, J. and Faulkner, D. (1998) *Strategies for Cooperation: Managing Alliances, Networks and Joint Ventures*, Oxford University Press.

Childerhouse, P. and Towill, D.R. (2003) 'Simplified material flow holds the key to supply chain management', *OMEGA, International Journal of Management Science*, 31(1): 17–27.

Childerhouse, P., Aitken, J. and Towill, D.R. (2002) 'Analysis and design of focused demand chains', *Journal of Operations Management*, 20(6): 675–89.

Childerhouse, P., Hermiz, R., Mason-Jones, R., Popp, A. and Towill, D.R. (2003) 'Information flows in automobile supply chains: present industrial practice', *Industrial Management and Data Systems*, 103(3): 137–49.

Choi, T.Y. and Hong, Y. (2002) 'Unveiling the structure of supply networks: case studies in Honda, Acura and DaimlerChrysler', *Journal of Operations Management*, 20(5): 469–93.

Cigolini, R., Cozzi, M. and Perona, M. (2004) 'A new framework for supply chain management: a conceptual model and empirical test', *International Journal of Operations Management*, 24(1): 7–41.

Croom, S.R. (2000) 'The impact of web-based procurement on the management of operating resources supply', *Journal of Supply Chain Management*, 36(1): 4–13.

DTI and Society of Motor Manufacturers and Traders (1994) 'A review of the relationships between vehicle manufacturers and suppliers', February.

Fields, J.M and Meile, L.C. (2008) 'Supplier relations and supply chain performance in financial services processes', *International Journal of Operations and Production Management*, 28(2): 185–202.

Fisher, M. (1997) 'What is the right supply chain for your product?', *Harvard Business Review*, March–April: 105–16.

Fisher, M., Hammond, J., Obermeyer, W. and Raman, A. (1997) 'Configuring supply chain to reduce the cost of demand uncertainty', *Production and Operations Management*, 6(3): 211–25.

Frohlich, M.T. and Westbrook, R. (2001) 'Arcs of integration: an international study of supply chain strategies', *Journal of Operations Management*, 19(2): 185–200.

Gattorna, J. (ed.) (1998) *Strategic Supply Chain Alignment: Best Practice in Supply Chain Management*, Gower.

Groucutt, J. and Griseri, P. (2004) *Mastering e-business*, Palgrave Macmillan.

Hagel, J. III and Brown, J.S. (2005) 'Productive friction: how difficult business partnerships can accelerate innovation', *Harvard Business Review*, February: 83–91.

Hald, K.S. and Ellegaard, C. (2011) 'Supplier evaluation processes: the shaping and reshaping of supplier performance', *Journal of Operations and Production Management*, 31(8): 888–910.

Handfield, R.B. and Krause, D.R. (2000) 'Avoiding the pitfalls in supplier development', *Sloan Management Review*, 41(2): 37–50.

Holcomb, T. and Hitt, M. (2007) 'Toward a model of strategic outsourcing', *Journal of Operations Management*, 25(2): 464–81.

Lee, H.L. (2002) 'Aligning supply chain strategies with product uncertainties', *California Management Review*, 44(3): 105–19.

Liker, J.K. and Wu, Y.-C. (2000) 'Japanese automakers, US suppliers and supply chain superiority', *Sloan Management Review*, 42(1): 81–93.

Lowson, R.H. (2003) 'How supply network operations strategies evolve: composition, competitive priorities and customisation', *International Journal of Physical Distribution and Logistics Management*, 33(1): 75–91.

Mason-Jones, R. and Towill, D.R. (1997) 'Information enrichment: designing the supply chain for competitive advantage, *Journal of Supply Chain Management*, 24(7): 17–23.

Nassimbeni, G. and Sartor, M. (2006) *Sourcing in China: Strategies, Methods and Experiences*, Palgrave Macmillan.

Rudberg, M. and Olhager, J. (2003) 'Manufacturing networks and supply chains: an operations strategy perspective', *OMEGA, The International Journal of Management Science*, 31: 29–39.

Salvador, F., Forza, C., Rungtusanatham, M. and Choi, T.Y. (2001) 'Supply chain interactions and time-related performance: an operations management perspective', *International Journal of Operations & Production Management*, 21(4): 461–75.

Smeltzer, L.R. and Carr, A. (2002) 'Reverse auctions in industrial marketing and buying', *Business Horizons*, March–April: 47–52.

Tan, K.C., Lyman, S.B. and Wisner, J.D. (2002) 'Supply chain management: a strategic perspective', *International Journal of Production & Operations Management*, 22(6): 614–31.

Vickery, S., Calantone, R. and Droge, C. (1999) 'Supply chain flexibility: an empirical study', *Journal of Supply Chain Management*, 35(3): 16–24.

Weeks, M.R. and Feeny, D.F. (2008) 'Outsourcing: from cost management to innovation and business value', *California Management Review*, 50(4): 127–46.

Wu, Y.C. (2003) 'Lean manufacturing: a perspective of lean suppliers', *International Journal of Operations & Production Management*, 23(11): 1349–76.

Youngdahl, W., Kannan, R. and Dash, K.C. (2010) 'Service offshoring: the evolution of offshore operations', *International Journal of Operations and Production Management*, 30(8): 798–820.

9 INFRASTRUCTURE CHOICE

THIS CHAPTER DISCUSSES...

SUMMARY

- Infrastructure is used to help manage delivery systems and support markets.
- It comprises a number of complex interacting elements that need to be aligned to both business and market needs. Some examples of the aspects involved are functional support, operations planning and control systems, IT systems, work structuring, and procedures, payment and reward systems, and organizational structure.
- Where infrastructure is managed with little strategic debate between functions, it can lead to unconnected, uncoordinated, functionally biased and reactive developments.
- Functions may resist infrastructure developments because these often challenge their roles, responsibilities and activities. To overcome this, decisions must be based on data or evidence of actual current and future market requirements and how well current aspects of infrastructure support these and the improvements that proposed changes will bring.
- Businesses must make incremental infrastructure developments based on continual market reviews. Step changes should be avoided wherever possible because they are costly, disruptive, difficult to get right and difficult to change once made.
- Cross-functional teams have to be empowered to identify improvement areas with high returns, compare alternative developments, consider all elements and make incremental changes.
- Many organizations make inappropriate infrastructure decisions. Examples of these are managing through specialist functions, creating functional silos, supporting delivery systems from a distance, paying and rewarding inappropriately, creating too many management layers and reducing line executives' roles and responsibilities.
- To overcome these problems, businesses must redefine functional objectives based on a cross-functional market review supported with data. They must challenge existing management structures, redefine roles and responsibilities, pay and reward based on skills and performance, reduce overheads, flatten management structures and set up cross-functional improvement teams.
- Once the appropriate infrastructure has been developed, it must be managed to support business and market needs. Three critical areas of management focus should be quality conformance, inventory and operations scheduling systems.

BUSINESS OBJECTIVES	MARKETING STRATEGY	HOW DO YOU QUALIFY AND WIN ORDERS IN CHOSEN MARKETS?	OPERATIONS STRATEGY	
			Delivery systems choice	Infrastructure choice
Sales revenue growth Survival Profit Return on investment Other financial measures Corporate social responsibility targets Environmental targets	Product/service markets and segments Range Mix Volumes Standardization versus customization Leader versus follower alternatives	Price Quality conformance Delivery: speed reliability Product/service range Design leadership Technical support Brand name New services and products–time to market	Choice of delivery systems Trade-offs embodied in these choices Make-or-buy decisions Capacity: size timing location Role of inventory in the delivery system	Operations scheduling systems IT systems Procedures Work structuring Organizational structure

Notes

1 The entries in each column are to provide examples and are not intended to be a definitive list.

2 Although the steps to be followed are given as finite points in a stated procedure, in reality the process will involve statement and restatement, because several of these aspects will impinge on each other.

3 Column 3 concerns identifying both the relevant order-winners and qualifiers for customers or markets/market segments.

Figure 9.1 Framework for reflecting operations strategy issues in corporate decisions

In addition to selecting and developing the necessary delivery systems for a business, operations also needs to choose and develop appropriate aspects of its infrastructure, as illustrated in Figure 9.1. The role of these two categories of investment within operations is somewhat similar to that of bricks and cement when building a wall. While bricks (the delivery systems) are the centrepiece within its design and construction, cement (the infrastructure) binds and holds the structure together.

The task of the various elements that make up infrastructure is to help to manage efficiently operations' various day-to-day tasks and/or help support the relevant order-winners and qualifiers of the company's markets for which operations is responsible. As highlighted earlier, infrastructure choices are typically large (involve major investment) and fixed (they are

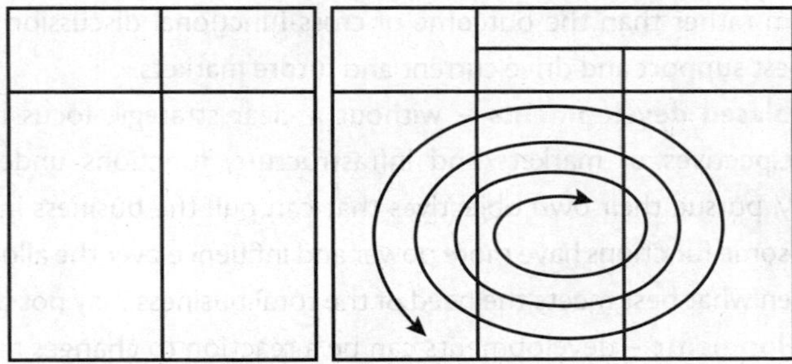

Figure 9.2 Strategic awareness ensures businesses identify market changes and develop the capability to support them

expensive to modify and take a long time to change). Thus, the need to make infrastructure choices that meet the needs of markets is as critical as the choice of appropriate delivery systems and, for some companies, more so.

Markets are dynamic and constantly changing, and businesses need to identify these changes and develop the necessary capabilities to support them (see Figure 9.2). While a company's infrastructure investment is sizeable in total, it is typically made up of a range of smaller elements. Taken individually, each element is often easier and less expensive to modify than the delivery systems used to provide the required services and products. For this reason, businesses often tend to meet market changes or refine their current approach to supporting the needs of customers by modifying and realigning elements of its infrastructure. Only if improvements to meeting market needs cannot be met through such infrastructure developments will subsequent delivery system investments be made.

ISSUES TO CONSIDER WHEN DEVELOPING INFRASTRUCTURE

It is important to consider a number of issues when developing infrastructure:

- **Complex and interacting elements** – operations infrastructure comprises a set of complex interacting elements. Modifying any one element will typically impact other elements and the overall, strategic capability of the operation.
- **Managing by functions** – companies traditionally manage the complexity that comes with size by breaking the organization down into smaller parts. Technically similar activities are grouped into functions. The logic for this is based on the principles of economies of scale and control through specialists.
- **Strategic debate between functions** – functional areas are managed separately and work together on tactical or operational issues. However, strategic debate around current and future market requirements and how to develop the appropriate infrastructure to support them needs to be a regular item on the corporate agenda.
- **Connected and coordinated developments** – without strategic debate then infrastructure developments will typically be the result of individual functions reacting to demands

placed on them rather than the outcome of cross-functional discussion about how the business can best support and drive current and future markets.

- **Functionally biased developments** – without a clear strategic focus based on cross-functional perspectives of markets and infrastructure, functions understandably, but inappropriately, pursue their own objectives that can pull the business in different directions. Because some functions have more power and influence over the allocation of investment funds then what best meets the need of the total business may not be the outcome.
- **Reactive developments** – developments can be a reaction to changes that have already occurred. To avoid this, businesses should continually review current and future market needs and make proactive developments to support or drive markets in a desired direction.
- **Functional resistance to change** – infrastructure developments often involve changing the size, responsibilities and activities of functions. This can lead to changing existing functional management structures and moving to cross-functional service/product or customer-based teams. Functional managers may well resist such changes by presenting a strong case for maintaining existing structures and arguing their case with a clarity that is based on the certainty of the status quo. It is important that these debates and discussions concern how best to support markets rather than the needs and perspectives of functions.

INFRASTRUCTURE DEVELOPMENT

When developing infrastructure, businesses must ensure they:

- **Continually review markets** to identify current and future needs. This enables companies to make decisions about how best to develop infrastructure to support or drive current and future markets.
- **Continually develop infrastructure** to ensure that changing current and future market needs are met. Because markets are continually changing, operations infrastructure will become misaligned with customer needs when developments stop or fall behind.
- **Make incremental changes** – where markets are continually reviewed, then the necessary elements of infrastructure can be incrementally developed to support or drive them. Structures, controls, systems and procedures can be modified, simplified or eliminated where required and on an ongoing basis. Step change is only necessary when elements of infrastructure have become significantly misaligned with market needs. This may result from a significant change in the competitive dynamics of markets, but is typically more likely to be due to a lack of development or market awareness over a long period of time.
- **Avoid step changes** – by making incremental changes, companies can usually avoid step changes. Step changes are costly, disruptive, difficult to get right and difficult to change once made. Also, the need to make such large changes implies that the market has not been well supported for a period of time.
- **Empower employees to make changes** – continuous incremental development is easier to bring about with local responsibility for identifying improvements and implementing subsequent developments.

- **Use cross-functional teams** to review and develop infrastructure. This happens more readily in organizations where service, product or customer-based teams are in place. In functionally structured organizations, cross-functional teams would first have to be established to identify and then implement improvements.
- **Focus on areas of high return** – identify the areas with highest strategic impact to ensure that businesses get the best return from their resources; 80 per cent of benefits typically come from 20 per cent of developments.
- **Compare alternative developments** – identify and select developments based on their benefits and costs.
- **Consider all elements** because they are complex and interact with each other.

Organizational issues

As emphasized throughout this chapter, infrastructure is central to the effectiveness and efficiency of an organization, and choosing the appropriate infrastructure is key to effectively supporting markets. However, many organizations make infrastructure choices that result in a number of issues. Some of these are now discussed, although the relevance and importance of each aspect varies, depending on the markets served and delivery systems supported.

Managing through specialist functions

Most organizations create specialist support functions to provide advice and guidance to their line functions. With this central provision, companies hope to maximize the utilization of their skills and resources based on the principle of economies of scale. While this is true for high-volume, steady-state markets, most companies now operate in lower-volume and more dynamic markets where the principle of economies of scale is less than ideal (see Chapter 7 on focus for a more detailed explanation). As a result, companies that manage their business through specialist functions tend to experience major difficulties including:

- **Differing functional perspectives** – line and support functions view business needs differently. As a result, delivery systems can often be inadequately supported. To redress this issue, support functions have developed approaches that are classed as being either user-oriented, user-sensitive or user-friendly. However, the attitudes and perspectives that have resulted in the existing lack of fit take time to change.
- **Differing functional objectives** – differing functional market and business perspectives result in dissimilar functional objectives and priorities. Although each function is clear about what it needs to do, this may not be consistent within and between functions.
- **Unclear roles and responsibilities** – the roles, responsibilities and purpose of line and support functions need to be clear. Without this clarity, priorities and relationships can be misinterpreted. For example, line managers will often, and understandably, seek specialist support to improve weaknesses within their area of responsibility, either as a reaction to some recent event or as part of long-term improvements. Where such demands are not planned into specialists' budgets and resource allocations tensions can arise. Equally, line managers can focus too much on day-to-day activities and end up delaying decisions about

longer-term developments until they become urgent. Both situations create problems unless there are clear roles and responsibilities within line and support functions. Without these, misunderstandings and criticism often result, which may lead to less amicable relationships and less productive outcomes.

- **Functions not aligned with each other** – differing objectives and perspectives often lead to functions pointing in different directions and focusing on different goals. Where line functions do not fully know what they require or fail to adequately think through their needs, support functions make assumptions and second guess solutions. Only when the reality of what is provided is tested against everyday use and requirements does the gap between needs and provision become clear.
- **Markets are not supported** – where functional rather than market needs drive the business then this eventually leads to less focus on customer needs and may well result in a loss of market share and future sales and profits.

Given these difficulties, companies need to review the question, 'Is control through specialists appropriate to their business and the needs of their markets?' This must be a systematic evaluation rather than the '0–100 management'[1] responses that can often characterize too many of the changes made in businesses. The use of specialist groups and other approaches such as order-winner, service, product or customer-based teams will probably be the most appropriate way to organize and manage a business. Distinguishing those tasks that are clearly specialist in nature from those that are operational in orientation will start the necessary process of asking where the responsibility for tasks would best reside.

Creating functional silos

The decision to manage through specialist functions often results in silos where functions work independently from each other and only make cross-functional decisions at senior levels within the organization. Because specialist functions are measured and judged by how well they meet the targets agreed and set by the business, they understandably pursue their own objectives and goals. As a result, helping and developing operations delivery systems to better support the needs of the company's markets is not always at the top of their agenda.

Figure 9.3 shows the growth of specialist roles and responsibilities in recent years. This often comes from a desire for 'organizational neatness' rather than a review of how best to support markets. Activities that were once integrated into line functions have been moved into specialist areas (Phase 1) and an independent reporting structure then evolves (Phase 2). The result is barriers and difficulties in reintegrating support and line activities.

Supporting delivery systems from a distance

As activities move from line functions to specialist provision, the latter functions grow and are often physically relocated away from the line function activities (the essence of a business). When this happens, line functions, such as operations, are then supported

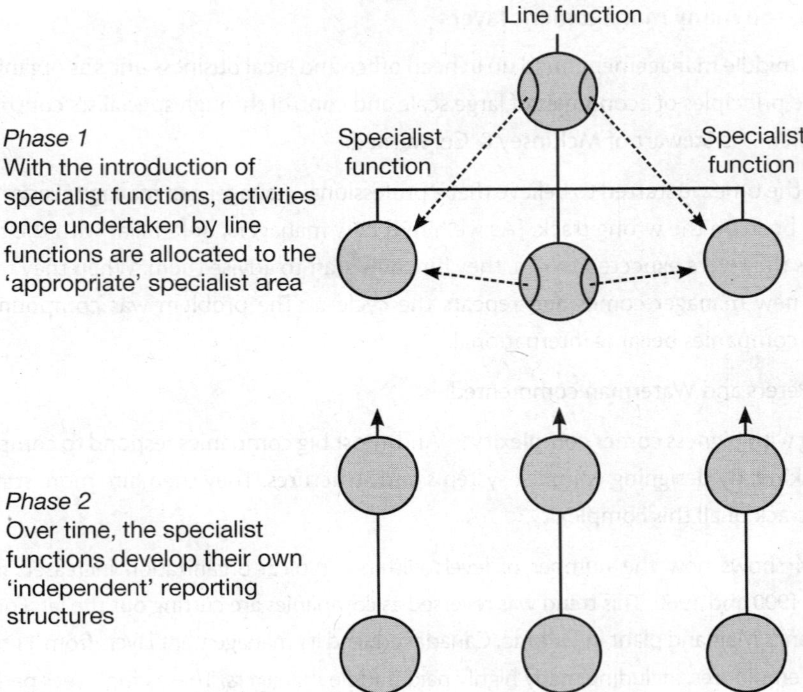

Figure 9.3 Typical phases in the evolution of specialist functions in an organization

by specialists that are not close at hand, with executives believing that they can manage effectively from a distance by using controls and systems. Such arrangements, however, fall short of the best way to support the principal activities of a business and the needs of customers. These approaches assume that factors such as unplanned events, disruptions, unforeseen patterns of demand and the need to meet the short lead-time requirements of customers are easy to handle and can be catered for by and within operations. But to manage the reality of the uncertainties that characterize most businesses it is also important to see and feel how an operation is working. For this reason, some support activities can be provided best when located in or close to the delivery systems they are designed to support.

Paying and rewarding inappropriately

Companies must recognize and reward executives on their relative importance and contribution to a business. People need to be attracted into key jobs and rewarded on their direct impact on the success of the business. Instead, salary structures and promotion opportunities reflect a perceived employee scarcity, assumed contribution and market rates. Consequently, people are attracted to support functions away from the line activities so critical to business success. Equally, payment and reward systems tend to be based around jobs rather than individuals. Such approaches create inflexibility and barriers to change.

Creating too many management layers

Layers of middle management build up in head office and local business units as organizations grow. The principles of economies of large scale and control through specialists contribute to this problem. As Stewart of McKinsey & Co. warned:

> Since the time we started to believe that a professional manager can manage everything, we've been on the wrong track. [As we hired] new managers, unfamiliar with the businesses they were expected to run, they hire new staff to advise them. When they move on, a new manager comes and repeats the cycle ... The problem was compounded when companies became international.[2]

And, as Peters and Waterman commented:

> Along with bigness comes complexity ... And, most big companies respond to complexity in kind, by designing complex systems and structures. They then hire more staff to keep track of all this complexity.[3]

Figure 9.4 shows how the number of levels within a typical organization increased fourfold between 1900 and 1960. This trend was reversed as companies are cutting out the fat. For example, DuPont's Maitland plant in Ontario, Canada reduced its management layers from 11 to 6 and shed 700 employees, including many highly paid middle managers. These employees performed well, but their roles did not add value and slowed down decisions and actions. Before the change, 90 staff reported to an operations manager through 6 supervisors. This was reduced to 40 staff and no supervisors. The staff now order tools directly from suppliers when they need them without waiting for authorization from senior managers. Also, customers now telephone the plant directly to discuss orders, rather than having to go through DuPont's head office in Toronto and four layers of bureaucracy. This has resulted in better support for line activities and customers.

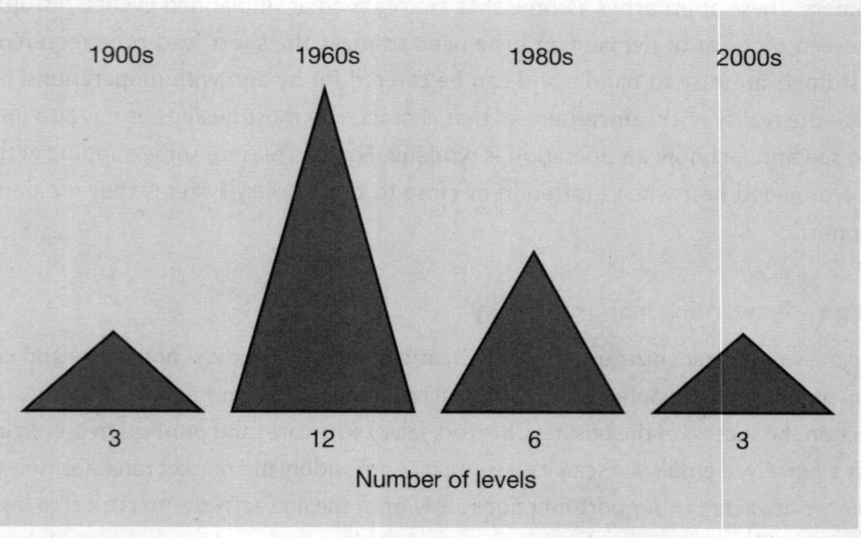

Figure 9.4 The number of levels within a typical organization at different times

Although there are obvious benefits from reducing management layers, it is important to address the task thoughtfully. Cutting staff, eliminating frills and reducing overheads needs to be addressed with care. Too often, all managers are asked to reduce staff levels by the same percentage without considering the impact on the level of market support. Corporate or central functions are often left intact because they direct the restructuring process without adequately or vigorously questioning their own roles. Applying similar across-the-board changes is not the way to go. The organization must be reshaped to become more effective and efficient. This requires careful surgery of both line and support staff based on an assessment of current and future market needs. Only then can appropriate functions, responsibilities and staff levels be determined.

Reducing line roles and responsibilities

As companies create support functions, they split out planning and evaluating activities from the 'doing' aspect of a job. Figure 9.5 shows such a separation. Operators become focused on providing services or making products and are no longer involved in planning or evaluating aspects of the job. This leads to a number of downsides:

- **Reduced responsibility** – staff are less responsible for planning and evaluating activities. For example, providing service/product quality conformance is no longer seen as the ultimate responsibility of the person providing the service or product itself.
- **Lack of empowerment** – staff are not able to make changes or improvements. Their job is simply to provide the services or products. However, often the best improvement ideas come from those whose task it is to provide the service or product.
- **Lower motivation** – as power and responsibility is taken away from staff, they feel less involved and less motivated.
- **Inflexible capacity** – when 'doing' activities are not required in a period, staff cannot be moved onto planning or evaluating functions. As a consequence, these staff either wait for work or are less effectively used elsewhere in the organization.

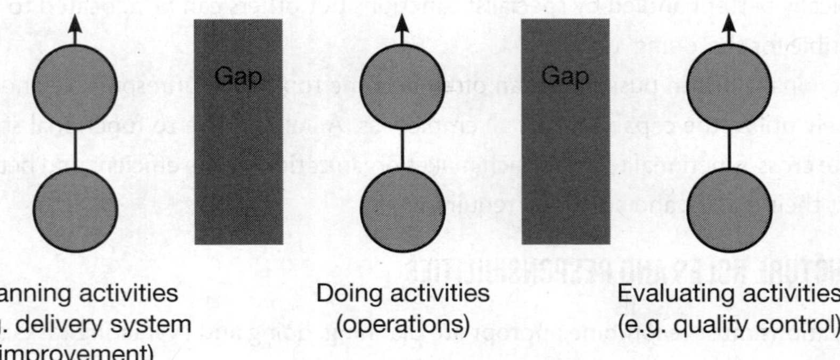

Figure 9.5 The separation between planning and evaluating activities created by organizational structures

To help rectify this development, companies need to recombine elements of planning and evaluating activities with the doing tasks. This works well when it forms part of a move to reduce management layers and restructure roles and responsibilities so as to empower 'doing' staff to be responsible for key decisions. Support functions provide advice and expert opinion but the final decision rests with the executive responsible. For example, while the human resources function would design and manage the recruitment process the ultimate decision on which candidate to hire would be made by the executive to whom the person will report.

DEVELOPING INFRASTRUCTURE

To compete effectively, firms must develop infrastructure that reflects current market needs and can adapt to future changes. Figure 9.6 shows a number of developments that overcome the organizational issues outlined in the last section and help businesses to create better infrastructure support for delivery systems, processes and markets.

DEFINE FUNCTIONAL OBJECTIVES

Functional objectives must reflect how best to support the current and future market order-winners and qualifiers, and this cross-functional market view will identify the capabilities to be developed and the functional objectives to be set. Discussing how to support markets means that objectives reflect customer and individual functional perspectives as well as clearer objectives being developed that are aligned to markets and customer needs. Functional roles, responsibilities, performance measures and reward systems can then be developed to reflect these objectives.

CHALLENGE EXISTING MANAGEMENT STRUCTURES

To re-shape existing management structures, organizations need to challenge current reporting systems, attitudes and expectations. For example, companies need to consider which tasks are best managed by specialist functions in terms of providing support for the business's delivery systems and markets. Some support tasks, such as negotiating suppliers' contracts, are typically better handled by specialist functions but others can be allocated to those staff responsible for the 'doing' tasks.

Functionally driven businesses can often become top heavy, unresponsive and unable to effectively utilize the capabilities of all employees. An alternative to functional structures is to create cross-functional teams, which makes organizations more efficient and better able to support their market and customer requirements.

RESTRUCTURE ROLES AND RESPONSIBILITIES

Organizations must recombine appropriate planning, doing and evaluating tasks to increase the responsibility, empowerment and motivation of line functions. Figure 9.7 shows how roles and responsibilities increase for line functions and decrease in support areas. 'Doing' staff become more motivated as they take responsibility for tasks such as delivery system

Aspect	Issue	Development
Organizational structure	Managing through specialist functions can result in differing functional perspectives, differing functional objectives and unclear roles and responsibilities	Set functional objectives, roles and responsibilities using cross-functional perspective of market order-winners and qualifiers (developed in Chapter 3)
	Functional silos are created where functions work independently from each other and only make cross-functional decisions at senior levels in the organization	Create cross-functional teams
	Too many management layers	Reduce overheads and flatten organizations by pushing responsibility as far down the organization as possible
Functional support	Insufficient specialist support for line functions because they are measured against their own targets, goals and objectives rather than how well they help the delivery system to meet customers' requirements	Create cross-functional teams and restructure roles and responsibilities to recombine planning, doing and evaluating aspects of a job
	Delivery systems are supported from a distance because support activities are relocated away from the 'doing' activities	Relocate support activities to work close to the 'doing' functions
Payment and reward systems	These do not reflect relative executive importance and contribution to the business	Pay and reward staff based on the contribution to the business task of meeting customer market requirements
Operations planning and control	Businesses split out planning, doing and evaluating aspects of the job. Staff responsible for undertaking the 'doing' roles do not have planning or evaluating roles as part of their job. Their ideas on improvement and reducing waste are lost to the business while they are less motivated and empowered	Restructure roles and responsibilities to recombine planning, doing and evaluating aspects of a job. Set up improvement teams

Figure 9.6 **Indication of how developments can be used to address infrastructure issues**

improvement, scheduling and quality control. Equally, specialists are released from non-specialist work, and activities become easier to coordinate.[4] Although these changes bring small returns in themselves, the cumulative effect can be, and typically is, significant.

As mentioned earlier, DuPont's Maitland plant significantly changed its employees' roles and responsibilities when it reduced management layers from 11 to 6 and shed 700 employees.

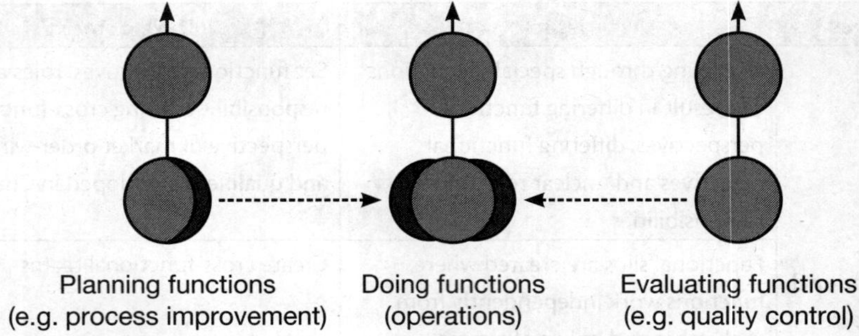

Figure 9.7 Incorporating appropriate planning and evaluating steps into the doing tasks

Previously, customer quality conformance complaints were handled by head office, but now the operator who made the product goes to see the customer and decides how to correct the problem. Problems are cleared more quickly and customers are better supported. Operators are also trained in computer technology and develop new systems as required.[5]

PAY AND REWARD BASED ON THE IMPORTANCE AND CONTRIBUTION OF TASKS TO BUSINESS SUCCESS

Payment and reward systems need to reflect the relative importance and contribution of the tasks to business success. The reward systems need to be designed so as to attract people into key jobs and reward them based on their business contribution. It is essential to evaluate the relative worth of jobs in the light of their contribution to meeting market and customer needs.

REDUCE OVERHEADS AND FLATTEN ORGANIZATIONS

Overheads will be reduced and organizations flattened as businesses challenge existing management structures and redefine roles and responsibilities. Companies need to push planning and evaluating responsibilities as far down the organization as possible by investing and developing the people involved in 'doing' activities. This will reduce overhead costs while increasing staff flexibility, resource utilization, decision-making effectiveness and employee motivation. Making a business more effective and efficient requires careful pruning of both line and support staff. As part of this process, organizations must look at their business and market needs before reducing their management layers and realigning tasks.

USING IMPROVEMENT TEAMS

Improvement teams tap into employee ideas and empower them to make the incremental changes that continuously improve businesses and keep them efficient and aligned with markets. Quality circles emerged in postwar Japan when they were struggling to meet quality conformance targets. Since then, similar teams have been used by organizations to improve other performance aspects such as reducing costs, improving on-time delivery performance

Aspect	Operation classification	
	World-class	Other
Percentage participation	80	54
Meetings per month	4	3
Suggestions per employee	17	12
Percentage of suggestions accepted	79	13

Figure 9.8 Employees are significantly more involved in world-class operations

and shortening lead times. Improvement teams are a key factor in the performance of many Japanese companies. Consequently, businesses in other countries have adopted this approach in an attempt to achieve similar benefits. There is a danger that such initiatives are introduced because they are fashionable rather than as a sound and suitable approach to improve businesses and better support current and future markets. Without a clear focus, these initiatives often fail to gain business support or direction and typically are discontinued after a time.

Improvement teams tap into the most underdeveloped asset of many companies – the ideas and contributions of their staff. Figure 9.8 shows how world-class automotive component companies use staff to suggest and implement improvements more than non-world-class competitors.[6] For these approaches to be successful managers need to genuinely commit to continuous improvement principles and work with their staff. A participative management style must be used to support improvement activities without interfering with the self-initiating and self-managed style that underpins the success of these approaches.

MANAGING INFRASTRUCTURE

Once the appropriate elements of infrastructure have been developed, businesses need to ensure that the organization as a whole is orientated and managed to support the needs of both the business and its markets. This embraces a wide range of aspects and this section looks at three important elements of managing infrastructure: quality conformance because it is usually either a market order-winner or qualifier; inventory because it is typically a substantial asset on a company's balance sheet; and scheduling systems because they represent a significant investment and help set the performance parameters of operations.

MANAGING QUALITY CONFORMANCE

In most markets quality conformance is either an order-winner or a qualifier and probably impacts on market share more than any other single factor. For example, Japanese companies at some point since the 1980s systematically increased quality conformance levels in many sectors (for example, automobiles, televisions and electronics) and by subsequently changing customer expectations gained market share. They typically achieved this by targeting markets where quality conformance was, at the time, a qualifier. They then entered these markets and provided products having significantly fewer defects and, in so doing, changed the dimension of quality conformance into an order-winner. Unable to meet those higher quality-conformance levels, competitors started to lose market share. In response these competitors then set about improving their own levels of quality conformance, with the outcome being that the role of quality conformance in these markets has now reverted back to that of a qualifier.

TASK AND RESPONSIBILITY

Managing quality conformance concerns the responsibility for setting performance levels, meeting these targets and measuring and seeking ways to improve current levels of performance. The allocation of some or all of these tasks varies for different types of service delivery systems and manufacturing processes. As shown in Figures 9.9 and 9.10, in some systems these tasks are combined with 'doing' activities whereas in others they are separated.

In the provision of non-repeat services these tasks are combined with the 'doing' activities involved. With repetition and associated volumes, however, quality-related tasks become increasingly separated from the 'doing' activities with external checks becoming part of the way in which performance levels are maintained, as well as using specialists to improve standards of provision.

Similarly, special products are handled by either project or jobbing processes where the task and responsibility for quality conformance rests with the person delivering the product. In continuous processing, quality checks are built into the process itself. However, in batch and line, the doing and evaluating tasks and responsibilities are often separated and, as a result, conformance levels may drop. Where this happens, businesses need to consider how they are able to recombine the doing and evaluating activities in order to redress this problem. As mentioned earlier, challenging existing management structures, redefining roles and responsibilities and setting up improvement teams are ways to achieve this.

Service delivery system type		Quality conformance	
		Task	**Responsibility**
Non-repeat		Highly skilled staff are typically involved in agreeing the service specification	The staff providing the service are responsible for the task of achieving quality conformance targets
Repeat	Low volume ↓ High volume	As volumes increase the service specification is set ahead of time. The server's role is to deliver the service to the agreed specification allowing for any agreed levels of server discretion	The staff delivering the service are responsible for meeting the agreed specification. Internal checks will be in place and in some high-volume businesses (e.g. franchises) these will be supplemented by additional checks undertaken by central functions

Figure 9.9 Varying quality conformance tasks and responsibilities by service delivery system type

Process type	Quality conformance	
	Task	Responsibility
Project and jobbing	Highly skilled people deliver the product or service and ensure conformance levels are met	The person delivering the product or service is also responsible for quality conformance
Batch and line	Doing and evaluating tasks are separated to deskill the doing aspect of the job and reduce labour costs. Inspection and quality control functions evaluate whether conformance levels are met	Inspection and quality control functions are primarily responsible for quality conformance
Continuous processing	Quality specification is set and checked by the process itself. Operators may check and monitor the process to ensure conformance levels are met	Conformance levels are controlled by the process itself. Operators may be responsible for ensuring conformance levels are met

Figure 9.10 **Varying quality conformance tasks and responsibilities by process choice**

SELECT APPROACH TO MANAGING QUALITY

Once tasks and responsibilities are established, businesses must decide to take a reactive or proactive approach to managing quality:

- **Reactive approach** – services and products are checked during their delivery to see if they meet target conformance levels. If levels are not met, changes to the process are made.
- **Proactive approach** – delivery systems and processes are continually monitored and redesigned to ensure poor quality services or products are never delivered. This ensures minimal cost of rectification, scrap, returned products and repeating the delivery of services.

The reactive approach tends to occur in batch or line processes where the doing and evaluating tasks are separated. However, this can be overcome by challenging management structures, redefining roles and responsibilities and setting up improvement teams.

Combine quality assurance and quality control tasks

Just as companies separate doing and evaluating activities, they also separate responsibility for performing the quality assurance and quality control tasks. Quality assurance involves developing quality standards, establishing management structures, determining roles and responsibilities and setting up procedures to ensure that quality conformance target levels are met, whereas quality control is the role of ensuring that specifications are met. As when splitting doing and evaluating tasks, this separation of roles can induce in those responsible for providing the services or products a lack of responsibility, empowerment and motivation. To redress this, companies need to recombine assurance and control aspects and start to merge them with doing tasks. Challenging existing management structures, redefining roles and responsibilities and setting up improvement teams will help facilitate such changes.

Develop a quality-improvement culture

Businesses need to recombine quality assurance and control tasks and reintegrate them with doing activities. The Malcolm Baldrige National Quality Award found that, although respondents in Europe and the US identified quality as their number one competitive priority, they still kept the doing and evaluating activities separate from one another. Baldrige examiners (using the categories in Figure 9.11) found senior managers were committed to quality, but were

> surprised to find they come up short at the other end of the organizational chart. Many companies with high-profile reputations for quality have been told to do more to empower their employees as well as their upper ranks.[7]

Reallocating the task and responsibility for quality conformance and moving to a proactive approach leads to significant cost, customer and employee benefits. However, it will not happen overnight because cultures and traditions are difficult and slow to change. It is interesting that, while Western companies consider product quality as their number one competitive priority, Japanese respondents in the same survey of manufacturing features placed it fourth. They are apparently now looking at other priorities to give them a competitive edge. Unless radical changes are made, it seems that Western companies will always be playing 'catch up' with their Japanese counterparts.

INVENTORY

To enable delivery systems to work effectively they need to be kept stable and cushioned from the inherent instability and uncertainty that characterize markets and customer demand. Inventory is one mechanism used in this cushioning process. Other such mechanisms include order backlog, proactive capacity, forecasting, scheduling, process improvement, demand management and capacity management, as shown in Figure 9.12. (See Figure 8.21 and the accompanying narrative for more information on cushioning.)

Category	Points
Leadership	120
Strategic planning	85
Customer and market focus	85
Measurement, analysis and knowledge management	90
Workforce focus	85
Operations focus	85
Results: business/organizational focus	450
Total	1,000

Figure 9.11 Baldrige National Quality Award (points allocation by category, 2016)

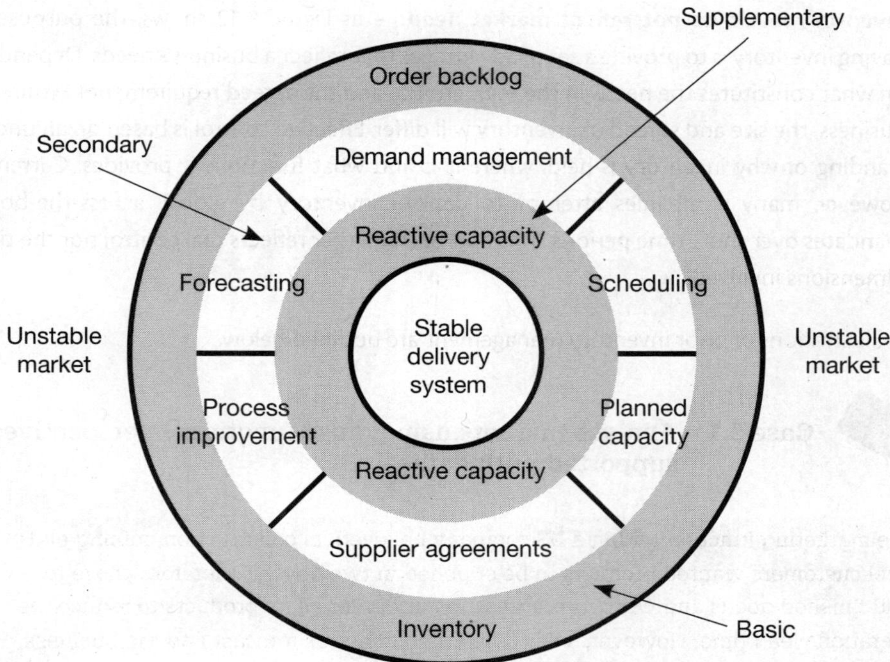

Figure 9.12 Three levels of mechanisms to cushion delivery systems from unstable markets

Issues with current management practices

Inventory accounts for 30–40 per cent of the total assets of many companies; in some (such as retailing) it can be considerably higher. However, while investment decisions such as those concerning systems developments and equipment are carefully monitored, the level of analysis and attention given to controlling levels of inventory is generally too little and too late. Issues with current inventory management practices include:

- **Uncontrolled increases** – day-to-day activities often increase inventory. These increases are not controlled or managed until after they have happened.
- **Infrequent stock counts** – many companies take few complete physical stock counts, often as little as twice a year to coincide with financial accounting periods.
- **Inaccurate stock counts** – as the stocktaking date approaches, companies often deliberately hold off purchases, bring forward deliveries and physically move existing inventory to other parts of the business to show a more favourable financial position.
- **Stocktaking is seen as a chore** – companies often regard stocktaking as a chore rather than an opportunity to collect valuable data, allowing it to be better managed.
- **Only analysed for accounting purposes** – inventory is usually analysed by its process stage such as raw material, work-in-progress or finished goods. This is to enable its value to be calculated as an input into drawing up profit and loss accounts and balance sheets. Thus, stocktakes are seen as a provider of accounting information rather than as data for controlling inventory.

- **Inventory levels do not reflect market needs** – as Figure 9.12 shows, the purpose of having inventory is to provide a set of advantages that reflect a business's needs. Depending on what constitutes the needs in the marketplace and the agreed requirements within the business, the size and spread of inventory will differ. Effective control is based on an understanding of why inventory is held, where it is and what functions it provides. Currently, however, many companies attempt to control inventory by global, across-the-board mandates over short time periods. This approach neither reflects real control nor the time dimensions involved.

Two illustrations of poor inventory management are outlined below.

Case 9.1 – Analyse markets using cross-functional perspectives supported with data

The marketing function within a US company believed its construction, mining and steel customers wanted products to be supplied in two days. It therefore chose to hold finished goods and work-in-progress inventory for all its products to reduce the operations lead time. However, sales failed to increase as forecast and the business was left with high levels of slow-moving inventory. An operations strategy review highlighted the inventory and questioned whether a two-day lead time was actually required by customers. In-depth customer discussions and analysis of the orders they placed on the business showed that less than 15 per cent of orders were required in two days. Inventory could therefore be reduced or eliminated for most products. This led to an inventory reduction of 46 per cent, releasing a significant amount of cash and reducing costs while maintaining market support.

Case 9.2 – Do not issue across-the-board inventory reduction directives

A company decided to reduce inventory by 15 to 20 per cent across all its business units. However, one business unit supplied optional features for vehicles to customers who wanted to minimize the time when these vehicles would be unavailable for use. To meet the short lead time requested by customers, operations held raw material and subassembly inventory so it could assemble the final product to order within two days. By reducing inventory it could not support this market and would therefore lose many of these high margin sales. After significant discussion, the corporate directive was eventually rescinded.

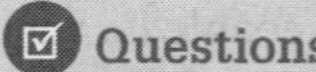

1 In what ways are the situations outlined in Cases 9.1 and 9.2 similar?
2 What key principles are illustrated by these two cases?

Categories and types of inventory

Inventory is used by different functions for a number of reasons. The categories and types of inventory include:

- **Corporate** – safety stock to guard against supply uncertainties such as national or international strikes.
- **Sales and marketing** – to meet demand uncertainty, customer agreement to hold minimum stocks on specified products or the launch of a new product.
- **Purchasing** – bulk buying to secure quantity discounts.
- **Operations** – decouple processes so they can be run independently from each other (decoupling), allow processes to produce different batch sizes (cycle), inventory due to a decision to outsource processes (pipeline), meet demand fluctuations (capacity related) or guard against demand or supply uncertainty (buffer).

Category	Type	Benefits
Corporate	Safety	Safeguards against supply uncertainties such as national or international strikes
Sales and marketing	Demand uncertainty	Ensures demand is met even if demand forecasts are inaccurate
	Customer agreement	Meets customer requirements such as holding safety stock on a customer site to ensure demand is met and lead times reduced
	Product launch	Allows demand spikes to be met when products are launched
Purchasing	Quantity discounts	Supports price when it is an order-winner by reducing material cost through bulk buying
Operations	Decoupling	Separates one process from the next so they can be run independently of each other and therefore be used more efficiently
	Cycle	Allows process to run different batch sizes/order quantities to reflect set-up times, customer order sizes and call-off patterns. Increasing production run lengths reduces set-up costs and increases capacity utilization
	Pipeline	Allows the company to outsource one or more processes and utilize capability and capacity not present in-house
	Capacity related	Meet anticipated future sales by making inventory in low sales periods and selling in the high sales periods. This stabilizes demand and increases capacity utilization
	Buffer	Protects against unpredictable changes in demand or supply to ensure service levels are maintained. Note that inventory levels above this requirement are 'corporate safety stocks'

Figure 9.13 Benefits of using inventory by category and type

Figure 9.13 shows the benefits of different inventory categories and types. When choosing to invest in inventory, businesses need to be aware of their reasons and the benefits they hope it will bring. They should also consider the alternatives available to them (see Figure 9.12) because different cushioning mechanisms may be more appropriate to meet certain conditions and requirements. Essentially, the main benefits of using inventory are:

- *Reduce raw material cost* – achieving quantity discounts by bulk buying products
- *Reduce operations cost* – by levelling schedules and increasing both capacity utilization and saleable productive time
- *Reduce operations lead time* – by eliminating material lead time or certain process stages
- *Improve delivery performance* – by buffering against demand and supply uncertainty
- *Meet high demand levels* – such as high seasonal demand or launching a new product
- *Meet customer-specific agreements* – for example holding consignment stock at a customer site.

Disadvantages of using inventory

While using inventory brings benefits, disadvantages are also involved:

- **Cash** – inventory ties up cash within a business that could be better invested in other areas such as equipment or systems.
- **Cost** – businesses also incur costs by holding and managing inventory such as space, storage, heating, monitoring, insurance and transporting.

Inventory is the most appropriate method to cushion delivery systems for certain businesses and markets. But, organizations may be better investing in one or more of the alternative mechanisms outlined in Figure 9.12 (and explained more fully in the accompanying narrative to Figure 8.21) as mechanisms are better suited to different order-winners and qualifiers, demand volumes, levels of uncertainty, and breadth of product range.

Managing inventory

To address the issues with current inventory management practices, companies need to change a number of aspects:

1. **Use inventory to support markets** – based on the market review outlined in Chapter 4, organizations can decide to use inventory to support markets. For example, bulk buying achieves quantity discounts and supports the order-winner of price while holding inventory at various stages in a delivery system reduces lead times and supports delivery speed requirements.
2. **Establish inventory targets and functional responsibilities** – once it is clear how inventory should be used to support markets then target holdings and functional responsibilities can be established. For example, purchasing with regard to bulk buying decisions, sales inventory due to actual demand not meeting sales forecasts or inventory increases due to an operations' decision to outsource processes. Targets and responsibilities must be continually reviewed as markets are always changing.

3 **Analyse and manage inventory by cause** – instead of analysing inventory by the stage in its process, businesses need to understand why inventory was created using the categories and types outlined in Figure 9.13. Once targets and responsibilities are established, inventory levels can be monitored and managed by cause rather than process stage. Knowing why inventory is present in a delivery system identifies the cause and allows adherence to existing rules or guidelines to be tightened or rules and guidelines to be changed.

Reducing inventory

Organizations find that factors such as past mismanagement of inventory or changes in demand often lead to excess inventory. Reducing this holding involves the following steps:

1 **Identify large inventory holdings** – this can take the form of a rough assessment of current inventory holdings rather than a detailed stocktake. From this, areas can be identified for a more detailed analysis of a stage in the process and by cause.

2 **Analyse process stage and cause of inventory** – determine the process the inventory has just left and the one it will go to next. Then identify why the inventory was present and determine its value (£s/€s/$s).

3 **Identify improvement areas** – a Pareto analysis will almost certainly show that 20 per cent of the inventory items account for about 80 per cent of its total value. Companies can then focus on reducing and effectively managing this 20 per cent while using simpler controls for the other low value items.

4 **Use other cushioning mechanisms** – businesses need to bear in mind that inventory has been created for a reason. If it decides to use one or more of the other cushioning mechanisms shown in Figure 9.12 then the consequence is that inventory can be reduced because market support is maintained by the other mechanism(s). When choosing between alternative approaches then the cost and cash implications of investing in other mechanisms must be compared to the benefit of reducing inventory. Improving operations is always a balance between reducing cost, releasing cash or improving market support, as shown in Figure 9.14.

5 **Change management rules and procedures** – when the position has been analysed and the decisions made, the final steps are to use up any excess inventory and then change the rules to stop excesses recurring.

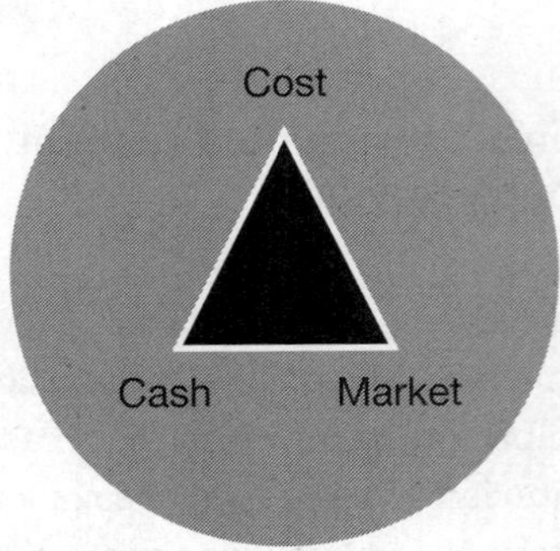

Figure 9.14 Balance between improving the cash, cost and market support of operations

SCHEDULING SYSTEMS

System investments can too often be driven by a panacea approach rather than considering how best to support the needs of the business and its markets. The high cost and fixed nature of these investments make them essential to securing short- and long-term prosperity and helping to support the dynamics of markets. It is essential, therefore, that investments in systems are made with an understanding of the business and its markets. Without this understanding, a company may find that these expensive and time-consuming investments fail to realize their full benefits. Three illustrations of inappropriate investments are now provided.

Case 9.3 – Computer system makes operations more expensive and less effective

A medium-sized US furniture company makes high-volume standard products using simple process technologies with few operations and little work-in-progress inventory. Customer lead times are short and met from finished goods inventory. Production is controlled with a central scheduling system, manual shop-floor controls, visual checks and verbal communications between departments. To improve equipment utilization, productivity and shop-floor order tracking, the company decided to install a computer-based shop-floor control system with automated order tracking, queue control and capacity planned features. The system cost about $0.75 million and was justified on increased sales from faster order fulfilment and tighter finished goods inventory management. However, it was subsequently found that the computer system neither made the process faster nor better controlled. It only increased paperwork, increased overheads and diverted supervisors away from key management tasks.

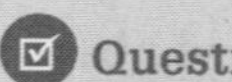

Questions

1. Analyse the original systems, controls, checks and methods of communicating between the different departments. Why did these procedures work?
2. Why do you think that the computer system the company installed did little to improve the work flow?

Case 9.4 – Systems not modified to meet changing business and market needs

A European telecommunications company developed its technology by moving from electromechanical to electronic-based products. The decision was made to outsource the manufacturing and assembly for the new electronic-based components. Previously, operations managed and controlled a wide range of complex internal processes with high work-in-progress inventory. Now it manages a range of suppliers with high component inventory. However, it did not modify its existing scheduling system to meet these significantly different business needs. The system was unable to manage and control the new operation, and this resulted in increased cost, poor delivery performance and lost market share.

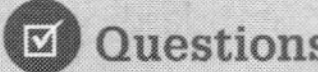

1 Explain the different control and scheduling tasks between making and assembling the range of electromechanical products and the task the company needs to manage for its electronic-based products
2 Why does the existing scheduling system fail to meet the different requirements?

Case 9.5 – One system used to support different market needs

A UK aerospace company manufactures a wide range of products at varying stages in their life cycles. It chose to invest in a comprehensive, standard computer-based system to manage and control all its products. Its varying product and customer requirements meant that the system was costly to develop and install and expensive to maintain. System development, installation and training cost $8 million and lasted for over two-and-a-half years. There were also high ongoing running and support costs. A review of the system after it was installed showed that it met the needs of its original equipment manufacturer (OEM) products, but not its spares business. Simpler master scheduling, materials planning and shop-floor controls would better support the spares business. There was no need for the order tracking, queue control and priority despatching features required by OEM products; 60 per cent of the development and installation investment cost was unnecessary.

 Question

1 Why did the system meet the scheduling needs of the OEM part but not the spares part of the business?

Selecting the appropriate planning and control system for a manufacturing company

As with all aspects of infrastructure, scheduling systems should be used as a support for the needs of the business and its markets. Based on the cross-functional market review outlined in Chapter 3, businesses must decide how to develop operations schedules, plan their materials and control shop-floor activities. Figures 9.15, 9.16 and 9.17 show alternative approaches for different markets and some of the key points are now discussed.

- **Make-to-order, assemble-to-order and make-to-stock operations scheduling** – a business will need to choose either one or a combination of these approaches to support its markets, as shown in Figure 9.15. The make-to-order approach suits markets with

Strategic variables			Master scheduling approach		
			Make-to-order	**Assemble-to-order**	**Make-to-stock**
Markets	Product	Type	Special	→	Standard
		Range	Wide	→	Narrow
	Individual product volume per period		Low	→	High
	Delivery	Speed	Difficult	→	Easy
		Reliability	Difficult	→	Easy
Operations	Process choice		Jobbing or low-volume batch	→	High-volume batch or line
	Managing volume and mix changes		Order backlog	Work-in-progress inventory	Finished goods inventory
	Meeting delivery speed requirements		Reschedule orders	Reduce process lead time	Eliminate process lead time

Figure 9.15 Linking the master scheduling approach to operations and market needs

low-volume, wide-ranging special products. Operations uses a jobbing or low-volume batch process, manages changes in sales volume and product mix with order backlog and reschedules orders to meet delivery speed requirements. By contrast, a make-to-stock approach suits high-volume, standard products with a narrow range. Operations uses a high-volume batch or line process and holds finished goods inventory to meet demand changes and delivery requirements. An assemble-to-order approach is used when market characteristics fall between these two extremes. Here, work-in-progress inventory is used to reduce the process lead time to enable demand changes and delivery requirements to be met.

- **Time-phased or rate-based materials planning** – time-phased planning suits low-volume, special products involving a wide range and using a jobbing or low-volume batch process, as shown in Figure 9.16. No inventory is held, order backlog is the basic cushioning mechanism used (see Figure 9.12) and operations' overheads are low because skilled operators plan and schedule activities themselves. The process is able to cope with product mix changes, but a long process lead time and the use of order backlog to help manage demand and capacity imbalances mean delivery speed and schedule changes are difficult to meet. By contrast, a rate-based approach suits a narrow range of high-volume, standard products that are made using high-volume batch or line processes. Operational activities have been automated and deskilled to reduce labour cost, but this means the system is less able to cope with product mix changes. Overheads are a higher cost percentage and finished goods are used to meet delivery requirements and handle schedule changes.
- **Push or pull shop-floor control** – in markets with high-volume, standard products, orders can be pulled through the shop floor using Kanban systems to control material flows

Strategic variables			Material planning approach	
			Time-phased	**Rate-based**
Markets	Product	Type	Special	Standard
		Range	Wide	Narrow
	Individual product volume per period		Low	High
	Ability to cope with product mix changes		High	Limited
	Delivery	Speed	Difficult	Easy
		Schedule changes	Difficult	Easy
Operations	Process choice		Jobbing or low-volume batch	High-volume batch or line
	Cost reduction sources	Overheads	No	Yes
		Inventory	No	Yes

Figure 9.16 Linking materials planning approach to operations and market needs

and finished goods to meet delivery requirements, as shown in Figure 9.17. By contrast, low-volume specials are made by skilled operators who control the flow of orders as they are pushed through the shop floor. This is a complex task with typically high changeover costs between jobs, but demand increases are more incremental and easier to meet.

Strategic variables			Shop-floor control approach	
			Push	**Pull**
Markets	Product	Type	Special	Standard
		Range	Wide	Narrow
	Individual product volume per period		Low	High
	Demand variability	Volume	Easy Incremental	Difficult Stepped
		Product mix	High	Low
	Delivery	Speed	Schedule change	Finished goods inventory
		Schedule changes	More difficult	Less difficult
Operations	Process choice		Jobbing or low-volume batch	High-volume batch or line
	Cost reduction sources	Overheads	No	Yes
		Inventory	No	Yes
	Changeover cost		High	Low
	Control	Key feature	Order status	Flow of materials
		Basis	Person or system	System
		Ease of task	Complex	Easy

Figure 9.17 Linking shop-floor control systems to operations and market needs

Good practice examples

Figure 9.18 shows examples of how planning and control systems can be used to support markets with different needs. Company A supplies a wide range of customized low-volume products where orders are won on product design and delivery speed while using raw material and work-in-progress inventory to reduce the process lead time. Products are made on low-volume batch processes with high precision work undertaken by skilled operators. The key operations tasks are meeting high product design specifications, controlling high labour costs and reducing long process lead times. It uses make-to-order and assemble-to-order approaches to schedule production, although the long process lead time means that work often starts before orders have been confirmed. Material is planned using a time-phased approach against known or anticipated orders. Extra material is ordered to cover scrapped items and some raw material and work-in-progress inventory is held to reduce the operations' lead time. Orders are pushed through the shop floor using skilled operators to manage delivery priorities. The company is very successful because all aspects of its planning and control system are aligned to its markets.

By contrast, Company B competes on price and delivery speed for a narrow range of high-volume standard products. It uses a high-volume batch process and holds finished goods inventory at its distributors to meet seasonal demand profiles and short customer lead times. The process is automated, has short set-up times and manufactures small batch sizes. Because price is a key order-winner, operations continually reduce material, overhead and inventory costs. To fully utilize resources, products are made to stock using a fixed three-month production plan and capacity is finitely planned. Materials are planned using a rate-based approach against forecasts. Orders are pulled through the shop floor using a Kanban and JIT approach to minimize raw material and work-in-progress inventory. This planning and control system successfully meets its price and delivery speed market requirements.

Aspect		Company	
		A	B
Market	Characteristics	• Low-volume products • Customized products • Wide product range • Short product life • Customers give demand forecast and then call off order against it	• High-volume products • Standard products • Narrow product range • Seasonal demand • High level of new product introduction • Changing product mix
	Order-winners	• Product design • Delivery speed	• Price • Delivery speed
	Qualifiers	• Delivery reliability • Quality conformance • Price	• Quality conformance • Delivery reliability • Product design

<table>
<tr><td rowspan="6">Operations strategy</td><td rowspan="2">Operations</td><td>Features</td><td>• Low-volume batch process
• Long process lead time
• Use raw material and work-in-progress inventory to reduce process lead time
• High precision work
• High labour cost (60 per cent total)
• Uncertain process and product</td><td>• High-volume batch process
• Short set-up times
• Small batch sizes
• Use finished goods inventory held at distributors to meet demand changes
• Low-cost manufacturing
• Low labour cost
• High material cost</td></tr>
<tr><td>Task</td><td>• Meet product design and quality specification
• Reduce process lead time
• Control labour cost
• Deliver on time</td><td>• Reduce material and overhead costs
• Manage finished goods inventory
• Reduce raw material and work-in-progress inventory</td></tr>
<tr><td rowspan="4">Planning and control system</td><td>Master production scheduling</td><td>• Make to order and assemble to order
• Manufacture to known and forecast customer orders
• Rough cut capacity planning due to long process lead time</td><td>• Make to stock
• Manufacture to forecast customer orders
• Fixed three-month production plan
• Finite capacity planning</td></tr>
<tr><td>Material planning</td><td>• Time phased
• Material purchased or manufactured for known and forecast orders
• High product obsolescence risk
• Extra material ordered to cover scrapped items
• Raw material inventory held to reduce operations lead time</td><td>• Rate based
• Material purchased or manufactured against forecast
• Finished goods inventory held to eliminate operations lead time and meet seasonal demand</td></tr>
<tr><td>Shop-floor control</td><td>• Push system
• Skilled operators schedule and track orders
• Despatch and production control staff liaise between customer and operators to manage delivery priorities
• Capacity planned by work centre</td><td>• Pull system
• Kanban system
• Just-in-time material flow
• Low raw material, component and work-in-progress inventory</td></tr>
</table>

Figure 9.18 The relevant operations tasks and operations planning and control system investments of two companies serving different markets

Question

Consider these two examples and explain how the scheduling systems meet the needs of the different businesses and their markets.

Infrastructure comprises a complex set of interacting activities that need to fulfil the day-to-day tasks they are designed to provide while being aligned to the company's delivery systems and markets. Because organizations often split their support activities into specialist areas, they are in danger of creating functional silos where, unless there is a full and comprehensive discussion about the needs of the business and its markets, the result may well be unconnected, uncoordinated, functionally biased and reactive developments. Furthermore, such approaches lead to situations where many organizations support delivery systems from a distance, reduce line roles and responsibilities, pay and reward inappropriately and create too many management layers. To realign infrastructure to markets, businesses need to redefine functional objectives based on a cross-functional market review supported by data. Using these objectives, businesses must challenge existing management structures, redefine roles and responsibilities, pay and reward employees based on the importance and contribution of tasks to business success, reduce overheads and flatten management structures. Business developments must be made on an ongoing basis by cross-functional teams monitoring market needs, identifying improvement areas, comparing investment alternatives and developing infrastructure. Step changes should be avoided because they are costly, disruptive, difficult to get right and difficult to change once made.

PANACEAS DON'T WORK

Generic strategic solutions assume that businesses have similar characteristics and support markets with similar needs. This is not so. Organizations have to develop their own solution that is based on their own business and market requirements. The Toyota Production System (TPS) is an example of how to do this. It successfully manages the three major phases in Toyota's business – the before phase (its suppliers), the owned phase (its own processes) and the forward phase (the sale of cars through its networks). It stabilizes the before and owned phases by holding finished goods inventory in the forward phase of its business. This cushions operations from the market and allows Toyota to reduce raw material and work-in-progress in its own processes and those of its suppliers. This releases cash that can be invested elsewhere in the business and reduces operating costs, so increasing profits.

To achieve this, TPS recombined planning and evaluating with doing activities and empowered operators to identify and make improvements. As improvements were made, processes were simplified, as was the infrastructure used to manage them. Visual controls and Kanbans replaced computer-based systems, making it easier for operators to plan and evaluate activities. There were significant cash, cost, quality conformance, delivery and product design improvements and markets were better supported. The ongoing incremental nature of these developments means they are more efficient, effective and sustainable than a stepped approach to securing change. Many companies trying to imitate this approach do not appreciate how developments have been made and why they are successful.

DEVELOPMENTS MUST BE BASED ON A CLEAR STRATEGY

A clear operations strategy enables infrastructure to be developed from a common base and in a common direction to meet a common requirement. Historical and personal views fall by the wayside and are replaced by clear strategic thinking. This ensures that current and future business and market needs are met. Without a strategy-based approach, developments are based on personal judgements, fixed ideas and specialist arguments about what they can provide rather than what the market requires.

BUSINESSES MUST CHALLENGE EXISTING APPROACHES

Businesses must challenge their organizational structures and redefine roles, responsibilities, authorities, specialist functions and all other aspects of infrastructure. Konsuke Matsushita summed this up in a speech he made to a group of Western managers in 1985, challenging them to rethink existing approaches. An extract from that speech is presented in Case 9.6.[8] While some organizations have made changes and improvements since the 1980s, others are still far behind. One thing is certain – to be successful in the future, companies must adapt to markets and effectively use all their resources.

Case 9.6 – Konsuke Matsushita on why the West will lose

"We are going to win and the industrial West is going to lose: there is nothing much you can do about it, because the reasons for your failure are within yourselves.

Your firms are built on the Taylor model; even worse, so are your heads. With your bosses doing the thinking, while the workers wield the screwdrivers, you are convinced deep down that this is the right way to run a business. For you, the essence of management is getting the ideas out of the heads of the bosses into the hands of labour.

We are beyond the Taylor model: business, we know, is now so complex and difficult, the survival of firms so hazardous in an environment increasingly unpredictable, competitive, and fraught with danger that their continued existence depends on the day-to-day mobilization of every ounce of intelligence.

For us, the core of management is precisely this art of mobilizing and pulling together the intellectual resources of all employees in the service of the firm. Because we have measured better than you the scope of the new technological and economic challenges, we know that the intelligence of a handful of technocrats, however brilliant and smart they may be, is no longer enough for a real chance of success. Only by drawing on the combined brainpower of all its employees can a firm face up to the turbulence and constraints of today's environment.

This is why our large companies give their employees three to four times more training than yours; this is why they foster within the firm such intensive exchange and communication; this is why they seek constantly everybody's suggestions and why they demand from the educational system increasing numbers of graduates as well as bright and well-educated generalists, because these people are the lifeblood of industry.

Your 'socially minded bosses', often full of good intentions, believe their duty is to protect the people in their firms. We, on the other hand, are realists and consider it our duty to get our own people to defend their firms, which will pay them back a hundredfold for their dedication. By doing this, we end up by being more 'social' than you."

CASE STUDY

Riviona Bank

'We're all very proud of our success over the last ten years, but we need to keep this up!' explained Michael Jones (Chief Executive) to his Executive Board. 'To continue to survive we need to grow sales by another 63 per cent over the next three years [see Case Figure 9.1] without taking on any more staff. I know this is a big challenge, but I think we've got the right team in place and the recent changes in Customer Services should help us do this.'

PRODUCTS AND MARKETS

'Working with a marketing consultant, we've identified ten segments to grow', explained Jim White (Sales and Marketing Director). 'Case Figure 9.2 shows how they fall into four groups, the percentage of the UK customers in each segment and how we plan to increase sales.'

'Whilst Case Figure 9.3 shows the number of savings customers we have and how

€billion	Year end							
	−4	−3	−2	−1	0	1	2	3
Mortgages	–	7.1	10.9	10.6	13.9	18.8	23.1	27.4
Savings	3.4	8.2	9.2	9.8	10.2	10.3	11.2	11.9
Total	3.4	15.2	20.1	20.4	24.1	29.1	34.3	39.3

Note: Current year is Year 0.

Case Figure 9.1 Historical and forecasted book value

Segments	% UK market	Growth strategy
Money worth managing		
Serious wealth	0.9	Attract more customers
Owners/investors	1.2	Sell more products to existing customers
High salary	0.7	Attract more customers
Small time borrowing		
Aspiring mid-market	7.2	Sell more products to existing customers
Wives on a budget	6.7	Attract more customers
Prospering flatmates	4.8	Attract more customers
Equity accumulation		
Nesting mothers	4.8	Attract more customers
Women flying high	1.8	Attract more customers
Men behaving well	3.2	Sell more products to existing customers
Urban enterprise	3.2	Sell more products to existing customers

Note: All financial products can be sold within all these segments.

Case Figure 9.2 Ten growth market segments

Savings products	Number of customers		
	Savings	With mortgage	
		Offset	Other
Personal			
One product			
Direct	240,165	335	7,212
Notice	46,538	23	687
Bond	2,106	–	4
ISA	11,447	24	335
Two products			
Direct & Notice	32,490	48	812
Direct & Bond	2,086	1	20
Direct & ISA	15,272	34	812
Notice & Bond	95	1	7
Notice & ISA	2,529	3	50
Bond & ISA	44	–	–
Three products			
Direct, Notice & Bond	857	3	9
Direct, Notice & ISA	4,109	13	155
Direct, Bond & ISA	244	–	3
Notice, Bond & ISA	79	–	3
Four products	165	–	7
Direct, Notice, Bond & ISA			
Business			
One product			
Direct	37,144	–	–
Notice	9,547		
Bond	355		
Two products			
Direct & Notice	3,084	–	–
Direct & Bond	459		
Notice & Bond	412		
Three products	256	–	–
Direct, Notice & Bond			

Notes

1 'Direct' savings can be withdrawn without notice.

2 'Notice' savings require 30-days' notice before withdrawal.

3 'Bond' is a savings bond.

4 ISAs and mortgages are not sold to business customers.

5 'Offset' customers only pay interest on the balance of their savings and mortgage.

Case Figure 9.3 Current savings and mortgage customers

many products they currently buy from us. We currently only sell discounted and fixed mortgages, but there are plenty more products that we could offer customers (see Case Figure 9.4) through different channels (see Case Figure 9.5).'

CUSTOMER SERVICE

'Customer Service manages all the phone, internet and written contact with our customers', explained Jane Gillanders (Customer Service Director). 'This requires managing four main activities (as shown in

Product by lender	Sold last year			
	Jan	Apr	Jul	Oct
UK total				
Discount	71,175	62,481	71,630	58,277
Fixed	38,351	37,376	38,783	45,892
Tracker	30,460	30,326	30,144	28,232
Premium	22,420	25,150	22,452	23,778
Standard	11,234	10,257	10,578	14,174
Capped	2,447	2,217	1,890	1,436
Other	41,812	38,180	41,446	46,734
Riviona Bank				
Discount	1,775	2,187	2,841	3,668
Fixed	613	554	537	454
Other	168	486	53	166

Note: The current average UK mortgage s €150,000

Case Figure 9.4 Mortgage products sold last year

Channel	Monthly sales	
	Volume	€000s
Mortgage		
Introduced		
Independent Financial Advisor	1,981	215,803
Mortgage Intermediary	516	56,642
Estate Agent	82	8,416
Other	53	3,980
Direct	317	450
Savings		
Introduced	1,495	2,123
Direct	1,913	2,716

Case Figure 9.5 Typical monthly sales by channel

Case Figure 9.6) so that we meet our objectives, targets and customer demand whilst also supporting any marketing initiatives we are running at that time (see Case Figure 9.7). Most of our processes are currently paper-based, which isn't very efficient. We're planning to move to an electronic document management system in the next couple of years, but we need to re-engineer our processes first so we don't simply automate our current inefficient processes. Staff find these changes very unsettling so we always have to keep explaining why we're making the changes, what this will involve and where we're at on our journey. Some people think we've changed too many things in the last

Activity	Description
Mortgage sales	Make outbound calls selling mortgages and receive inbound calls from new customers
Mortgage new business	Receive new mortgage applications (by mail, phone, email or through the website), make agreement in principle (AIP), confirm this in writing, complete financial checks, coordinate third-party property valuations, send formal offer and release funds. This usually takes 35 days, with a formal offer given after 20 days
Mortgage servicing	Servicing existing mortgages by amending customer details, managing overpayments, deferring repayments (for some products) or rerunning financial checks
Savings new business	Receive new savings applications, complete simple financial checks and set up account on the computer system
Savings servicing	Amend customer details and manage customer deposits and withdrawals

Case Figure 9.6 Key customer service activities

Issue	Description
Meet objectives and targets	Service (85 per cent of calls answered in 15 seconds, <3 per cent of calls abandoned, 90 per cent of written mortgage AIP in 1 day if all information is available and 90 per cent in 5 days if not), cost and sales targets
Meet demand	Forecasting demand and ensuring that there is sufficient resource to meet it while also controlling costs
Support marketing initiatives	Provide sufficient resource to meet the demand created by marketing initiatives
Improve efficiency	Plan to introduce an electronic document management system as most processes are still paper-based, for example mortgage applications, house valuations and customer communications
Manage people	Explain why roles are becoming more cross-functional and sales based, the changes required and where we are on the journey

Case Figure 9.7 Current customer service challenges

couple of years, but we'll fall behind our competitors if we don't keep moving forward.'

BEFORE THE RESTRUCTURE

'Prior to the restructure earlier this year', Jane explained, 'the Call Centre handled all phone and internet customer contact and processed simple applications and servicing requests (see Case Figure 9.8). More complex mortgage activities were then handled by the Mortgage New Business team who managed third-party activities, made formal offers, released funds and managed other written customer contact. However most savings activities were relatively simple and were handled by the Call Centre.'

'This approach had several advantages. For example, demand fluctuations for each product could be managed across the Call Centre, call lengths were easier to forecast

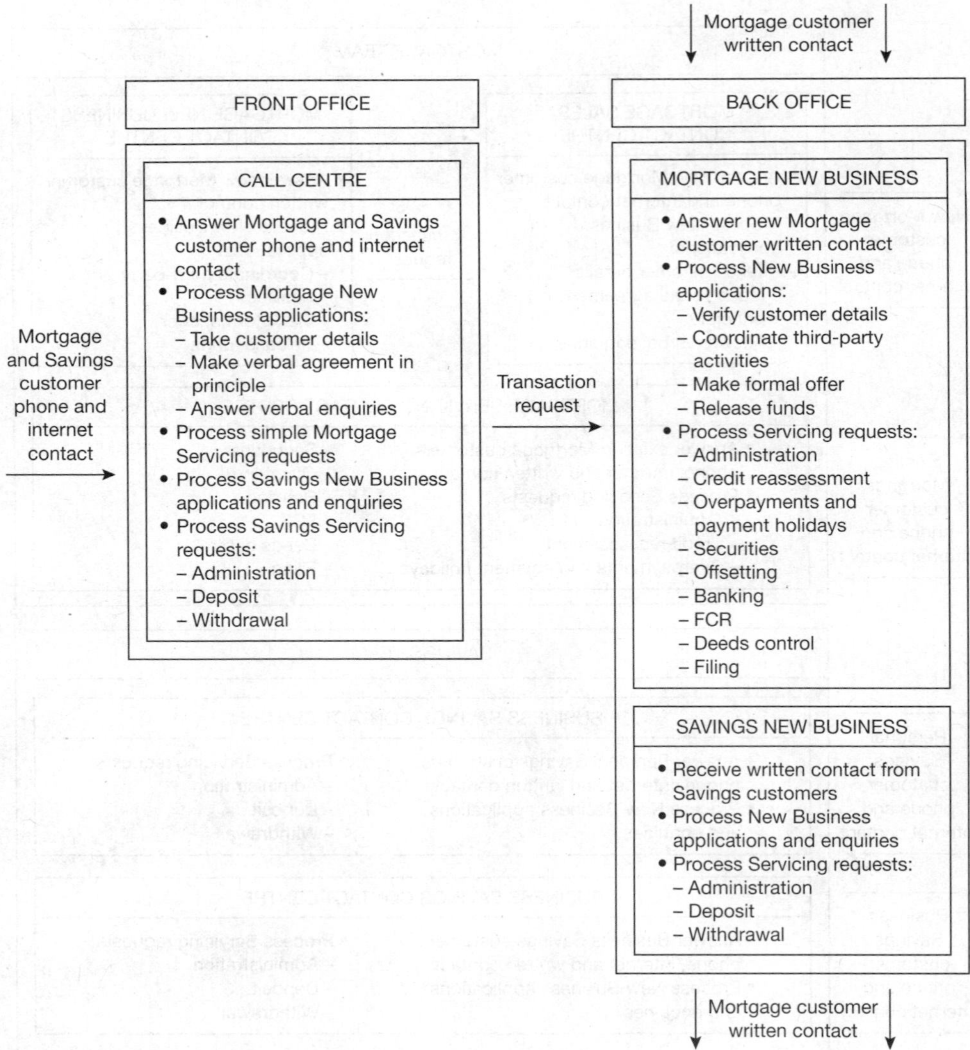

Case Figure 9.8 Before the restructure

because they were similar and could be handled by lower-skilled staff. However, there were lots of handoffs between the different teams, many customer requests were delayed when they were transferred, it was difficult to move staff between the different teams and people only saw their part of the process and didn't understand how it impacted the customer.'

AFTER THE RESTRUCTURE

'Earlier this year,' Jane explained, 'we set up Contact Centres where each team completes all the activities necessary to process a customer request (see Case Figure 9.9). Within Mortgage New Business, Personal Savings and Business Savings, there are smaller teams who manage a group of

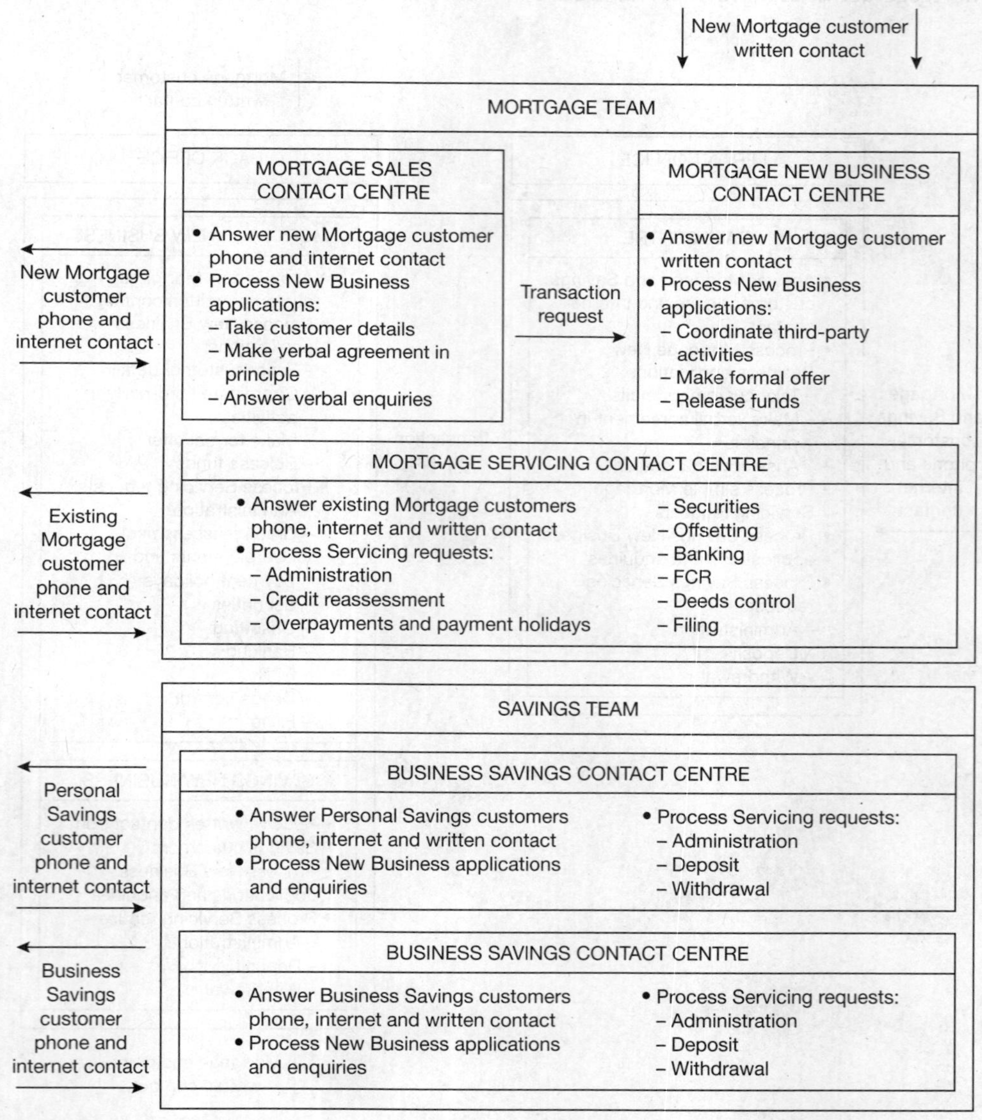

Note: Twilight Contact Centre covers both the Mortgage and Savings teams Monday to Friday from 5pm to 10pm.

Case Figure 9.9 After the restructure

customers categorized by the first letter of their surname (A to F, G to O or P to Z), whereas within the Mortgage Servicing Contact Centre, staff are split into customer accounts, securities and banking deed teams. To do this, we had to relocate most of the staff so each team could sit together and we're starting the long process of cross-training everyone to create the right flexibility in each team. Once this is done, we're hoping teams will become more productive and flexible so we can meet our service, cost and sales targets (see Case Figure 9.10).'

THE FUTURE

'Meeting our targets over the next four years is going to be a real challenge, but I think we've got the right strategy in place to do this', reflected Michael Jones. 'The question is can we bed down the changes we've already made whilst also moving the business forward? We can't afford to stay still for too long or our competitors will overtake us.'

QUESTIONS

1 Are Riviona's corporate objectives realistic?

2 What are the implications for Customer Service?

3 What are the advantages and disadvantages of the recent Customer Service restructure?

Aspect	Description
Increased productivity	Reduced double handling (between teams), less idle time as agents complete back office tasks when calls are low and understand whole process so can start improving it
Increased flexibility	Across tasks within each Contact Centre
Improved service	Improved speed of answering calls, written AIPs and less abandoned calls
Easier to train staff	Easier to identify needs and tailor training to each individual or team
Increased sales	All staff have customer contact, better understand their needs and should be able to cross-sell them other products while serving them

Case Figure 9.10 Rationale for restructure

DISCUSSION QUESTIONS

1 Whereas changes to existing or the introduction of new service delivery systems and/or manufacturing processes are readily recognized as necessary, infrastructure changes more often appear questionable and overstated, both in terms of levels of investment and the timescales involved. Discuss.

2 Businesses can make infrastructure developments that are either incremental or stepped in nature. Explain the advantages and disadvantages of these alternative approaches using examples other than those described in this chapter.

3 Outline the advantages and disadvantages of using inventory within a business. Give examples other than those described in this chapter.

4 Outline the three levels of mechanisms that can be used to cushion delivery systems from unstable markets. How can the different mechanisms be used? Give examples to illustrate your points.

5 'Cross-functional teams must be empowered to identify improvement areas with high return, compare alternative developments and make incremental changes.' Explain this statement using examples other than those described in this chapter.

6 Give four examples of corporate inventory. Each example needs to be the responsibility of a different function. Explain the purpose and benefits of your examples and how you would monitor and control this investment.

NOTES AND REFERENCES

1 The expression '0–100 management' was developed to highlight the pendulum-like response to problems/solutions or advantages/ disadvantages that typifies many executives and/or organizations. Instead of one extreme or another they need to reposition their response/position on a gradual and continuous basis.

2 Stewart, M. (2009) 'Masters of illusion', *The Independent*, 16 September.

3 Peters, T.J. and Waterman, R.H. Jr (1982) *In Search of Excellence: Lessons from America's Best-run Companies*, Harper & Row.

4 A key feature of quality circles is that those involved not only implement their ideas but also evaluate the gains they yield.

5 Stoffman, D. (1998) 'Less is more', *Business Magazine*: 97–8.

6 Andersen Consulting (1990) 'The Lean Enterprise Benchmark Project', Cardiff Business School/University of Cambridge.

7 Burrows, P. (1990) 'Five lessons you learn from (Baldrige) Award entrants', *Electronic Business*, 15 October, pp. 22–4.

8 Matsushita, K. (1985) 'Why the West will lose', Extracts from remarks made by Mr Konsu Matsushita of the Matsushita Electrical Industrial Company to a group of Western managers, Industrial Participation, Spring, p. 8.

EXPLORING FURTHER

Barber, F. and Strack, R. (2005) 'The surprising economics of a people business', *Harvard Business Review*, 83(6): 80–90.

Berry, W.L. and Hill, T.J. (1992) 'Linking systems to strategy', *International Journal of Operations & Production Management*, 12(10): 3–15.

Bryan, L.L. (2007) 'The new metrics of corporate performance: profit per employee', *McKinsey Quarterly*, 1: 57–65.

Burrows, P. (1990) 'Five lessons you learn from (Baldrige) Award entrants', *Electronic Business*, 15 October: 22–4.

Carr, L.P. (1992) 'Applying cost of quality to a service business', *Sloan Management Review*, 33(4): 72–8.

Cobb, J.C., Samuels, C.J. and Sexton, M.W. (1998) 'Alignment and strategic change: a challenge for marketing and human resources', *Leadership & Organization Development Journal*, 19(1): 32–43.

Hammer, M. and Champy, J. (1993) *Reengineering the Corporation: A Manifesto for Business Revolution*, Harper Business.

Hayes, R.H. and Wheelwright, S.C. (1984) *Restoring Our Competitive Edge: Competing through Manufacturing*, John Wiley & Sons.

Hill, A. and Brown, S. (2007) 'Strategic profiling: a visual representation of internal strategic fit in service organisations', *International Journal of Operations & Production Management*, 27(12): 1333–61.

Hill, T.J. (1998) *The Strategy Quest*, AMD Publishing.

Hughes, M., Hughes, P. and Morgan, R.E. (2007) 'Exploitative learning and entrepreneurial orientation alignment in emerging young firms: implications for market and response performance', *British Journal of Management*, 18(4): 359–75.

Hyland, P.W., Mellor, R. and Sloan, T. (2007) 'Performance measurement and continuous improvement: are they linked to manufacturing strategy?', *International Journal of Technology Management*, 37(3/4): 237–53.

Kaplan, R.S. and Norton, D.P. (2004) 'Measuring the strategic readiness of intangible assets', *Harvard Business Review*, February: 52–63.

Kaplan, R.S. and Norton, D.P. (2007) 'Using the balanced scorecard as a strategic management system', *Harvard Business Review*, July–August: 150–61.

Leisen, B., Lilly, B. and Winsor, R.D. (2002) 'The effects of organisational culture and market orientation on the effectiveness of strategic marketing alliances', *Journal of Services Marketing*, 16(3): 201–22.

Morris, D.C. and Brandon, J.S. (1993) *Re-engineering your Business*, McGraw-Hill.

Obeng, E. and Crainer, S. (1994) *Making Re-engineering Happen*, Pitman.

Olsen, E.O., Zhout, H., Lee, D.M.S. et al. (2007) 'Performance measurement systems and relationships with performance results: a case analysis of a continuous improvement approach to PMS design', *International Journal of Productivity and Performance Management*, 56(7): 559–73.

Rayner, B.C.P. (1990) 'Market-driven quality: IBM's Six Sigma crusade', *Electronics Business*, 15 October: 26–30.

Roy, R., Souchoronkov, P. and Griggs, T. (2008) 'Function-based cost estimating', *International Journal of Production Research*, 46(10): 250–62.

Senju, S. (ed.) (1992) *TQC and TQM*, Asian Productivity Organization.

Stahl, M.J. and Bounds, G.M. (1991) *Competing Globally through Customer Value*, Quorum Books.

Ulrich, D. and Smallwood, N. (2004) 'Capitalizing on capabilities', *Harvard Business Review*, June: 119–27.

Ulrich, D. and Smallwood, N. (2005) 'HR's new ROI: return on intangibles', *Human Resource Management*, 44(2): 137–42.

10 DEVELOPING A BUSINESS CASE

THIS CHAPTER DISCUSSES...

SUMMARY

- No matter how good your strategy, you still need to convince decision makers, supporters or influencers to give you resources and support or take action. A good business case is critical for doing this.
- First you must understand how strong your organization is and the opportunities or threats it faces by comparing its performance over time with competitors, other organizations with whom your customers interface and companies using a similar strategy to yours in another industry.
- Business model innovations have the most impact. You need to work out how to change your cost or revenue structure by investing differently or working with your customers/suppliers in a different way.
- It is often easier to remove a problem than try to fix it. For example, can you get customers to serve themselves rather than trying to improve how you serve them?
- Consider the costs, benefits and risks of all potential investment options before pitching to investors. They will want to pick from a number of options, and yet know which one you support.
- Tell a story that engages your investors, one that is simple enough for them to remember and that they can tell to other people. They will ask themselves: Why am I here? What do you want from me? Does the return justify the investment? How did you get to your numbers? Do I believe in the idea? Do I believe in you?

INTRODUCTION

No matter how good your strategy, you still need to convince decision makers, supporters or influencers to give you resources, support or take action. A good business plan is critical for doing this. The first step is understanding how your recent performance compares with your objectives, competitors and organizations competing in other industries to understand the health of your company and the opportunities or threats it faces. Then identify alternative investments that are necessary to sustain or improve your performance. You must ascertain and understand the expected cost, benefit and risk of these different options before you can explain why you chose one, what you want from your investors, what they will get in return and the risks involved. Once you know which investments you want to make, then you can start to develop your proposal by thinking about what you want to happen, who the audience is and what they will ask. You might need to develop different proposals for different audiences depending on the story you want to tell them and what you want them to do after they have read or heard it. You then need to present your story in a form that engages your audience, convinces them to do something and is simple enough for them to remember so they can tell it to other people. Finally, you need to track the costs and benefits of the investments you make so you can manage risk, adapt your ideas and share your learning with other people. This chapter helps you work out how to do this by explaining the points you need to consider at each stage and showing examples of approaches taken by other organizations.

UNDERSTANDING CURRENT PERFORMANCE

To understand why an investment should be made and the impact it could have, you first need to determine what the organization is trying to do (its objectives), key stakeholder requirements it has to meet, how it currently performs and any opportunities or threats it faces. Analyses to help you do this are now discussed.

CORPORATE OBJECTIVES

The first step is to show what the organization is trying to do. For example:

- **Sales growth** – do you want to increase revenue in existing markets? Or move into new ones?
- **Survival** – are you simply trying to survive?
- **Profit** – do you want to increase profits of existing services and products? Or develop new, more profitable ones?
- **Return on investment** – what return on debt and equity do investors require?
- **Inventory turns** – how often do inventory levels need to 'turn' so cash does not get tied up?
- **Debtor (or Accounts Receivable) levels** – how quickly are invoices paid to ensure cash flows through the business?
- **Environmental targets** – do you want to reduce your environmental footprint? Do you have a corporate social responsibility programme?
- **Social targets** – do you want to improve your impact on society? Examples include improving customer safety, staff safety, fair employment policies within the supply chain, fair pricing and non-exploitation of developing countries.

STAKEHOLDER REQUIREMENTS

Next you need to show the requirements of different stakeholders and how your investments will help to better meet them. To do this, you need to:

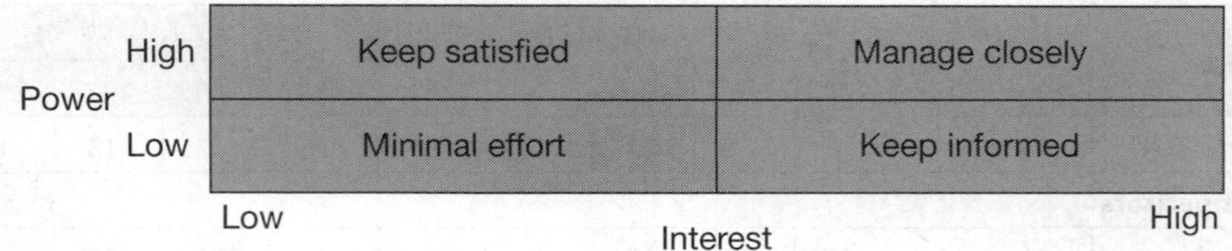

Figure 10.1 Mapping stakeholder power and interest

1 **Identify key stakeholders** – typically your owners/shareholders, employees, suppliers, customers and the societies in which you operate. However, there may be others to consider as well, such as governments and legal or environmental bodies.
2 **Identify stakeholders' power and influence** over the decisions you have made and map them onto the power and interest matrix shown in Figure 10.1 where:

   – **Power** – is the ability of individuals or groups to persuade, induce or coerce others to follow a certain course of action.
   – **Interest** – shows how much each group wants to impress its views and expectations on your organization's purpose and the choices it makes.

3 **Identify needs and requirements** – it is important to look for potential areas of conflict. For example, shareholders may want short-term financial performance whereas employees are more concerned about the organization's long-term social and environmental impact.
4 **Show impact** – how does meeting stakeholders' needs affect your revenue or income? For example, do they provide funds (or other resources), buy services/products or can they prevent others from doing this?

BUSINESS HEALTH

It is necessary to understand the organization's financial health and which investments can sustain and/or improve this. It is useful to check various performance trends relative to competitors and other external benchmarks such as sales revenue, sales volume, operating profit, operating costs and customer satisfaction scores. Good questions to ask are: What is going on in the market? How is the business performing relative to competitors and other external benchmarks? Have any significant changes occurred? What threats or opportunities have these created? Example analyses are now discussed using data from Southwest Airlines. (This information comes from a case study in Hill, A. and Hill, T. (2012) *Operations Management*, 3rd edn, Palgrave Macmillan.)

Sales revenue trends

Are sales increasing or decreasing? How does this vary by market segment relative to competitors? Useful analyses include:

- **Sales revenue trend** – Figure 10.2 shows that Southwest has the fourth largest sales revenue (out of five airlines) in its market.

Airline	Sales revenue ($billion)										
	1999	**2001**	**2003**	**2005**	**2007**	**2009**	**2010**	**2011**	**2012**	**2013**	**2014**
Southwest	5	6	6	8	10	10	12	16	17	18	19
Competitors											
American	16	16	17	21	17	20	22	24	25	26	43
Delta	15	13	14	16	15	28	32	35	37	38	40
United	18	16	15	17	20	16	34	37	37	38	39
Alaska	2	2	2	2	3	3	4	4	5	5	5
US Airways	9	8	7	7	7	11	12	13	14	15	–
Continental	8	8	7	11	11	13	–	–	–	–	–
Northwest	10	10	9	12	10	–	–	–	–	–	–
America West	2	2	2	3	3	–	–	–	–	–	–
Competitor average	**10**	**9**	**9**	**11**	**11**	**15**	**21**	**23**	**24**	**24**	**32**

Notes

1 Delta merged with Northwest in 2008.

2 United merged with Continental in 2010.

3 Southwest merged with AirTran in 2010.

4 American merged with US Airways in 2013.

Figure 10.2 Southwest Airlines' sales revenue compared with its major competitors (1999–2014)

- **Market share (percentage of sales revenue) trend** – Figure 10.3 shows how, although Southwest's market share has increased from 6 to 13 per cent over the previous 15 years, it is still smaller than its competitors.
- **Sales revenue relative to competitors** – Figure 10.4 compares all the airlines' sales with Southwest's performance in 1999. This shows that Southwest's growth is greater than its competitors' and has been achieved organically rather than through acquisition. However, it does raise concerns about Southwest's ability to compete in the future as its competitors become larger and stronger.

Sales volume trends

Are sales volumes increasing or decreasing? How does this vary by market segment relative to competitors? Useful analyses include:

- **Sales volume trend** – Figure 10.5 shows that, although Southwest's volume has increased more than the overall market in the last five years (35 versus 28 per cent), it has decreased relative to its competitors. It was the second largest airline in 2009, but in 2014 it is the second smallest (fourth out of five).
- **Sales volume market share against competitors** – Figure 10.6 shows that Southwest's market share doubled between 1999 and 2007, but remained constant for the next seven years.

Airline	Market share (% sales revenue)										
	1999	2001	2003	2005	2007	2009	2010	2011	2012	2013	2014
Southwest	6	7	7	8	10	10	10	12	13	13	13
Competitors											
American	19	20	22	21	23	20	19	19	18	19	29
United	21	20	19	18	20	16	29	29	28	27	27
Delta	18	16	18	16	15	28	27	27	27	27	27
Alaska	2	2	3	2	3	3	3	3	3	4	3
US Airways	10	10	8	7	6	10	10	10	10	11	–
Continental	10	10	9	11	11	12	–	–	–	–	–
Northwest	12	12	11	13	10	–	–	–	–	–	–
America West	3	3	3	3	3	–	–	–	–	–	–
Competitor average	**12**	**12**	**12**	**12**	**11**	**15**	**18**	**18**	**17**	**17**	**22**

Figure 10.3 Market share as a percentage of sales revenue (1999–2014)

Airline	Sales revenue (% Southwest's 1999 sales revenue)										
	1999	2001	2003	2005	2007	2009	2010	2011	2012	2013	2014
Southwest	100	117	125	160	208	219	256	331	361	380	401
Competitors											
American	340	330	367	436	484	421	468	507	524	549	908
Delta	315	279	300	340	306	593	671	741	774	802	845
United	381	341	315	367	425	345	718	784	784	802	823
Alaska	37	37	43	51	65	72	81	91	98	106	106
US Airways	179	174	143	152	136	221	251	276	292	317	–
Continental	169	168	155	235	224	267	–	–	–	–	–
Northwest	208	203	194	260	202	–	–	–	–	–	–
America West	46	43	47	72	58	–	–	–	–	–	–
Competitor average	**209**	**197**	**195**	**239**	**238**	**320**	**438**	**480**	**495**	**515**	**670**

Figure 10.4 Sales revenue analysis (1999–2014)

- **Sales revenue per customer** – Figure 10.7 shows that Southwest's sales revenue per customer is significantly lower than its competitors. This is appropriate given its strategy is to compete on price. However, it would be a concern if this wasn't its strategy.

Airline	Millions of domestic passengers carried										
	1999	2001	2003	2005	2007	2009	2010	2011	2012	2013	2014
Southwest	65	74	75	88	102	101	131	129	134	133	136
Competitors											
American	82	78	89	98	98	86	105	106	108	109	197
Delta	106	94	84	86	73	161	163	164	164	165	170
United	87	75	66	67	68	56	146	142	140	139	138
Alaska	14	14	15	17	17	16	17	18	19	20	29
US Airways	56	56	41	42	42	59	60	61	61	64	–
Continental	44	43	39	43	49	46	–	–	–	–	–
Northwest	55	52	52	57	54	–	–	–	–	–	–
America West	19	20	20	22	16	–	–	–	–	–	–
Competitor average	**58**	**54**	**51**	**54**	**52**	**71**	**98**	**98**	**98**	**99**	**134**
Total market	**528**	**506**	**481**	**520**	**519**	**525**	**622**	**620**	**627**	**630**	**670**

Figure 10.5 Number of domestic passengers (1999–2014)

Airline	Market share (% sales volume)										
	1999	2001	2003	2005	2007	2009	2010	2011	2012	2013	2014
Southwest	12	15	16	17	20	19	21	21	21	21	20
Competitors											
American	16	15	19	19	19	16	17	17	17	17	29
Delta	20	19	17	17	14	31	26	26	26	26	25
United	16	15	14	13	13	11	23	23	22	22	21
Alaska	3	3	3	3	3	3	3	3	3	3	4
US Airways	11	11	9	8	8	11	10	10	10	10	–
Continental	8	8	8	8	9	9	–	–	–	–	–
Northwest	10	10	11	11	10	–	–	–	–	–	–
America West	4	4	4	4	3	–	–	–	–	–	–
Competitor average	**11**	**11**	**11**	**10**	**10**	**13**	**16**	**16**	**16**	**16**	**20**

Figure 10.6 Market share as a percentage of domestic passengers (1999–2014)

– **Sales volume against competitors** – Figure 10.8 shows that, although Southwest's sales volume doubled over the 15 years, it declined relative to its competitors in the last five years. This could be a problem because its strategy is to compete on price and having high sales volume is critical for reducing its operating costs. The airline might need to find other ways to compete as it no longer has a volume advantage.

Airline	Sales revenue per passenger ($)										
	1999	2001	2003	2005	2007	2009	2010	2011	2012	2013	2014
Southwest	73	75	79	86	97	102	92	121	128	135	140
Competitors											
United	207	215	226	259	296	292	233	261	265	273	283
Delta	141	141	169	187	199	174	195	214	222	230	235
American	196	201	196	211	234	232	211	226	230	239	218
Alaska	126	126	135	142	181	213	225	240	245	250	172
US Airways	151	147	165	172	154	177	198	214	227	234	–
Continental	182	185	188	258	217	274	–	–	–	–	–
Northwest	179	184	177	216	177	–	–	–	–	–	–
America West	114	102	111	154	171	–	–	–	–	–	–
Competitor average	**162**	**163**	**171**	**200**	**204**	**227**	**213**	**231**	**238**	**245**	**227**

Figure 10.7 Sales revenue by passenger (1999–2014)

Airline	Sales volume (% Southwest's 1999 sales volume)										
	1999	2001	2003	2005	2007	2009	2010	2011	2012	2013	2014
Southwest	100	114	115	135	157	155	202	198	206	205	209
Competitors											
American	126	120	137	151	151	132	162	163	166	168	303
Delta	163	145	129	132	112	248	251	252	254	254	262
United	134	115	102	103	105	86	225	218	215	214	212
Alaska	22	22	23	26	26	25	26	28	29	31	45
US Airways	86	86	63	65	65	91	92	94	94	98	0
Continental	68	66	60	66	75	71				0	0
Northwest	85	80	80	88	83	–	–	–	–	–	–
America West	29	31	31	34	25	–	–	–	–	–	–
Competitor average	**89**	**83**	**78**	**83**	**80**	**109**	**151**	**151**	**152**	**153**	**205**

Figure 10.8 Sales volume analysis (1999–2014)

Profit trends

Are profits increasing or decreasing as a percentage of sales revenue? How does this vary by market segment relative to competitors? Useful analyses include:

- **Operating profit trend** – Figure 10.9 shows that Southwest is the only airline to consistently make a profit over the 15-year period. However, competitors' profits increased

Airline	Operating profit ($billion)										
	1999	2001	2003	2005	2007	2009	2010	2011	2012	2013	2014
Southwest	0.8	0.6	0.3	0.5	0.8	0.3	1.0	0.7	0.6	1.3	2.2
Competitors											
American	1.0	(2.6)	(1.4)	(0.4)	0.8	(1.0)	0.0	(1.1)	0.0	(1.6)	4.2
United	1.4	(3.7)	(1.6)	(0.2)	0.4	(0.7)	1.0	1.8	0.0	1.2	2.4
Delta	1.7	(1.0)	(1.2)	(1.2)	1.0	(0.3)	2.2	2.0	2.2	3.4	2.2
Alaska	0.0	0.0	0.0	0.0	0.1	0.3	0.5	0.4	0.5	0.8	1.0
US Airways	0.2	(1.2)	(0.4)	(0.2)	0.5	0.1	0.8	0.5	0.9	0.4	–
Continent	0.5	(0.3)	0.0	0.0	0.6	(0.1)	–	–	–	–	–
Northwest	0.8	(0.8)	(0.3)	(0.9)	1.1	–	–	–	–	–	–
American West	0.2	(0.4)	0.0	(0.1)	0.0	–	–	–	–	–	–
Competitor average	**0.7**	**(1.3)**	**(0.6)**	**(0.4)**	**0.6**	**(0.3)**	**0.9**	**0.7**	**0.7**	**0.8**	**2.5**

Figure 10.9 Operating profit (1999–2014)

Airline	Operating profit (% sales revenue)										
	1999	2001	2003	2005	2007	2009	2010	2011	2012	2013	2014
Southwest	17	11	5	7	8	3	8	4	4	7	12
Competitors											
Alaska	1	4	1	0	4	8	12	10	11	16	20
American	6	16	8	2	4	6	1	5	0	6	10
Delta	12	7	8	7	7	1	7	6	6	9	6
United	8	23	10	1	2	4	3	5	0	3	6
US Airways	2	14	6	3	8	2	7	3	6	3	–
Continental	6	4	0	1	5	1	–	–	–	–	–
Northwest	8	8	3	7	12	–	–	–	–	–	–
America West	9	21	1	4	1	–	–	–	–	–	–
Competitor average	**6**	**(12)**	**(4)**	**(3)**	**5**	**(1)**	**6**	**4**	**5**	**5**	**10**

Figure 10.10 Operating profit as a percentage of sales revenue (1999–2014)

significantly after 2010 because they increased sales volumes and reduced costs by merging with other airlines.

- **Operating profit trend as a percentage of sales revenue** – Figure 10.10 shows the significant improvement in performance by Alaska from 2010. Figures 10.5 and 10.7 suggest that this was achieved by reducing costs (by increasing sales volumes) rather than by increasing prices, but Southwest needs to understand this in more detail because it might identify some ways it can improve.

Operating cost trends

Are operating costs increasing or decreasing as a percentage of sales revenue or sales volume? How does this vary by market segment relative to competitors? Useful analyses include:

- **Company operating cost trend** – Figure 10.11 shows that Southwest's operating costs as a percentage of sales volume (per available seat mile) increased significantly between 1999 and 2011, but stabilized thereafter.
- **Operating cost compared with competitors** – Figure 10.11 also shows that Southwest's cost advantage was eroded after 2009 and Alaska then had the lowest costs in the industry. More worrying are American's cost reductions since 2011 because they compete in more of Southwest's markets. They could become a real threat if this continues.

Customer satisfaction trends

These trends provide some indication of the future financial performance because satisfied customers usually lead to increased future sales. Key questions to ask are: How does the business measure customer satisfaction? Does it simply measure complaints, or is it more proactive than that? Are these satisfaction levels changing over time? How do these compare with its competitors? Useful analyses include:

Airline	Operating costs per available seat mile (in cents)										
	1999	2001	2003	2005	2007	2009	2010	2011	2012	2013	2014
Southwest	6.6	7.5	7.9	8.3	9.1	10.3	11.3	12.4	12.9	12.6	12.5
Competitors											
Delta	9.0	10.1	12.9	13.1	10.6	12.3	12.7	14.1	15.0	14.8	15.9
United	9.7	12.4	12.4	12.9	13.8	11.1	12.5	13.1	14.1	14.3	14.0
American	9.4	11.9	11.5	12.0	9.6	12.2	12.6	14.3	14.3	13.7	13.4
Alaska	10.2	10.2	9.8	10.9	12.2	11.8	12.1	13.1	13.1	12.8	12.2
US Airways	12.4	14.2	14.0	13.9	10.9	11.1	13.0	14.0	14.0	13.3	–
Continental	9.0	10.3	9.8	13.1	10.2	15.2	–	–	–	–	–
American West	7.3	9.3	7.9	11.5	12.9	–	–	–	–	–	–
Northwest	9.3	11.3	11.4	15.2	10.4	–	–	–	–	–	–
Competitor average	**9.5**	**11.2**	**11.2**	**12.8**	**11.3**	**12.3**	**12.6**	**13.7**	**14.1**	**13.8**	**13.9**

Figure 10.11 Operating costs (1999–2014)

- **Customer satisfaction trend against competitors** – Figure 10.12 shows that Southwest's customers are consistently more satisfied than those of its competitors. However, Delta and American's customer satisfaction levels have increased since 2011, while Southwest's have remained the same. They could become a real threat if this continues.

External benchmarks

As well as benchmarking against competitors, it is also important to compare performance with the other organizations with whom your customers interface. This is important for retaining customers because they might consider moving to competitors if, for example, they receive a better service from them than from you. Equally, organizations might move into your industry to leverage a capability they have developed. For example, Virgin moved into industries with a reputation for poor customer service such as rail, mobile phones and the internet. External benchmarks, therefore, help identify with whom customers compare you and who might move into your market with a similar strategy to yours. These benchmarks also help you to estimate the potential benefit of any investments you propose so as to stop a threat or take advantage of an opportunity. Useful analyses include:

- **Industry customer satisfaction comparison** – Figure 10.13 shows that there is a low customer level of satisfaction across the airline industry. It could, therefore, be targeted by a retail or shipping company providing higher levels of satisfaction and wishing to move into a new market.
- **Company customer satisfaction comparisons** – Southwest competes on its service design and has the highest customer satisfaction ratings in its industry (see Figure 10.12). However, Figure 10.14 shows that most companies with the highest customer satisfaction in their industry outperform Southwest. Organizations such as Amazon and Costco who

Airline	Percentage of customers satisfied											
	1999	**2001**	**2003**	**2005**	**2007**	**2008**	**2009**	**2010**	**2011**	**2012**	**2013**	**2014**
Southwest	72	70	75	74	76	79	81	79	81	77	81	78
Competitors												
Delta	68	61	67	65	59	60	64	62	56	65	68	71
American	64	62	67	64	60	62	60	63	63	64	65	66
United	62	59	63	61	56	56	56	60	61.	62	62	60
US Airways	61	60	64	57	61	54	59	62	61	65	64	–
Continental	64	67	68	70	69	62	68	–	–	–	–	–
Northwest	53	56	64	64	61	57	57	–	–	–	–	–
Competitor average	**62**	**61**	**66**	**64**	**61**	**59**	**61**	**62**	**60**	**64**	**65**	**66**

Note: Alaska and American West figures are not available.

Figure 10.12 Customer satisfaction (1999–2014)

Source: American Customer Satisfaction Index, www.theacsi.org.

Industry	% customers satisfied											
	1999	2001	2003	2005	2007	2008	2009	2010	2011	2012	2013	2014
Restaurant	NA	NA	NA	NA	81	80	84	81	82	80	81	82
Internet retail	NA	77	84	81	83	82	83	80	81	82	78	82
Shipping	79	78	79	81	81	82	82	83	84	82	84	81
Search engine	NA	65	71	76	75	80	83	77	80	79	76	80
Retail	NA	73	74	74	75	76	77	78	79	78	80	79
Personal computers	72	71	72	74	77	75	74	75	78	78	80	79
Supermarkets	74	75	74	74	76	76	76	75	76	77	78	76
Banks	68	72	75	75	78	75	75	76	75	77	78	76
Hotels	72	71	73	73	71	75	75	75	77	77	77	75
Airlines	63	61	67	66	63	62	64	66	65	67	69	**69**

Figure 10.13 Industry customer satisfaction comparison (1999–2014)
Source: Based on American Customer Satisfaction Index, www.theacsi.org.

compete on both low cost and service (like Southwest) are particularly threatening. Therefore, it is important for Southwest to identify and understand what they can learn from them.

- **Company sales revenue comparisons** – Figure 10.15 shows that Southwest's sales revenue is smaller than the other organizations shown in Figure 10.14. This suggests that Southwest's market might not be large enough to attract these organizations. However, their size will give them a low-cost advantage if they do.
- **Company profit (percentage of sales revenue) comparisons** – Figure 10.16 shows that Southwest has a medium level of operating profit compared with the other organizations. This makes it attractive for some (such as Amazon, Costco, Fedex and Walmart), but not others (such as Nordstrom and McDonald's). Southwest should also look at 'high-margin' organizations to understand how they have achieved this. For example, how does McDonald's reduce costs so it can compete on price, but still make a 29 per cent profit margin?

Overall business health

From these analyses a number of conclusions can be drawn about Southwest's business health:

- **Customers like its services and products** – customer satisfaction is the highest in its industry and its sales revenue and sales volume have increased significantly over the last 10 years.
- **Good cost control** – it manages its operating costs well so it can compete on price but still make a profit.

Company	Industry	% customers satisfied											
		1999	2001	2003	2005	2007	2008	2009	2010	2011	2012	2013	2014
Nordstrom	Retail	76	76	NA	NA	80	80	83	82	84	84	83	86
Amazon	Internet retail	NA	84	88	87	88	86	86	87	86	85	88	86
Apple	Personal computers	72	73	77	81	79	85	84	86	87	86	87	84
Costco	Retail	79	76	80	79	81	83	81	82	83	83	84	84
Google	Search engine	NA	NA	82	82	78	86	86	80	83	82	77	83
FedEx	Shipping	83	82	82	84	84	85	84	85	83	82	85	82
UPS	Shipping	79	78	79	82	81	83	82	82	85	81	84	82
Marriott	Hotel	77	77	76	76	79	78	77	80	79	78	82	81
eBay	Internet retail	NA	82	84	81	81	78	79	81	81	83	80	79
Southwest	**Airline**	**72**	**70**	**75**	**74**	**76**	**79**	**81**	**79**	**81**	**77**	**81**	**78**
Dell	Personal computers	76	78	78	74	74	75	75	77	77	81	79	76
Wal-Mart	Supermarket	NA	NA	NA	70	71	68	71	71	69	72	72	71
McDonald's	Restaurant	61	62	64	62	64	69	70	67	72	73	73	71

Figure 10.14 Company customer satisfaction comparison (1999–2014)

Company	Industry	Sales revenue ($billion)											
		1999	2001	2003	2005	2007	2008	2009	2010	2011	2012	2013	2014
Wal-Mart	Supermarket	138	191	245	285	345	374	401	408	421	447	466	476
Apple	Personal computers	6	5	6	14	25	37	43	65	108	157	171	183
Costco	Retail	27	34	42	52	63	71	70	76	87	97	103	110
Amazon	Internet retail	2	3	5	8	15	19	25	34	48	61	74	89
Dell	Personal computers	18	32	35	49	57	61	61	53	61	62	57	NA
Google	Search engine	0	0	1	6	17	22	24	29	29	46	56	66
UPS	Shipping	27	30	33	43	50	51	45	50	53	54	55	58
FedEx	Shipping	17	20	22	29	35	38	35	35	39	43	44	46
McDonald's	Restaurant	13	14	16	19	23	24	23	24	27	28	28	27
Southwest	**Airline**	**5**	**6**	**6**	**8**	**10**	**11**	**10**	**12**	**16**	**17**	**18**	**19**
eBay	Internet retail	0	1	2	5	8	9	9	9	12	14	16	18
Marriott	Hotel	9	8	9	11	13	13	11	12	12	12	13	14
Nordstrom	Retail	5	6	6	8	9	8	8	9	10	12	12	13

Figure 10.15 Company sales revenue comparison (1999–2014)

Company	Industry	Operating profit (% sales revenue)											
		99	01	03	05	07	08	09	10	11	12	13	14
Nordstrom	Retail	35	33	35	37	37	35	35	37	37	37	36	36
McDonald's	Restaurant	25	19	18	21	17	27	30	31	32	31	31	29
Apple	Personal computers	6	(6)	(0)	12	18	17	28	28	31	35	29	29
Google	Search engine	(68)	8	7	24	25	19	28	29	33	23	23	22
eBay	Internet retail	(2)	19	29	32	8	24	17	22	20	21	21	20
Southwest	**Airline**	**17**	**11**	**5**	**7**	**8**	**4**	**3**	**8**	**4**	**4**	**7**	**12**
UPS	Shipping	12	13	13	14	1	10	8	11	11	2	13	9
Marriott	Hotel	11	5	4	6	9	6	(1)	6	4	8	8	8
FedEx	Shipping	7	5	7	8	9	5	2	6	6	7	6	8
Wal-Mart	Supermarket	6	6	6	6	6	6	6	6	6	6	6	6
Dell	Personal computers	11	8	8	9	5	6	5	4	6	7	5	NA
Costco	Retail	3	3	3	3	3	3	3	3	3	3	3	3
Amazon	Internet retail	(37)	(13)	5	5	4	4	5	4	2	1	1	0

Figure 10.16 Company profit comparison (1999–2014)

- **Strong financial position** – compared with its competitors, it is in a strong financial position and has returned a profit every year for the last 10 years.
- **Competitive and declining market** – however, its market is declining and becoming more competitive. As a result, although it is the most profitable airline in this market its margins are significantly lower than businesses competing in other markets.

Given these findings, we need to propose investments for Southwest to consider:

- **Improve market support** so that it can attract (and retain) more customers, increase prices or move into new more profitable markets.
- **Reduce costs** to increase the margins of its existing services and products.

IDENTIFYING ALTERNATIVE INVESTMENTS

Once the corporate objectives, stakeholder requirements and current health of the business are understood, the alternative investments required to sustain or improve the current position of the organization can be developed. Businesses can invest in nine main areas (see Figure 10.17) to improve their short- or long-term performance:

- **Leadership** – changing or developing their leadership capability so, for example, they are better at leading and involving people, making decisions, driving results, managing and influencing stakeholders and developing and implementing strategy.
- **Objectives** – changing what the business is trying to do by making its objectives more ambitious, better aligning them with stakeholder expectations (especially customers because they are usually the primary source of revenue), or making them more consistent across different levels and functions so that everyone is trying to do the same thing.
- **Market research** – understanding current or future customer needs or trying to predict how customers might respond to new developments (such as new services/products or how they are delivered). It is important to understand both the customer voice (what they say they want) and their behaviour (what they actually want) because these may be different. Organizations attract customers by appealing to their voice (through sales and marketing), but retain them by supporting their behaviour (through service/product delivery and after-sales support).
- **Service or product** – develop a new offering to meet an existing market need or to create a new market; modify an existing offering to better meet existing market needs; extend the existing service/product range to increase the life cycles; or reduce existing offerings to refocus resources or eliminate unprofitable services or products.
- **Structures** – change the management, organizational and power structures within the business that determine where managers are focused (processes, markets or a combination of the two), where resources are located (centrally or near customers) and who decides where and how resources are invested.
- **Systems** – develop new systems for managing information or performance, or rewarding and developing people.

Aspect	Typical investment
Leadership	• **Capacity** – number of leaders • **Diversity** – knowledge, experience, capability and style of leaders • **Capability** – ability of leaders, for example, to lead people, make decisions, drive results, manage/influence stakeholders and develop/implement strategy • **Focus** – where they spend their time and what they consider important
Objectives	• **Ambition** – performance targets • **External fit** – with stakeholder expectations, especially those who fund the organization (such as customers, shareholders and public bodies) • **Internal fit** – across the different functions and levels within the organization
Market research	• **Customer voice** – what do they say they want (important for winning them) • **Customer behaviour** – what do they actually want (important for retaining them) • **Test new offering** – how will they respond to a new service/product, structure, system or process
Service or product	• **Create new markets** – new offering developed and introduced to change customer behaviour and create a new market • **Meet existing market needs** – new offering developed to meet an existing need • **Modify existing offerings** – adapt current offering(s) to better meet existing needs • **Extend existing range** – leverage existing brands to, typically, extend the life of existing services/products • **Reduce offerings** – stop delivering some services/products and supporting some customers
Structures	• **Management focus** – processes, customers or a combination of the two • **Resource location** – allocated to customers/processes or centrally located • **Power** – who decides where resources are invested and what activities/areas receive investment
Systems	• **Information** – how information/knowledge is captured, managed and shared • **Performance** – measures used and importance given to each measure • **Reward** – how people are rewarded and recognized • **Development** – how people are assessed and developed (such as appraisal, mentoring and development systems)

Processes	• **Front office** – processes with customer contact such as customer management and service/product delivery • **Back office** – internal processes without customer contact such as processing paperwork and managing interactions between functions • **Channels** – how customers interact with you (face-to-face, telephone or internet) • **Capacity** – number of orders and customers that can be processed • **Flexibility** – range of services/products and demand levels that can be delivered • **Technology** – process automation and equipment used by customers or servers • **Inventory** – products made or purchased ahead of demand
People	• **Capacity** – number of people • **Capability** – technical, managerial and people skills • **Culture** – beliefs, attitudes and behaviours encouraged and rewarded by the organization
Suppliers	• **Capability** – ability to help support your customers and meet your objectives • **Collaboration** – work with suppliers to share capabilities/resources, access new markets and develop new offerings

Figure 10.17 Typical investments

- **Processes** – change how services/products are delivered to customers (which includes both front- and back-office activities); the choice of channels for customers to interact with the business; the level of capacity, flexibility and technology in these processes; or whether products are made or purchased ahead of demand and held in inventory.
- **People** – number of staff, their skills (technical, managerial and people) and the culture (beliefs, attitudes and behaviours) within the organization created by aspects such as how they are controlled, success and failure stories told and structures, systems and processes used to run the organization.
- **Suppliers** – as well as investing internally within an organization, investments can be made externally in suppliers (or other partnering organizations) to develop their capabilities, share capabilities/resources, access new markets or develop new offerings.

Although your proposal is likely to focus on only a few of these areas, it is important to consider them all because you might get a better return from investing elsewhere or your existing capability might limit the impact of the investment you propose. You should also work out whether you get a greater or faster performance improvement by changing one aspect of your organization before another. For example, you could change your structures to focus managers on customers so as to better understand their needs before developing new services, products or processes to support them; or perhaps you should enable customers to self-serve rather than improving your customer service (see Case 10.1 explaining how Uber has transformed the taxi industry); or you could release cash first (by reducing inventory or your enquiry-to-cash lead time) before investing in new structures, systems or processes. This will help you think through the sequence of investments you should make to ensure you do not waste resources fixing a problem that could be removed altogether or may not even be relevant in the future. Even if you decide your proposed investment is still the right one for the business to pursue, the investment board (who will review your proposal or plan) will want to see that you have explored a number of different options before deciding upon the one you propose.

Case 10.1 – Uber

In less than five years, Uber has transformed the taxi industry in over 80 cities in 57 countries with over 500 employees and sales of $10 billion in 2014. It is just one example of the 'shared economy' that emerged after the 2008 credit crisis in which organizations (such as Uber and Airbnb) enable customers to rent expensive assets (such as cars and rooms) from people who own them (such as taxi drivers and home owners), but are not using them.

To do this, Uber gives customers free mobile software enabling them to see how long it will take a taxi to get to them and how much it will cost to take them to where they want to go. After ordering a taxi, customers can track it on a map on their phone and they receive a text when the car has arrived. Although the driver does not receive a customer's phone number, they can still contact them by calling through Uber if they are unable to find them. Customers' credit cards (on their account) are automatically debited after passengers reach their destinations (Uber takes 20% of this) and a receipt is emailed to them. The passenger and driver can then rate each other based on the experience they received.

This approach has completely changed the taxi industry. Previously customers had to pre-book a car in advance or hope they could hail one on the street. Instead, Uber uses smartphone GPS systems to match passengers to drivers, and algorithms and 'heat maps' (showing where customers are located) to work out how many drivers it needs in an area at a particular time to ensure most customers get a taxi in less than five minutes. The cost of the journey is typically much lower than other taxi services, but Uber will increase prices in periods of high demand (such as New Year's Eve) to encourage more drivers to go onto the road. As a result, it creates a simpler, faster and more enjoyable experience for its drivers and customers.

www.uber.com

 **Questions**

1 How is Uber transforming the taxi industry?
2 What could other organizations learn from this?

UNDERSTANDING EXPECTED COSTS, BENEFITS AND RISKS

People are more likely to give you resources, support you or take action if you can explain the expected costs, benefits and risks of implementing your proposed investment. To help them understand what you want from them, what they will get in return and how you reached your conclusions then you need to show:

- **Different options** – overview the expected costs, benefits and risks of a number of alternatives before highlighting in which one you think the business should invest. This should include the options of 'doing nothing' (what happens if you do not invest?) and 'investing more resources' (could greater benefit be achieved more quickly and at what point will investing more resources not create a greater or faster impact?). Research[1] has shown that people are twice as likely to invest in an idea to prevent a loss rather than to create a benefit. Therefore, you need to show the advantages lost by not investing in your idea. Figure 10.18 shows how different service or product investments create different costs, benefits and risks depending on whether they are to create a new market, meet an existing customer need, modify an existing offering or extend an existing range. This analysis is key to thinking about the investment: what resources will be required to implement your idea? what benefits will it bring and what is the risk that the costs

Example	Cost	Benefit	Risk
Create new market	**High** • Forecast future needs • Design the new offering • Develop new delivery system • Market and advertise the new offering • Educate salesforce to sell the new offering	**High** • Little or no competition • High sales potential if design the right offering and can persuade customers to buy it • High margins as no similar offerings exist	**High** • High and uncertain design costs • Unknown demand • Need to change customer behaviours • Market might not want the offering • New technology (product and process) and channels (sales and distribution)
Meet existing market need	**Medium** • Customer needs are established and known • Design the new offering • Develop the new delivery system • Market and advertise new offering • Educate salesforce to sell the new offering	**Medium** • Medium or low sales potential as competition already exists • Medium or low margins as similar, competitor offerings exist or could easily be developed	**Medium** • Demand is known and established • New technology (product and process) and channels (sales and distribution)

Figure 10.18 Costs, benefits and risks of different service or product investments

Example	Cost	Benefit	Risk
Modify existing offering	**Low** • Customer needs and service/product designs are known and established	**Low** • Low sales potential due to existing market share of competitor offerings • Low margins as similar competitor offerings exist	**Low** • Demand and process technologies are known and established • New product technology and channels (sales and distribution)
Extend existing range	**Low** • Leverage existing customers, designs and delivery systems • Customer needs, service/product designs and delivery systems are known and established	**Low** • Low sales potential due to market share of existing offerings and competitors • Low margin as similar competitor offerings exist	**Low** • Demand, technology (process and service/product) and channels (sales and distribution) are known and established

Figure 10.18 (Continued)

might be higher or the benefits lower than predicted? For example, are you trying to do something you have never done before? From whom can you learn? Which internal or external stakeholders (such as employees or customers) need to behave differently for your idea to work and how willing are they to do this? What are your competitors doing? How easily can they see and copy your idea and what future technologies (service, product or process) or legislation could limit the impact of your idea? Only when the costs, benefits and risks of alternative investments are known can you determine which ones to propose.

- **Link to overall business strategy and objectives** – how does your proposed investment support the organization's objectives? For example, does it fix a problem, take advantage of an opportunity (such as a new market, service/product or process technology), respond to a threat (such as a new competitor) or reduce a risk (such as a potential future quality or legal issue).
- **Clear assumptions** – as investments become more complex, more assumptions and estimates have to be made to determine their expected costs and benefits. These assumptions should be explained up front so that they can be discussed and debated. Conducting a pilot study will help test your assumptions before making the full investment. You should also track costs and benefits after the investments are made to reduce the risk that these assumptions can create.
- **Financial return** – although there will also be non-financial benefits, people are more likely to support an investment if they command a financial return. Most investors like to know the 'payback period' to show how long it will take to recoup their investments.

- **Be ambitious** – you need to fix a problem or take advantage of an opportunity large enough to engage your audience and where they would get a significant return even if you did not hit your targets. For example, Thierry Breton (CEO at Atos, an IT services provider) set an ambitious goal for staff to stop using internal emails within two years (see Case 10.2).

Case 10.2 – Atos: Zero emails

In 2011, Thierry Breton (CEO at Atos, an IT services provider) commissioned a study to measure the weekly email traffic of a sample of its employees. It found 73 per cent spent one-quarter of their time managing emails (most received or sent over 100 emails a day), 82 per cent struggled to keep up with the volume and 58 per cent felt it wasted time and added little value. Worryingly, the problem increased as employees became more senior, with managers receiving over 200 emails a day (of which 10 per cent were considered to be useful) and spending up to 20 hours a week managing their emails. Thierry was amazed by the findings and announced that Atos would have 'zero emails' by 2013.

Over the next two years, Atos introduced several collaboration and social media technologies (such as Office Communicator, Atos Wiki and Livemeeting). Now 97 per cent of its 76,000 employees participate in 7,500 communities, posting almost 300,000 items and viewing some 2 million pages per month. Although it did not hit its ambitious target, emails did reduce by 60 per cent while people spent 25–30 per cent less time managing them. During the same period, overhead costs reduced from 13 to 10 per cent of sales revenue, net cash increased by €1 billion, sales revenue increased by 26 per cent (from €6.8 to €8.6 billion) and operating profit increased from 6 to 7 per cent of sales revenue. Although not all these improvements were a direct result of the 'zero emails' initiative, they are connected. Atos believes the success came from improving how people work together and serve their customers through four key steps:

1. **Set objectives and deadlines** – it was important to set a clear deadline and publicly announce what it was trying to do.
2. **Invest and commit** – it invested 500 times more than most organizations do in similar initiatives and linked bonuses (10 per cent) and performance evaluations to how well emails were reduced.
3. **Explain the reasons for change** – managers clearly explained how emails waste time for everyone and are not always effective.
4. **Collect and share success stories** – such as how a service desk in Brazil resolved customer issues 30 per cent faster, which increased both customer and employee satisfaction.

at.atos.net/content/dam/de/documents/atos-whitepaper-zeroemailcompany.pdf

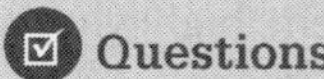

Questions

1. Why do people send so many emails?
2. What can other organizations learn from Atos's initiative?

Although it only reduced emails by 60 per cent over the following two years, it would not have achieved that reduction without such an ambitious target.

- **Find resources** – people are more likely to support ideas that quickly become 'self-funding'. Therefore, it is important to work out whether any of your actions will free up resources (people and/or cash) so they can be invested elsewhere. For example, could you release cash trapped within the business by reducing the customer-to-cash lead time, debtors or inventory? Or, could you free up people by improving processes or changing priorities? If so, then take these actions first.
- **Manage risk** – investors like to understand how you are going to learn and adapt to unplanned events or developments as you implement your ideas. Ideally, they would rather invest in an already-tested idea so you can show the impact it had in one area (such as a market or service/product) and why you think it would have a similar impact in another one (the investment you propose).
- **Best and worst case scenarios** – it is important to remember that the true costs and benefits of any investment are unknown, and so you should show the best and worst case scenarios before explaining how you plan to maximize your return and minimize your costs. It is important to show how you will learn and adapt as you implement your ideas in case the assumptions you made to calculate the expected costs and benefits were incorrect.

DEVELOPING YOUR PROPOSAL

Once the expected cost, benefit and risk of alternative investments are known then you can start putting together your proposal. But first, you must consider two key questions:

- **What do I want to happen as a result of my proposal?** What is not happening that you want to change? Who could help change this (decision makers, supporters or influencers)? How could they help you (resources, support or help spread your ideas)? And, what do you want them to do (give feedback, provide resources or take action)? You might need to develop different proposals for different audiences (or stakeholders) depending on the story you want to tell them and what you want them to do after reading or hearing these.
- **Who is the audience and what questions will they ask?** Your audience will ask themselves: Why am I here? What do you want from me? What will I get in return? Does the return justify the investment? How did you get to your numbers? Do I believe in the idea? Do I believe in you? Your proposal needs to answer all these questions to convince your audience to do what you want them to do.

Figure 10.19 gives tips for developing your proposal, but you will need to determine which aspects are more important for which audience. For example, if your investors are 'risk averse' then you will need to spend longer showing that you understand the problem, highlight the opportunity costs or risks of not investing in your proposal and demonstrate how your ideas have worked elsewhere. However, if they are looking for a large return then you will need to spend longer showing the high ambition of your proposal, the return they will get and how you will learn as you go along.

- **Understand the problem** – it is easy to find a solution once you understand the problem
- **Challenge existing views and perspectives** – do not just accept hearsay in the business because it might not be correct. Always check opinions with data and evidence
- **Be ambitious** – the person or panel to whom you are presenting your idea want to invest in something that makes a large enough return to justify them looking at it
- **Take risks** – you only get a return by taking a risk and doing something new
- **Find resources** – can you free up resources (people and/or cash) that you could invest elsewhere? For example, you could release cash trapped within the business by reducing the customer-to-cash lead time, debtors or inventory, or you could free up people by improving processes or changing priorities
- **Show how your ideas have worked elsewhere** in different markets, locations or industries. People prefer to invest in a proposal for an idea that has already worked elsewhere
- **Test your recommendations** – present your recommendations to people who will implement them, understand how to implement them and/or the costs, benefits or risks of implementing them. You can use their feedback to modify your recommendations, confirm the costs/benefits/risks you propose or show the challenges to overcome (if they do not agree with your ideas)
- **Learn as you go along** – build in ways to learn during the investment so you can reduce risk and respond to changes that might occur. This is particularly important when you are trying to do something new, such as creating a new market or using a new process technology. It is often better to make incremental changes so you can learn as you go along than try to create a breakthrough improvement
- **Build barriers** – think about how competitors will respond to your investment. In particular, what will stop ones with more resources taking your idea and doing it better than you? Use investment to create capabilities that competitors will struggle to imitate. Often this will come from making a large number of small improvements rather than making one big one

Figure 10.19 Tips for developing your proposal

PRESENTING YOUR PROPOSAL

Figure 10.20 gives tips for presenting your ideas. It is critical to explain at the beginning of your presentation what you want from your investors (or audience) and what they will get in return. It is surprising how many people forget to do this because they want to save their recommendations until the end and build up to them, and gradually showing how they have got there. However, your audience wants to know where you are taking them so they know what questions to ask along the way in order to understand why you are taking them there and how you worked out the route. That is why you need to explain straight away the costs,

- **What do you want and what is the return** – potential investors will want to know at the beginning of your proposal the costs, benefits and risks of the investment(s) you propose. You should also explain the assumptions you have made when calculating these figures so they can be debated, discussed and understood
- **Present options** – investors want to understand the costs, benefits and risks of all the investment options available so they can choose between them
- **Show how you reached your conclusions** – investors want to know the research you have done and how you have reached your conclusions so as to check that you have thought broadly and have conducted rigorous research (with data and evidence) that challenged and tested people's views along the way

Tell a story – a good structure to follow is: (1) talk about the problem, (2) explain how it could be, (3) suggest some actions; and (4) explain what it will be like after they have been implemented. Steve Job's presentation at the iPhone launch is a good model to follow, as discussed by Nancy Duarte in her TedXtalk:

www.ted.com/talks/nancy_duarte_the_secret_structure_of_great_talks

- **Engage your audience** – a good approach is to use the 'And, but, therefore' technique
- **Make it memorable** – create a memorable moment within your presentation by thinking about what you want people to talk about afterwards
- **Keep it simple** – most people struggle to remember more than three things, so keep your message simple. For example, three actions are required to fix three problems, which will lead to three benefits. Leaving things out makes what is left simpler and stronger
- **Make it visual** – think creatively about how to tell your story to make it more engaging and memorable rather than simply filling your slides with repetitive text
- **Test your presentation** – present your ideas to someone who understands how the panel will operate and has won investment in the past
- **Practise** – practise your presentation, record it and watch it. You need to know your subject inside out, present well and be able to answer the questions you expect to be asked

Figure 10.20 Tips for presenting your proposal

benefits and risks of the investment(s) you propose and the assumptions you have made to calculate these figures, so that they can be debated and discussed within the presentation. Once the audience understands this, you can then show them how you reached your conclusions by explaining the research you have done and how you have checked and tested opinion with data and evidence along the way. You need to convince them that you have explored all the different investment options and that the numbers you are presenting are as accurate as they can be.

Remember you are telling a story which needs to engage your audience and is simple enough for them to remember so they can tell it to other people. Even if they are the key decision makers, they will still need to convince other people to take action to support or implement your ideas. To help you think about how you might do this, Case 10.3 describes *South Park*'s number one rule of storytelling, suggesting you should use the words 'but', 'because' and 'therefore' to connect the different parts of your story. These links force you to think about 'why' and 'so what', which will arrest your investors' attention. Case 10.4 also shows Pixar's rules of storytelling, which illustrate the importance of thinking about the audience, rewriting and simplifying your story once you know the ending and analysing stories you like in order to understand why they work and what you can learn from them. Case 10.5 then describes how you can make your presentation memorable, visual and simple by taking ideas from some great TED talks. Links to these presentations and a brief description of what they contain are shown in the Exploring Further section at the end of this chapter. Finally, Case 10.6 shows the power of a good story in which two researchers purchased $128.74 worth of objects off eBay, added a story to them and then re-sold them on eBay for $3,612.51.

Case 10.3 – *South Park*'s number one rule of storytelling

South Park's creators and writers Trey Parker and Matt Stone explained to students in a 'storytelling strategies' class at Tisch School of the Arts at New York University the importance of looking at the 'beats' of the story to see which words connect them.

They suggest that your story will be boring if you use the words 'and' or 'then' to connect its different parts. For example, this happened 'and' this happened 'then' this happened. Instead they suggest using the words 'but', 'because' and 'therefore' to make it more interesting. So, you would say this happened, 'but' this happened, 'because' this happened, 'therefore' this happened. The story immediately becomes more interesting and also forces you to think about 'why' and 'so what', which will grab your investors' attention.

Randy Olsen (www.youtube.com/watch?v=ERB7ITvabA4) takes this idea and applies it to business presentations claiming that: 'Stories are fun AND may seem complex, BUT they all have a similar structure, THEREFORE they lend themselves to templates.'

www.nytimes.com/video/arts/television/100000001039812/a-clip-from-stand-in.html

Questions

1 Why are 'but' and 'therefore' better words to connect the different parts of your story?
2 Think about a recent presentation you have made. How would this idea have changed what you talked about?

Case 10.4 – Pixar's rules of storytelling

1. People admire ambition rather than achievement
2. Focus on what your audience is interested in, not what you think is fun
3. You will not know what the story is about until you are at the end of it. Then you will have to go back and rewrite it
4. Simplify. Focus. Eliminate detours. You will feel like you are cutting valuable stuff, but you are not
5. Work out the ending before the middle because that is hard to get right and needs setting up early on
6. Finish your story, even if it is not perfect, and make sure you write a better one next time
7. When you are stuck, work out what would not happen next to help you get unstuck
8. Pull apart the stories you like, work out why you like them and use those ideas in your stories
9. Write your story down. Otherwise it stays in your head, never improves and is never heard
10. Discard the 1st, 2nd, 3rd, 4th and 5th idea you think of – get the obvious ideas out of the way and then focus on finding something different
11. Have an opinion
12. Why are you telling this story? What is your burning belief? Why should people know about it?
13. If you were in this situation, how would you feel? What would you do? Honesty creates credibility
14. What are the stakes? Why should we root for this character? What happens if they do not succeed?
15. No work is ever wasted. If it is not working let it go and move on – it will be useful later on
16. Know the difference between doing your best and being fussy. Your story needs testing, not refining
17. Take a story you do not like and make it into one you do like. What did you change?
18. Your audience has to identify with your situation and your characters
19. What is the essence of your story? What is the simplest way to tell it?

Questions

1 Why are these rules useful for helping you develop a story?

2 Look at a recent investment proposal you have written. How would these ideas have changed how you approached it and what you talked about?

Case 10.5 – Some great TED talks

TED is a great source of presentation tips and good practice. Some good ones to learn from are:

- **Create a memorable moment** – Bill Gates (2009) released some mosquitoes and said, 'There is no reason why only poor people should be infected.' Only afterwards did he say the mosquitoes were malaria free.
- **Make it visual** – Lisa Kristine (2012) used pictures rather than words.
- **Talk in threes** – many presentations talk in threes. For example, Kevin Alloca (2011) talks about the three reasons why YouTube videos go viral, Don Norman (2003) explains the three ways that design makes people happy, Tom Wujec (2009) talks about three ways the brain creates meaning, Tim Leberecht (2012) discusses three ways that brands lose their identity and Ric Elias (2011) talks about three types of people who might steal your data.
- **Break up your slides and data with stories** – Bono (2013) links his charts, graphs and photographs with stories to engage his audience and make his message more memorable.
- **Teach them something new** – the most viewed TED presentations do this. For example: the surprising science of happiness (Dan Gilbert, 2004), how to live before you die (Steve Jobs, 2004), schools kill creativity (Sir Ken Robinson, 2006), your elusive creative genius (Elizabeth Gilbert, 2009), how great leaders inspire action (Simon Sinek, 2009) and the power of introverts (Susan Cain, 2012).

Links to these presentations and a brief description of what they contain are shown in the Exploring Further section at the end of this chapter.

www.ted.com

Questions

1. Which of these presentations do you like? Why do you like them?
2. How could you use some of these ideas in your own presentations?

Case 10.6 – The power of a good story

Two researchers, Rob Walker and Joshua Glenn, purchased $128.74-worth of objects off eBay, added a story to them and then re-sold them on eBay for $3,612.51. For example, a torch (flashlight) bought for $1.99 was re-sold for $20 after the following story was added:

'The thing about flashlights – and really, if we are inclined to be completely honest, the thing about any of the objects that we carapace ourselves with, that we use to hedge ourselves in – is that they are, more or less, interchangeable. As long as they function as they are meant to function, we hardly notice them. Nine times out of ten, one object of a near-identical make can be substituted for another without anyone noticing until it's too late.

I'll go ahead and say it again, despite knowing you will choose to believe what you have already chosen to believe. This is my flashlight. You can see for yourself that it's in perfect condition. No sign of excessive wear, no indication of it having been used for any purpose other than what the manufacturer intended: viz., the illumination of other subjects and objects swallowed up in the dark. Admire the way the chrome of the casing shines evenly. The incomparable gleam of the dimpled reflector, uncracked and perfect. There is no discolouration to the ribbed grip, no trace of rust or dirt or of any other substance such as, say, blood.

Admittedly, it has been clicked on and turned off. The flashbeam has been directed in first one direction and then another. But it has never been wielded as if it were a club. Such a flashlight has never done any damage to anything, to anyone. It is a simple, uncomplicated object, free of any relation to clots of blood or clumps of hair, chips of bone or hunks of gore. Where the other flashlight, the one allegedly found in the drawer of my kitchen, came from, I cannot venture to guess. It has nothing to do with me. It is not my flashlight. This is my flashlight, not that one.

Until you accept that, officer, we are not likely to get anywhere.'

www.significantobjects.com/evidence

 **Questions**

1. How did the story help to increase the value of the torch?
2. How could you use some of these ideas in your own investment proposals?

TRACKING COST AND BENEFIT

Too often organizations heavily scrutinize an investment before it is made, but do not track the cost or benefit it creates. However, it is critical to do this for a number of reasons:

- **Managing and reducing risk** – any investment requires assumptions to be made because you are trying to do something new. The higher the risk you take (and the greater the benefit you try to create), the more assumptions you will need to make. However, this risk can be managed and often reduced by tracking costs/benefits and comparing them with your original plan to understand whether the assumptions you made were correct so you can modify your plan.
- **Adapting and changing your ideas** – you may need to change your plan depending on the impact your actions have (cost and benefit), how your stakeholders (such as employees and customers) and competitors respond to them or if there are any developments you did not expect (such as new technology or legislation). This might mean reducing investment, investing in other areas or increasing investment to get you there faster than your competitors or before new legislation is passed.

- **Learning** – investments are complex decisions and difficult to get right so it is critical to learn from your decisions so mistakes are not repeated and good practice is shared. Web-based (or other) forums enable people to ask questions which can then be answered by people who have fixed similar problems or exploited similar opportunities. It is also useful to share learning through, for example, external or internal publications.

Organizations make investments to improve performance so they can better support market needs (or other stakeholder requirements) and meet their objectives. To do this, you must first understand the health of your organization by comparing its performance over time with competitors, other organizations your customers interact with and companies using a similar strategy to yours in another industry. This will help you understand how strong your organization is and the opportunities or threats it faces. Remember customers compare you with the other organizations they interact with (both personally and through work), not just your competitors or how well you served them last time. If they have a great experience with Uber or Apple, then they will want a similar experience with you. Often your biggest threat is someone entering your market with a completely different business model. Uber is a threat to everyone, but also an idea that we can all learn from. Good questions to ask yourself are: What is our cost structure? What are our competitors' cost structures? Could we change this if we invested differently? Or worked with our customers and suppliers in a different way? Is anyone else already doing this in another industry? This will help you think about how you might remove a problem rather than fixing it. For example, could you get customers to serve themselves rather than fixing how you serve them?

It is important to consider all available investment options to ensure you are making the right one and can present your investors with alternatives. Your investors will ask themselves: Why am I being approached? What do you want from me? Does the return justify the investment? How did you get to your numbers? Do I believe in the idea? Do I believe in you? Your story needs to engage them and be simple enough for them to remember so that they can tell it to other people. You might need different proposals for different audiences depending upon what you want them to do after reading or hearing it. You will also need to track costs and benefits after making your investments so as to manage risk, adapt your ideas and share your learning with other people trying to fix similar problems or take advantage of similar opportunities.

Fowlers of Earlswood

'Over the last two years we have increased sales and profits by improving the design of our existing products and introducing new ones [see Case Figure 10.1]. Our next task is to review our current processes and look for ways to release cash trapped within the business so we can make investments to further increase sales or reduce costs', explained Adrian Fowler (CEO of the cheese maker, Fowlers of Earlswood).

BACKGROUND

Founded in Derbyshire in 1670, Fowlers of Earlswood is the oldest cheese-making family in England, handcrafting its award-winning cheeses for over 14 generations. Currently, it makes three types of cheese (see Case Figure 10.2) using the same processes (see Case Figure 10.3) to supply retail and wholesale customers (see Case Figure 10.4). Three years ago, it decided to grow wholesaler sales after realizing retailers are more expensive to serve (retailer orders are 20 times smaller than wholesalers, which increases distribution, packing and administration costs) and competitive (most sell a variety of cheeses including their own) so sales tend to plateau after two years.

Performance (£k)	Year			
	−3	−2	−1	Current
Sales	475	475	485	500
Operating profit	85	85	90	100
Costs				
Material	240	240	240	245
Direct labour	80	80	80	80
Overheads	75	75	75	75
Inventory				
Raw material	3	3	3	5
Work-in-progress	7	7	7	10
Finished goods	145	155	170	185

Note: All finished goods inventory is 'hard cheese' at different stages of maturity. Currently there is £100k at 0–12 months maturity, £40k at 12–17 months and £45k at 18–29 months.

Case Figure 10.1 Financial performance

Cheese	Maturity (months)	Annual sales (£k)				Selling price (£/kilo)	Contribution (% sales)
		−3	−2	−1	Current		
Soft	N/A	50	50	50	50	7.90	50
Blue	N/A	–	–	10	25	7.90	50
Hard	3–11	175	175	175	175	5.00	20
	12–17	150	150	150	150	6.00	35
	18–29	100	100	100	100	7.90	50

Note: Contribution = Sales – (Materials + Direct labour).

Case Figure 10.2 Sales and contribution by product

Manufacturing

To make cheese, milk (taken from Fowlers' cows) is pasteurised, cultured, heated, cured and matured before it is then cut, packed and despatched to customers. Deciding how long to mature a hard cheese is a critical decision because it increases its selling price, but ties up cash.

Cutting and packing

The shelf life of cheese starts when it is cut. Most cheese is therefore 'cut to order' by hand into 16 to 20 portions per round that are then bagged, sealed, labelled and returned to stock before being sent to a customer.

Case Figure 10.3 Current processes

Market	Year			
	−3	−2	−1	Current
Retailer				
Customers (#)	85	80	75	70
Sales (£k)	240	225	200	185
Operating profit (£k)	30	25	20	15
Inventory (£k)	25	25	20	20
Debtors (£k)	45	40	40	35
Wholesaler				
Customers (#)	3	4	5	6
Sales (£k)	235	250	285	315
Operating profit (£k)	55	60	70	85
Inventory (£k)	130	140	160	180
Debtors (£k)	55	60	70	80

Case Figure 10.4 Sales, costs and profit by market

PROPOSED INVESTMENTS

To further increase sales, reduce costs and release cash, Fowlers of Earlswood looked at the investments shown below.

CUTTING MACHINE

The first option was to purchase a £40k machine to cut the cheese, which was previously cut by hand. This would reduce the time to cut the cheese by 20 per cent for each order and also reduce the excess product included in each order from 15 to 5 per cent because the cheese would be cut more accurately. Also, because the cheese shapes would be more uniform, it would be possible to fit 36 packs (rather than 30) in a box and 80 boxes (rather than 65) on a pallet, which would reduce the average packing time of each order by 20 per cent, with 60 orders packed in a normal week. The typical material and direct labour cost for each order is shown in Case Figure 10.5.

Although the cutting machines would be able to cut twice as many packs per week without any additional staff, there would be no reduction in staff because the machine would still need to be supervised. Also, it would take 15 (rather than 10) minutes to change over between different cheese types because the cutting machine would need to be cleaned (normally 25 times a week) and serviced at a cost of £1k per year.

PACKING MACHINE

The second option was to purchase a £5k packing machine because cheeses are currently packed by hand. This would be linked to the new cutting machine because cheese needs to be packed as soon as it is cut to increase its shelf-life. However, while the cutting machine will cut 20 packs per hour, the packing machine can only pack 15 packs per hour. Therefore, there would need to be a holding area for 300 products between the two machines. It would also take 20 (rather than 15) minutes to change over between cheese types because the packing machine would need to be cleaned (normally 10 times a week) with service costs of £500 per year. At an annual cost of £10k, the machine could also vacuum pack cheeses to increase

Cost (£)	Year			
	−3	−2	−1	Current
Material	55	60	65	80
Direct labour				
Manufacturing	3	4	5	6
Cutting	5	5	5	5
Packing	6	6	5	5
Despatch	6	6	5	5
Total	20	21	20	21
Total	75	81	85	101

Note: Labour costs do not include set-up times.

Case Figure 10.5 Typical material and labour costs per order

Cheese type	Shelf-life (days)	
	Hand packed	Machine packed
Soft	28	36
Blue	28	42
Hard	70	110

Case Figure 10.6 Increased shelf-life by vacuum packing cheeses

their shelf-life (see Case Figure 10.6), which would enable Fowlers to cut and pack products ahead of demand.

Although the packing machines would be able to pack four times as many packs per week without any additional staff, there would be no reduction in staff because the machine still needs two people (one at the front and one at the end) to use it.

MATURATION STORAGE

The third option was a £10k refurbishment of the maturation storage rooms, which would enable soft and blue cheeses to be stored separately (reducing contamination) and increase the hard cheese storage area from 100 to 300 packs.

CREDIT CONTROLLER

The final option was to employ a part-time credit controller at £200 a month to chase customers' unpaid invoices. From previous experience of doing this himself, Adrian Fowler estimates this would result in invoices being paid 10 days earlier.

LOOKING FORWARD

'We hope these investments will help make us stronger going forward by reducing costs or increasing sales', reflected Adrian. However, we need to fully understand the cost, benefit, playback and risk of each one before implementing them.'

QUESTIONS

1. Determine the cost, benefit, payback period and risk of each proposed investment
2. Which one(s) would you suggest they implement and in what order?
3. Looking at their performance, are there any other investments you think they should consider?

NOTE

1 See Kahneman, D. and Tversky, A. (1984) 'Choices, values and frames', *American Psychologist*, 39(4): 341–50.

EXPLORING FURTHER

Journal articles

Amabile, T.M. and Kramer, S.J. (2011) 'The power of small wins', *Harvard Business Review*, 89(5): 70-80. What is the best way to motivate employees to do creative work? Help them take a step forward every day. The key is to learn which actions support progress, such as setting clear goals, providing sufficient time and resources, and offering recognition. On the flip side, small losses or setbacks can have an extremely negative effect.

Chesbrough, H.W. and Garman, A.R. (2009) 'How open innovation can help you cope in lean times'. *Harvard Business Review*, 87(12), 68–76. This article proposes that 'open innovation' can play an important role in helping companies in a challenging business environment. Open innovation allows intellectual property, ideas and people to flow freely both into and out of an organization and includes placing some of its assets and projects outside.

Kahneman, D. and Tversky, A. (1984) 'Choices, values and frames', *American Psychologist*, 39(4), 341–50. Discusses why people tend to prefer avoiding losses to acquiring gains.

Kaplan, R.S. and Norton, D.P. (2007) 'Using the balanced scorecard as a strategic management system'. *Harvard Business Review*, 85(7/8), 150–61. The balanced scorecard contains financial performance measures that report what has already happened and non-financial measures that help predict what might happen in the future. This article examines how a balanced scorecard can be used to link current actions with tomorrow's goals.

Washburn, N.T. and Hunsaker, B.T. (2011) 'Finding great ideas in emerging markets', *Harvard Business Review*, 89(9): 115–20. A new kind of manager, a 'global bridger', can help companies take advantage of the innovative energy that permeates emerging markets.

Books

Duarte, N. (2012) *HBR Guide to Persuasive Presentations*, Harvard Business Review Press.

Gallo, C. (2014) *Talk like TED*, Macmillan.

TED talks and YouTube videos

Alloca, K. (2011) *Why videos go viral.* YouTube's trends manager explains three reasons why videos go viral.

www.ted.com/talks/kevin_allocca_why_videos_go_viral?language=en

Bono (2013) *The good news on poverty (Yes, there's good news).* Bono shares some inspiring data showing that the end of poverty is in sight, if we can harness the momentum we have created.

www.ted.com/talks/bono_the_good_news_on_poverty_yes_there_s_good_news?language=en

Cain, S. (2012) *The power of introverts*. Susan Cain argues that introverts should be encouraged and celebrated because they bring extraordinary talents and abilities to the world.

www.ted.com/talks/susan_cain_the_power_of_introverts?language=en

Duarte, N. (2011) *The secret structure of great talks*. Nancy Duarte draws lessons on how to make a powerful call-to-action from speeches such as 'I have a dream' and the iPhone launch.

www.ted.com/talks/nancy_duarte_the_secret_structure_of_great_talks

Elias, R. (2011) *Three things I learned while my plane crashed*. Ric Elias tells the story of when the plane in which he was travelling crash-landed in the Hudson River in New York in January 2009.

www.ted.com/talks/ric_elias?language=en

Gates, B. (2009) *Mosquitos, malaria and education*. Bill Gates asks us to consider two big questions and how we might answer them.

www.ted.com/talks/bill_gates_unplugged?language=en

Gilbert, D. (2004) *The surprising science of happiness*. Dan Gilbert challenges the idea that we'll be miserable if we don't get what we want. Instead, he suggests we feel truly happy when things don't go as planned.

www.ted.com/talks/dan_gilbert_asks_why_are_we_happy?language=en

Gilbert, E. (2009) *Your elusive creative genius*. Elizabeth Gilbert discusses what we expect from artists and geniuses – and suggests we all have a genius inside us.

www.ted.com/talks/elizabeth_gilbert_on_genius?language=en

Jobs, S. (2005) *How to live before you die*. At his Stanford University commencement speech, Steve Jobs (CEO and co-founder of Apple and Pixar) urges us to pursue our dreams and see the opportunities in life's setbacks – including death itself.

www.ted.com/talks/steve_jobs_how_to_live_before_you_die

Kristine, L. (2012) *Photos that bear witness to modern slavery*. For two years, photographer Lisa Kristine travelled the world to document the harsh realities of modern-day slavery of, for example, miners in the Congo or brick layers in Nepal.

www.ted.com/talks/lisa_kristine_glimpses_of_modern_day_slavery?language=en

Leberecht, T. (2012) *3 ways to (usefully) lose control of your brand*. Online chatter and spin mean there's a constant, free-form conversation happening about you that you have no control over. Tim Leberecht offers three ideas about to accept this and even design for it.

www.ted.com/talks/tim_leberecht_3_ways_to_usefully_lose_control_of_your_reputation?language=en

Norman, D. (2003) *3 ways good design makes you happy.* Design critic Don Norman turns his incisive eye toward beauty, fun, pleasure and emotion, as he looks at design that makes people happy.

www.ted.com/talks/don_norman_on_design_and_emotion?language=en

Olsen, R. (2013) *The and, but, therefore template of storytelling.* Stories are fun AND may seem complex, BUT they all have a similar structure, THEREFORE they lend themselves to templates.

www.youtube.com/watch?v=ERB7ITvabA4

Robinson, K. (2006) *Do schools kill creativity?* Sir Ken Robinson makes the case for creating an education system that nurtures (rather than undermines) creativity.

www.ted.com/talks/ken_robinson_says_schools_kill_creativity?language=en

Sinek, S. (2009) *How great leaders inspire action*. Simon Sinek has a simple but powerful model for inspirational leadership all starting with a golden circle and the question 'Why?'. His examples include Apple, Martin Luther King, and the Wright brothers.

www.ted.com/talks/simon_sinek_how_great_leaders_inspire_action.html

Wujec, T. (2009) *3 ways the brain creates meaning.* Information designer Tom Wujec talks through three areas of the brain that help us understand words, images, feelings and connections. In this short talk, he asks: How can we best engage our brains to help us better understand big ideas?

www.ted.com/talks/tom_wujec_on_3_ways_the_brain_creates_meaning

INDEX

Reader – please note that page references in **bold** highlight the principal coverage of that topic within the book.

E

F

G

H

I

J

K

L

M

R

S

T

U

V

W